Human Resource Development

Human Resource Development

Process, Practices and Perspectives

Stephen Gibb

University of Strathclyde
Department of HRM

Second Edition

First edition published 2002
Second edition published 2008 by
PALGRAVE MACMILLAN
Houndmills, Basingstoke, Hampshire RG21 6XS and
175 Fifth Avenue, New York, N.Y. 10010
Companies and representatives throughout the world

PALGRAVE MACMILLAN is the global academic imprint of the Palgrave
Macmillan division of St. Martin's Press, LLC and of Palgrave Macmillan Ltd.
Macmillan® is a registered trademark in the United States, United Kingdom
and other countries. Palgrave is a registered trademark in the European
Union and other countries.

ISBN-13 97814039987327
ISBN-10 14039987327

This book is printed on paper suitable for recycling and made from fully
managed and sustained forest sources. Logging, pulping and manufacturing
processes are expected to conform to the environmental regulations of the
country of origin.

A catalogue record for this book is available from the British Library.

A catalog record for this book is available from the Library of Congress.

10   9   8   7   6   5   4   3   2   1
17   16   15   14   13   12   11   10   09   08

Printed in China

Contents

List of figures

List of tables

Preface

The second edition retains the overall approach of the first, but has been modified in structure and content. Most obviously the title has evolved to reflect contemporary usage, from 'learning and development' to Human Resource Development (HRD). Reviewers of the draft of this second edition, to whom I owe a debt of gratitude, noted that these modifications also meant an extension of the breadth and depth of treatment. They wondered if this changed the basic character of the book, and the level at which it could be used. I believe that in essence it is still the same, as I have sought to preserve a balance between two demands. One is the demand for a text to support those approaching this subject in a pragmatic way, with a concern to complete study in this area as part of their undergraduate development or professional development. The other is the demand from those seeking a text that is more challenging, an opportunity to explore for themselves ideas as well as operational realities, and hear what authors have to say about these subjects in context. The second edition demonstrates an abiding concern with supporting and challenging, identifying and exploring the core propositions which form the deep and serious interest that successful people, companies and countries have about supporting and managing HRD at work.

What's new in the 2nd edition at a glance

- **New chapters** on learning in groups, diversity, learning development providers, and strategic HRD
- **Major revisions** to the chapters on HRD partnerships, theory in HRD and HRD strategies
- **New cases** with **discursive questions and model answers** to introduce and conclude the chapters
- **Mapping of contents** against CIPD standards

In the past managing HRD has been integral to creating wealth and opportunity, transforming lives and advancing on the highest goals that people set themselves. It has been a key driving force in shaping our societies, and a catalyst for economic growth and opportunity. Organisations that are successful in managing HRD are better placed to meet their goals and fulfil their purposes, becoming assets to the societies they work within, fostering greater productivity and an improving quality of life. The continuance of that wealth creation and opportunity depends upon the management of HRD, now more than ever as the scale and extent of expertise needed to confront what lies ahead grows. An awareness of this increases for me the level of interest in understanding better why and how HRD can be managed. I hope that such enthusiasm is something that helps animate this treatment of the subject. I have focused on five HRD education value propositions for undergraduate and postgraduate learners alike who are spending time gaining knowledge and understanding about HRD;

- HRD education contributes directly to society by facilitating economic development and service; graduates and postgraduates learning about HRD will have responsibilities for those ends.
- Through HRD education it is possible and necessary to inspire and involve all kinds of people in engaging with HRD education, and for those who learn about HRD to value and work for diverse aims.
- HRD education provides graduates with a portfolio of competences that facilitates meaningful contributions to organisations engaged in a variety of enterprises and pursuits, and provides significant life-long economic benefit to graduates.
- HRD education produces well-rounded graduates who can help to strengthen the connection between business and society.
- HRD education helps to produce and disseminate cutting edge ideas and theories that facilitate the advance of organisational efficiency and effectiveness. HRD education provides a fertile environment for the development and incubation of research, reflective inquiry and new ideas.

There are modifications and enhancements to the structure and content in this second edition. These are intended to help better support learning about HRD. They seek to better combine the values of the human sciences within the disciplines of business and management. One stronger message, that I am ever more convinced needs to be promoted, is that students of HRD need to become much more design conscious, and design savvy. They need to be more aware of how thinking about design and being a designer can help them to arrive at solutions to problems and make decisions that produce effective HRD. This, in my experience, is as important in the students' development as the grasp of theory and the appreciation that comes from understanding theory coherently.

I am conscious of seeking to engage learners through powerful cases. It is an assumption for me that exploring highly visible and well documented cases can engage learners of all learning styles. Often the cases that arise in HRD are cases in which there have been errors and deficiencies, resulting in high profile individual, organisational or national problems. For some this kind of case, with its negative overtones, was presented too often in the first edition, giving an imbalanced tone and colour to the textbook, even though the aim was to highlight the significance of effective HRD. I have sought to redress that.

The other major design challenge that faced me in the first edition persists and increases: the lack of 'content stability' in HRD. Texts aiming to be introductory are dated as soon as they are written. Erosion and creation, simultaneous at all levels, surrounds us from the most practical to the most theoretical. New institutions, practices and initiatives bloom and old ones fade. In the first edition I emphasised that organisational practices evolve and change with bewildering frequency, that government policy is subject to constant review, and even the apparently established content of learning theory offers little in the way of solid ground. I remain committed to adopting a constructivist position (or rationale) as a personal anchor and response amid all the change. Dyed-in-the-wool constructivists recognise, accept and welcome such ferment. For learners approaching the area fresh and anew, with a demand for basic learning, this ferment is less welcome. Getting beyond it needs active participation in proposition and problem-based learning, working directly themselves on process issues and questions about practices that are relevant and engaging, and which develop their confidence in themselves as learners who are growing and changing. Hands-on HRD at work activity and observation of the actual organisational world of work provide the best wellsprings of experiences that can enable such learning. Models, concepts and cases are substitutes for that, available as resources that many can take the time to look and pore over, and explore in safety without the turbulent flow of action and consequence that accompanies process and practice in organisations. Even so, the best models, concepts and cases are the results of others' observations and speculations about workplace and organisational experiences, not authoritative and definitive accounts of organisational reality. As such these 'constructions' of others should be approached as open to question, challenge and change. 'Critical' study of organisations, models, concepts and cases is a way of doing that, and is necessary to get beyond reliance on others' constructions. But critical thinking is not sufficient to construct your own secure understanding. That takes time and experience and action.

Acknowledgements

I am greatly indebted to the reviewers of this second edition, for their feedback. Many colleagues, and students have been instrumental in sparking dialogues around and providing insights into HRD process, practices and perspectives over the years. They are too numerous to mention individually, but I thank them all. Of course the responsibility for any remaining errors or omissions is mine.

Every effort has been made to trace all the copyright-holders, but if any have been inadvertently overlooked the publishers will be pleased to make the necessary arrangements at the first opportunity.

Mapping of the text to CIPD Standards (brief outline)

Operational themes	1	2	3	4	5	6	7	8	9	10	11	12	13	14	15	16
The integration of HRD activity into the organisation	H	H	R	R	R	R	H	H	N	H	H	R	H	R	H	R
The provision of a value-adding HRD function	H	R	H	R	R	R	H	R	R	H	R	R	R	R	H	R
HRD's contribution to the recruitment and performance management processes	N	H	R	N	N	N	N	H	N	R	N	N	H	R	R	R
HRD's contribution to the retention of employees	N	R	N	N	N	N	N	R	N	N	N	N	N	R	N	N
HRD's contribution to building organisational capacity and facilitating change	R	H	R	R	R	R	H	H	N	R	R	R	H	R	H	H
The stimulation of strategic awareness and development of knowledge	R	R	R	R	R	H	H	R	R	R	R	H	H	R	H	R
The design and delivery of learning processes and activity	R	R	H	H	R	R	H	H	H	H	R	R	R	R	R	R
The evaluation and assessment of HRD outcomes and investment	R	N	N	N	H	R	R	R	N	R	R	R	R	R	R	R
The role and tasks of the ethical practitioner	R	R	R	R	R	H	R	R	H	N	N	R	H	H	N	R
The importance of continuing professional self-development	N	N	N	N	R	R	R	H	N	R	N	N	R	N	R	N

H = Highly relevant   R = Relevant   N = Not relevant

An extended set of CIPD standards can be found in Appendix 1.

Dedication

To Jen, Sam, Joe, for all so far,
and on with the odyssey

Introduction to human resource development

| By the end of this chapter you will be able to: |

- define the core concepts associated with HRD in work and organisations;
- identify the main elements of a model of the HRD process;
- describe the major practices associated with HRD in work and organisations;
- outline how perspectives shape understanding HRD as a feature of work and organisation.

Introduction

The following job advertisement, for a head of Human Resource Development in a major organisation, was placed recently:

"Railco is investing heavily in staff training and development, to ensure the business exceeds at all levels of customer service first time, every time … you will champion, enable and support practical organisational change via training, learning and development, thereby making a direct impact on the business. With a huge infrastructure and traditional outlook, we are seeking an individual who can design, develop and implement learning strategies to drive culture change and enhance values. Within the context of a unionised workforce you will develop programmes to make a measurable impact on the business, inspiring the whole workforce to buy-in to an ethos of focus on customer service. Your first class relationship management skills will enable you to push ideas through, making things happen both on a strategic and hands-on level…you should possess contagious enthusiasm, a passion for results and have the gravitas and credibility to influence and drive organisational change at the highest level."[1]

The significance and role of HRD at work in the world of practice is well articulated in a concise way here. First, it is of value and of interest as something that can have a major impact. Second, successful management of HRD involves specialist knowledge and skills of the professional process. Third, it also involves more general abilities to push ideas through, to make things happen, to have credibility and to be able to drive change. These are the central themes which mark HRD as an area demanding study and which set the context for those approaching such study, whether experienced in organisational realities or a new student (see Resources Box 1.1.). Appreciating this big picture of what learning about HRD can mean from the outset is essential as a reference point for learning about all the different aspects of HRD.

1.1 HRD and involvement in organisational change activities

- There is almost universal agreement (93%) that a consideration of the learning and development implications of change is critical to its success.
- Only 29% of respondents feel that the learning and development implications are considered 'important' when their organisations plan major change initiatives.
- Thirty-three per cent of respondents report that they're not involved in the planning process for change until after all the major decisions have been taken, and 9% of respondents said the learning and training department isn't involved at all.
- Many respondents feel that this exclusion is because training implications are not thought through (54%) and 46% believe it's because they're not considered key stakeholders in organisational change.
- Over 80% of respondents feel that greater involvement could result in higher employee satisfaction and improved business results.

CIPD, *Learning and Development, Annual survey report 2006.*

The recognition and status of HRD in the workplace as a significant process, worth great attention and investment, has been hard won over time. Several important bodies and networks have contributed to this. They include the Academy of Human Resource Development (AHRD), The Chartered Institute of Personnel and Development (CIPD) and the American Society for Training and Development (ASTD). Their influence is a clearer agenda for learning about HRD at work (Strategic View Boxes 1.1, 1.2 and 1.3). However, that recognition and status is only as secure as the evidence and arguments which can be developed as business and management evolve. The guardians of learning and development in society – the great institutions of schooling and universities – have always understood their mission as central to securing a better future for all. The position of learning and development in the workplace has not been so esteemed. In the past 'training' was perceived to be practically-based, usually brief and occupation-focused. In the pragmatic, practical and cost-conscious contexts of work and organisation the infrastructure of training was, ideally, like a machine for developing the operational capability of the workforce. The world of work was to be a place where well-trained workforces used their skillsets, embraced organisational change to improve flexibility and innovated with the use of new technologies. One sign of changing

1.1 CIPD standards for people working in HRD

- Cooperate with stakeholders in developing policy and plans which are integrated with the wider HR and business strategy
- Advise on developing a well-managed HRD function
- Contribute to HRD that will aid recruitment and performance

- Promote learning and disseminate knowledge
- Design and provide effective learning using technology as appropriate
- Meet or exceed legal and ethical requirements in practices
- Continuously develop their own expertise and credibility

1.2 CIPD standards; knowledge and understanding

- Integration
  - Business environment and internal context
- Value-adding HRD function
  - For organisation and individuals, in projects, using consultants
- Induction and performance management
- Career and management development

- Support for change in structures, roles and environments
- Stimulation of innovation and creativity
- Design and delivery of HRD processes
- Evaluation of outcomes and investments
- Ethical practitioner

1.3 CIPD suggested curriculum in HRD

- Environment
  - Global and local
  - NVET policy
  - Internal environment; structure and culture
- Value adding; potential and issues
  - Business focus, HRD roles, budgets
- Supporting other HR processes
  - Recruiting, performance, relations, retention
- Change
  - Re-skilling, multi-skilling, adaptability, culture

- Challenging routines
  - Sharing and disseminating knowledge
- Design and delivery
  - New technologies, monitoring programmes
- Evaluation
  - Data and information sources, payback
- Ethical practitioner
  - Information and guidance, creating awareness, statutory standards

times is that this position seems to have been reversed. There is a questioning of the value and impact of schools and universities as the most significant institutions of learning in society. HRD at work is the means by which the new guardians of development will help secure a better future for all. The workplace is more esteemed as a site of learning, with lifelong learning replacing initial education as the rallying banner for the 21st century.

In the past the language of training and skills was prominent, and is still used in many instances. However, theory and practice have moved on, emphasising broader concepts and themes. Here we adopt an organising framework of process, practices and perspectives (see Figure 1.1) in which each domain interacts with another.

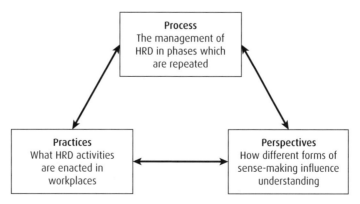

Figure 1.1 Overview of the structure of the book

There is no linear beginning–middle–end structure to the HRD triangle in the workplace; but textbooks do have to adopt such a structure. Here we begin with the core, recurring HRD process, manifest in varying and evolving kinds of practice which are guided and influenced by the perspectives of professionals, learners, governments and others.

In this introductory section the key concepts are listed and explained:

- Human resource management (HRM)
- Human resource development
  - Learning, Training, Education, Development
- HRD process
- HRD practices
- HRD perspectives
  - Performance management
  - Talent management

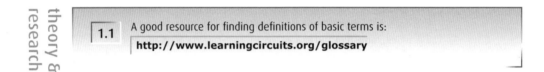

theory & research

1.1   A good resource for finding definitions of basic terms is:
http://www.learningcircuits.org/glossary

Human resource management (HRM)

You will often see the term 'HRD' used in conjunction with HRM, and sometimes synonymously. However, the term 'HRM' itself has various connotations and meanings. Usually it is used to define a particular approach to the management of people at work, and is contrasted with other approaches, such as the more conventional terms 'personnel management' or 'industrial relations'. In this sense HRM is seen as being a more managerial and restricted set of activities, focusing on employees as individuals and playing down the traditional employee relations role, conflict and the legitimacy of trade unions.

In this book I use HRM in a general and neutral sense to mean the whole of people management, the combination of employee resourcing, employee relations, employee reward and HRD concerns in business and management. HRD is thus one key function of the broader HRM of an organisation; it is not an isolated and stand-alone activity. Organisations' strategies and policies for attracting and retaining staff, and the ways in which stakeholders define their different and common interests at work, can have a great impact on HRD policies and practices. The scope of this text is to consider the HRD process, the practices associated with it, and perspectives relevant to exploring the nature of HRD at work in more detail.

Human resource development

Human resource development (HRD) is now commonly used as the organising term for discussion and analysis of workplace learning. It has a range of possible meanings which will be considered here (McGoldrick et al 2002, Harrison and Kessels 2003).

In some cases HRD is simply a different title for the same content as a conventional text on workplace training, learning and development. For other writers it signifies a broader and more encompassing definition of the scope of concerns of those studying learning in business and management (Walton 1999, Wilson 2001). In exploring HRD in either sense the roles of psychology, economics and systems theory can be widely acknowledged (Swanson and Holton 2001). In Piskurich et al (2000) the term is used primarily in the former sense, defining the general of study in which learning, development and training in the workplace are the subjects of interest.

Learning is conventionally defined as a change in an individual's level of knowledge, skill or attitude. We will explore later how a wide range of meanings with differing implications cluster around the idea of learning. What such change entails – and how to initiate, guide and control it –has generated much discussion among those whose job it is to manage learning, researchers and theoreticians, and entrepreneurs looking to market new learning solutions. Underlying all this diverse activity is the tension between the stress of practice – being able to manage learning – and the search for structured and secure understanding of learning. The last is the animator of the abiding interest in elaborating a science of learning. Being scientific in this context means simply giving a certain and definitive account of facts and relations, enabling rational and intelligent control for specific purposes. The pursuit of a 'science of learning' continues to exercise all those who seek to make learning happen better, faster or more effectively.

Training has been defined as learning and development undertaken for the purposes of supporting development and maintenance of operational capability in employment: skills for work and in work, on-job or off-job, to enable effective performance in a job or role. Training was thought of as separate from education and development. Training was a specific kind of formal learning provided in the workplace or preparation for a discrete job and/or role. The study of training in this sense has been dominated by the discipline of economics, associated with the analysis of skill formation and demand and supply in the context of general and business economics.

Education has been defined as a form of learning and development associated with academic learning, undertaken in dedicated educational institutions in the pursuit of qualifications, usually in advance of employment. Even as such learning has come to be more closely associated, in some cases, with employment, the participants in education are treated as students of bodies of knowledge, being taught by teachers in institutions. The nature and evolution of educational institutions and roles in the context of work, employment and organisations continues to be a significant area of concern and debate. Increasingly, some areas of academic education may be more related to learning for work, but not all. Education, and academic learning and development, still have broader and deeper aims: to promote learning for life and in aspects of life not connected with work and employment. Research in education, as a major institutional feature of society, remains a significant site for investigating learning and development.

Development has been distinguished from both training and education. It has been defined as learning which changes the whole person in some substantial way and helps people to grow, not just to change their vocational skill level or academic knowledge. Development is a task that faces people at all times, from childhood throughout the lifespan. It can become central at critical points such as the changes from childhood to adulthood, from early adulthood to mid-life, and from mid-life to later-life. These provide the more dramatic transitions; but there are other lesser experiences of transition within these where learning may be critical to the direction a person follows. In the context of work and organisations, 'development' was usually reserved to describe what was, in effect, learning for managers and professionals. There was a status issue involved. These groups, with career paths, had a course of development to follow; not just periods of vocational training. Employees were to be trained; managers and professionals were to be developed. Development tended to signify higher status and more sophisticated forms of learning and growth. Now personal development is becoming an integral part of working life for many employees, and the concept of development is being applied more broadly throughout work, employment and organisations. Development, and the growth it entails, is of interest as a domain of learning involving many more in the workforce.

This introduction to meanings makes a simple point. Describing the core terms in use signposts several areas of study, each complex in its own right, each with a stake in making up a full and useful understanding of learning and development at work. Skills and economic factors, the psychology of development, the social and institutional features of education: these all contain the seeds of an interest in knowledge and professionalism, development and ethics, learning and science.

The HRD process

A business process is a sequence of complementary activities intended to achieve a specified set of organisational objectives. The definition adopted here is that HRD involves a **process** of observation, planning, action and review to manage the cognitive capacities, capabilities and behaviours needed to enable and improve individual, team and organisational performance in work organisations (see Figure 1.2).

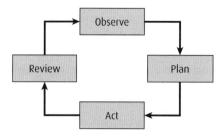

Figure 1.2 The HRD process

HRD begins with a phase of observation involving the assessment of HRD needs at work. This can be done at various levels and in various ways. It then involves planning, focusing on setting objectives for HRD at work interventions to achieve specific kinds of results. It subsequently requires action, in professionally delivering HRD at work using a range of methods and techniques. The process is completed by review, when HRD experiences and outcomes are evaluated; from testing what learners have learned to calculating costs and benefits. This cycle of activities forms the **HRD process** (see Theory & Research Box 1.2).

1.2 | *HRD process modelling*

Process modelling and understanding HRD at work should be done with the *caveat* that these categories of analysis can obscure, and become an obstacle to appreciating as a whole, the larger picture. By analogy, any work of art can be described in terms of its constituent colours of cyan, magenta, yellow and black. No art critic or historian would attempt to describe any real painting like that; pictures have to be appreciated as a whole. Likewise, while HRD in organisations may be composed of parts in these categories of process, a straight and mechanical application of them to describe cases can be as misleading.

Gratton and Ghoshal (2006; p. 6) have taken this further and suggested an important distinction that can be of use here – the distinction between 'best practice' processes and 'signature' processes.

> The search for, and adoption of, best practice processes is a crucial component in the creation of a high performance company....The more effective these processes are the more likely the company is to enjoy a competitive advantage.... what our research into high-performing companies shows, however, is that the adoption of best practice processes only gets you a seat at the table; it is not enough to assure you of winning the game...for sustained competitive success, however, something extra is required. We have discovered that other types of processes, which we call signature processes, are crucial. Signature processes are different from best practice processes. They are processes that evolve internally from executives' values and aspirations, while best practice refers to ideas developed outside the boundaries of the business unit or company.

In the context of that bigger picture HRD is the part of people management that deals with the process of facilitating, guiding and coordinating work-related learning and development to ensure that individuals, teams and organisations can perform as desired. A new recruit to a manufacturing company and an established senior manager assuming a new leadership role in a large multinational bank have different learning needs which present distinctive challenges. Nevertheless the HRD process involved will have some common, core features. Coming to know core parts of the HRD process, and being able to deal with them effectively, is a significant part of HRM in work organisations. The nature of organisational learning needs will also be distinctive, varying with the strategy, structure and culture of the organisation. The ability to analyse these is also a significant part of general HRM.

In other words, a uniform 'best practice' is not the be all and end all. In identifying needs, planning, delivering and evaluating HRD there might be distinctive and diverse 'signature' processes. Operations Box 1.1 identifies issues about the origins, development and core of best practice and signature processes in organisations in general. This model can be used as a basis for considering HRD processes as well.

Gratton and Goshal are suggesting that, as well as validating a range of signature processes rather than copying one version of best practice, learning about signature processes may actually reverse some common prescriptions of modelling best practice. To nurture signature-process development, there is a need to:

- Acknowledge that best practice is good, but not good enough;
- Look within an organisation rather than search externally for best practice;
- Become sensitive to and elaborate on those processes in a company about which people are passionate;
- Be more in tune with the organisation's values and beliefs.

| 1.1 | Best practice and signature process modelling compared |

	Best practice modelling	Signature process modelling
Origin	Starts with external and internal search for best practice processes	Evolves from a company-specific history
Development	'Bringing the outside in' Needs careful adaptation and alignment to the business goal and industry context	'Bringing the inside out' Needs championing by executives
Core	Shared knowledge from across the sector	Organisation values

Source Gratton, L. and Goshal, S. (2006) *Signing up for Competitive Advantage: How signature processes beat best practice*, London, EPSR/ESRC.

Enhanced process analysis in HRD can be informed by this. 'Best practice' may be applied in identifying needs, design, delivery and evaluation, yet, for any specific, real organisation, simply following this is not sufficient for advancing performance and competitiveness. Instead an awareness of the history and scope for signature processes, for doing things differently based on what has evolved within an organisation – which is different from best practice – can also improve the organisation's performance.

Practices

HRD at work in organisations typically involves major kinds of practice – what is done – for facilitating, guiding and coordinating HRD. The management of practice is the second major feature that is essential to developing effective performers in work and organisations. Practices include, for example:

1. on-the-job learning experiences at the workplace;
2. organisation-based/external short training courses;
3. 'learning partnerships', such as coaching or mentoring;
4. e-learning: either computer-based or in a 'learning centre'.

| 1.2 | Changes in workplace learning |

- On-the-job training is identified as the most effective form of learning by 39% of respondents.
- Eighty-five per cent believe that training is now more geared to meeting the strategic needs of the business than it was a few years ago.
- Nearly four-fifths report that learning and training now incorporates a much wider variety of activities (79%) and almost three-quarters agree that their jobs now involve a greater element of consultancy (74%).
- Only a quarter believe that e-learning has significantly altered learning and training offerings (25%).
- Two-thirds believe that learning and training is now taken more seriously by senior and line managers (63% and 68% respectively) and over half (58%) believe the learning and development department has far more credibility than in the 1990s.
- The implementation of new programmes to develop the roles of line managers is the most common change to workplace learning practices in the past 12 months.

Source CIPD, *Annual survey on Learning and Development 2006*

There are formal practices, such as training courses, and informal practices, such as peer coaching and mentoring. On-the-job training is defined here as training given at the desk or place where the person usually works. Off-the-job training is defined as training away from the immediate work position, at the employers' premises or elsewhere. It includes all forms of courses, as long as they are funded or arranged by the employer. If we look at techniques for HRD service delivery in organisations, the typical approach is to use internal and external off-the-job training. HRD at work is dominated by the delivery of short courses, typically of 1–3 days' duration.

How these practices emerge, are supported and managed, and change as organisations, technologies and priorities change creates a great demand for understanding learning and managing the behaviour of a range of stakeholders, from individual learners to specialist training organisations (see Resources Box 1.2).

Perspectives

How different people perceive the domain of HRD, and how those perceptions interact to determine what is seen as possible and desirable, is the third force that can impact on HRD at work. Where these perceptions can be applied to a group, and are relatively coherent and stable, we can call them 'perspectives' – points of view from which to consider and explore a subject. In HRM the simplest form of perspective is to consider the points of view of the employer and the employee, or the organisation and the individual. These are coherent and stable, if somewhat abstract. A more sophisticated differentiation of perspective extends to identifying stakeholders. In HRD at work these would include different kinds of learners, institutions of learning, government, professional bodies, trade unions, and others concerned with work. In this book a number of high profile and powerful perspectives will be considered. The selection is not exhaustive, but they do represent the major stakeholders and their high priority concerns.

Performance management

HRD needs to be set in the wider operational context of organisational performance management. HRD is a means to an end, not an end in itself. That end is usually acknowledged to be getting better results from the organisation, teams and individuals by understanding and managing performance within an agreed framework of planned goals, objectives and standards. HRD in this context is only one, albeit important, means of achieving organisational goals, objectives and standards. HRD is one of the complex social and technological systems which combine to produce functioning organisations, and, in seeking change, HRD often stirs up unexpected difficulties as it encounters the wider performance concerns embedded in socio-technical systems.

Talent management

Much activity and discussion in HRD is couched in terms of talent management and development (Tulgan 2001, Rothwell and Kazanas 2003). The emergence of this perspective represents an evolution of thinking on succession planning among the senior echelons of organisations, extending to values about identifying potential and working on that throughout the organisation. In some cases talent management will mean what is done with the development of people towards or in the senior echelons of the organisation; in others it will mean what we refer to here as HRD, the development of all in the workforce.

HRD in context

There has been increasing interest in effective HRD at work over recent years. This has been the outcome of argument and evidence about the connections between HRD and effective organisations. Individuals and organisations were agreed to be entering an era when adaptations to the onset of a learning society and a knowledge economy were argued to mark the way ahead. We can think of learning societies as communities dependent on the lifelong learning of all their members. This contrasts with industrial societies, which required most of their community to participate only in basic education. We can think of knowledge economies and learning societies as those in which wealth creation depends on the application of know-how alongside the manufacture of goods and provision of services. In this context the evidence was that HRD at work becomes more than a minor function of HRM, and is treated as one of the essential and critical tasks confronting individuals and organisations.

There has been no overnight success for HRD. The belief that HRD was a 'good thing' was manifested throughout the last century in frequent exhortations for employers to invest in their people, for government to invest in new schemes and initiatives to improve workforce development, and for all individuals to embrace lifelong learning in one form or another. These exhortations grew louder from the 1960s onwards. Yet HRD has often been overshadowed by other management and HRM concerns. At times industrial relations problems have dominated social and economic thinking, and consequently people management problem-solving. At other times people management was dominated by employee-resourcing concerns arising from changes in organisational and employment structures, such as the rise of flexible firms, and the establishment of 'new deal' employment practices and policies. It is often only when these industrial relations and employee-resourcing concerns slip off the organisational 'radar' that HRD gains the prominence many HR practitioners feel it merits. For many the 1990s saw employers embracing HRD, and a host of government schemes and initiatives launched whose goal was to improve workforce development for those in work and those preparing for work.

The provision and quality of HRD at work are currently acknowledged as key factors in adapting to change – economic change, social change, organisational change and technological change. As the traditional industries with their old forms of knowledge and skill base declined, new knowledge and skill bases had to be established to enable job creation and growth. In a context of dealing with unemployment and aspirations to eliminate historical discrimination and inequalities, the foundations for the social inclusion agenda were established. And as work organisations changed from standard bureaucracies with classic divisions of labour to flatter structures for lean, world-class manufacturing or service delivery, so a new agenda for HRD at work was needed, both as a means of effecting such change and as a consequence of it. And finally, as new technologies, particularly information technologies, were invented and adopted, so a whole range of other changes to organisations and jobs required new HRD at work.

This promotion of a critical role for HRD at work shows no signs of abating. Indeed there are signs that the importance of HRD at work is still increasing. This prominence may be unstable: it might be threatened if the industrial relations or work and employment situation were to worsen. However, at present the proponents of the learning society, of knowledge economies, of flexible organisations and careers, and the developers of new technologies all agree that the future will see greater demands upon employers, governments and individuals to participate in and improve HRD. It is in this context that HRD can claim to be a significant and challenging part of the future of HRM – much more than a passing concern for everyone except those aspiring to be specialist trainers who had to learn 'how to train' people.

Furthermore, HRD at work seems to offer the ultimate win–win outcomes for everyone. In an era characterised by the volatility of the change to a learning society and a knowledge economy there is logic to this approach. Effective HRD at work promises to provide the levers that can be manipulated in order to control the future of work and organisation to ensure individual career success and competitiveness for those currently prosperous, and a route to prosperity for those currently 'struggling to get by' or 'going nowhere'.

For those with a more sceptical approach to such consensus in areas of management, this may all sound too good to be true. The sceptics have a point, and, to avoid the pitfalls of succumbing to the rhetoric of some with a lot to gain from over-promoting HRD, we need advocates who can give a balanced and professional view; those with the ability to reflect critically on HRD, using what the human sciences have to offer; on the problems of HRD strategies in organisations; on how National Vocational Education and Training (NVET) policy is made; on the potential of e-learning; and on how to connect HRD with the theory and practice of knowledge management.

Conclusion

The theory and practice of HRD is characterised by a dilemma, that of being simultaneously lauded and questioned. It is commonly supported – cited as part of the solution to securing the best possible future – but also challenged to demonstrate its relevance to business and to fulfilling value-adding criteria, especially among strategists concerned with the future of the whole enterprise. Behind these concerns is the simple truth that, although HRD is a necessary condition for success, the practices it entails are not a sufficient condition for effective performance or success. For HRD at work to be a part of securing the future it needs to be embedded in the strategic and performance management heart and head of the organisation, an integral part of dealing with strategic threats and opportunities by building on internal strengths and overcoming weaknesses. Linking HRD to the key strategic drivers of organisation can deliver the promised returns of HRD at work, and those who can manage HRD are to be valued since they may play a major role in its success.

resource

| 1.3 | **Key quote** In times of drastic change it is the learners who inherit the future. Those who have finished learning find themselves equipped to live in a world that no longer exists. |

Eric Hoffer

Being equipped to live in the world of the future rather than one that no longer exists (see Resources Box 1.3) is a real challenge facing many people in thousands of workplaces throughout the world. Exploring HRD in work and organisations is a major feature of modern management and organisation because of the demands this adaptation creates. Among the key decisions to be made about the workforce, central to the problem-solving which permeates managing and right at the heart of understanding transitions and change, is the question 'what are the right kinds and levels of learning and development that we need to have?'. If those needs are recognised and dealt with the conviction that success and sustainable competitiveness is always founded on investing on the right kinds and levels of learning and development can be supported and extended for the good of people and organisations, and for national and global success.

resources

1.4 | *UK training spend and budgets*

- Seventy-three per cent of organisations have a training budget, with the average spend per employee being £469.
- Organisations employing less than 100 people spend more per head on training (£898) than those with more than 500 employees (£344).
- Private sector organisations spend an average of £488 per employee, compared to £447 in the public sector and £438 in the voluntary sector.

Source CIPD, *Annual Survey on Learning and Development 2006*

References

CIPD (2006) *Annual Survey on Learning and Development*, CIPD, London.

Garger, E. (1999), 'Goodbye Training, Hello Learning', *Workforce*, vol. 78, no. 11.

Gibb, S. and Megginson, D. (2000) 'New Employee Development: Successful innovations or token gestures?', *Personnel Review*, vol, 29, no 4.

Gratton, L. and Goshal, S. (2006) *Signing up for Competitive Advantage: How signature processes beat best practice,* London, EPSR/ESRC.

Harrison, R. and Kessels, J. (2003) *Human Resource Development in a Knowledge Economy*, Basingstoke, Palgrave Macmillan.

IPD (2000) *Success Through Learning: The argument for strengthening workplace learning*, IPD Consultative Document.

Johnson, S. et al (2000) *Learning Pays; The Bottom Line*, National Advisory Council for Education and Training Targets.

Martin, G. et al (2001), 'Company Based Education Programmes: What's the pay-off for employers?', *Human Resource Management Journal*, vol. 11, no. 4.

McGoldrick, J., Stewart, J. and Watson, S. (2002) *Understanding Human Resource Development: A research based approach*, London, Routledge.

Piskurich, G.M. et al (eds) (2000) *The ASTD Handbook of Training Design and Delivery*, New York, McGraw-Hill.

Rothwell, W.J. and Kazanas, H.C. (2003) *The Strategic Development of Talent*, Amherst, HRD Press.

Swanson, R.A. and Holton, E. F. (2001) *Foundations of Human Resource Development*, San Francisco, Berret-Koehler.

Tulgan, B. (2001) *Winning The Talent Wars*, New York, W.W. Norton & Co.

Walton, J. (1999) *Strategic HRD*, London, Financial Times/Pitman.

Wilson, J. (2001) *Human Resource Development*, London, Kogan Page.

URLs

American Society for Training & Development

www.astd.org

Academy of Human Resource Development

www.ahrd.org

Chartered Institute of Personnel and Development

www.cipd.co.uk

Q

| concluding short case question | *Developing 'customer focus* |

In recent years your company has been subjected to increased competition, and the CEO has responded to this by seeking to develop a more customer-focused workforce. As the HR director you have been asked how HRD could contribute to achieving that goal.

With particular reference to the ideas introduced here about the HRD process, what would you suggest are the priority areas of action that are likely to need addressing?

A

| concluding short case answer |

Answers should consider priorities for action in the four main process areas of HRD: identifying needs, designing effective learning activities, delivering these and evaluating the HRD.

They should first set the HRD process in context. The first contextual issue is how training has always been an important concern in improving performance in the workplace, but that now promoting learning and development is often seen as an integral part, not only of effective performance, but also of maintaining job satisfaction and improving employee retention rates. The second aspect of context is that, despite these forces for HRD, the realities are often that organisations may respond to competition with strategies such as downsizing and cost-cutting which mean that HRD activity may be cut back. It is not unusual for this 'stop–start' and 'off–on', 'love–hate' vacillation about HRD to produce confusion and bad practice in even the most basic activities in organisations which appear to be busy with HRD activity.

Here the performance focus is 'customer focus', and the CEO is switched on to exploring HRD's potential to change this. In this case the first part of the HRD process is the needs analysis phase. What is the organisation currently doing on customer focus? The strategic concerns around 'customer focus' should be unpacked and made more explicit, providing a framework for developing training around knowledge, skills and values. What are the different levels of need across the organisation as a whole for specific occupational groups (front line staff or support staff, for example) and for each individual? Having taken all these levels into account a training plan to translate the business objective into the workforce's capability, skills/competence, is necessary. When it comes to identify training needs for an individual, whoever is working with the individual to define those needs must keep in mind the organisation's overall objectives and how that training contributes towards them. It is also important to recognise that identifying the need also involves convincing staff that the need exists and should be met. If people do not understand how their HRD is tied into their company's overall business goals they may not feel committed to it. For a training programme to work effectively, it is vital that employees understand its impact not only on their personal development, but also on overall company development.

The design phase comes next: having identified a set of needs a professional and considerate development of activities is required. Some needs may be tackled through sourcing off-the-shelf e-learning packages, some may need a series of workshops to be created; others may require individual 1-to-1 coaching and/or mentoring.

continued overleaf

A

Given the need to balance elements of cognitive capacity, capability and behaviour in addressing 'customer focus', all kinds of activity can be designed. The important thing is to show an awareness of a need to combine all these three elements, whether e-learning, a workshop or coaching is to be used.

The delivery phase – actually doing the development – is an opportunity to use some combination of instruction and facilitation to motivate, engage and affect the learners effectively. That may be done by using specialist trainers, by involving managers and/or by involving other staff. For a major exercise on a central competence, such as customer focus, it is likely that a combination of all three, with internal and external specialists, will be used. The variations in control, quality and cost that these represent have to be balanced.

'Internal' solutions can be relatively straightforward and inexpensive to arrange. In other situations it may be appropriate to involve specialist providers, and many products/services exist in the training marketplace.

The final phase is evaluation which has several functions in this context:

- Have the training interventions been appreciated by staff and have they met the aims sought?
- Has there been a measurable improvement in skill and knowledge? Some of the HRD an organisation provides may be certificated, and there might be scope for aspects of that in this case, although the company-specific context might present a constraint on the value of this kind of development and its certification.
- Does the training that has been provided away from work transfer back to the workplace?
- Is the cost of the training on customer focus producing the expected benefits and changes in performance and productivity? The various stakeholders, from senior management through the trainers themselves to the workforce, will want to be clear that any deficiencies in training are remedied and any benefits are recognised.
- Can the company put itself forward for an award, for example, to capitalise on this investment in training?

In conclusion, an effective answer should seek to reflect on what completing the HRD process for this specific need – customer focus – shows us; that reference to the HRD process enables a disciplined approach to the basics to be followed, increasing the likelihood that HRD will meet business objectives.

HRD is a means to an end not an end in itself. Has the HRD delivered produced the performance required? The answer can also indicate that each HRD project, like this one on customer focus, is shaped by, and in turn helps to shape or change, the organisation's culture. In this way HRD is felt to play a central part in raising motivation and satisfaction levels at work. Personal development may ensure an employee feels a valued part of an organisation, no matter how big or small, and no matter what his/her job function is. If organisations can make investing in learning a part of their business strategy and provide formal, individualised learning for each person, they may see returns that can exceed the expected increased productivity and drive.

The HRD process is only a guide. It may become a hindrance if people become too focused on organising the process rather than managing learning. In theory the HRD process model will help to manage learning by helping to guide and direct good practice and ensuring that training is the best it can be. But such formal training is not the be-all-and-end-all. There is also workplace learning, and encouraging employees to take responsibility for their own development, above and beyond structured training.

Notes

1. Railco job ad, head of learning and development, *The Herald*, 23 September 2005.

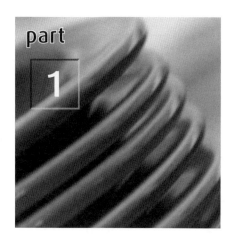

Process

A process can be thought of as a series of phases repeatedly used in making or achieving something, which can be modelled and controlled. The overall HRD process is illustrated graphically overleaf. It shows the four main phases:

Assessing needs	Objectivity
Developing HRD experiences	Designing
Delivering HRD	Actions
Evaluating HRD	Quality

Each of these phases is explored in sequence. Within each of the major phases there are actions which are usually required to complete each major phase. These can be analysed with regard to both 'hard' and 'soft' features. The 'hard' features are those involved in organisational performance, the techniques and practical, technical, operations in use. The 'soft' features are those involved in the organisational environment, which requires these techniques to be applied thoughtfully rather than mechanically, in social settings.

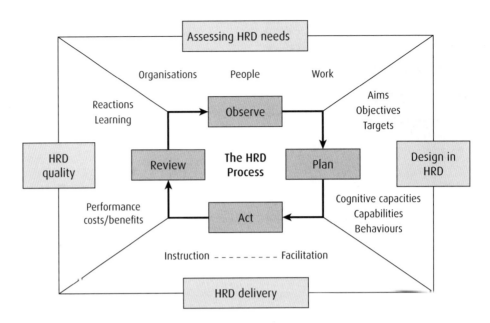

Figure P1.1 The overall HRD process

HRD needs: people,
work and organisations

> **By the end of this chapter you will be able to:**
>
> □ describe the first phase of the HRD process, assessing needs;
> □ identify different causes for performance gaps, including those related to HRD;
> □ describe and analyse three areas of potential HRD need: organisational, work or occupational, and personal;
> □ relate HRD needs analysis to the broader performance management process and concerns of individuals and organisations;
> □ use skills and techniques to identify HRD needs.

Q

> **introductory exercise**
>
> You are HRD director of an organisation that has recently been the subject of some adverse publicity following a high profile court case in which accusations of sexual harassment of women in your organisation were proven. Your CEO has asked you to come up with 'a training course' to eradicate the problem of sexual harassment.
>
> Put down some thoughts on the advice you would give the CEO about how you might go about 'assessing' HRD needs in this situation.

Introduction: the performance management process and context

The first phase of the HRD process we identified in chapter 1 is to assess and identify HRD needs. It is self-evident that, unless needs can be perceived and articulated, there can be no effective management of HRD. What is less obvious is that what is observed, and who is doing the observation, can influence if and how HRD emerges as an option among a range of responses to observed performance problems (see Figure 2.1). These assessments of need come from an interplay of organisational, work and individual factors, each of which calls for a careful and considered observation of situations and circumstances.

The assessment of needs does not happen in a vacuum, it always arises in a context. Figure 2.1 provides a graphic overview of the broad performance management context for the observation of HRD needs in the workplace: the possible human causes of performance gaps, and interventions to deal with them. It is important to realise that Figure 2.1 demonstrates that there is a range of possible causes and interventions in observing performance problems. Some of these are not attributable to deficits in human resources, or are not best resolved through continuing the HRD process onto its subsequent stages. First and foremost interventions need to be weighed for their appropriateness (see Operations Box 2.1). These broad concerns are the context within which to describe and analyse the first phase of observation and assessment of the HRD process.

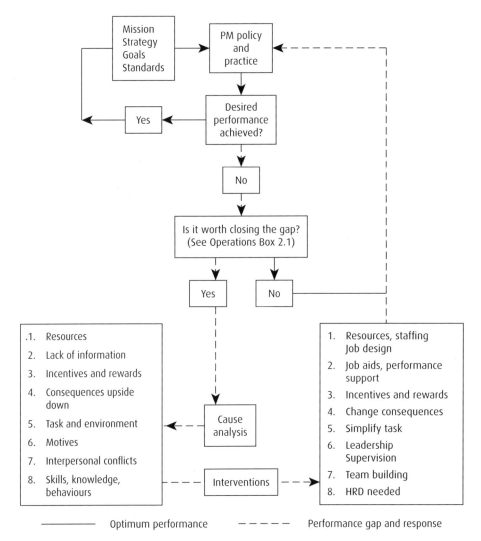

Figure 2.1 Performance management analysis

Source Based on Ford 1999

Figure 2.1 shows that, where a performance gap is identified, the first question is 'Is it worth closing the gap'? This requires some sense of context and an estimation, or calculation, of costs and benefits. For a performance problem that is mission critical, where the benefits of closing the gap are considerably greater than the costs, this is clear. Equally, where the performance problem is an apparently minor concern for which a 'quick fix' is available, but which might take a lot of resources and time to deal with through training, the approach will be clear. The more difficult and challenging situations arise are those which are less black and white.

2.1 | *Are performance gaps worth closing?*

Identifying performance gaps does not necessarily mean that actions, HRD-related or otherwise, have to be taken. The following stepwise analysis shows one way of structuring the observation of any gap that exists to consider whether, and what, action is needed:

1. **Define** specifically whose performance is at issue: which person, or which group.

2. What is the actual performance **discrepancy**? Describe the actual and the desired performance.

3. **Estimate the cost** in such a way that a solution can be found which costs less than the consequences of living with the problem. Is the problem worth solving? Is it a big enough problem to bother about? How much does the problem cost? What happens if you ignore the problem?

4. Options other than full HRD include:

    a. Is it possible to apply a **fast fix**? If a light goes out we try changing the bulb first rather than calling out an electrician.
    b. Do the people involved **already know how** to perform effectively? Could they perform in the past? Are the tasks performed often? Perhaps better feedback is needed, or some refresher practice or job aids.
    c. Are expectations clear, and are resources adequate? Is performance quality visible, and is **feedback** on performance being given?
    d. Consider **task changes** as solutions: simplify the task, remove obstacles to performance.
    e. Are the '**consequences**' properly balanced? Or are people in some way rewarded for doing things wrong? List all the negative and positive 'consequences' of poor performance from the point of view of the people involved.

5. Do the poor performers have the **potential** to change?

6. If it seems after all this that the performance gap is worth closing, and HRD is appropriate, then describe the **training solutions** and calculate the costs. Select the most practical and cost-effective HRD solution and implement it.

Source Mager, 2000.

Performance context

The next concern in HRD needs analysis, which is often neglected, is to consider the full range of possible theoretical frameworks and explanations for and responses to any performance gap.

For as well as the practical challenge of identifying genuine HRD needs there is often another kind of challenge early on, an intellectual problem of bias and perspective in observing performance at work reflecting the influence of movements and systems in thinking about organisational performance. The way that patterns in organisational performance are perceived may take different forms depending on how key people in the organisation see and think about performance management and the appropriate interventions that are consistent with them. Theory & Research Box 2.1 sets out some different ways of seeing and thinking about performance management in an organisation. These perceptions reflect and embody deeper assumptions about management and change, and will influence how company strategies and HR policies for performance management are enacted.

These options about observing patterns in organisational performance offer different ways of defining and translating the basic goals of the organisation into different levels of responsibility, including unit, team and individual performance tasks and challenges. They also offer different ways of thinking about the performance management process of planning goals, setting objectives, and agreeing measurable standards or activities in organisations. These lenses and ways of thinking about organisational performance will influence the extent to which HRD needs are observed and assessed: that is, they define the type and shape of the issues that will be identified and encountered. By using these approaches, explicitly or implicitly, organisations will be able to observe and identify certain kinds of gap between their desired performance and their actual performance.

theory & research

2.1 | Different lenses for thinking about performance management and HRD

Identifying a core value proposition for the business. This involves determining the value streams in a business; the extent to which the business model is, for example, brand- or cost-driven. Determining the core value provides an underlying context for success, and what managers need to work on to achieve it; making the brand perform or controlling and reducing costs are not mutually exclusive, but the concerns they highlight about managing performance can be distinctive (see Finkelstein et al 2006).

Identifying key performance indicators (KPI). This involves setting specific, measurable, attainable, time-bounded objectives for a range of activities in the organisation. This is the model of performance management that many people have, and which many organisations adopt. It is associated with conventional top-down strategic management in the private sector, and with value-for-money initiatives in the public sector.

Kaizen, TQM. This involves developing, planning and monitoring systems to achieve continuous improvement. It is most associated with successful manufacturers, with origins in Japanese companies.

Becoming 'excellent' or 'world class': adopting, or establishing, the standards of the best in order to compete. This is associated with, for example, the work of Peters and Waterman (1990) on 'excellence' and, in the contemporary context, with standards such as the European Quality Management Foundation (EQMF).

High-commitment organisations. This involves ensuring that the workforce is fully and enthusiastically engaged in achieving the tasks of the organisation. It is associated with trends to develop organisational cultures that embody this concern, often focused on customer service.

Business process re-engineering. This involves reviewing organisational structures to achieve tasks faster with fewer resources. It is associated with the 'flattening' of hierarchies, 'downsizing' of workforces, and 'outsourcing' of activities.

Developing balanced scorecards. This involves identifying measures across a broad range of areas to monitor and evaluate. It is associated with the work of Kaplan and Norton (1996). They identify four areas that need to be balanced: translating the vision, feedback and learning, business planning, and communicating and linking.

Learning organisation. This involves keeping abreast or ahead of the competition by ensuring that the organisation has an effective collective learning process that facilitates change and innovation. It is associated with the work of Senge (1990) in the USA and the ideas of Pedler et al (1991) in the UK.

Organisation development. This involves using behavioural sciences to diagnose and solve organisational problems. It is most associated with the 'academic' literature on management and organisations (e.g. Robbins 1993) and the use of 'action research' projects, in which researchers and managers work together.

Objective and subjective factors in assessing needs

Objective observations of needs centre on defining levels of expected performance and performance gaps in tangible and quantifiable ways. They may be based on financial results, productivity or product/service quality levels (see Resources Box 2.1).

2.1　*People and productivity*

Productivity is the average output produced by inputs, a combination of human and capital resources. We can describe it in economic terms – for example, in manufacturing measuring the number of goods produced per hour – or in terms of customer satisfaction. One UK survey found that 36 per cent of organisations measured productivity formally, 22 per cent measured it informally, 21 per cent used both formal and informal measures, and 22 per cent did not measure it all (see Table 2.1).

Measure	Organisations (%)
Customer satisfaction	24
Output per head	16
Output per hour per head	13
Sales/turnover per head	12
Profit per head	11
Output	10
Output per £ invested/ROI	10
Other	2

Table 2.1 Productivity measures

Countries can be compared in productivity terms. Differences may reflect issues in capital productivity, a lack of investment in HRD or structural differences such as having more part-time and temporary staff. A lack of HRD can be seen as a principal barrier to increased productivity.

Source: NOP World, 2004.

In defining and measuring objective productivity criteria, some general problems with obtaining accurate information at reasonable costs are encountered. There can also be problems specific to sectors, where productivity may be less dependent on internal organisational factors and more on external factors. Even where such contextual challenges are overcome the use of objective data on its own is often of limited use in HRD needs analysis. It is usually only meaningful when compared with some internal or external benchmark standard, and/or with trends over time. It is this comparison, rather than stand-alone, absolute observations, that generates effective assessments of HRD needs. To take a simple example, the level of sales a sales person achieves will not indicate whether there are performance issues; it is only when we compare that person's sales with those of other people in the same organisation, or in similar companies, that we may see whether a difference exists which warrants being called a performance gap.

The challenge, then, is to establish norms for performance. Measures of central tendency, such as arithmetic means and deviations from these means, provide the control limits and standards of acceptable performance. If an organisation's performance as a whole lies outside these standard thresholds, then its viability will be doubtful. If a retailer is failing to make as much sales revenue per person employed or per area of retail space as its competitors, or perhaps as other stores in the same group, then this is usually a signal that something significant needs attention. Trend analysis in performance is also possible: tracking trends over time can be one of the most useful sources of information about tangible gaps in performance.

However, what is objectively measurable isn't necessarily all that is important or meaningful in assessing needs. And the attempt to become more forensic in identifying needs can distract from providing effective HRD. Subjective perceptions may also be used, and may indeed be more useful. Subjective perceptions about performance, usually described as attitudes and feelings, can be collected and interpreted to identify where performance issues arise. These subjective perceptions may come from customers, the workforce, managers, or from more general management research. For example, managers may form perceptions in the course of their work, through conducting staff surveys, or by getting feedback on individuals from a range of sources in the course of performance appraisal. Perceptions may also be derived from focus group discussions among managers, staff and customers on important performance themes and issues. These perceptions may be cross-checked through surveys of customers or other stakeholders.

Subjective perceptions of need usually remain private information inside the organisation, or inside the unit or team, in contrast to the publicly available objective observations and measures. One of the issues with using and including subjective perceptions and measures of need is their reliability. Norms for subjective perceptions can be established, and many of the model employer surveys now in common use seek to do that. Again, trends over time are more valuable than snapshots.

Levels of analysis

Whether objective or subjective approaches to assessing need are taken, there are other influences on methods for HRD needs analysis, thinking about, observing and measuring organisations and their goals. Variation occurs in terms of sectors: for example, for-profit organisations often observe and measure clear financial measures whereas not-for-profit organisations may be more 'values-based', for example valuing being compassionate and caring, and concerned to link HRD to achieving that. Variations in perception, observation and measurement will also exist according to the different business strategies followed by organisations; depending on the relative importance of, for example, innovation, quality or cost-leadership strategies. The underlying challenge is to identify, observe and measure the key strategic drivers of performance before investing in any HRD. Without specifying relevant and specific performance improvement outcomes – no matter how much is to be spent on HRD or how professional HRD delivery may be – the prospects for sustained impact from HRD activity will be poor.

Observing and assessing HRD needs is the first phase in providing the learning opportunities required to achieve the goals, standards and objectives of the organisation. These can be articulated through organisational, team and individual levels of analysis.

Organisational needs

In discussing and analysing overall organisational effectiveness, senior directors, managers and others naturally consider the extent to which HRD needs may exist. In dealing with the identification of HRD needs at the organisational level it should be stressed that this is a particular example of a general activity; research to inform problem-solving and decision-making. The methods and techniques of data collection and analysis are not unique to the identification of HRD needs.

For example, we can analyse performance management concerns that relate specifically to HRD at work by defining the goals, standards and objectives of the organisation in terms of performance management concerns in three categories (see Strategic View Box 2.1).

strategic view

2.1 | *Three kinds of organisational HRD need*

Based on Boydell and Leary (1996).

Goals	Standards	Objectives
Implementing	doing things well	competence
Improving	doing things better	excellence
Innovating	doing new and better things	pioneering

exercise

2.1 Select an industry sector, for example, food retailing, fashion, or banking. Using the categories 'Implementing', 'Improving' and 'Innovating', identify one example of an organisation from each sector that is engaging with each of these levels of performance management. Who are the examples in the sector of pioneers, the excellent and the competent? What differences in observing HRD needs do you think these different kinds of organisation would have?

One kind of organisational need is that of the whole organisation, which we can define as needs that are common to all members of the organisation. Everyone, from the top to the bottom and across all units, may need HRD of a particular kind. This might include induction or basic health and safety training. Other common examples are learning about new information systems or new product introductions. If organisational restructuring is proposed, in the course of which jobs and job specifications will change, the cognitive capacities and capabilities required will also have to change. Or, as often applies in restructuring exercises, culture changes are also sought, and these may necessitate major behavioural and attitudinal changes among all employees to align with the desired new culture.

Often, in this regard, organisations have completed their own internal mapping of competence. These are outlines of the key qualities and behaviours associated with effective performance in the workforce as a whole. They can be used for many purposes, from compiling selection profiles to development planning and reward.

Second, organisational HRD needs may be defined in terms of a performance gap that is seen to affect the organisation as a whole, not just a part of it. With this kind of organisational need assessment, gaps between desired performance and actual performance can come in many shapes and sizes. In the pursuit of effective performance – which may be defined as either doing things well, doing them better or doing them differently – an HRD issue may become a central strategic issue, and of major concern to the organisation's senior management team. Classifying the kinds of concern about organisational effectiveness can lead to identifying HRD needs at the organisational level in many areas (see Strategy Box 2.2).

| 2.2 | *Organisational effectiveness, from Bramley 1991* |

Achieving goals
- Increasing product/service quality
- Increasing output
- Increasing productivity

Satisfying customers
- Improving organisational image
- Reducing complaints
- Increasing proportion of on-time deliveries

Increasing resourcefulness
- Increasing share of market
- Increasing employee versatility
- Moving into new markets

Improving internal processes
- Increasing group cohesiveness
- Increasing quality of supervision
- Increasing managers' abilities

Much information may already be available within the organisation, in the form of plans and data sources about all these kinds of concern, thus limiting the need for original observation and research in assessing HRD needs. In undertaking a needs analysis it should be the business needs that provide the rationale for what is to be done, not what a training manager or anybody else with a professional view thinks might be useful. Many stress this point, because otherwise there is a threat that trainers and training managers may drift into providing 'more of what has been done already', maintaining a catalogue of courses as a ready-made solution to performance problems. Such familiar and easy-to-manage catalogues or menus of courses may even be popular with managers and staff, but they can be out of touch if they are not founded on proper needs analysis and a general analysis of the environmental factors that impinge on the organisation and its development.

| 2.2 | *Existing plans and data* |

1. **Human resource plans**: data on future demands for staff to ensure that there is a supply of the right kinds of people, whether that means maintaining a steady state, expanding or rationalising. From these, we can derive some perceptions of the extent and kind of HRD needs – for example the replacement rates of certain kinds of role.
2. **Succession planning data**: identifying concerns with employee flows related to promotions, retirements and leavers.
3. **Reviews of critical incidents**: organisations often experience and analyse unforeseen events that turn out to be of great importance. By reviewing such 'accidents', good or bad, and discrepancies, they develop a database for learning.
4. Management **information systems**: data from various sources are collated and can be integrated to support analysis for decision-making. In manufacturing, for example, enterprise resource planning systems provide managers with data on real-time performance.
5. Individual **performance appraisal** systems and records: performance reviews based on attainment of targets offer a potentially rich source of information about HRD needs. However, it is possible to have the trappings of a performance management system, particularly an individual appraisal system, without the data from that being collated and processed for the management of HRD.

Existing sources of information and other HR systems that may be relevant to a needs analysis are set out in Operations Box 2.2. If no existing sources of information are available, then identification of HRD needs may become the source of information for others to use in their own contexts, as well as identifying HRD needs. If, for example, there are performance problems that catalyse HRD needs analysis, but there are no current measures of productivity with which to gauge the impact of any HRD, then such measures will need to be developed. Thus, analysing HRD needs may have important implications for motivating and driving performance management in general.

Work and occupation analysis

HRD needs can also be observed at the level of areas of work and occupation. In this respect there is an abundance of frameworks to chose from. Government, other agencies and companies often conduct exercises to map and specify the skills and knowledge needs of an area of work or an occupation. Professional associations and bodies do the same for almost every area of work, from general management to customer service. The resulting comprehensive maps, often defined as 'competence' frameworks, are needed to inform the design of vocational courses and qualifications for those who aspire to work in that area or occupation. They specify what is needed to be able to perform to the standards expected in employment. These general maps may not exactly match the behaviours that any specific organisation needs or expects from people in those roles. Nonetheless, someone who holds a qualification in a particular area may have demonstrated sufficient competence for an organisation to infer equivalent competence in its specific sphere of concern.

Where more general HRM plans and systems *do* exist in an organisation it is usual to find that some kind of job analysis has been undertaken. These may range from simple job specifications to more structured job grading schemes. Job specifications typically identify roles, key tasks, competences and performance standards. Job and task analysis will have been used to create these specifications, and HRD needs can be logically and directly derived from them. It makes economic sense to use such existing reference points, based on traditional forms of scientific job and task analysis of existing data about jobs and competences. However, there are concerns with these, and one major problem with depending on these kinds of job specification and analysis is that they produce an inflexible notion of needs related to discrete job families. This model often seems outmoded and inappropriate alongside contemporary views of changing organisational structures and cultures that emphasise flexibility, innovation, project and teamworking.

At a national level, specifications for occupational categories can be highly detailed and very well defined, and integrated into many development systems and activities, such as career guidance and advice. These occupational categories can be used to characterise overall supply and demand in the labour market and associated systems such as further and higher education. Accordingly, various institutions have an interest in defining and managing the HRD needed to provide the year-by-year replacements in occupations, depending on expansion or contraction in the particular area of work in the short and long term. On the basis of such forecasts governments provide funding for HRD in educational institutions, and organisations provide their own HRD for those pursuing careers in occupations they depend on.

Job analysis

Within organisations, job, task and occupational analyses are required to support HRM systems in many areas of practice, ranging from templates for recruitment processes to performance appraisal systems and rewards (see Figure 2.2). Some suggest that, even where job specifications already exist, a distinct HRD needs analysis may raise issues about the validity and reliability of these specifications. This is because it can be dangerous to assume that existing models of work and occupation can be directly adopted for the purpose of HRD needs analysis. Examining existing job specifications for their robustness in the HRD context means understanding something of methods of job analysis.

Job analysis is, in essence, any systematic procedure used for obtaining detailed information about a job. The methods may vary, but they should all produce the following outcomes:

- specifications that have 'face validity' – that is, they are acceptable to current job-holders and their managers;
- clear role definitions specifying the purposes and main functions of the job;
- specification of key tasks – describing the main parts of the job;
- specification of competences – what people need to know and be able to do to perform the tasks;
- specification of performance standards – what will be measured and reviewed.

These outcomes can help to identify what HRD will be relevant, and where HRD efforts might need to be focused. As will be discussed in chapter 3, they can also be used to help structure the planning of HRD, by suggesting areas where specific aims, goals

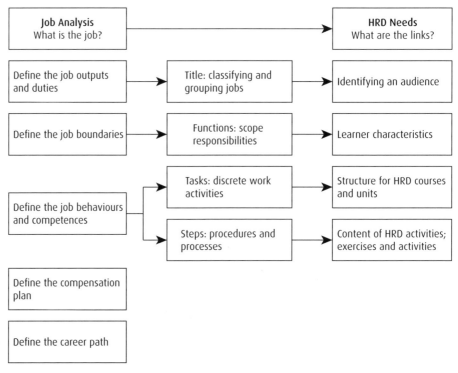

Figure 2.2 Job analysis and links to occupational HRD

and objectives for HRD activities will be needed. Sometimes, though, a performance gap seen to be associated with the way a task or occupation is managed is not relevant for HRD needs analysis at all.

A framework for analysis is needed where jobs or tasks must be reviewed in order to identify HRD needs. For instance, examples of job outputs could be 'to take orders over the phone', 'to assemble a piece of furniture' or 'to write marketing reports'. Duties related to these kinds of output can be described using job analysis. These descriptions may vary from the general to the highly specific. In the examples cited above, the resulting titles might be 'call centre operator', 'furniture maker' or 'marketing manager'.

Boundaries are the limits to the job, delineating where responsibilities end. These are the interfaces with other jobs and roles in the organisation at which job-holders must interact to achieve overall outputs. For example, call centre operators will not manage budgets, furniture makers will not sell chairs, and marketing managers will not design the products. These tasks will all be part of other jobs.

Behaviours are defined in this context as the observable actions involved in performance, whereas competences are defined as the capabilities underlying effective performance. When describing jobs, we usually use a mixture of behavioural and competence statements, though some jobs emphasise one rather than the other. For example, furniture-making will focus on behaviours, whereas management and professional roles are more often described in terms of competence, because they involve the application of capacities that are not directly observable. A good example would be a medical doctor: he or she cannot guarantee to produce the outcome of a 'successful' operation or course of treatment – that is, a healthy or 'live' patient. What doctors can, and should, guarantee is that, in dealing with patients, they follow the procedures laid out for such operations or courses of treatment in a competent fashion.

Personal level HRD needs

HRD needs assessment would be a blunt and ineffective instrument if it were confined to a generic analysis of organisational or occupational needs. Not everyone whose work includes the same or similar tasks, whether new or existing staff, will have the same kinds or degrees of HRD need. A 'one-size-fits-all' approach, which is a consequence of analysing only at the organisational or occupational level, is pejoratively known as sheep-dip training. Everyone is processed through the same things, regardless of their individual needs. Yet the workforce is not a flock of cloned sheep to be shepherded through HRD.

Perceiving and assessing HRD needs correctly and accurately at an individual level is also critical. Where an individual person has a great personal need for learning, the HRD provided is usually a success. Where there is little or no personal need, the HRD, no matter how well designed and delivered, is going to be perceived as a waste of time and resources. To reduce waste and concentrate resources on using HRD to improve the performance of the organisation and the individual, the personal-level needs must be accurately identified and worked with.

One way to identify individual needs is to compare individuals with standards. If clear organisational, task or occupation descriptions and standards are defined, then individuals can be assessed against them. Some individuals may need more development in some aspects of the task need than in others; obvious occasions being induction and following any major change.

Personal needs can also be identified at various critical gateway points. The first gateway is the exploration of applicants' experience and qualifications during the selection process. The second gateway will be some form of performance appraisal during employment. There is a wide variety of performance appraisal methods, but their common purpose is to identify how far individuals meet expected and desired performance standards. A third gateway might be the use of assessment centres to identify HRD needs, whether for selection, placement, appraisal or career development during employment. A fourth gateway might be the management of career development, up the promotion ladder and across posts and tasks.

As with the organisational identification of HRD needs in a performance management context, some sources and responses to individual performance concerns do not lead into HRD design and delivery (see Resources Box 2.2). These are performance issues attributable to other factors.

The aim is to analyse HRD needs that connect systematically with personal performance issues over at least an annual cycle, rather than reacting 'as and when' personal issues arise. In the past this depended upon line managers being concerned with HRD provisions as they discussed and planned the work of their staff. Increasingly, employees are being expected to take more responsibility for identifying their own HRD needs through some kind of personal development planning process.

2.2 | Personal performance gaps; possible causes

Reasons why people do not perform	Responses
They've forgotten how to do it	*Job aids* to remind people how to do what they already know how to do; for example, checklists
They don't know what is expected	*Information*: clarify what is expected in the job
They do not have the authority, tools, time or space	*Give permission to perform*, providing not just responsibility for results but also authority to achieve these
They don't get feedback	Give feedback – people need specific feedback on how they are doing to help them attain what is desired and expected
Documentation is poorly designed, inaccessible	*Improve documentation*; manuals and materials to help or non-existent people do their jobs
Work station is badly designed	*Change the workplace* from being 'just assembled' to being carefully designed for optimum performance
Punished or ignored for doing it right. Rewarded for doing it wrong. Nobody notices if they do it right or wrong	Ensure no 'upside down' consequences; provide rewards for desired performance and punishments for failing to perform. The individuals concerned can see these 'consequences' as upside down if doing it right gets the person 'punished' (embarrassment, ridicule, more work, frustration, boredom) and failing to do it right brings rewards (peer approbation, less work, easier life).
Organisation makes desired performance difficult or impossible	Change organisational structure; to deal with boundaries which are producing 'turf wars' or confusion

The three dimensions of HRD needs

It is widely agreed that effective performance in work roles requires the development and combination of a number of constituent factors. How these factors are determined will shape how HRD needs are defined, and there is less agreement on how these factors ought to be defined. One long-held view has the tripartite identification of Knowledge, Skills and Attitudes (KSA) as the constituent factors. Any assessment of needs will lead to one or a combination of these. Kraiger et al (1993) also recognised three domains, but they defined them as:

- *cognitive learning* – needed for activities to enhance the acquisition and application of knowledge;
- *skills-based learning* – the ability to execute a sequence of behaviours smoothly;
- *affective learning* – changes in attitude and motivation.

Kraiger et al (op cit) further recognised that needs in the cognitive domain could have three forms:

- *verbal learning*, in the form of declarative knowledge (know-what);
- *procedural knowledge* (know-how);
- *tacit knowledge organisation*, structuring or mapping such knowledge.

For a long period there has been in-depth discussion of 'competence' as a unifying concept that might replace such tripartite frameworks for describing needs. Competence maps tend to cluster HRD needs together under umbrella behaviours, with a relegation of concerns about knowledge. Despite the widespread uptake of competence frameworks in organisations, a concern with differentiating different dimensions of HRD need persists.

Here the three dimensions will be defined in terms of:

Cognitive capacities: forms and aspects of intelligence, conceptualised as the processing and possession of information in the brain, and higher-order neurological abilities;

Capabilities: the practical abilities involved in work roles, either inherent in a person or developed through practice and experience;

Desired behaviours: from motivation to perform to 'social skills', enabling effective interaction, mediated by the affective; which can be conceptualised in terms of attitudes, values or 'emotional intelligence' (EI).

These three dimensions of performance may be linked to HRD needs in all kinds of organisation, across all kinds of occupation and all kinds of people. They are evident in the simplest role in the most basic, small organisation up to the most complex role in a technologically sophisticated multinational firm. At this stage a brief exposition of these elements and their role in HRD needs analysis is appropriate.

Cognitive capacities

Effective performance depends upon the presence, development and use of cognitive capacities, knowledge and understanding. How cognitive capacities are conceived – how intelligence, knowledge and understanding are believed to work – reflects ideas about the way the brain's functions can be modelled. For Kraiger et al (op cit) cognitive learning has three forms:

- verbal learning, in the form of declarative knowledge (know-what);
- procedural knowledge (know-how);
- tacit knowledge organisation, structuring or mapping such knowledge.

Specifying needs at this level, then, is to identify the elements of 'know-what', 'know-how' and tacit knowledge that might be significant. In general, models aim to present a simplified version of a complex reality so as to enable purposeful interaction with that complex reality. This is true of models of the brain and cognitive capacity. They may share some common factors, such as information processing, but in important respects they can diverge significantly, producing quite different implications for identifying HRD needs in terms of managing knowledge and understanding (see Theory & Research Box 2.2).

The issues revolve around debates about how forms and aspects of intelligence are needed in work roles. Some work roles may require specific or specialist forms of intelligence or complex thinking skill because the work is complex and requires the independent use of thinking and judgement in a context of substantial responsibility, where there may be little prior knowledge available, and where the person doing the work has to act autonomously. Other work roles may require very little specialist intelligence or thinking skill; all that is needed to perform these roles is an awareness and memorisation of only the most basic of instructions. Such work roles may be fully

theory & research

2.2 | *Three models of the brain*

In exploring the change in human activity from hunter-gatherer to the sudden burst of art, technology and religion that occurred around 30 000 years ago, the archaeological record shows an increase in brain size. But the change was not just about the brain getting bigger, there was a change in architecture as well.

Model 1   The brain is like a sponge, able to soak up information. This model implies that the bigger the sponge the more intelligent the person – and some sponges are better than others. However, unlike sponges that just absorb, minds can also compare and combine.

Model 2   The brain is like a computer; it takes data, runs programs, and provides outputs. The same 'program' is running in the background all the time; this is a general-purpose learning program. Different minds are like different specifications of computer, with varying speeds, capacities, and software.

Model 3   The brain is like a Swiss army knife: it has a central system (the knife case) and several independent special tools (the knife blades) that can be used for various purposes. These 'tools' are present at birth, built into the brain, and are 'opened out' for use if experience requires them. For example, interpersonal abilities are stimulated through the building of alliances and developing friendships, learning about the use of cunning and deception.

These three different models can be used to explain the development of the mind in historical terms, and as a process that is reprised in the development from child to adult:

- first the sponge, the general-purpose intelligence, 'soaking up' phase of learning among children;
- then the computer', a core general intelligence in central control and using several modules during development into adulthood;
- finally the Swiss army knife, the emergence and use of 'specialised' tools in the right context by experienced mature adults.

Source Mithen, 1996.

scripted, with no requirement to do anything other than repeat a series of set behaviours or acts of communication.

Alternatively the brain can be modelled as a holistic system governed by a master cognitive capacity. The processing power of the brain and its actions are also the subjects of divergent analyses. One study identified 35 different frameworks for generic thinking skills, defined as capacities in information-gathering, building understanding and productive thinking

Cognitive capacities are most commonly discussed in the context of HRD in terms of developing knowledge and understanding. They are what people gain by studying for a work role before they engage in it, and what they get from experience over time while in the role. Knowledge and understanding both precede performance, and evolve alongside it. As neurological study of the brain and continuing analysis of the nature of forms and aspects of intelligence and thinking advance the modelling of cognitive capacities, and how to enhance them, will continue to exercise and animate HRD both in theory and in practice.

Capabilities

To perform to the standards expected in employment, individuals and organisations require more than certain levels of knowledge and understanding; they require capabilities. Capabilities are the practical skills or competence that people need to achieve the required performance. While much discussion and study in this area continues to use the concept of skill (for example in skills surveys, discussing skills shortages and skill gaps), the terminology is evolving. In an era of workforce development and lifelong learning, the identification of terms such as capability can accompany or supersede the discussion of skills. The term 'skill' is often used loosely. They are usually measured in terms of occupation or qualification. Both ways have the merit of being relatively straightforward to measure and readily understood. More recently there has been much greater emphasis on what are variously termed key, core and generic skills, including:

- literacy and numeracy;
- general management skills;
- communication and customer handling skills;
- information handling skills;
- teamworking, etc.

These types of skill are frequently emphasised when employers are asked about their skill needs. Much of our thinking about how skills might be linked to productivity and performance also relies on these more general and qualitative aspects of skill. Yet these terms are nowhere near as well-established as 'occupation' and 'qualification', either in terms of a consensus about what they mean or on how best to measure them (see Theory & Research Box 2.3).

Capability is the practical performance of a work role. It is either inherent in the person and/or developed through practice. Capability may be considered at three levels, outlined in more detail in a later chapter:

- underpinning capabilities – literacy and honesty;
- intermediate capabilities – communication and motivation;
- overarching capabilities – teamworking and customer orientation.

2.3 | Other terms in use; Economics and psychology

The concept of skill is most strongly embedded in economic theory. To be skilled is, first, to be able to do something basic to an adequate or good standard. A skill is then a discrete and simple building block of performance and productivity, which exists or is absent. However, skill is often also referred to as 'expertise' in tangible, physical and observable actions: being highly skilled is associated with being an expert in complex physical activities. A craftsman who wielded tools was skilled; a dancer who could complete complex steps was skilled. Nowadays, in economies dominated by knowledge- and service-based industries, much performance at work depends on less tangible 'skills' such as information-handling and interpersonal relations. To classify these as skills is legitimate for some uses but questionable for others. Skill is then a complex of many things associated with expertise and a comprehensive and authoritative level of ability. This multiple sense of 'skill' can lead to confusion; for example, is a skills shortage a shortage of the simple building blocks of performance or a shortage of expertise?

The concept of competence, imported from psychology, became widely used as an alternative to skills, and many organisations have created sets of competence descriptions for their workforces. Competence in this sense comprised the key attributes desired and expected of superior performers. It involved setting out a list of core qualities and standards by which all staff in an organisation might be evaluated or appraised, equally and consistently.

The third dimension

Finally, as well as identifying and developing the cognitive capacities and capabilities required for performance, it has long been emphasised that there is an important third determinant of performance where needs may be identified. This may be defined and discussed in terms of forming attitudes, developing 'soft' social skills, or, increasingly, developing emotional intelligence (EI). Attitudes are the settled ways of thinking and feeling about someone or something – positive and negative orientations about the world. Social skills are the 'soft' skills associated with effective interpersonal behaviour. EI refers to awareness and management of emotions in order to act effectively in relationships and social situations (Goleman 1995).

What these different constructs have in common is a shared concern with recognising and making transparent the *affective* influences on behaviour in social situations – in the HRD context, workplace behaviour. To get the desired forms of behaviour in the context of work performance we must develop the right kinds of attitudes, soft skills, or EI. The ways people perform in work roles are determined not only by what they know (explicitly or tacitly) or what they can do (basically or expertly) but also by how they feel. So the way people actually perform can vary significantly, even if they have similar levels and types of cognitive capacity and capability.

Observing HRD: skills and issues

The perception and assessment of HRD needs in the context of performance management constitute the first step in initiating HRD so that people can do things well, or do them better, or do new and better things. We can combine these categories of performance concern and levels of HRD into a matrix that maps all the areas (see Figure 2.3) where HRD needs may be assessed in order to ensure comprehensive and complete foundations for HRD in the organisation.

		Area of need		
		Organisational	Group/Occupation	Individual
Level of business benefit	1 **Implementing: doing things well** · Cognitive · Capability · Behaviour	Meeting current organisational objectives	Working together to meet existing targets and standards	Working at the level of core standards
	2 **Improving: doing things better** · Cognitive · Capability · Behaviour	Setting higher objectives and reaching them	Continuous improvement within teams	Meeting current organisational objectives
	3 **Innovating: doing new and better things** · Cognitive · Capability · Behaviour	Changing objectives and strategies	Working across boundaries to create	Working differently and more creatively

Figure 2.3 Performance concerns and assessing HRD needs

Source: Based on Boydell and Leary 1996

Effective HRD needs analysis will be based on considering and managing all these aspects. The assessment of HRD needs – whether by managers or by HRM professionals – is a challenge. As an activity it requires a range of generic capabilities:

- **Process capabilities:** setting goals, making plans, and reviewing and evaluating the progress of HRD needs assessment for an organisation, a group or an individual.
- **Content capabilities:** getting information, analysing it and making sense of it, using tools derived from research methods, such as interviews or surveys, to help collect and analyse objective data about performance.
- **Relationship capabilities:** maintaining relationships with people during the HRD needs assessment. They are both the skills of being empathetic with learners and managers and others, and the skills of being assertive, to confront and challenge people.

As line managers are increasingly being made responsible for establishing training needs within their company or organisation their behaviours are important. This reflects a general trend in which line managers are assuming, if sometimes reluctantly, more responsibility across a range of people management and HRM issues. This trend has a number of implications.

First, the ability to assess HRD needs is not unique to HRD specialists: it is a particular application of generic skills, such as benchmarking, surveying the learning climate, and relating HRD to strategic change and models of organisation development (OD).

Second, there is much more to observing and assessing HRD needs than merely using standard data collection techniques. The 'technical' aspects of research and data collection are only part of the process; the political and relationship aspects of assessing needs are equally important.

Third, HRD needs assessors often have to make optimal use of limited resources to consider a range of diverse and relevant HRD concerns. Few organisations have the luxury of 'over-investment' in HRD that meets all possible existing and future needs. Instead, most organisations have to struggle with 'under-investment', where resource constraints mean that identified needs are not always met. Nevertheless, it is essential that HRD needs are accurately identified.

Fourth, assessing needs can be often be a sensitive issue for the organisation as a whole, for groups in it, and for individuals. These sensitivities arise because the identification of HRD needs always involves investigating gaps between expected performance and actual performance. Anxieties about being judged to be falling short of expected performance can interfere with and offset the forces pushing for gaps to be properly identified and dealt with.

Fifth, the time, effort and skills required to collect data and gather useful information from it are often not resourced properly. The problem is not usually that needs are not observed or assessed at all; it is more likely that there are shortcomings in identifying the gaps that do exist. So there may be good organisational-level analysis identifying strategic objectives and needs, but there may be inadequate operational-level analysis of expected versus actual performance, or assessment of individual needs in personal performance review. Errors can exist in the process of observing and assessing needs at all these levels, as with any observation-based research process. The consequences of errors can be over-training, under-training, or meeting perceived needs rather than individuals' actual needs.

The solutions to these potential sources of error are self-evident. They include assessing HRD needs in a systematic way while remaining proactive; having written plans, but also being flexible; having central organisation, but also supporting local action in observing and assessing needs. In the area of occupations and jobs the concern is to keep up with changes, continuous development, standards and certification. In the individual domain the concern is to ensure that there are positive developmental relationships between employees, managers and others so that HRD needs can be analysed and explored openly.

Areas of contemporary debate

Even where perceiving HRD needs is done effectively there may still be problems with improving organisational, work and personal performance. It is not possible to anticipate or observe all needs in advance, no matter how skilled the analyst or how much time is devoted to collecting the right kinds of information. Dealing with and responding to emergent needs is important. Alongside the challenge of emergent needs there are other challenges for HRD, two of which are particularly relevant to performance management and the assessment of HRD needs.

First, there is the challenge of deconstructing the contemporary consensus on HRD needs analysis (Rainbird 2000): the assumption that training and skills should be made responsive to employers' needs for increased productivity and flexibility. This is the rationale of performance-management accounts of HRD needs assessment. But do the steps being taken to interpret those needs from this perspective have unwanted consequences that will cause tomorrow's problems? In other words, might the solution become the problem, as short-term needs capture investments at the expense of longer-term visions? Arguably, it is the needs of tomorrow – which most employers may not be concerned with, or may say that they cannot be concerned with given the short-term pressures to satisfy capital markets – that matter most. So who *is* going to identify those needs and provide the appropriate HRD to meet them?

Also, how far is there an empirical link between training, skills and competitiveness, to justify the obsession with defining HRD needs in terms of the needs of current businesses? The emphasis on defining and meeting business needs for HRD through training and skill may be distorting investments in HRD – investing in activities that bolster existing businesses' short-term needs for profitability at the expense of longer-term change and the future of the economy. HRD needs might be assessed quite differently if a longer timescale were adopted. For example, consider the marginalisation of employees' needs to operate in an era of lifelong learning as free agents. HRD needs may have to be defined in the context of responsiveness to employers' economic demands, but what about social concerns such as equity and equality? This interpretation of the subtext of relating HRD needs to performance management forms part of the critical approach to HRD that sees the workplace as an arena in which different interests, within a balance of power, are contested.

Second, there is a view that there is a wider context for the direction of the modernisation of work. This needs to be acknowledged and critically analysed, as it sets the agenda for arguments about the content and quality of HRD needs analysis and learning at work. The assessment of HRD needs sits in this wider context, not just within the performance management systems of individual organisations, but also within the wider direction of change in societies and economies. The analysis of HRD needs should not presume that the future will be like the past with, for example, forms of work practice requiring the analysis of jobs into discrete tasks producing profiles of distinctive jobs. Rather, the changing nature of work in a 'post-Taylorist' era, where employee autonomy rather than close control is the hallmark of many jobs, must be taken into account when considering what amounts to a real and important HRD need.

Conclusion

The perception and assessment of HRD needs is the initial phase of the HRD process. The quality of what happens in this phase sets the foundation for all that follows; for good or for ill. Done effectively, it may determine real needs, clearly and comprehensively. Done imperfectly, it may neglect to identify real needs, or provide an inadequate understanding of needs. This could affect just one individual, or a discrete team, or perhaps the whole organisation.

This phase of the process takes place within the broad context of performance management in the organisation. If it is done properly, then HRD needs will be more likely to relate to real and significant performance concerns. If attention is paid to all three levels of needs assessment, then the subsequent phases of the HRD process are more likely to provide positive outcomes for investments in HRD: that is, to address real and important gaps between expected performance and actual performance. Success in the HRD process depends on the quality of analysis of what is involved in organisational performance, task performance and individual performance. It depends upon a coherent and integrated performance management system as a whole.

To analyse organisations, tasks, jobs, occupations and professions stakeholders must be able to access or develop data sources, business plans or competence profiles of occupations, or individual performance reviews. They must also be aware of how changes in structure and culture, or the introduction of new technologies and processes, will change the learning needs of those in the role, both now and in the future.

The design and implementation of effective performance appraisal systems should include the fit with requirements for HRD needs assessment. Bottom-up assessments of need, from individuals in dialogues with their managers, have to be reconciled with top-down thinking about future needs, from the strategic analysis of HRD needs, in planning for optimum use of limited resources to satisfy both individual and organisational interests.

| 2.3 | HRD needs analysis matters |

In a study of 61 hospitals, researchers found a strong association between HRD practices and patient mortality. Greater extent and sophistication of appraisal systems were closely related to lower mortality rates, and there were also links to the quality and sophistication of training and the number of staff trained to work in teams.

The survey gathered data on four areas: hospital characteristics, hospital HRM strategy, employee involvement strategy, and HRM practices and procedures. Chief executives and HR directors completed the whole questionnaire, and other occupational groups answered on HRM practices and procedures. Ninety per cent of all these people had training needs assessed annually. Some staff in some hospitals received no appraisal, but more hospitals failed to provide training in conducting appraisals.

Measuring mortality rates was a difficult process: geographical and regional variations might influence these, reflecting factors such as socio-economic status. Hospitals in poor areas might not attract the high flyers.

The final results showed that there was a relationship between HRM practices and mortality, with appraisal having the strongest correlation. Why should this be so? How can HRD needs analysis, as found in appraisal, improve the hospitals' performance? The researchers concluded that if an organisation has HRD policies that focus on effort and capability, develop people's capabilities, encourage cooperation and innovation in teams among most, if not all, employees, then the whole system functions and performs better. Managing all staff well, not just medical and nursing staff, gets good performance.

The researcher's conclusion was that a significant improvement in appraisal, to attain the standards of the best, would be equivalent to 1090 fewer deaths per 100 000 admissions. This does not invalidate the need to employ more and better medical staff, but it does emphasise how much all the staff in the working community affect performance.

Source: West 2002

Multiple-choice questions

2.1 Which of the following are potential non-training reasons for performance gaps?
A. Employees are not receiving feedback on performance.
B. There are 'upside down' consequences for performing poorly.
C. There is too much expectation of a high performance being the norm.
D. Training courses have been of a poor quality.

2.2 Which of the following statements about HRD needs analysis are true?
A. The best way to measure HRD needs is to find some quantitative measure of organisational, occupational or individual need.
B. Organisational training needs can be defined either as those shared by all members of the organisation or as those concerning performance gaps affecting the organisation as a whole.
C. It is often possible to use existing job specifications as starting points for occupational HRD needs analysis.
D. Three generic capabilities are used in observing HRD needs: process capabilities, content capabilities, and relationship capabilities.

References

Bartram, S. and Gibson, B. (1994), *Training Needs Analysis: A resource for identifying training needs, selecting training strategies, and developing training plans*, Aldershot, Gower.

Boydell, T. and Leary, M. (1996) *Identifying Training Needs*, London, CIPD.

Bramley, P. (1991) *Evaluating Training Effectiveness*, London, McGraw-Hill.

Chiu, W. et al (1999) 'Re-thinking training needs analysis: A proposed framework for literature review', *Personnel Review*, vol. 28, no. 1/2.

Finkelstein, S., Harvey, C. and Lawton, T. (2006) *Breakout Strategy: Meeting the challenge of double-digit growth*, New York, McGraw-Hill.

Ford, D. (1999) *Bottom Line Training*, Houston, Texas, Gulf Publishing Co.

Goleman, D. (1995) *Emotional intelligence: Why it can matter more than IQ*, London, Bloomsbury.

Kaplan, R. and Norton, D. (1996) 'The Balanced Scorecard', *Harvard Business Review*, January–February.

Kraiger, K., Ford, J.K. and Salas, E. (1993) 'Application of cognitive, skill-based and affective theories of learning outcomes to new methods of training evaluation', *Journal of Applied Psychology*, vol. 78, pp. 311–28.

Mager, R. (2000) *What Every Manager Should Know About Training*, Chalford, Management Books.

NOP World (2001) *People and Productivity*, London, Investors in People.

Parsons, D (1997) *A Qualitative Approach to Local Skills Audits*, Skills and Enterprise Briefing, Issue 6.

Pedler, M. et al (1991) *The Learning Company: A strategy for sustainable development*, London and New York, McGraw-Hill.

Peters, T. and Waterman, R. (1990) *In Search of Excellence*. London: Harper & Row.

Rainbird, H. (2000) *Training in the Workplace: Critical perspectives on learning at work*, Basingstoke, Macmillan

Robbins, P. (1993) *Organizational Behaviour*. London, Prentice Hall.

Rothwell, W.J. and Kazanas, H.C. (1992) *Mastering the Instructional Design Process*, New York, Jossey-Bass.

Senge, M. (1990) *The Fifth Discipline*. London, Doubleday.

West, M. (2002) 'A matter of life and death', *People Management*, 21 February, 30–35.

Wolfe, P. et al (1991) *Job Task Analysis: Guide to good practice*, Englewood Cliffs, NJ: Educational Technology Publications.

Q

concluding cases

Review the following brief cases showing, first, some good experiences and then some bad experiences.

Identify which aspects of assessing needs appear to have been well or poorly done in each case.

What does this tell you about the roles and skills involved in assessing needs?

Some good learning experiences

John cited a total customer satisfaction (TCS) course as being effective. This was a company-wide course that used well-trained facilitators. A lot of thought was put into the course environment and room layout. There was good use of different media, and a blend of thinking and doing. There were many group exercises involving teamworking. There was even an after-course reception dinner, and follow-up involving developing and swapping action plans.

continued overleaf

Q

Paul experienced an induction process when he moved from one retailer to another. One of his new key objectives was to understand the store financial report. He arranged a one-to-one meeting with his line manager, who explained it step-by-step, line-by-line. He could relate this to what he knew from his previous experience, and understand the new (to him) method of reporting financial information. He could get immediate clarification of any questions from an experienced person.

Chris described learning how to do the 'store walk' as a manager in a supermarket. This was an on-the-job experience with his store manager who did it every day. The store manager explained the benefits of doing this store walk daily – for Chris's own awareness, for staff awareness, and ultimately to benefit the customers. The walk was structured at a good pace, and he summarised each stage and referred to relevant issues. The manager got Chris's input by asking 'what if?' questions. Chris was encouraged to take notes; afterwards he was asked to communicate these to the manager, and the manager clarified issues Chris had misunderstood. On the next occasion Chris had to lead the store walk, with the manager asking him questions.

Jill talked about the importance of relationships. As someone aspiring to promotion she had the opportunity to shadow a senior manager on the job for 2 days. The manager, who was also female, was prepared to discuss general issues, almost like 'mentoring', rather than just go through the tasks. She was very self-aware, and was able to highlight 'good' and 'bad' characteristics of her own management style, which Jill found very useful and informative. It also dispelled some of the fear that Jill had about aspiring to promotion.

As a student Simon had the near-universal experience of learning to serve food in a restaurant and work behind a bar for the first time. He had no experience of either, and was thrown in at the deep end, getting coaching from other members of staff. The best way to learn was actually to do the tasks in the real environment. It was stressful, but he felt that he could learn at a faster pace this way.

Some bad learning experiences

Paul had the ineffective experience of being given a one-page handout on changes to the disciplinary process and authority levels. He did not understand the terminology, although he knew the outline of the process. He had to request clarification on the detail and terminology, and he had to wait for this information, thus delaying his ability to understand and follow the new procedures.

For Fiona an ineffective learning experience was an evening course in typing. She was at university at the time, and did not have either the motivation or the time to complete the course. She was not really interested in the subject, although she could see benefit in knowing how to type. She paid for the whole 12-week course, but lasted only 3 weeks.

John cited a poor in-organisation course. The materials used were out of date, and there was only one facilitator delivering the course in a limited style. The pre-course objectives were unclear, and there was no variety of thinking and doing on the course. There was no time for delegates to mix, and the facilities were cramped and uncomfortable. There was limited connection to John's work role, and no follow-up after the workshops.

For Jim an ineffective course was one delivered by a senior manager on a specific topic relevant to his job as a senior civil servant: drafting for ministers. The course had been promised for a number of years, but was delayed time and again. This constant delay meant that training on the topic became a source of ridicule, which was vented against the senior manager, who eventually did come to deliver the course. His behaviour further annoyed the trainees: he was late for the start of the course, was ill prepared, allowed himself to be interrupted by phone calls during the course, and delivered confusing information. He constantly 'lost the thread', resulting in attendees feeling that they had learned nothing. The delayed course had been worse than no course at all.

For Lorraine an ineffective learning experience was attending a one-day in-house course on basic employment law, delivered by an employment lawyer. The course content was devised in-house, but was aimed at managers with no HR background, so as an experienced HR person she found the course to be of little use.

concluding cases continued

For Mike an ineffective experience was his company's course on the new computer system. A lot of information was rushed or missed because the trainer felt the trainees ought to have known it anyway. The trainer was unfamiliar with the materials, and jumped about from subject to subject. The trainees felt they could not ask questions as there was no time, and because they were afraid of looking stupid. It left them with no confidence at all about using the system, and having no faith in the trainer.

For Simon ineffective learning was in the use of the front-of-house computer system. This was learned on the job, with reference to a training manual. He learned how to do each task, but often not until he had made a mistake and had to phone a very expensive help-line to fix it. A few hours with someone trained in the system would have helped him to learn the basics.

introductory short case on sexual harassment answer

If your thoughts included aspects of the three levels, organisational, work and individual, you would have been on the right lines. If it included covering all the areas of cognitive capacity, capability and values that too would have been well thought. And if you had recognised that it would have required a mix of reference to objective issues, such as the law in this area, plus attention to subjective factors, how people would respond to exploring areas like this, you would have covered all the bases in advance of reading the chapter. If you did not get all of those straight off, then you can now hopefully see how they all are relevant.

First the problem should be put in context. What is the business issue here? Partly it is a financial one, as the cost of having allegations like this proven can be considerable. Partly it is one of 'image'; the employer brand is tarnished by these kinds of cases being publicly aired. Partly it is a question of ethics; the great majority of managers and staff will find such behaviour unacceptable, and will be concerned that they are not considered to be perpetrators of such behaviour. Partly it is a legal issue; what needs to be done by a reasonable employer in order to seek to prevent and deal with such problems.

These contextual issues will all affect how any HRD initiative will be seen, and welcomed or otherwise, by managers, staff and others. The business need, as ever, ought to be central, so that everyone understands that an HRD response is appropriate, rather than confining a response to threats of discipline and punishment of transgressors. And the need is not just about complying with legislation, but about rooting out unacceptable behaviour and promoting a positive culture for working life for all.

The kinds of aims and objectives that might be appropriate need to be clarified. The different aspects of cognitive capacity, behaviour and value-oriented change should all be addressed as these are all relevant. The elements of cognitive capacity will be to do with understanding legislation and company policies, with different levels of need existing for managers and the workforce as a whole. Some form of workshop is usually appropriate for this. Attention to skills and expertise, and changing behaviour, so that previously accepted practices are stopped and alternative forms of behaviour respecting others are reinforced, is evidently needed. Ways of opening up behaviours to change revolve around facilitating discussions and variations on role-playing to model and practise desired behaviours. There will always be an underlying need to address questions of value and attitude, to reinforce the change and remove the possibility of staff temporarily conforming to new expectations only to relapse at later stages.

The topic and aim here would suit a combined approach. The inclusion of both instruction-oriented and facilitation-based methods is relevant and should be clearly indicated. There is a potential role for specialist trainers, external providers and line managers, with associated systems, such as access to counselling also possible.

continued overleaf

introductory short case on sexual harassment answer continued

Finally, some early thinking needs to be done on the question of evaluation. The obvious target is the reduction of sexual harassment cases; the broader, more positive issue is promoting equal opportunities. The question of costs and benefits needs to be considered, alongside the less tangible matters of public image and reputation among stakeholders.

In conclusion, a good answer will seek to integrate these, suggesting, for example, that it would be a mistake to focus solely on assessing needs around changing male behaviour by instructing people on the letter of the law and seeking compliance with that, in order to reduce the risk of facing harassment cases and the costs that entails. Instead HRD needs assessment can be seen as an opportunity to meet everyone's needs and initiate a general process, including facilitating values and culture change, for the greater and longer-term good of the company as a whole.

Designing for HRD: principle and applications

learning
objectives

By the end of this chapter you will be able to:

□ define and develop aims, objectives and targets for HRD activities;
□ describe the themes and issues involved in planning HRD activities;
□ incorporate methods for developing cognitive capacities, capability and behavioural change;
□ critically evaluate the overall design of typical HRD activities;
□ design engaging and stimulating HRD activities.

introductory case study   *Transfusion*

A company producing and bottling alcoholic drinks at various sites employed around 1500 people. There was a history of adversarial employee relations in the company. In an increasingly competitive environment it adopted a strategy based on what it called a 'change agenda'. This involved a change to flexibility, shared responsibility, continuous improvement, more customer focus and teamworking. These were the characteristics that the company needed to be a pioneering and innovative organisation. Associated with this was a process of intensive and extensive HRD. 'Transfusion' was the name given to the major HRD event the company designed to meet the demands of their broader change agenda.

The HRD was planned as a series of three-day workshops for all staff. These workshops would use dramatic techniques to challenge and break old norms of rule-following and task orientation. They were designed to help staff develop a more holistic view of and commitment to the new organisational culture, along with a new entrepreneurial ethos in the company. This training event was seen by staff as almost evangelical, requiring them to confess their weaknesses before moving on to embrace the new values. Up to 50 people drawn from various locations attended each event. On day 1, as participants entered the room, loud music was playing, and during the day learning points were illustrated with clips from major motion pictures. These were intended to stir up a quasi-religious fervour, providing a quite different experience from the way that previous company seminars had been run. The other sessions included guided fantasy exercises, Tai Chi practice, and used forms of dramatised group interaction.

The event was planned to engage with the whole person, not just limited elements of knowledge or skill. The days started at 7.30 am and went on until late at night. Only healthy food and drinks were made available for refreshment. There were 'spotlight sessions', when participants were put on a stage with the room in darkness and asked to tell the group their values, hopes and fears. This encouraged many to reveal astonishing

continued overleaf

disclosures: divorce, deaths and serious illness. At the end of each day there was a 'ho' session, mimicking traditional North American Indian practices. Participants sat cross-legged and had to access a symbolic stick to be able to talk; when they were finished they called 'ho' to signal it, and everyone else had to respond likewise.

At the end of the process the directors of the company felt that Transfusion had 'done it': it had broken down barriers, taken away inhibitions, and given people a real buzz. Young team leaders were more ready to talk and interact. The HR manager commented that 'people who would have been seen as cynical were jumping and singing and dancing and whooping because they thought it was brilliant.' Apparently no-one had a negative view. Research done 18 months later confirmed this overall positive assessment of the HRD event. The planning and design had worked. The need to meet the demands of the change agenda, in a company that had had severe employee relations problems, had been satisfied (Beech et al 2000).

Introduction

Having successfully identified HRD needs, the next phase of the HRD process is to plan and design HRD experiences that will address those needs. As with assessment of needs, planning and designing are generic activities. The design management aspects of developing HRD experiences have much in common with other applications of planning and design management. The specific concerns for HRD planning and design include:

- determining aims, objectives and targets for HRD;
- using combinations of activities to achieve different kinds of change; and
- synthesising activities into a holistic and integrated programme that engages learners and produces the desired results.

There is no single best way to design HRD. Nor is there a simple, formulaic way to arrive at a good design. Rather good design emerges from giving time and care to design thinking (see Strategic View Box 3.1). More than many other areas of HRM, HRD requires the development of a design consciousness and capability. This does not mean that you need to be or become a creative genius, but it does mean that if you develop designer cognition, capabilities and behaviours you will be better placed to understand and work successfully in HRD situations on a case-by-case basis. The planning and design phase is initially concerned with the preparation of a blueprint. That blueprint may be for a day-long training programme, a week-long programme or for various kinds and lengths of HRD. The preparation of a blueprint is a discrete design activity, following on from the specification of need. It parallels what happens elsewhere; for example, once the need for a building, a product or a new service is established then blueprints for buildings, products or services are needed to guide their actual construction.

Designs in many areas of practice are abstract two-dimensional models, using symbolic means, such as drawings, to prefigure the construction of real-world three-dimensional, structures and forms. The design process here is one of building more and more detailed specifications of what people want and what is possible so that ideas

3.1 | *Design and design thinking...*

'Design' can be a bit of a catch-all term, with different people using it to mean different things. Many concentrate on the aesthetic aspects of design, the look and feel of objects. While this is important, it is wiser to view it more as a way of thinking, and hence to use the term 'design thinking'. Attributes of design thinking include: questioning, creativity, innovation, and communication:

Questioning: designers in all sectors, from engineering to fashion, tend to question things a lot. They 'soak up' information from their environments and store it in a less judgemental or hierarchical way than non-designers. Good ideas are much more than the sum of their parts – combining seemingly 'useless' bits of information can give you a world-beating idea. This ability, inherent in all of us, is effectively eradicated from most through the education system. The links between a questioning mind and creative mind are important, and these are skills rather than 'talents'.

Creativity: either the combining of existing ideas and concepts in original ways (new-to-the-world/sector/ market) or more rarely the development of 'brand new' ideas and concepts.

Innovation: the development of ideas and concepts into something real, new-to-the-world/sector/market. Creativity you can do in your head, innovation involves the physical world – and usually other people too.

Communication: the ultimate element in successful design, as it is through the communication of ideas and concepts, via drawings and specifications, that imagining becomes design. Design can be defined as this act of communication because, while painting your living room is just painting your living room, producing drawings and specifications for how you want your living room painted makes you an interior designer.

Source Lawson 2000

can be translated into something tangible in order for actual, real-world, construction to begin. The blueprints that are created for HRD products, services and events are usually made up of statements using language rather than line drawings. However, they serve the same purpose: to make ideas manifest so that they can be discussed and refined in advance of a commitment to constructing and making the learning happen, implementing it. The point is that designers raise their constructions first in the mind. The discipline of doing that effectively is the key to good design in any field.

Planning and design tasks in HRD will range from the straightforward (see Operations Box 3.1) to the highly complex: from how to plan and design a single on-the-job training experience for an individual through to developing events such as the 'Transfusion' event described in the opening of this module. Such structures and forms illustrate that starting with fairly conventional HRD needs and specifications, including concerns such as better teamworking, can lead to the planning and design of HRD that is unusual, innovative and challenging.

Whether the design outcomes will be conventional forms of HRD, such as a class-based session, or experimental ones such as a computer-based game for learning, the heart of the planning and design phase is the same. It requires the establishment of aims, objectives and targets to structure the design and construction of the learning experience. This involves two kinds of design capability. First, the analysis associated with the craft of determining and writing aims, objectives and targets; and, second, synthesis, the craft of balancing and unifying different elements into an the HRD experience to support the development of cognitive capacities, capabilities and desired behaviours.

Crafting aims, objectives and targets

Planning and design in HRD is, initially, about the preparation and refinement of explicit, written statements to act as foundations for the design process. These statements provide the public, common and agreed foundations for the further development of form and content, whether of course and lesson plans for classroom-based instruction programmes, of a mentoring programme or of a multimedia simulation. The art of doing this well is to include both the acquisition of skill and understanding knowledge during learning and also the development of attitudes, values and identities.

3.1	*Basics and elaborations on a simple structure for an HRD session*

For HRD activities in the classroom the simplest design structure is a narrative flow; an event with a beginning, a middle and an end. Each of these parts has its well-recognised design challenges.

In the beginning learners are often uncertain and can be distracted. There is a need to set the scene and state the topic while creating and maintaining rapport. It is possible to gain attention through standard opening techniques: for example, use a question, a quotation, a story, a factual statement, a dramatic statement, a curious opening, a checklist.

The middle. This is where the 'work is done' to put over the content using a structured approach. The prescriptions for doing this are to:

- Maintain learner attention; stress relevance, use visual aids, involve people, be enthusiastic.
- Obtain acceptance: be clear, precise, demonstrate.
- Handle objections, and take questions.
- Use exercises: get people to work as individuals, in pairs, or syndicates

The end. End on a high note, pulling the session together, identifying action points, and signing off (with a question, a quote, or a story).

Such a simple narrative structure provides a template and reference point around which different 'plots' may evolve as the HRD process is designed.

More originality and creativity in design will follow by working on the following features:

□	Involvement	Is this an active or a passive experience, involving the learners?
□	Meaningful	Will the learners be doing things that are relevant, within their capabilities and necessary to reach a goal they have?
□	Control	Who exercises control? Is it complete trainer control, or shared, or complete learner control?
□	Constraints	There is always limited time and resources, but find ways around these; respect, but outwit constraints.
□	Feedback	Provide feedback; give information on progress, positive results throughout the experience
□	Edit!	Make good use of media; look at your plan, and ask whether you could get the same result if you dropped something.
□	Double check	that what you do will meet the learners' needs; make the experience good for them, not for you as the trainer.

It can be useful to look at a learning event you have experienced, or are designing, and rank it on a 1–10 scale on these features.

3.1 | Event diagnostic

To what extent were these criteria met in the learning experience, with 1 being not at all met and 10 being 'fulfilled as much as possible'.

	1	2	3	4	5	6	7	8	9	10
Involvement An active experience, involving the learners?										
Meaningful Did learners do things that were relevant, possible, and helping to reach a goal they had?										
Control Was control shared?										
Constraints Were they outwitted?										
Feedback Was feedback provided throughout the experience?										
Edited Was good use made of media; concise?										
Not Just Trainer Comfort Did the experience meet the learners' needs rather than the comfort of the trainer?										

The same principles of planning and design will apply across all design contexts, but each offers special challenges. For, as with all design, there is a general structure for good practice and aspects that are particular to the context and materials being worked with. These can be described in various ways, usually with three levels being specified. In HRD this general context and structure entail developing and specifying statements in the form of aims, objectives and targets. These are the blueprints that allow learning events to be constructed and refined in advance of their being built or delivered.

This good practice structure for HRD design has to be seen as an ideal. The rigour it requires may not always be followed in real life and organisational situations. Short-cuts are often taken. For example, one kind of shortcut is simply to 'import' an existing design, copying and imitating what has already been done somewhere else. So if an organisation identifies a need to help team-leaders to perform better it may simply buy in a stock team-leader training programme. Such shortcuts are attractive, widely used, and are often good enough. This shortcut means buying in someone else's design efforts. It may, however, mean importing as many problems as solutions if the design does not actually address the core areas that the specific situation and group need to have addressed.

When organisations cannot just import a solution from already known 'designed courses' they have to design their own. The challenge first encountered early in the design process is to avoid obscuring an initially well-identified HRD need. The design should provide a structure for articulating the form and content for HRD, but

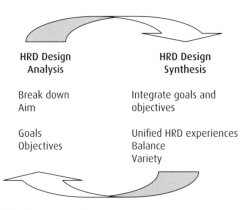

Figure 3.1 HRD planning and design

the process can interfere with fulfilling the need if vague statements divert attention from a focused treatment of the need. This may happen where a designer reaches too quickly for a favoured design solution instead of thinking through the aims, objectives and targets.

To avoid this pitfall attention is to be given equally to two things: analysis and synthesis (see Figure 3.1). Analysis as part of the design process involves starting with the general 'whole', defining an overall aim and then breaking that down into constituent parts –goals and more specific objectives – that can be used to structure the actual form and content of HRD experiences. The product of analysis in design are the specific objectives and outcomes around which the HRD will be built. Synthesis is also required to contain and place together all these different parts in an integrated HRD experience from which people will learn. The result of this is the construction of a balanced, practicable and high-quality learning experience; whether that synthesis is a good off-job training, mentoring or a multimedia programme.

Analysis in design: identify aims, objectives, targets

The first element of analysis is finding the aim that best meets the identified needs (see Operations Box 3.2). Aims are what we want the learning to do: general statements of desired conditions or states to which interventions are directed. Aims are high-level statements of intent which provide the broad foundations and boundaries for further design work. Aims in HRD are not meant to be directly measurable. The use of amorphous terms such as 'learn', 'know', 'understand' is acceptable at this level of initial analysis. An aim is often expressed as a single sentence.

> "The aim of this course is to equip managers with the skills and knowledge
> to be health and safety consultants."

For example, if a performance gap is attributed to people not having the technical skills to do their job well then an HRD need has been identified. An aim might then be to 'improve technical capabilities in work roles'. As long as whatever then follows is anchored to that aim the HRD development process will not stray far from relevance. If the wrong aim is articulated then whatever design is done subsequently – no matter how good in itself – will not take people on track towards closing the performance gap.

3.2 | Defining aims, objectives and targets

Terminology	Example
Aim (or Goal) A general statement of a desired condition or state to which an intervention is directed	To introduce coaching as a new role in the company
Objectives More specific statements that describe what the intervention should accomplish. They support the overall aim	To provide employees with ideas and incentives to implement coaching as a way of working, supporting and teaching within their role
Targets Each objective should have a specific target. There should be an indicator that the target has been achieved and a means of verification, usually by measuring or observing an outcome. Indicators can be quantitative or qualitative	To have 15% of staff in all stores active as coaches To raise customer satisfaction levels by 20% as a result of coaching support

After having identified an appropriate aim for an important HRD need, the next step is to define some objectives. Objectives or outcomes tell learners what is expected and show what is liable to be assessed They provide a framework for constructing course content. They are what we expect the learner to get from the course and be successful. In much education with a syllabus base, objectives mainly relate to the acquisition of a catalogue of knowledge, and knowing the syllabus. In other areas they are more behavioural: what the learner will be able to do, and the manner and quality of doing, and how it can be assessed in practice.

This second level of analysis is needed to translate the aim into discrete and manageable parts that can then be further broken down into what we will here call 'targets'. The concern here is that people developing HRD often draft out some vague and fuzzy outcomes and badly expressed objectives. If these are too imprecise they will fail to provide a guideline for the further refinement and structuring of an HRD experience, that is, they are not specific enough to drive the next step of setting targets. A process for establishing objectives is outlined in Operations Box 3.3.

Objective, or outcomes, can be divided into three types:

- enabling   necessary to be able to perform;
- terminal   a consequence of the HRD;
- application   the practical reason there is a concern with this issue.

This way of modelling helps to define prerequisites, the kinds of learning that learners must already have, or which they will need to undertake, before engaging with the focal HRD under design. The focus of design and construction is then concerned first with the enabling objectives, if appropriate, through separate HRD events, or with addressing them along with the terminal objectives. In the former case several HRD events might be designed and developed for appraisal and team-building, whereas in the latter case a single event that included something on all of these might be designed.

Enabling objectives	e.g. appraise, lead, handle conflict, build teams
↑	
Terminal objectives	e.g. motivate staff
↓	
Application objectives	e.g. to meet customer requirements for quality of service

Figure 3.2. Forms of objective

This method of defining objectives can result in a range of statements; from a single set objective for an aim to several interrelated objective statements. The result will depend on the complexity of the performance issue and the scale of the HRD required. One planning and design rule-of-thumb is to have no more than seven objective statements for any particular HRD aim. More than this is inadvisable, as it complicates communications with others about the HRD. It also means that the further analysis of specific targets becomes a much more complex exercise. Developing a myriad and complex set of objective statements is not an expression of good design, it is a substitute for good design. The identification of up to seven objectives related to an aim can, then, provide the entry point for the third level of analysis.

3.3 | Defining objectives clearly

1. State the objective in terms of *outcomes* (what is to be achieved) rather than stipulating how it is to be done.
   This means describing the result of learning – *what* will tangibly be different as a consequence of learning. This is contrasted with putting the cart before the horse by trying to think about 'how' to get somewhere when they have not specified where 'there' is. For example, if the objective is 'to improve motivation by fixing employee attitudes', specifying *how* to get from poor to positive attitudes in order to change motivation before defining the desired result – *what* will tangibly happen if motivation is improved. Phrasing objectives clearly in terms of outcomes – of what is expected – is also essential for communicating with managers and potential learners. They should be able to see how their performance will be impacted by HRD. For example:

Unclear objectives specifying 'how'	Clearer objectives (Outcomes – 'what')
Fix attitudes	Adopt a responsible attitude towards work
Be more motivated	Reduce levels of absenteeism

2. In setting clearer objectives it is also helpful to list the performances that are desired, as they may still be imprecise at this stage. This can be achieved by brainstorming, mind-mapping or any other similar techniques. For example, to work on staff 'to hold a responsible attitude towards their work', these performances might emerge:
   □ Deal with customers courteously.
   □ Get work done on time.
   □ Keep work area uncluttered.
3. Having generated a list of performances, prioritise to select the primary objectives, then identify and delete those items on this list that are too abstract to be measurable, or revise them until they are measurable.
4. Having gone through this process of listing, selection and refinement, ask the question: 'If someone did all these things (that the HRD event could cover) would that provide the performance that is wanted?' Is there anything more to add? This is a test to see whether you have finished defining objectives.

The final step, the third level of analysis, is to craft 'targets' specifying the results desired. Targets are statements of the specific outcomes to be achieved by training, stated from the point of view of the learner. Planning and design targets are needed for three main reasons:

- to provide the focus for detailed HRD design;
- to communicate the purpose of the HRD to learners and others;
- to establish the context for measurement and evaluation.

Targets are the specific statements of intention that define measurable outcomes for the learner. They indicate the specific cognitive capacities, capabilities and behaviours that need to be demonstrated for learning to have occurred. Guidelines for developing HRD targets from objectives include:

- Specify the target behaviours involved using an action verb:
  not   'understand how to motivate people'
  but   'be able to *motivate staff*'

- Specify a statement of content using a noun to describe a task:
  not   'to motivate staff'
  but   'to motive staff and *reduce customer complaints*'

- Provide a statement of conditions and standards; quantity (how much), quality (how well), time (how long):
       'to motivate staff and reduce customer complaints by 10%'

If it is difficult to identify a direct and apparent, explicit target behaviour this may indicate that the objective involves more abstract learning. In this case, determine a behaviour that requires performance of an activity showing application of the abstract learning, e.g. for health and safety awareness, 'list and explain safety rules.

The final concern with this level of analysis is that, having generated a number of targets, there is another prioritising process to work through. This is needed to prioritise targets into a set and establish a hierarchy defining enabling, terminal and application targets (see Figure 3.3).

	Examples (of the objectives of managers motivating staff)
Prerequisites	communication skills, knowing quality
Enabling objectives ↑	appraise, lead, handle conflict, build teams
Terminal objectives ↓	motivate staff
Application objectives	to meet customer requirements for quality of service
Targets/Results	To decrease customer complaints by 10% To increase customers by 10%

Figure 3.3 Organising objectives and targets: the example of 'managers motivate staff'

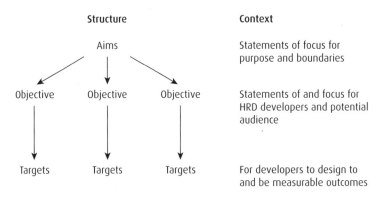

Figure 3.4 Aim, objective and target statements

As a result of this kind of analysis an HRD learning experience could now be confidently moved on to a design, based on the enabling, terminal and application objectives and targets. This stage of analysis has established some criteria for measurable evaluation. Figure 3.4 provides a graphic overview of the analysis side of the planning and design process, and Resources Box 3.2 provides some ideas of the time it takes to design different options.

3.2 Design time ratios for estimating costs

Design element	Content type	Design time : learning time
Participant manual	Familiar, non-technical	3:1
Participant manual	Unfamiliar, technical	6:1
Leader's guide	Familiar, non technical	2:1
Leaders guide	Unfamiliar, technical	4:1
Visuals/overheads	Simple, text-based	1:1
Visuals/overheads	Complex, graphic-based	5:1
Videos	Simple, voice over, one location	50:1
Videos	Complex, live audio, many locations	150:1
CBT	Simple, text-based	50:1
CBT	Complex, graphic-based	300:1
Multimedia	Simple, graphic-based	150:1
Multimedia	Complex, video-based	500:1

Source Ford 1999.

The synthesis dimension: design and the different dimensions of learning

Having outlined these analytical issues it is important to recognise that design is not a 'science', based on formulas and guidelines, to be achieved by following set procedures alone. That is evident from looking at other areas of knowledge and practice where design thinking has been recognised as an issue for much longer. In areas like graphic, product and building design, principles have been suggested, but these remain domains for the 'artful'. Knowles (1984) entitled the opening chapter of his seminal text on adult learning 'the art and science of helping adults learn'. What he meant by 'art' was that the process as well as the content has importance; setting the right climate and involving learners. Resources Box 3.3 shows a set of ideas about how artful aspects of principles for good design in HRD can be suggested as the heart of what is put together, or synthesised, following the analytical phase.

resources

| 3.3 | *'Excellence in Learning; Design Guidance'* |

Relevance

The real concerns of the audience are engaged:

- By applying the result of training needs analysis
- When the relevance and context is clear
- By effective learning and/or value for money with measured benefits
- When there are defined business benefits and impact

Retention

The knowledge and understanding has impact:

- At the right time for a learner
- When there are clearly defined and achievable learning objectives linked to business benefits
- If the presentation is engaging, interactive and includes a range of activities to suit all learning styles

Response

The learners are able to do something new when:

- Training is the best solution to a problem
- The right media and methods for the audience are used
- Technology is embraced where it will add value

Repetition

Useful learning can be applied in other contexts:

- Transferable to the workplace
- Informal as well as formal

In achieving this synthesis in HRD design there is usually an interest in having some balance between each of the key areas of need we discussed briefly in chapter 2: cognitive capacity, capability and the affective dimension. The different kinds of need present different kinds of design challenge.

In determining objectives and targets for 'cognitive capacity', the cognitive categories and levels suggested by Bloom (1965) provide one frame of reference for designing HRD in detail. In analysing capability objectives in learning and performance, a tripartite model of employability, vocational capacities and overarching capabilities can be referenced. Finally, with regard to analysing desired behaviour objectives in learning and performance, a model of the affective elements involved in performance can be outlined with options to design for changing attitudes, values and/or emotions. These particular frames of reference raise some more general questions about design. We will discuss their shortcomings by using constructivist interpretations of knowing and learning, and the concept of emotional intelligence (EI).

To deal with cognitive capacity design issues first, there are concerns with establishing or improving knowledge as a focus for HRD in the workplace (see Operations Box 3.4). The term 'knowledge' is used in the HRD design context to mean a range of cognitive capacities. Narrowly defined, knowledge is only one constituent part of a spectrum, defined as organised, factual information. It is clearly misleading to assume that 'knowledge' in this sense contains all possible cognitive capacities. In the effective performance of many roles there are aspects of cognition beyond the possession of organised bodies of fact.

3.4 | *Design for promoting active learning*

When seeking to design for:
- Knowledge of how: skills – procedural memory
- Knowledge of what: facts – declarative or propositional memory
- Knowledge of context: – social and organisational understanding

The following are helpful directions:
- Doing something helps embed knowledge and transfer from short-term memory to long-term memory.
- Rehearsal can involve uploading (using) or downloading (processing such as taking notes).
- Rehearsal can be physical or mental processing into meaningful constructs which can happen in a social context.
- Learning is effective through tasks involving mental manipulation plus a physical component and a social component such as group discussion.
- Desk-based recalling, summarising, preparing notes for others, apply to new problems, compare.
- Practical/research; interview, role play, exercises.

These ideas directly connect the design of HRD with thinking about how people 'know' the world and act in it as accomplished performers. This is not dependent solely on 'knowledge' in the form of organised, factual information. Performance may require people to make judgements and decisions when factual information is uncertain, contradictory or unavailable. And performance may require people to depend on the use and application of 'multiple intelligences', not just an awareness of a few memorised facts. We tackle these issues more thoroughly in chapter 6 on learning theory. Here we focus on some issues of cognitive capacity as it impacts on design concerns.

Bloom (op cit) developed a taxonomy of cognitive capacities for use in designing educational experiences (see Figure 3.5). This has been a long-established framework for describing a range of outcomes, and as a guide to the form and content of learning experiences, According to one estimate, there are around 35 different frameworks in use, but the classic model has a number of advantages. One benefit is the simple modelling of a hierarchy that can be easily applied to a range of performance domains and learning contexts. 'Knowledge' is the most basic factor, with 'evaluation' being the most complex.

Cognitive Capacity	Typical Statement Form	
Knowledge	state, list, identify	**Surface**
Comprehension	explain, give examples	↑
Application	demonstrate, solve	
Analysis	describe	
Synthesis	design, create	↓
Evaluation	appraise, contrast, critique	**Deep**

Figure 3.5 Bloom's taxonomy of cognitive factors

In Bloom's taxonomy (see Figure 3.5), 'knowledge' is a term for the baseline or entry-level cognitive capacity involved in human performance: the capture and retention of information as a prerequisite of being able to do something. But the capture and retention of information provide a necessary but not sufficient condition for effective performance. Some kinds of performance rely purely on knowledge; some require the capacity to evaluate. The performance of a call centre operator can be knowledge-based, pre-programmed and scripted; the performance of a surgeon in the middle of an operation will be based more on evaluation (and corrective action).

So, there is more to doing than knowing, and often there is more to performance than the possession of information. Effective performance associated with an increasing degree of difficulty and complexity draws upon other cognitive capacities:

- *Evaluation* – the ability to judge the value of material for a given purpose; to assess, evaluate, argue, validate, criticise.
- *Synthesis* –the ability to put parts together to form a whole; to design, formulate, develop, organise.
- *Analysis* – the ability to break material down into component parts; to analyse, compare, contrast, investigate.
- *Application* – the ability to use learned material in new and concrete situations; to relate, show, demonstrate.
- *Comprehension* – the ability to grasp the meaning of new material; to explain, discuss, review, interpret.
- *Knowledge* – the ability to recall previously learned material; to define, identify, list.

3.4 A lexicon of objectives

Evaluation

judge	compare	determine	assess	revise
criticise	recommend	measure	evaluate	

Synthesis

compose	plan	construct	design	make	predict
hypothesise	formulate	propose	develop	invent	incorporate

Analysis

interpret	test	analyse	distinguish	differentiate
examine	investigate	scrutinise		

Application

exhibit	solve	interview	simulate	apply
employ	demonstrate	operate	calculate	experiment
practise	illustrate	show	dramatise	

Comprehension

translate	restate	summarise	discuss	describe	retell
recognise	explain	express	identify	locate	report

Knowledge

know	relate	define	label	repeat	specify
record	cite	list	enumerate	recall	tell
name	recount				

In the area of capabilities, 'knowing how' does not always translate into 'being able to'; the possession of cognitive capacities does not ensure effective performance. A person must also have constituent capabilities, which are defined here as the discrete abilities involved in effective performance. In principle the simplest division of capabilities is into three categories: capabilities with data, with people, and with things. Finer sets of distinctions can be made. These may elaborate upon differences between types of data, types of people, and types of thing. Thus we can make a distinction between quantitative data (numerical) and qualitative data (statements, meanings); between people in external roles (customers) and internal roles (staff); between simple things (use of basic computing applications) and complex things (the control of a complex machine).

Finer and finer distinctions can be made, and there is no obvious limit to this, apart from the practical one of enumeration (Harvey 1999). From a measurement perspective, it becomes increasingly difficult to collect reliable and valid data with increasing numbers and degrees of abstraction of capability categories. One study grouped over 12 000 occupations using highly abstract data and people capabilities, and concluded that only five occupational clusters – five different kinds of capability – existed. However, within each of these mega-clusters of occupations there was a tremendous degree of variability in actual work activities, rendering the description of any specific job using these terms effectively useless for any practical purpose, such as advising people on career paths or developing training plans.

theory & research

> **3.1** It is not enough, for example, for a doctor to 'know' that certain symptoms may indicate the presence of a specific disease, otherwise there would be automatic diagnosis machines that could respond to descriptions of symptoms. Instead there are long queues at general practitioner practices because real doctors have to be able to analyse various sources of data and symptoms, and put those analyses together to diagnose and evaluate an appropriate course of action. No machine can do this, though the development of call centres and interactive websites for heath-related queries can provide a degree of service without the usual full set of (expensive) cognitive capacities found in trained doctors.

Figure 3.6 provides one framework for mapping such capabilities. This map of capabilities suggests that capability-related objectives for HRD can be identified at three levels: underpinning capabilities, intermediate capabilities, and overarching capabilities. Underpinning capabilities are those that, broadly speaking, are expected as a consequence of primary and secondary education, including literacy and numeracy. As such they may seem to be irrelevant for HRD at work. However, it is widely acknowledged that some people have problems with attaining these underpinning capabilities in education, meaning that they are an issue in many workplace contexts. Many people enter the workforce lacking in numeracy, literacy and certain personal characteristics, such as influencing skills.

Intermediate capabilities are capabilities in occupation-specific roles, and the generic capabilities relevant to most mature adults in employment, and in life generally. These capabilities are most usually associated with training at or for work. They often form the heart of vocational qualification systems, and can be thought of as skills in the traditional sense. Work seen as being either low-skill or high-skill will vary at this level of capability.

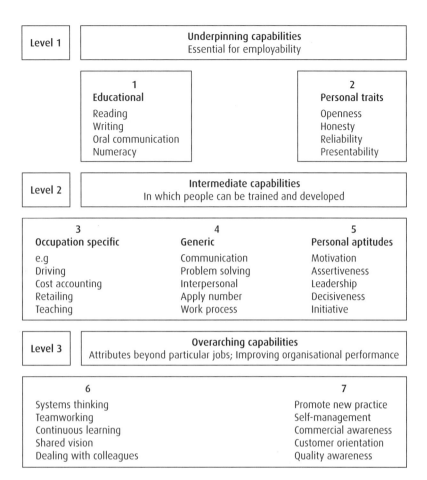

Level 1	Underpinning capabilities Essential for employability	

1 **Educational** Reading Writing Oral communication Numeracy	**2** **Personal traits** Openness Honesty Reliability Presentability

Level 2	Intermediate capabilities In which people can be trained and developed

3 **Occupation specific** e.g Driving Cost accounting Retailing Teaching	**4** **Generic** Communication Problem solving Interpersonal Apply number Work process	**5** **Personal aptitudes** Motivation Assertiveness Leadership Decisiveness Initiative

Level 3	Overarching capabilities Attributes beyond particular jobs; Improving organisational performance

6 Systems thinking Teamworking Continuous learning Shared vision Dealing with colleagues	**7** Promote new practice Self-management Commercial awareness Customer orientation Quality awareness

Figure 3.6 Capabilities

Source Parsons 1997

theory & research

3.2 | *Validity issues*

Maps of capabilities, such as those outlined in Figure 3.6, can be considered in terms of their validity in providing a means of designing useful HRD activities. Determining validity is the process of estimating the extent to which correct and accurate inferences can be derived from the scores or profiles generated by using the model. Such instruments may be classical psychometric tests or more general assessments of capabilities, such as a framework for performance appraisal based on an annual review of objectives by a manager and an employee. The former tend to be subject to formal validation studies whereas the latter are simply evaluated in terms of their usefulness in getting results.

An instrument that provides correct and accurate inferences is valid: for example, a selection test is said to be valid in allowing inferences about the potential job performance of an applicant to be derived from its use. An instrument that does not allow correct and accurate inferences is, thus, invalid. Continuing with the selection example, a psychometric test used in a selection process that does not allow inferences about the applicant's potential job performance is invalid. A similar test can be applied to models of capability.

Overarching capabilities are those attributes associated with people taking on responsibility for their own work and self-development, rather than being instructed to work or develop by others. These capabilities were once thought to be relevant only to people working as supervisors and managers, but they are now seen to be essential to all employees, and to form the core of new and advanced employability. From an HRD design point of view, most importantly, they are capabilities that need to be developed in concrete workplace situations. They cannot easily be learned and developed in other circumstances such as the classroom.

theory & research

| 3.3 | *Competence frameworks* |

Competence can be defined as the capabilities of superior performers. The demand on HRD strategies is to go beyond *doing things well* and move on to *doing things better* and *doing better things,* and this could be based on a mapping and development of competence. Many organisations have sought to develop their own maps of competence. Competence-based HRD systems are designed to help blind a set of initiatives to a set of managerial and workforce behaviours in order to lead to some future desirable state, usually improved performance. These systems are also often meant to provide a coherent framework for the integration of various HRM processes and initiatives, as well as being the focus for HRD strategy.

Finally, the identification of aptitudes, or affective factors, as a third dimension of development presents design challenges for HRD. The reason for including this third dimension is that effective performance is a consequence not only of what people know and think, and what they can do, but also of how they actually behave because of how they feel, and how they manage their feelings These affective influences on people and performance can often make the critical difference between good and poor performance, because affective influences on people are the prime controllers or drivers of behaviour (see Theory & Research Box 3.4). If affective factors are so critical for performance it is essential that they are addressed in the design of HRD experiences and the setting of objectives. In the HRD context affective factors influencing behaviour are commonly discussed in regard to three constructs:

- **changing attitudes**: patterns of personal likes and dislikes that can be measured and changed;
- **developing values**: basic beliefs about right and wrong that will influence what people will pursue and what they will or will not do;
- **emotional intelligence**: the effective handling of emotions to enable effective interpersonal relations.

To study only an isolated individual, abstracted from his or her social context, or to study people only as parts of systems without any individual agency, is of limited use when analysing performance issues and designing HRD at work. The former is a weakness attributed to the field of individual psychology, the latter is the weakness attributed to much of sociology. Social psychology stands between the assumptions and foci of these two sciences, and is defined as the study of human behaviour in interpersonal relations and groups. Social psychology draws on the concept of attitudes, which lies at the heart of much design practice in HRD. Attitudes were established in early social psychology as a focus for research and discussion of the

3.4 *Perspectives on the affective*

In the nineteenth and early twentieth centuries psychological theories gave primacy to 'affect' in explaining much human behaviour. People were thought to be at the mercy of various drives and passions which might erupt and overwhelm reason and rationality.

As behaviourism became more dominant in the field, affect was more and more discounted. There were those who wished to exclude affect from the 'scientific' study of people altogether. Even recently, with the ascendancy of cognitive psychology, humans have still been viewed as essentially problem-solvers whose thinking processes operate rather like a computer. Indeed the growth of Cognitive Behaviour Therapy (CBT) is premised on the theory that it is patterns of thought which sustain problematic emotional responses (such as phobias, anxieties and other debilitating conditions). Treatment of such conditions does not necessitate deep analysis of their root causes, rather it needs patterns of thinking to be changed – then the 'symptoms', the debilitating emotional responses of phobias and so on, will fade.

Often in such a modern view, affect is seen to matter, if at all, as a regrettable 'flaw' in an otherwise perfect cognitive machine.

On the other hand, the current rise in popularity of ideas about multiple forms of intelligence, including the concept of emotional intelligence, has seen the full cycle completed, because affect is once again seen as a primary factor in human behaviour which can be studied scientifically and incorporated in development experiences.

interface between psychological and sociological processes – between interaction and persuasion or group membership and prejudice. Attitudes are enduring predispositions to evaluate objects, people, or institutions favourably or negatively. They provide for patterns of behaviour based on the interaction of three elements:

- cognitive components: elements of perceptions;
- affective components: elements of feelings;
- conative components: elements of patterns of action and experience.

Attitudes are formed either from general experience through exposure to situations in the course of life, or from direct conditioning by which others seek to structure their development deliberately; from parents through peers to educators and then, of course, employers. They are the domain in which the dynamics of balance and dissonance are played out. People are naturally inclined to hold attitudes that are consistent with their perceptions and behaviour, and feel troubled if there is dissonance between what they perceive, what they feel, and what they do. These connections open up paths of influence for those concerned to shape attitudes.

In attitude theory, then, shaping or changing attitudes requires us to influence what people perceive, what they feel, and what they do, either singly or in combination. Usually, behaviour will tend to be adjusted to remove dissonance. However, there are problems with the concept and shaping of attitudes. First, measurement is difficult: because attitudes are not directly observable it is necessary to use scales and questionnaires to define and explore them. Thus the validity and reliability of these scales and questionnaires becomes an issue. Second, there are concerns based on evaluating arguments about managing attitude change. There is often agreement on the ideal behaviours – for example, it is right to try to reduce attitudes such as prejudices – but there is much less agreement on what is required to effect such change. In order to change attitudes, is it better to use the central route, providing for people to be exposed to and weigh up arguments, or the peripheral route, which involves using emotion to arouse dissonance and change behaviours? Anti-drug campaigns provide a good example of this dilemma: is it better to provide information about drugs and let people weigh up the arguments, or should emotive messages about the dangers of drugs be promoted more forcefully?

Yet it is also the case that people's avowed attitudes may be related only loosely to their actual behaviour: for example, there are those who hold prejudiced views but not actually act in prejudiced ways. Because people's behaviour is constrained by laws and rules, by knowing other's attitudes, by the relative importance of the issue at hand, and by perceptions of social pressures, the existence of an attitude may not actually be a good guide to how someone will behave. Someone may demonstrate all the attitudes expected of, for example, a chartered accountant, but then behave in an unprofessional way; or they may fail to have these attitudes, but still act in a professional way. These kinds of concern qualify the importance of attitudes as a potential driver of behaviour, and restrict the scope for and usefulness of attitude change as a part of HRD at work (see Theory & Research Box 3.5).

| 3.5 | *Attitude change factors* |

The following variables are all important when attempting to design in objectives around attitude change in the context of HRD and work roles:

- **Communicator credibility**. Do the people attempting to change learners' attitudes have expertise, and are they trustworthy? If HRD experiences are managed by people who are not perceived as experts and trustworthy, any attempt at attitude change is likely to fail.
- **Communicator attractiveness**: that is, their attractiveness to the person whose attitudes are to be influenced. The ability to have rapport with a person or group is essential in HRD.
- **Extremity of message**. Greater attitude change requires more extreme messages.
- **Use of one-sided or two-sided, debate-style, forms of argument**. Many HRD experiences need to be given a structure in which either a one-sided presentation (of instruction) or scope for debate and discussion is needed. Using the wrong method in the wrong circumstances will frustrate and confuse.
- **Use of fear**. People will change their attitudes if threats can be articulated to favour attitude change.
- **Different social situations**. Group situations are better at eliciting attitude change than interpersonal face-to-face settings, and public situations are better than private. This is one reason why many HRD experiences involving attitude change are organised in groups.
- **Influence of prior events**. For example, being forewarned that attitudes will be confronted can lead people to self-inoculation against change. In the management of attitude change through HRD it should not be kept 'secret', but the potential for self-inoculation can mean that time is needed to 'open people up' in HRD events.

The concept of values provides another avenue for thinking about the design of HRD, taking into account the role of affect in behaviour that is relevant to performance and HRD at work, and to the setting of objectives. A value can be defined as an enduring belief that a specific mode of conduct or end-state of existence is personally or socially preferable to an opposite or converse mode of conduct or end-state of existence. Values embody basic beliefs about what is right and what is wrong: they both express and control the behaviours of community members for stability within the community.

The community of a specific workplace also requires people to accept and abide by core values. More specifically, explicit values can impact upon organisational, professional and personal performance. It is often considered important that core organisational values should be identified and propagated: organisations define their core values and disseminate them widely to staff and others. These are sometimes called 'Big 'V'' values (Leonard-Barton 1995) to distinguish them from 'small 'v'' values, which inform interaction and behaviour. Small 'v' values are evident in professional work roles in the form of ethical guidelines: doctors, lawyers, teachers and others must abide by these above all else, or they will be disciplined and barred from practising. Personal values about what is right and wrong, about duty and virtuousness, are invariably at the core of people's sense of personal identity and self (Morris 1965, Davidson 1972).

Values are important because they have the potential to be executive guides for all of a person's actions, attitudes and judgements, with reference to ultimate ends and to issues beyond their immediate goals. While values may be easy to identify and promulgate, they are not necessarily mutually supportive. For example, there are potential contradictions in being both thrifty and charitable. They are both worthy behaviours in the right context and at the right time, but may conflict at certain times and in certain contexts. It is through the resolution of these value conflicts, either consciously or unconsciously, that a hierarchical arrangement is established in a person or group and evolves as a value system. A value system is a rank ordering of values that serves to resolve social and personal conflict and direct the selection of alternatives where choices have to be made. The analytical interest in values has been inspired by exploring different value systems – within specific cultures and between different cultures.

The connection with HRD design is the importance of planning for and designing objectives related to values. Core organisational, occupational and individual values, such as teamwork, quality and creativity, are identified and propagated. Occupational values are relevant and necessary for competent performance of a specific job, and professional values provide ethical guidelines. Personal values, and their fit with the organisation and occupational roles, may be areas where HRD is required.

Finally, the emotional aspects of work and performance have long been acknowledged as important for performance in many jobs and organisational settings, and the topic is now assuming greater prominence in business and management as a whole. This has in part resulted from the rise of stress as a prominent health and safety issue in many organisations. An analysis of the kinds of emotional demand being made on staff, and ways of mitigating these, has been seen as highly relevant to responding to the stress epidemic. Concern with emotion is also a reflection of a long-standing concern for human relations within effective teams and relationships at work. Emotion is not just an issue for work and performance in situations where employees may be exposed to high degrees of stress and trauma. All forms of work and performance have emotional contexts. There are emotional aspects of effective performance for holiday representatives in a beach resort, employees in customer call centres, as well as in nursing and care in hospitals.

Operationalising emotion can be done simply: there are four core feelings: 'mad, bad, sad or glad'. These can be expanded upon (see Theory & Research Box 3.6). The ways in which performance at work involves experiencing and containing anger, elation, anxiety/fear, disgust, grief, happiness, jealousy/envy, love, sadness, embarrassment, pride, shyness, shame, or guilt can be important in providing areas for HRD design to include and not to ignore (Hochschild 1983, Fineman 1993).

3.6	Eight basic emotions		
□ Fear	□ Sorrow	□ Disgust	□ Anticipation
□ Anger	□ Joy	□ Acceptance	□ Surprise

Source Plutchik 1980.

Finer distinctions can be made, of variations and expansions on these emotions (see Resources Box 3.5). In the context of HRD at work the concern is that performance may be affected if positive emotions are not activated and negative emotions are not contained and controlled. In context effective performance may require people to potentially feel angry or embarrassed or disgusted, or to avoid getting angry, embarrassed or disgusted.

3.5	Personal and interpersonal emotions		
Personal emotions			
Joy	Suffering	Pleasure	Pain
Content	Regret	Relief	Aggravation
Cheerfulness	Dejection	Rejoicing	Lamentation
Amusement	Dullness	Aesthetic	Taste
Hopelessness	Fear	Courage	Cowardice
Rashness	Caution	Desire	Indifference
Dislike	Fastidiousness	Wonder	Pride
Humility	Vanity	Modesty	Insolence
Interpersonal emotions, feelings in relationship			
Friendship	Enmity	Sociality	Courtesy
Love	Hatred	Resentment	Anger
Sullenness	Benevolence	Malevolence	Threat
Pity	Gratitude	Forgiveness	Jealousy
Envy	Guilt		

Source Roget's Thesaurus 1987

There are a range of perspectives (Strongman 1996) on identifying and analysing emotions that are relevant to defining HRD objectives. One is to view emotions as physiological processes: that is, physical changes in the physiology of organisms. This kind of analysis explores the connections between, for example, fear and preparing for fight or flight. HRD design needs to be aware of such issues and aims to help people develop mechanisms for coping with these physiological processes in the context of work roles.

An alternative perspective is to view emotions as an influence on thinking, so that they are studied as a feature of the information-processing brain. Here the concern is the way in which emotions shape perception and thinking. HRD about emotion is needed to make people aware of, and take into account, the way that emotions can influence thinking. The patterns of emotion within social contexts, reflecting conditioning, are also studied as facets of socialisation in patterns of role behaviour – for example, with gender-based and cultural variations in appropriate emotional display, or 'big boys don't cry' and 'women are nurturing' expectations. HRD at work can then be about challenging this conditioning, and the stereotypes that go with it. Finally, emotions have been studied in the context of clinical dysfunction: as causes of or contributors to mental dysfunction, for example, depression. While insight about emotion can be found in this domain, HRD design and activity is not the appropriate environment for managing this kind of concern; other professionals are the proper people to investigate and deal with this form of influence of emotion on performance.

In the work and performance HRD context, current concerns arising from all these perspectives focus on the discussion of emotional intelligence (EI). Intelligence is the ability to define and pursue goals, and to overcome obstacles to achieve them. EI is the ability to appreciate the interpersonal dynamics involved in defining and pursuing goals and overcoming obstacles to achieving them. Performance gaps and HRD objectives can be related to gaps in EI. One framework for structuring analysis of EI is given in Strategic View Box 3.2. This suggests that EI requires, as a minimum, some awareness, complemented by personal experiences enabling empathy, and that it further involves being able to express emotions oneself. It, therefore, ultimately enables the control of emotions based on awareness, empathy and the ability to express. Without awareness there can be no experience, without experience there can be no expression, and without expression there can be no control.

strategic view

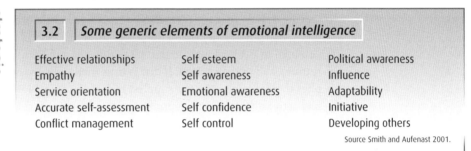

3.2	Some generic elements of emotional intelligence		
Effective relationships	Self esteem	Political awareness
Empathy	Self awareness	Influence
Service orientation	Emotional awareness	Adaptability
Accurate self-assessment	Self confidence	Initiative
Conflict management	Self control	Developing others

Source Smith and Aufenast 2001.

Finally, Figure 3.7 illustrates one framework for appreciating how different kinds of emotion can support learning in different phases of a learning experience. HRD design should include roles for all kinds of emotion to give highs and impact to learning.

Figure 3.7 Emotions and the learning cycle

Source Derived from Reilly and Kort 2003.

Reflections on HRD design

The preceding frameworks are examples of what can be termed 'content models' to guide the analysis of designing objectives for HRD activities across the three identifiable dimensions of needs. Content models suggest a framework of universal, general, fixed and set hierarchical structures. However they can be misleading, and may even lead to design practices which impede learning rather than supporting it. For example, there are problems with Bloom's taxonomy as a content model of cognitive capacities. The model assumes that, for humans, information is passively received by the senses, and that the more complex cognitive capacities are engaged only during certain kinds of activity, tasks and situations. The overall function of cognition is, thus, to help people discover an objective reality: that is, a reality that exists 'out there', independent of the person sensing it.

However, these assumptions about cognitive capacities are contestable. If people are not just passive cognition machines, passively receiving information through the senses, they may be seen rather as agents actively building up and constructing a view of reality based on their own experience and interests (see Theory & Research Box 3.7). The functions of cognition can then be interpreted as adaptive sense-making, serving to help manage the person's experience of the world, rather than just accessing an objective reality that is 'out there'. And this kind of sense-making in work is not confined to professionals undertaking difficult and complex tasks – it is an inherent feature of all human action. If that is true, then such a view of cognitive functions implies that learning even the simplest task is always achieved by people as sense-making, active agents, not as neutral cognition machines trying to memorise knowledge. Defining objectives for HRD experiences may impede the natural learning process rather than support it.

theory and research

3.7 | Constructivism and design

Constructivism has roots in philosophical debates about rationalism and empiricism. Rationalists argue that the individual human has no direct access to external reality, only to impressions of external reality. Thus people can only obtain information and use it through in-built cognitive principles which actively organise their experience, rather than behaving like machines that neutrally process it.

The psychologist Piaget, for example, developed a theory of the different cognitive stages through which a child progresses, building up an increasingly complex model of the world.

The cognitive principles evident in change during a child's development suggest that there is active construction of information and knowledge. The analysis implies that, when trying to structure and direct learning that involves establishing or developing cognitive capacities, there is much more to doing it well than cramming facts into brains.

The most noteworthy development of these ideas related to psychology and learning that is relevant to adults is seen in the work of Kelly and the concept of 'personal construct' psychology. This assumes people are active sense-makers, so it is first necessary to elicit and know people's existing personal constructs in order to clarify why they behave as they do. Only then is it possible to work on what needs to be challenged to change behaviour and help them learn. This is invariably an individual task, and is not about generic objectives.

With an objectivist view of cognitive capacities, the underlying proposition is that learning means obtaining, codifying and packaging the 'truth', whether that means accessing forms of defined knowledge or higher-order capacities such as critical evaluation. If cognition is a passive reflection of an external, objective reality learning can be so characterised. This view is then consistent with the idea that, and indeed implies, a process of instruction is the key to effective HRD design; learning about the truth from an authority. In order to obtain an image of reality (the subject) people must somehow receive the right information from the environment: that is, they must be instructed. In learning, people are acting like cameras which capture an image of how the world 'really' is in their brain. Trainers simply present them with the right images in the right sequence, and learning follows.

But this characterisation of people quickly runs up against a host of objections. Human brains do not act like mirrors or cameras. People are always actively generating different models of the 'world out there', reinforcing some observations of the outside world while eliminating others. This is a process of selection by the person, rather than a process of mirroring in the brain. The process of personal construction cannot be switched off and on; it occurs all the time. Sometimes it can be productive for learning and sometimes it can cause problems. It can be helpful where it leads people to new insights, as they check and test their versions of the world and come to useful and insightful conclusions. Alternatively it may reinforce mistaken views and delusions, leading people to reject learning, and changes in their cognition, capabilities or behaviour. What cognition or learning cannot do is to establish one best and true way of perceiving reality.

Contrasting assumptions about cognition are embodied in a constructivist view of learning. Knowledge, all other aspects of cognitive capacity, reflections on capability and behaviour emerge from and are embedded in what is personally constructed by the person, not by what is impressed upon them by external authorities. Such personal construction matters as individuals seek to control what they perceive in order to eliminate any deviations or perturbations from their own secure, existing and preferred model of the world. Thus people tend to 'see' and consider that which is relevant to their individual goals and actions and their own status quo, but tend to ignore that which they do not feel is relevant. The typical individual does not care about the 'truth' of the knowledge that an expert may try to communicate to them; they are rather more concerned about how much it disrupts their personal constructions. They may face up to and adapt to the changed ideas that come with new knowledge, or they may seek to compensate for perturbations in their existing models of reality by rejecting them.

Constructivist views of learning are deep, suggesting that there is more to the design challenge than communication in order to gain acceptance of new knowledge, capabilities or behaviours; it can be about overhauling or protecting a whole, constructed model of the outside world. That model may be more valid than the learner's own in some ways, but still not be accepted. Experts may indeed be right, and their information and knowledge, prescribed capabilities and behaviours may be valid, but people will still not adapt or change their own models – their own validated kinds of information and knowledge. The most important HRD design issue is then to help people to open and modify their own constructions rather than impose an expert's best construction on them. This is much more difficult to manage; it is easier to try to enforce a correct model, by citing authority, by asserting and by imposing.

> ### 3.8 | *Dissonance and Aha! moments*
>
> We may need to endure dissonance in a learner as a starting point of learning, including the experience of thinking or feeling that an existing world-view is wrong or inadequate. It is wrong to try merely to pack in more and more new knowledge, because it simply creates information overload. It is also wrong because people need time to adapt and adjust their model of the world as they go along a learning and development curve. If they are overloaded they will almost inevitably reject the new knowledge that others have been trying to instil. On the more positive side, a sign of such a qualitative change in their constructed model of the world arises with 'Aha!' learning moments, when it seems that they suddenly 'get' something that previously had eluded them.

Individuals' criteria for selection of the kind of information and knowledge they will accommodate may be 'coherence'-related; that is, the new information and knowledge agrees with their existing patterns of information and knowledge, what they already know. Or their criteria may be 'consensus'-related; that is, the extent to which they believe it is widely accepted in significant groups. This consensus dimension connects learning design with broader social construction ideas, which see more than intrinsic, personal cognition factors as shaped by social processes of communication and negotiation, part of the person's larger social construction of reality as the member of a group. HRD always occurs in and contributes to a social context.

A pragmatic interpretation of the constructivist view is that it alerts us to the ways in which the process and adequacy of learning requires more than an authority specifying information and knowledge profiles. In some areas where HRD design arises there may be expert-validated and accepted bodies of information and knowledge, and the kinds of cognitive capacities required for jobs and tasks. It is, nonetheless, often difficult to get people to learn, partly because of their pre-existing model of the world. The learning may act to perturb, so that new information and knowledge, or changes to behaviour, are resisted.

Conclusion

To plan and design for effective HRD it is necessary to establish aims, objectives and targets. These need to relate in a balanced way to the cognitive capacities, capabilities and behaviours required for effective performance in roles and organisations. Particular models for identifying these are available and used in practice, though they are all partial and biased in some respects, and we need to handle them with care.

To plan and design HRD well requires design thinking, which faces challenges in three areas: analysis, synthesis, and communication. The challenge of analysis is to break needs down into discrete 'developable' units of learning. The challenges of synthesis are about balance and variety in putting together designs for dealing with cognitive, capability and behavioural dimensions of learning. Communication is central to the whole process, requiring clarity and simplicity in definitions and statements. The structures suggested by an improved consciousness of design will help support personal change. It can be developed in various ways: intellectually exploring ideas such as the constructivist framework for thinking about the nature of learning and HRD design, and familiarity with general design principles and concerns (see Resources Box 3.5).

3.6 | *Design principles*

Principle	General Issues	Applied to HRD Design
Balance	What is to be made will need to be balanced, and design should be the time when the right balance is gauged. How much of one thing, and how much of another, to ensure balance?	What proportion of cognitive capacity, capability and behaviour is going to be right?
Contrast	Powerful images use high contrast, of dark and light, shapes or materials. Another way to show contrast is with contradiction This can provide muscle to get a message over.	Powerful learning can use high contrast: before and after, bad practice and good practice, light humour and serious stories.
Direction	People's experience of a newspaper, a building or anything else that is designed has to be 'directed' clearly, or they will feel lost.	Trainers need to lead learners through their HRD experiences without getting them lost or confused. Direction in learning is about the management of going in circles, but still making progress.
Economy	Getting down to the bare bones of the design, once all extraneous elements are eliminated, are you sure the message is clear?	If you are not, then the learners will not be either. And sometimes it is essential to send a large message with a small voice; there is no time or resource for anything else.
Emphasis	People are always telling stories that end with them saying 'And my point is this...' Although the story might be interesting, perhaps the point could be made with less embellishment and more structure.	If everything is emphasised, nothing is emphasised. When you create an HRD event, what point are you making? Where does the emphasis need to be?
Rhythm	Following a rhythm, a pattern, is central to all forms of communication. Without rhythm, communication is lifeless and drab. The principle of rhythm is as unavoidable as the element of contrast.	Good learning experiences have rhythm, a 'beat' that people can feel and which allows them to feel comfortable.
Unity	If form and content don't match goals, it all ends up an agony of self-defeat. Unity sounds like the crowning achievement of all the principles of design, but it's really no better than emphasis and no less than rhythm. Unity is judged on how well the event is received.	Elements must be employed effectively within a format. Success depends on the appropriate relationship of content within the format.

Source http://www.graphicdesignbasics.com

Multiple-choice questions

3.1 Which of the following sequences is the correct one for structuring the design of an HRD intervention?
   A. Identify objectives, then targets, then an aim.
   B. Identify an aim, then targets and then objectives.
   C. Identify targets, then objectives and then an aim.
   D. Identify an aim, then objectives, then targets.

3.2 Which of the following describe potential sources of poor HRD design?
   A. There is too much analysis of needs in terms of discrete cognitive capacity, capability and an affective dimension.
   B. The language used to express objectives is vague and fuzzy.
   C. Seeing people as passive 'cognition machines' that are ever ready to absorb new information.
   D. Seeing people as possessing a stable world-view that may need to be upset in order to enable learning.

References

Beech, N. et al (2000) 'Transient transfusion: or the wearing off of the governance of the soul?', *Personnel Review*, vol. 19, no. 4, 460–73.

Bloom, B.S. (1965) *A Taxonomy of Educational Objectives: Handbook 1; Cognitive Domain*, New York, McKay.

Davidson, P. (1972) 'Value Theory: Toward Conceptual Clarification', *British Journal of Sociology*, vol. 23, 172–87.

Fineman, S. (ed.) (1993) *Emotions in Organizations*, London, Sage.

Ford, D. (1999) *Bottom Line Training*, Houston, TX, Gulf Publishing Co.

Harvey, R.J. (1999) 'Job analysis', in M.D. Dunnette and L. Hough (eds), *Handbook of Industrial and Organization Psychology*, 2nd edn, Palo Alto, CA, Consulting Psychologists Press.

Hochschild, A.R. (1983) *The Managed Heart: Commercialization of human feeling*, Berkeley, CA, University of California Press.

Knowles, M. (1984) *Andragogy in Action*, San Francisco, Jossey-Bass.

Lawson, B. (2000) *How Designers Think: The design process demystified*, Oxford, Architectural Press.

Leonard-Barton, D. (1995) *Wellsprings of Knowledge*, Boston, MA, Harvard Business School Press.

Morris, C. (1965) *Varieties of Human Value*, Chicago, University of Chicago Press.

Parsons, D. (1997) 'A qualitative approach to local skills audits', *Skills and Enterprise Briefing*, Issue 6.

Plutchik, R. (1980) 'A general psychoevolutionary theory of emotion', in R. Plutchik and H. Kellerman (eds), *Emotion: Theory, Research, and Experience, Vol 1: Theories of Emotion*, New York, Academic, pp. 3–33.

Reich, B. et al (1976) *Values, Attitudes and Behaviour Change*, Methuen & Co.

Reilly, R. and Kort, B. (2003) 'The science behind the art of teaching science: emotional states and learning', working paper, Boston, MA, MIT.

Rokeach, M. (1970) 'Beliefs, Attitudes and Values: A theory of organisation and change', San Francisco, Jossey-Bass.

Smith, P. M. and Aufenast, J. (2001) 'Emotional competence at work; Implicit theories, a new model and supporting data', *British Academy of Management*, Cardiff.

Strongman, K. (1996) *The Psychology of Emotion: Theories of emotion in perspective*, 4th edn, New York, John Wiley.

| concluding case question | *Using game genres* |

The use of computer games for learning purposes is not new, but most of the applications to date have been for young learners with very few significant examples of adult learning through this medium. Yet we are now very much in the 'games generation' (Generation X) and many adults are now experienced video gamers. The most successful games in the market are designed for and purchased by adults in the age range 20 to 27.

Games are often classified by 'genre'. There are 44 classifications for games, but this is generally accepted to be too complex. There has been recent trend to reduce the number by combining related ones, resulting in a total of 7 genres that are more easily understood:

- Action and adventure
- Driving and racing
- First person shooter
- Platform and puzzle
- Role playing
- Strategy and simulation
- Sports and beat 'em ups

What kinds of HRD options might such games be used for?
What design problems would you foresee in using such games in adult learning in the workplace?

| concluding case answer |

There are some obvious options and some more imaginative ones.

Genre	Obvious Options	Imaginative options
Action and adventure	Decision-making in the course of action and adventure	Increase confidence in risk-taking; Structuring an entire learning event as an action adventure, a quest with challenges to be met and overcome
Driving and racing	Simulations for drivers of vehicles	Pressure learning in and for stress environments; improving reaction times and increasing sensitivity to background cues, providing thrills
First person shooter	Simulations for those using firearms	Completing a task in time enables an advancing threat to be fought off, e.g. touch typing fast enough to keep away a horde of oncoming Zombies
Puzzle games	Problem-solving skills	Structuring a piece of knowledge in a way that allows players to explore it over several rounds of puzzle-solving
Role playing	Strategies for interacting with other people	Creating complex groups and organisations that persist over time, in which participants' behaviour affects outcomes
Strategy and simulation	Developing and implementing strategies	Learning in a rapidly changing environment; creating entire worlds that evolve and change according to the decisions made by a team
Sports and beat 'em ups	Sports knowledge and tactics	Networked learning; making a learning event a 'league' or tournament in which teams can compete

coninued overleaf

A

The design problems would be several. Are these game genres promoting behaviours that some might object to; including aggression, risk-free recklessness? Can simulations be truly effective domains for dealing with people and soft skill issues?

The main areas of HRD interest, remember, are in topics like health & safety, communication, teamworking and leadership. Are these genres really good models for those, or might the 'game' get in the way of learning?

Games-based learning may only be really successful and widely accepted when the experience is comparable with that of leading games. That means that the experience must be within the game's paradigm, contrasting with the usual HRD situation of having clearly identifiable learning outcomes.

The majority of successful games have large-scale support available through online forums and websites. These allow sharing of hints and tips, 'cheats', patches and updates to the games. This level of support may be hard to sustain in a workplace. Many games also support the introduction of new characters and challenges as well as the development of the capability of characters and other resources. These are also items that are shared through the support networks.

The leading games in the market all have an after-market that is encouraged by the publisher. SDKs (Software Development Kits) are commonly available that enable third parties to develop and extend the core game by creating new scenarios, challenges, characters and resources. This development is organic in nature and a successful game can reach much further through the efforts of third parties than it ever could through the efforts of the publisher alone. The websites for these games often have many hundreds of add-ons available that have been created by players, groups and some commercial developers. Some of the most successful games in the market have been developed on the platform of another successful game or the 'games engine' that was developed for another game.

Managing workplace HRD in action

learning
objectives

By the end of this chapter you will be able to:

- describe the theory and practice of instruction and facilitation in delivering HRD;
- describe and analyse other forms of performance support relevant to HRD;
- critically evaluate the strengths and weaknesses of instruction and facilitation as methods of managing HRD;
- adopt and adapt instruction and facilitation methods in HRD.

| introductory case study | *CapitalAirport* |

CapitalAirport was a large, busy airport in a country that had become increasingly dependent on air travel. It served the nation's capital, and was run by a state-controlled company. In the previous five years there had been a virtual doubling of passenger numbers, and a big increase in freight. Staffing had not increased at the same rate, however, and there was strain on existing resources. Senior managers saw some key problems. Managers were concerned that many staff were not going out of their way to help customers; customer service did not seem to be a high priority. Increasing competition with services offered by other travel companies, both ferry and train, was a factor. Customer surveys presented a reasonably positive picture, but with a near-monopoly people could not vote with their feet. But the real threat was of privatisation if poor service was not improved. The company wanted to provide a quality service for passengers and other customers, but was not making any significant investments in training. It was known that some workers felt themselves undervalued, and were at best a 'necessary evil'. For example, the airport police service felt this; yet they were the biggest employee group in the organisation, and played a big day-to-day operational role. There was conflict between the police service and the operations department. Management felt that this whole situation needed changing.

It was decided that an HRD strategy aimed at improved handling of increased levels of service had to be set up. Three key activities were organised. First, consultants were hired to run a course on 'the human factor'. This off-site company-wide course involved getting employees to think about their careers, and life–work balance, and also included role-playing for dealing with customer service problems. Then, new customer service teams were introduced, based on quality circle principles to look at continuous improvement. Despite initial successes with these teams, relations in them deteriorated; two years on they had ceased to function. Finally there was another training programme: an event called 'the winning factor'. This was a one-day, organisation-wide event run at a nearby hotel. It consisted of a film presentation on dealing with customers, a workshop on identifying competitors and how well they delivered customer service, a play performed by airport staff, a question and answer session with the Chief Executive, and awards given at a ceremony to 'outstanding employees'.

continued overleaf

Managers and employees had strong views about this last aspect of the training, and it failed to have any positive impact. They thought of it as a demeaning programme, because it treated managers and staff like fools and insulted their intelligence. The people responsible for organising and running the programme were seen as two-faced: saying one thing and doing another. Some expressed very strong views that the event had been fraudulent and a disgrace. This reflected general discontent.

There were a number of interconnected reasons why the managers and staff were so irritated and provoked by this aspect of the training. However, the key issue seemed to be that the message being promoted in training was that all employees could be 'winners' and 'heroes' in the course of undertaking their day-to-day work. And, of course, winning should be accompanied by loud celebrations and applause, reminiscent of many US companies' employee-of-the-month schemes.

This portrayed a romanticised view of their work situations that bore no resemblance to the day-to-day reality, which, for the most part, was routine and hard work. Even on the training day itself only a few actually received awards. In fact employees struggled to meet customer needs. They were involved in exhausting and difficult interchanges with customers, who projected their anxieties and frustrations onto staff. They saw themselves very far from being winners in any sense, and could not see any way in which they might be winners in the future. Even the airport firemen, the most likely 'heroes', were struck by the incongruity of the idea of being 'winners'. Much of their time was spent in extreme boredom waiting for things to happen. What was so irksome was that the whole idea of the HRD strategy denied the reality of their day-to-day work. It seemed that managers did not want to know – and therefore did not care about – the employees. The managers seemed unable to acknowledge the realities of stress and boredom that characterised the employees' work. The HRD strategy of instilling in everyone the thought that they were 'winners' was at best deluded and patronising and at worst dishonest.

Introduction

Having identified an HRD need and subsequently planned and designed the structure and form for appropriate HRD, the next phase is to develop and deliver the HRD. There are a wide range of options and environments for practical delivery, including:

1. on-the-job learning experiences at the workplace;
2. organisation-based short training courses;
3. external short courses or learning events;
4. e-learning – computer-based or learning in a 'learning centre';
5. 'learning partnerships' such as coaching, mentoring.

HRD development and delivery may range from a single person developing a brief, one-off activity for a single employee to many people working in a team developing complex courses that are delivered to tens of thousands of people many times as a part of larger organisational projects. Whatever the scale of development and delivery there are common challenges around controlling costs, quality and time. And while the practical forms of delivery listed above may appear quite varied, and do indeed involve different kinds of action, they all use some combination of instruction and facilitation. Instruction is the process by which someone delivers a scripted, impersonal and 'closed' presentation to impart set ways of knowing, doing or behaving. In contrast, facilitation is about an individual or group being helped, through non-directive and improvised delivery methods, to improved awareness and change in their diverse, personal ways of thinking, doing and behaving. Instruction 'tells'; facilitation 'sells'.

These delivery methods are at opposite ends of the spectrum of ways to deliver effective HRD (see Operations Box 4.1), and we shall examine both in this chapter. To help fix what they can involve, exemplary kinds of delivery can be cited:

- instruction   HRD for health & safety matters, where standard and shared ways of knowing, doing and behaving are recognised and desirable;
- facilitation   HRD for leadership development, where different styles and personalised ways of knowing, doing and behaving are recognised and desirable.

4.1	A spectrum of delivery methods

Instruction	Facilitation
Impersonal	Personalised
Scripted	Improvised
Replicate the same	Each group different
Directive	Participative
Closed topics	Open Topics
Convergent	Divergent
Deficiency assumptions	Growth assumptions

The delivery methods spectrum is grounded in two contrasting assumptions about people: deficiency and potential. The deficiency assumption is that, for HRD to be effective, adult learners must recognise that they are deficient in some aspect of cognition, capability or behaviour, and therefore require an intervention to remedy the deficiency before performance is achieved. The alternative model is that adult learners have growth potential in some aspect of cognition, capability or behaviour, and they are willing to be helped to discover that latent ability and fulfil their potential. Delivery challenges reflect the management of learning as a process that is at times 'outside-in' and at times 'inside-out'. In other words, it can be directed both at instilling what is new and drawing out what is innate. This duality in delivery applies from the start of learning, from the earliest learning in child development and the role of the nursery teacher. It comes very much to the fore in adult learning and development, and managing this ambiguity is a perpetual source of tension and fulfilment in delivery.

Instruction

Instruction requires the direct transmission and development of predetermined kinds of cognitive capacity, standardised capabilities and explicit behaviours. The principles of such programmed instruction (Eitington 1984, Forsyth 1992, Mager 2000) emerge from theories and practice in how to shape and influence human development and end up in Instructional Steps (see Figure 4.1). These influence delivery from the memorisation of basic knowledge, trial-and-error practical learning for developing capabilities, and the conditioning and reinforcement of desired kinds of attitude and value.

A four-phase model of HRD delivery by instruction in the classroom outlines the most common recipe (see Figure 4.2). In most effective instructional experiences the emphasis is initially on cognition then on doing (practice) with affective dimensions implicit.

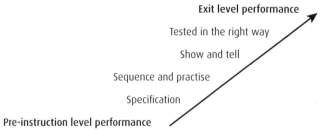

Figure 4.1 Instructional learning steps

Figure 4.2 Phases of the development and delivery of instruction

Specifications for delivery are determined, outlining in full and in detail what learners have to know and be able to do, and how they should act. Learning is then delivered, with these elements presented in the logical sequence, enabling practice. The instructor is required to play the role of showing and telling. Learners are then directly and formally tested on whether or not they have developed the cognitive capacity, capability and behaviours required.

There are various types of instruction including direct verbal instruction from managers and others in the course of work; self-instruction, using workbooks and learning packs; or instruction provided in specialist learning environments by trained instructors. The success of learning delivery depends on a well-sequenced experience which can be delivered by instruction. Principles for instruction, whichever mode is to be used, are suggested in Resources Box 4.1 and Operations Box 4.2.

The development of professional instructors is therefore seen as an essential and integral part of managing HRD. The professional development of trainers – the training of trainers – has in the past been concerned largely with proficiency in the process of instruction. Professional instructors are people who have a thorough knowledge of effective human performance and the learning required for performance in an area; they understand the how and why of the learning that trainees are experiencing. They also understand and use the principles of structured and programmed instruction in design and delivery. They are able to perform consistently over many learning events, and over time as instructors, to deliver instruction sessions and objectively assess learners. The challenges facing instructors are also universal, across sectors and roles and kinds of learners (see Operations Box 4.3). Good instructors are generally seen to be:

- Consistent in their ability to manage repeated delivery of the same/similar HRD processes;
- Meticulous and obsessively organised in order to ensure that all aspects of instruction are effective;
- Sympathetic to learners of different abilities;
- Patient with the process of showing and telling, trial and error;
- Objective in assessing others' knowledge, capabilities and behaviour.

| 4.1 | *Instruction principles* |

Instructional **objectives** must be set for all parts of the learning experience and for the whole learning experience. Instructional objectives must be embedded in structured materials, experiences or class-based sessions, whether for 1-day or 2–3-day courses, or for a programme lasting years.

- Instruction experiences must be both **comprehensive** and **simple**. Every single element must be included and systematically dealt with, through confirmation, stage by stage, until at the end the complete transmission of cognition, capability and behaviour is achieved.
- **Preparation** is the largest task in instruction: developing materials, presentations, simulations, and appropriate tasks so that all objectives are covered.
- In the delivery of instruction thought has to be given to **creating and maintaining interest** for the individual or the group. Materials have to be engaging, experiences have to be motivating, and class-based instruction has to be engaging.
- • Instruction culminates in an **objective evaluation** of the extent of learning. As objectives have been tightly set, it is possible to measure whether someone knows or does not know, is capable or is not capable, can behave appropriately or not. Trainees can be tested and deemed to be right or wrong in terms of performance-related cognition, capability and behaviours

| 4.2 | *Instruction delivery* |

A retail organisation decided it needed to improve stock flows and safety in its warehouses. The pre-instruction level of performance showed poor stock-flow management and evidence of unsafe practices. The organisation developed a programme of instruction to attain an improved level of performance that involved the following elements:

- **Cognition**: knowledge of set procedures, specifying what employees will do.
  They will store incoming stock in the right order in the right areas.
  They will know the correct procedures for lifting and using machinery.

- **Capability**: instruction in the one best way to do things – how they will do it.
  Employees will be shown how to manage stocks.
  They will be shown how to lift heavy loads following prescribed procedures.

- **Behaviour**: prescribed norms about why they should perform in these ways.
  Employees will follow proper procedures to ensure the smooth running of re-stocking, ensuring efficiency on all shifts.
  They will behave safely to ensure there are no accidents or injuries, keeping in mind the impact this has on the efficiency of the organisation and to meet its legal obligations.

In dealing with delivery to adult learners some of the characteristics of good instructors can present more fundamental problems (see Theory & Research Box 4.1). There are tensions between the principles of instruction and these features of adult learning.

theory & research

4.1 | *Instruction and adult learners*

Instruction	Adult learners
Get attention	Have different kinds and degrees of experience
Motivation	Can already perform many skills; get bored
Modelling	Seek to avoid pain and embarrassment; dislike feeling exposed
Timing	Pacing for different abilities; some bored, some lost
Practice and feedback	Feel exposed and vulnerable
Relevant practice	Through experience judge classrooms or cases are unrealistic
Reinforcement	Have own experiences to reflect on; dislike being 'taught'

operations

4.3 | *Challenges of instruction*

- Get attention – capture attention and keep it, get learners to respond
- Motivation – make clear 'what's in it for me?'
- Modelling – provide learning through imitation, 'do it the way I do it'
- Retention – manage retention of information and procedures
- Timing – keeping everything on schedule
- Practice and feedback – enable and manage trial and error
- Relevant practice – ensure practice is realistic and performance -related
- Reinforcement – reinforce the correct ways, extinguish the erroneous

Facilitation

The core meaning of 'to facilitate' is 'to make something easy or easier'. In the HRD context, what we are 'easing' is a change in knowing, doing and behaving (Berry 1993, Leigh 1991, Bentley 1994). 'Easing' is more appropriate than instruction partly because of the widely recognised nature of HRD for adult learners. They prefer working with those supporting their learning to being 'taught'. It is also partly because of the kinds of objectives and targets that are addressed through HRD at work. Here 'soft' skills and diverse styles in aspects of performance, such as management and leadership, preclude simple instruction as the one best way or a single model. Facilitation is also seen as appropriate because the logic of experiential learning has become accepted as a paradigm in workplace HRD (see Figure 4.3). Instruction is not an appropriate mode of managing learning. Facilitation is argued to be valid and useful as it helps those supporting HRD to use an experiential cycle model of learning (Kolb 1984).

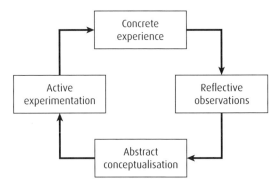

Figure 4.3 The experiential learning cycle

Facilitation is then an umbrella concept, and it has come to be associated with the clusters of methods that have evolved for supporting and challenging active adult learning, so that people are eased into discovering and learning by and about themselves rather than being 'told' what to do or think. Indeed for some (Daloz 1999) much of what really changes in adult learning is perspective, how things are perceived.

The experiential learning cycle theory emphasises that, for successful HRD delivery to occur, learners need to work through every part of the experiential cycle. It is not enough to only provide for one or two stages, as that is incomplete. Much traditional education, for example, has been critiqued because its delivery is based on abstract conceptualisation, teaching around theories. When it comes to 'real world' applications, much that is learnt in school, college or university seems to have been delivered ineffectively. Much training, in contrast, was critiqued for being only based on classroom concrete experience. Again, when it came to delivery, the training had not been enough preparation for the 'real world' of actual work, with the contingencies and circumstances found there. There was, thus, a need to build in time and opportunity for reflective observation and active experimentation, as well as concrete experience (practice) and abstract conceptualisation (theory).

Facilitation is sometimes perceived to be a more recently evolved delivery method in HRD, compared with instruction. In one respect the interest in facilitation is more modern, emerging as it does from the growth of values and systems of experiential learning that have permeated learning institutions since the 1960s. Yet the origins of the principles and practice of facilitation are also more ancient. Back in the origins of western civilisation, Socrates used to respond to learners seeking his wisdom by enlightening and infuriating them in equal measure through facilitation. He insisted to those who came to hear his great 'wisdom' that, far from being a font of all wisdom who could instruct others, he knew nothing. All that he could do was question those who thought they did know the answers. And, by examining their certainties as partial and wrong ways of understanding the world, he eased them into a state of 'productive confusion'. This had a greater impact than dispensing wisdom directly, and helped provide an opportunity and space for the critical exploration of ideas through dialogue, to ultimately improve their understanding and develop better knowledge and behaviour. Balancing support and challenge is still the key to understanding how facilitation can impact on adult learners.

Daloz (1999) suggests we should map the extent to which 'challenge' and 'support' are present in a development partnership to promote growth. Where there is neither much support nor challenge learners will experience 'stasis', or no growth. Where there is much support but only little challenge learners will experience only 'confirmation' and limited growth. Where there is much challenge but little support learners may choose to 'retreat', consequently not experience growth. Only where there is both support and challenge will learners potentially experience real growth and change.

In the modern context Rogers (1969) exemplifies those who have come to adopt facilitative techniques, and to argue that environments where 'space' for facilitation existed mattered more than providing direct instruction. This, indeed, was not just desirable but was essential for promoting learning in many educational and corporate settings. The dominant instructional approach was stifling, approaching learning as a task of filling up empty vessels with prescribed and standardised bodies of knowledge, discrete predetermined capabilities and behaviours. In such learning people were to be controlled, confined to fixed paths and subject to the authority of the instructor. Alternatively, Rogers argued, people should be 'free to learn' not stifled. Those responsible for learning had to engage not control, to inspire not dragoon, and to work with rather than 'on' the learner. It meant that learners had to experience learning and change by encountering significant experiences that were meaningful to them, not instructor-driven agendas of efficient teaching. If this was not done there was little hope of engaging learners with learning in any meaningful way.

The underlying challenge for Rogers was that learners were not engaged with learning, they were in the 'stasis' or 'retreat' quadrants . Classrooms in schools did not provide a positive learning environment; nor did training facilities in organisations. Schools, colleges and other learning environments had to be reformed to allow for and enable this freedom to learn. Like Socrates in his time, Rogers was issuing a challenge: to provide for and manage effective learning relationships that could overcome the challenges stifling participation in learning. In Socrates' time that stifling was the acceptance of unexamined assumptions about key ideas and concepts of the world and what it was like. In Rogers' time the stifling was a climate where there appeared to be an endemic lack of purpose, lack of meaning, and lack of commitment on the part of individuals – a climate where people were alienated not just from learning and educational environments, but more broadly from their societies. Facilitating learning was one way of reaching past and challenging these broader kinds of alienation.

Rogers concluded that there was a need to create communities of learners, where the 'educator' was facilitating change and learning, not instructing. This vision of learning communities is an abiding one, and it has flourished again recently in a way we will look at in chapter 13. The delivery challenge is for people promoting HRD to provide resources, develop learning contracts, organise groups and stimulate inquiry to get employees as learners to work together on real problems. In educational contexts this has meant movements to reform formal classroom teaching, examinations, and grading systems. Facilitators set the mood and enable learning, moving away from formal teaching roles to being in learning relationships. In HRD in workplaces, facilitation as a delivery method is reflected in the use of action learning with people together on real problems rather than sitting in classrooms (Megginson and Pedler 1992). Facilitation methods seem to have found a more favourable reception in the workplace than in education, which still remains largely structured around classroom-based, teacher-led systems.

The theory of experiential learning

Permeating the logic and language of the facilitative framework for delivery is the model of the experiential learning cycle. Like Rogers, Kolb was concerned with challenging and reforming big ideas about learning. Learning needed to be seen as a social process based on carefully cultivated and guided experience: this implied a move away from instruction in the classroom to other modes of learning in other circumstances. In this he was adopting the earlier ideas of others about experiences as providing the only firm foundation for developing useful knowledge.

Kolb adapted and applied this with a view to managing learning based on experience. He identified different aspects of what it means to talk about learning from experience, and discussed two dimensions of the way people interact with the world: learning structured as apprehension–comprehension, and knowledge structure as intention–extension. From these dimensions he derived four modes of learning. We have already seen that this had important implications for the reform of delivery, but this sparked a lot of research about another big idea: that a person could have a preference for one or other of these modes of learning.

The concept that people have preferred learning styles derived from the idea that they might have preferences for one part of the experiential learning cycle, and therefore be most comfortable when learning involved activities around that stage. This idea of learning styles as a factor that informs learners' interaction with learning has proven so popular that, in one study, Coffield et al (2004) noted that some 70 different models of learning styles had been developed. In practice only a few dominant models are used for exploring the preferences for learning, and the one proposed by Honey and Mumford (1982), based on Kolb's, is among the more popular (see Figure 4.4).

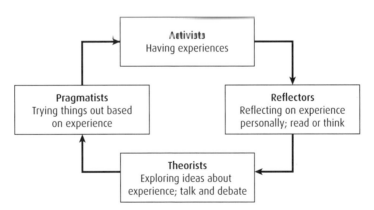

Figure 4.4 The experiential learning cycle and 'learning styles'

For Kolb the challenge of learning was one of integrative development; of people who were delivering learning appreciating the need to deal with all the elements of experiential learning to complete a learning cycle. Learners also needed to be aware of their individual preference, and therefore understand why some kinds or parts of learning suited them whereas others were more difficult; why some people preferred to read the book first then have a classroom discussion while others preferred to have the discussion before going away to read more about the subject. Learning styles are the key to understanding these different kinds of preferences.

The major implication is that learning delivery should involve actions across the full learning cycle, accommodating all learning styles and drawing upon facilitative methods as well as instruction. For example, an organisation may seek to build more effective teams because problems with an absence of teamwork are causing performance concerns. It may seek to facilitate the develop of teams by sending a group of people on an outdoors experience. This may involve:

- **Cognition**: knowledge about how effective groups work. This will come from an experience of being in a group and reflecting on its developments.
- **Capabilities**: exploring what it takes to be a leader in a group by giving people an opportunity to experience it for themselves. As they practise it, issues are raised about options for leadership and about their own abilities.
- **Behaviours**: exploring how to encourage and maintain communication even when difficulties with handling conflict in the group arise.

4.4 | Styles and delivery

People, including those delivering HRD, develop preferences which make them more comfortable with certain aspects of learning than others. These preferences can, in some situations, lead to a systematic distortion of the learning process as greater emphasis is placed on some aspects to the detriment of others. Here are some typical examples, using the terms of Honey and Mumford:

□ Preferences for experiencing can mean that delivery will include lots of activities, to the extent that learners never sit still but have to be rushing about, constantly on the go. This results in plenty of experiences and the assumption that having experiences is synonymous with learning from them.

□ Preferences for reviewing and theorising can mean that delivery may shy away from dealing with first-hand experiences, and most time might be spent in promoting thinking; learners postpone reaching conclusions for as long as possible whilst allowing for more and more data to be gathered. This results in an 'analysis to paralysis' tendency with plenty of pondering and little action. A preference for theorising will mean that delivery includes lots of discussion and debate.

□ Preferences for pragmatism can mean delivery focused on finding an expedient course of action and implementing it with inadequate analysis. This results in a tendency to go for 'quick fixes' by over-emphasising the planning and experiencing stages to the detriment of reviewing and concluding.

Source http://www.learningbuzz.com

Facilitators will aim to motivate and manage learning through the use of participative methods, and reflections on experiences that they nurture or arrange with the learner. The learning happens as the experiential cycle is running, not in relation to a preset and fixed agenda scripted entirely by the trainer. Learners are not empty vessels to be filled up; they come with pre-existing cognitive capacity and ideas, capability and behaviour. Changing these through HRD involves either adding ideas, capabilities or behaviour, or displacing erroneous ideas, bad habits or dysfunctional behaviour.

4.2 | *Learning styles frameworks*

How can you facilitate someone's learning if you do not know how they learn? This question has led to the description of learning styles. There is an extensive literature and research on this topic. One study (Coffield et al 2004) identified 71 different models of learning styles. The following 13 models were seen to be influential or potentially influential. They varied according to whether authors saw learning styles as constitutionally-based or open to change.

- Allinson and Hayes' Cognitive Styles Index (CSI);
- Apter's Motivational Style Profile (MSP);
- Dunn and Dunn's Model and Instruments of Learning Styles;
- Entwistle's Approaches and Study Skills Inventory for Students (ASSIST);
- Gregorc's Styles Delineator (GSD);
- Herrmann's Brain Dominance Instrument (HBDI);
- Honey and Mumford's Learning Styles Questionnaire (LSQ);
- Jackson's Learning Styles Profiler (LSP);
- Kolb's Learning Style Inventory (LSI);
- Myers-Briggs' Type Indicator (MBTI);
- Riding's Cognitive Styles Analysis (CSA);
- Sternberg's Thinking Styles Inventory (TSI);
- Vermunt's Inventory of Learning Styles (ILS).

A reliable and valid tool should encourage people not only to diagnose how they learn but also to enhance their learning by extending their repertoire. A good model can provide a 'lexicon' – a way of talking about their own and others' learning preferences, and how trainers and others can help or hinder these. There are problems, though. One is that studies on learning styles are small-scale, uncritical and inward-looking. There is a proliferation of concepts, dichotomies and, therefore, strategies. The models also have serious psychometric weaknesses. They should have evidence of internal consistency and test–retest reliability, and construct and predictive validity. Yet only one model meets all four of these criteria, and three meet none. Also, these models are sampling self-reports, which may be deluded or influenced by what they think others want to hear.

Despite the concerns, learning style instruments are widely used. Some of the well-known ones ought to be discontinued because of their poor validity and reliability. However, those with fewer defects should be researched further because they can act as agents for broader change, enabling dialogue between trainers and learners, and the support needed. There is a panoply of possible interventions though, not a simple choice. Professional judgement is needed, not personal preference or dogma.

The use of facilitation principles and methods with adult learners can create an environment in which the key issues are dealing with questions and responses, handling problem people, and maintaining rapport. Rather than having a set sequence like instruction, facilitation requires an awareness of principles:

- establishing the right environment;
- ensuring participation;
- confronting difficult issues;
- maintaining a focus on achieving objectives;
- managing the pacing of tasks and exercises.

For a facilitator, one of the challenges is handling 'difficult' people (see Resources Box 4.2).

4.2 | *Encountering difficult people in facilitated learning*

If the goal is to 'ease' learning by actively involving learners in the delivery of HRD, treating them as participants not passive spectators, a number of challenging kinds of behaviour can emerge that may interfere with facilitated learning. Identifying and managing these can be essential to successful facilitated HRD.

Behaviour	Issues
Showing off	Hogging the limelight, impeding others' contributions
'Heckling'	Undermining the trainer or others who try to participate
Rambling	Going on and on, wasting time and losing focus
Griping	Taking the opportunity of being asked to speak up to moan
Fighting	Discussions become a space where conflicts surface in the group
Whispering	Once speaking up is sanctioned some may begin a constant low level chatting, distracting others
Struggling	Those unable to express themselves will struggle to contribute
Silence	Those who are unable or unwilling to participate in activity and discussions

There are inherent challenges in delivering either pure instruction-based or facilitation-based learning (see Operations Boxes 4.5 and 4.6). Such problems are sometimes due to inadequate resourcing, with poorly prepared instructors or facilitators who are inexperienced. But even given adequate resourcing and effective needs assessment and design, there are still inherent challenges in using pure instruction or facilitation. The demand is to combine them in delivery – to have a balance – with structure and process incorporating elements of instruction and facilitation.

The core weakness of facilitation is, it seems, that more can go obviously wrong with trying to 'ease' learning than with instruction. Poorly delivered instruction may be hidden on the day because the learners are passive – only when it transpires that they have not learned what was desired, back at work, does the problem emerge. And poor instruction can be countered or redeemed by further learning in practice. This is often not the case with poor facilitation; it is evident immediately and can be really counter-productive, worse than a waste of time. The underlying challenge with facilitation is knowing about learners as individuals – getting and using information about them before and during the learning process. The 'trainer' may also have professional anxieties about losing control of the HRD process. The lone facilitator has challenges in managing to coordinate small group work, and in providing effective and useful feedback to many individuals; the gains are greater, and the risks are higher as well.

Facilitation also demands that learners approach learning in a way that they may be unfamiliar or uncomfortable with, given how much education and schooling is still managed. But facilitation is worthwhile where existing knowledge impedes assimilation of new knowledge; where habits that are already well-established impede practising new ways of doing things; and where values and attitudes are already deeply entrenched. These can all survive the most intensive periods of instruction untouched and unchanged, but some good facilitation can make a difference.

4.5 | The most common problems with the delivery of instruction

Problems	Causes
Dull (tell, tell, tell)	Too much information
No buy-in from trainees	Mandatory courses
Not real life	All theory, no practice
Falling behind or racing on	Goes at instructor's pace
Only get instructor's point of view	Only one instructor
Little chance to question and consolidate	Time and nature of instruction
Pitched at one level	Lack of preparation
Not adapting to different styles	Lack of time
Too authoritarian	Not knowing audience
Boring; Stand and deliver	The structure too rigid
One-way; teacher–class	Include interactivity
Limited/no feedback from audience	Check and get feedback
Lack of preparation/knowledge	Train the trainers
Poor presentation style and material	Improve styles, OHPs and handouts

For better instruction	
Define and convey clear aims and objectives	Encourage intervention
Improve materials (ensure up to date)	Encourage participation (ice-breakers, room layout, facilitation)
Prepare, make time, know audience	Work on presentation style
Vary styles within class	

4.6 | Facilitation delivery: problems and solutions

Problems	Solutions
Group dynamics	Need to know all types prior to start and be able to listen/observe
Some over-talkative	Tactfully stop talkative people
Some very quiet	Get all to contribute
Fears, personality, attitudes	Create a safe environment for learning
Perception of the learning	Will not be the same for all
Experience and opinions can hinder agreement on solution	Accept and deal with different experiences, managing conflict
Keeping it focused on objectives	Can involve questions before and at end of course
Facilitator is not competent	Facilitate for them, leadership in the group
Difficult to keep on track	Prior planning prevents poor performance; think about timings
Objectives not clear enough	Define clear objectives
Different levels/ kinds of needs	Respond flexibly to these
Lack of control	Ensure that the learning rather than personal agendas prevails
Motivation	How does this translate back to work?

Other delivery options: developing and delivering performance support

The delivery of HRD does not have to be confined to any of the formal practices such as a course or formal on-job training. There is an alternative way of approaching delivery. This is based on behaviourist psychology which, having being used to inform the design of programmed instruction, still saw disconnections between HRD and job performance. Well-conceived and designed programmes appeared to fail, with a pattern of regression to pre-training skill levels of performance. Initial vigour in performance after training often lapsed, with performance problems again coming to the fore.

Instead of concentrating on writing better aims, goals and objectives for cognitive capacities and capabilities, the focus shifted to thinking about the work context, and analysing more closely expected behaviours and the environments that reinforced these. The logic was that organisations had perhaps not defined expected behaviours clearly enough or built an organisational environment conducive to attaining these behaviours. This argument rested on a view of behaviour as human activity that can be seen, measured or described. There was a concern with identifying and dealing with specific behaviours, not generic or abstract issues of cognitive capacity, capability or affective factors. Thus results and the cause of results were not given equal weighting. A few vital behaviours were seen to account for effective performance and results, not a wide span of cognitive capacities, capabilities and emotional intelligence (see Figure 4.5).

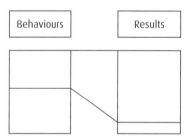

Figure 4.5 Key behaviours and results

The reaction to the behaviourist focus on instructional training was the need for more effective analysis of human performance problems, based on identifying and reinforcing key behaviours, and designing and developing environments that reinforced such behaviours. This core basic insight has been elaborated upon and 'reincarnated' in several forms, such as those models of 'excellence' articulated in some competency frameworks and the advocacy of movements such as Neuro Linguistic Programming (NLP) and, more recently, 'Positive Psychology'. It can be labelled the **behaviourist's ABC**, and in one guise or another it plays an important role in thinking about and delivering HRD in many contexts:

- **A**ntecedents: identify the causes of behaviour.
- **B**ehaviours: describe people's overt and actual actions.
- **C**onsequences: analyse what then happens as a result of the behaviour.

For example, staff might be instructed during health and safety training to wear hard hats on construction sites. Following such instruction, they might then wear the hard hats when returning to a normal work situation, only to be derided by their peers who do not wear them. This feedback does not reinforce the required behaviour, and indeed undermines it. It may then make sense to the person not to wear the hard hat in the first place to escape the derision of their peers.

This kind of outcome was taken as a paradigm for what was wrong with even the best-delivered training: it could not alter the dynamics of 'ABC' in the real world of the workplace, which undermined the transfer of learning. The antecedents that were most influential were not the instructions people were given in the classroom or their facilitated learning, but the environments in which they worked. These antecedents were seen to be the principal causes of the behaviour, and not the learning being provided on courses. So even the best-designed and carefully thought-out training programmes were seen to fail because they were not supported on the job. The consequence of this finding was a change in focus in dealing with performance gaps by developing interventions aimed at analysing and rearranging the outcomes of desirable or undesirable behaviours – for example by using reward systems to reinforce effort or output.

Behaviourists are renowned for denying the possibility of scientifically studying mental states – effectively, what goes on in people's heads – as a cause of behaviour. The notion of the ABC reinforces that because it does not require any overt analysis of thought processes. It implies that people behave the way they do because it 'makes sense' to them, even where it does not make sense to others who see their behaviour as dysfunctional. The consequences of behaviours have to be understood through the eyes of the beholder. Knowing about such perceptions and sense-making becomes all-important for influencing behaviour. Reinforcement of desired behaviours by managing consequences has to be seen from the perspective of the learner, not anyone else. If, for example, the payment outcomes of particular behaviours are valuable to them, then they will behave consistently with what is desired; if the outcomes are of little or no value to them, they are unlikely to.

Problems for an ABC form of delivery platform can arise in various ways. One is when organisations send mixed signals, asserting new aspirations but failing to alter existing systems of consequence; a deadly combination. So, for example, organisations may attempt to reorganise the work environment to elicit innovative behaviour by using performance-related pay, but at the same time they may still encourage bureaucratic adherence to existing ways of doing things by promoting people who follow those. Or organisations may seek to promote empowerment by training their managers to involve teams in decision-making, which is often aimed at improving long-term performance, but reward these managers for hitting short term targets. Under these circumstances, managers are likely to interpret their jobs and make behavioural choices in terms of what matters most to them, which is usually those behaviours that are actually measured – in this case short-term targets. The likely result is that managers would become directed to achieve targets rather than empowering, which was the aim of the HRD.

Other problems arise where there are positive consequences for the same behaviour in some conditions, but negative consequences in others. For example, new ways of army training were tried, based on self-instruction rather than instructor-led instruction. The trials of this new system went well, with learners completing the courses much faster than had previously been the case. But when the new system was put into more widespread use, the results were the opposite. Learners were taking as long, if not longer, to complete the training. The situation was investigated, and it was found that, when the learners finished, they were moved on to other work details. It was in their interest to delay finishing to avoid being sent on those other work duties. So the consequences did not elicit the desired behaviour, which was to complete training quickly.

One more common problem in the work environment that undermines the ABC delivery logic is the distance between behaviours and consequences. The further in time a consequence is from a behaviour the less impact the consequence will have. So, for example, many employees are held accountable for performance only at their annual performance review; the time period between much of their behaviour and the consequences emanating from these reviews is too great for them to see a direct link. The ideal is to provide consequences at the time of behaviour – small doses of positive or negative rewards at the appropriate time, rather than large doses much later. In particular, positive consequences ought to arise on an immediate basis.

If the ABC delivery approach is to be used in the workplace as an alternative to instruction or facilitation in order to support effective performance, feedback must be given. Feedback is about providing information regarding performance on goals; reinforcement is the desired effect of effective feedback. Performance gaps may be closed by appropriate reinforcement of desired behaviours using reinforcers rather than providing training. Effective feedback should be:

- immediate;
- goal-specific;
- expressed positively not negatively.

Feedback on performance problems will not work if:

- it is used as punishment;
- it is delayed or too late;
- given to someone not in control of the problem;
- given on the wrong variable, e.g. quantity not quality;
- it needs too much effort to record it.

Even so, the use of feedback and reinforcers will not have overnight effects. Shaping people's behaviours to be consistent with what is desired is about changing in the right direction, reinforcing improvement in the right direction, building upon success, and noticing and reinforcing improvements. Intermittent reinforcement is, in theory, the best strategy. Non-existent reinforcement or continuous reinforcement both fail to shape behaviour effectively. Non-existent reinforcement fails because, without consequences, the desired behaviours will diminish. Continuous reinforcement is not only impracticable and costly, but fails because the apparent certainty of consequence means there is no credibility for it as a reinforcer. The symbol of classic intermittent reinforcement is the behaviour of playing slot machines: the people who play them know that they will pay out some time, but they do not know when. The trick in designing machines that engage people is to reinforce their playing with intermittent wins. The work environment is similar. People should want to play the performance game because they know they will get positive consequences, but they are not sure exactly when – that way they keep playing.

Reinforcement of desired behaviour has to be complemented by the punishment and extinction of undesired behaviour. Punishment focuses on reducing or eliminating undesired behaviour, which is a more problematic concept than the provision of feedback for positive consequences. This is because the use of punishment creates long-term problems in relationships, and can lead to their disintegration. Moreover, people learn to tolerate punishments, and it has only temporary effects; on the other hand, it can extinguish other desired behaviours. Its use also generates a culture of excuses, and escape and avoidance behaviour. The intermittent reinforcement schedule effect also arises: if punishment is intermittent the behaviour continues at a higher rate. Above all, it cannot lead to the desired behaviour being established.

Conclusion

The delivery methods of instruction and facilitation are opposite ends of a continuum of HRD development. The elements of each are essential parts of the HRD practitioner's toolkit, and represent a continuing challenge for theorising. The development and delivery of HRD should follow the good practice principles of project management. These help to establish what must be done across a wide range of possible options for development and delivery. In addition, HRD specialists should also be aware of the factors that produce HRD deliverables. Finally, there is a need to understand how human behaviour is influenced. The behaviourist ABC provides a model of developments in organisation that might be appropriate; it provides an alternative to the formal provision of learning using either instruction or facilitation.

Q

| concluding case | *The drama of HRD delivery* |

Read the following case of a learning experience.

- □ What elements of instruction and what elements of facilitation can you see?
- □ What seem to have been the design flaws leading to problems in using this mode of delivery?
- □ What could be done to remedy these problems? Or should other modes of delivery be used?

A university[1] wanted some training on equal opportunity policies for its managers. The aim was to emphasise how important the policies were for the organisation's academic managers, particularly their heads of department. A day session was planned. The morning was to be taken up with instruction on the content of equal opportunity policies, and an exploration of how they applied to staff through recruitment, reward, career management, and to students.

The university felt that an instructional approach was a bit dry, and that it did not provide an opportunity for its managers to reflect on the 'realities' of trying to make these policies work. The afternoon was therefore devoted to an experimental use of experiential learning. The organisation invited a training company that employed actors to present a drama based on an equal opportunity issue. First they gave the audience some background information on an organisational scenario, and on two characters whom they would then meet and see involved in action. The scenario was built around a fictitious university. The characters were two lecturers, Philip and Angela, who were jointly supervising a PhD student. The audience were told some facts about these people, and then allowed to interrogate them to explore aspects of their personality and background. Then these two characters were seen in a scene.

The scene involved a confrontation between Angela and Philip. They were both supervising a female PhD student. Angela confronted Philip with the fact that he had been having an affair with the student, which had now broken up. The effect on the student was that she was thinking about not completing her PhD. Angela was infuriated that Philip had done this. Philip took the view that it was nothing to do with her or the university;

continued overleaf

what happened between consenting adults was their business. He thought the impact of the end of the affair could be managed to ensure she did not withdraw from her PhD. Philip, by the way, is a married man with children. The meeting ended with nothing resolved, and both parties clearly furious and upset.

Following the dramatic scene, the audience were expected to be able to discuss the behaviours of the two characters and explore the equal opportunity issues involved and how to resolve them. To do that they were expected to work in groups to discuss the issues before being allowed to question the characters again and explore some of their perceptions and motivations. They could ask the characters why they behaved in certain ways, how they felt, and suggest/discuss what could be done to resolve the matter.

The rationale for this type of exercise is that seeing a piece of theatrical drama over a conflict between people allows others to view a problem as being 'over there'. They can get emotionally involved and be disturbed, but still maintain a distance. They can reflect on what is going on – what the characters are doing wrong, and why things are taking the turns that they do – and discuss among themselves what the alternatives are. They can then get the characters to demonstrate what happens if alternative strategies are used.

This is a very powerful method, having much more impact than reading a case study, or even seeing a professionally produced and acted video of the right way and the wrong way to manage a situation. Having real actors playing characters who are there, right in front of you, and who can talk with you, disagree with you, respond to you as a person as you talk with them, is a powerful experience.

All this action is controlled by a facilitator, who stops and starts the theatrical action, and manages the discussions that the group have about the issues raised. The facilitator's objective is to encourage people to explore the behaviours that lead to problems, to appreciate the emotional aspects and conflicts involved in such interactions, and to seek insights that can be applied back to a manager's own job. What happens in the group as this is process develops is very important. The group can help each other learn by providing insights and sharing ideas. The individuals involved can also reflect, quietly and to themselves, upon their own perceptions and ideas.

If the method is used well, the learning that results can be of a very high quality. Where it may fail is that, instead of learning, people will find themselves emotionally charged, in dispute with each other and the facilitator, and confused about what they are doing and what they are learning.

On the afternoon that this session was run with heads of department from the university there was evidence of a mix of both these effects. Learning was achieved, but there was also conflict and confusion. There are various reasons for this. First, the group was half male and half female. It was obvious to an independent observer that there were differences between the men and the women in their reactions to the drama they witnessed. The men all agreed that Philip was morally wrong to do what he did. They chastised him for his behaviour. But one person who claimed to have a lot of experience in these matters hogged much of the discussion. He insisted that there was no point in heads of department taking these kinds of issues to senior managers, as nothing would be done about them. There could be no proof that anyone had done any wrong, and there would be no support for disciplining people who had behaved this way. He made this point time and time again: heads of department were powerless.

Meanwhile the women were more concerned that there seemed to be a male-dominated culture in the organisation, which resulted in a woman such as Angela, who was bothered by such behaviour, having no support. Indeed Philip had been her support in the organisation, against the others, before this incident. She was doubly let down by his behaviour and by seeing him in a new light. The women, it seemed, could empathise with this kind of situation – of being isolated when it came to confronting such problems. The manner in which Angela had confronted Philip had been ineffective. They were concerned to explore with her what else she might do. But they still somehow felt that no other option would have had any different outcome; he would still 'get away' with it.

This was all, on the surface, very good for the facilitator. The group were engaging in debates and discussion, and the matters they were discussing were opening up questions about the realities of promoting equal opportunity policy that the morning's instruction had not. But, on the other hand, the facilitator felt the session

| concluding case continued |

was failing. Every time she tried to get the group to do a task – for example to split up into groups and talk about a specific issue – they resisted, and queried the reasons for it. Some of this reflected the group: these were after all academics, albeit in a management role, nitpicking about the use of language, and the different meanings of words. They would spend their time in groups discussing these queries rather than completing the set task.

The facilitator regarded this as a form of hostility, but could not see how to deal with it. And while it was clear that certain group members were hogging the discussion while others were as silent as the sphinx, there did not seem to be time to deal with all these issues.

Events reached an important stage halfway through the afternoon. When the actors were quizzed following the scene, they responded to questions in a manner that was true to their character, reflecting back to people how their behaviour impacted on the character. This sometimes meant being pleasant or difficult. As a result, one participant had his line of questioning explored: the character of Angela took a 'how dare you' response to being asked whether she had had an affair with Philip herself. The point was to allow people to see the impact of their behaviours, and to challenge the way that people in the audience were behaving. But the person who had asked this question and received this reaction got very upset. After the actor had left the room, he accused the facilitator of being unclear about what was happening, leading to him looking like a fool because the character had clearly taken strong exception to his line of questioning. He accused other group members of not participating properly, leaving it to him and a few others to be exposed in discussions. This had the effect of showing that this was not a safe learning environment for him, as he felt upset. And it then made it an unsafe environment for others to participate: could they trust other people to listen to what they had to say without being challenged and put on the spot? Thereafter, a tension developed over the session, and the earlier sense of people being engaged with what was happening soon dissipated.

At the end of the day there was meant to be 15 minutes to review what people had learned, and how this could be applied to the workplace. Events ran over time, and there was only one minute left for review. When the facilitator asked what people had learned, the response from some of the dominant contributors was that such a scenario 'could not happen here'. If it did happen there would be nothing that heads of department could do, as they would get no support from the central management. Instead of time to discuss the points that were being made about the power, or lack of it, of heads of department, the discussion petered out. People left. In the lift lobby, however, some of the participants mingled with the actors, who were now out of character; they thanked them for providing an excellent afternoon's stimulating learning.

[1] Note: this was not the author's institution.

Multiple-choice questions

4.1 Which of the following statements are true?

A. Good instructors do not need to know much about the subject; they just need to be aware of the principles of effective learning.

B. The characteristics of adults as learners make them more likely to benefit from conventional instruction principles.

C. Most instruction follows a set sequence of phases.

D. Most instruction concludes with some form of objective evaluation of learning.

4.2 Which of the following statements are true of facilitation?

A. Facilitation is about forcing learners to be more active by making them speak out about their views.

B. A facilitator has to adopt a role that is quite different from that of a teacher or instructor.

C. All learning styles include a preference for participation in group problem-solving activities.

D. Facilitators have to be able to handle a variety of 'difficult' people while maintaining a positive learning environment.

References

Bentley, T. (1994) *Facilitation*, Maidenhead, McGraw-Hill

Berry, M. (1993) 'Changing Perspectives on Facilitation Skills Development', *Journal of European Industrial Training*, vol. 17, no 3, pp. 22–32.

Coffield, F., Moseley, D., Hall, E. and Ecclestone, K. (2004) *Should We Be Using Learning Styles? What Research Has to Say to Practice*, London: Learning and Skills Research Centre.

Daloz, L.A. (1999) *Mentor: Guiding the journey of adult learners*, San Francisco, Jossey-Bass.

Eitington, J. (1984) *The Winning Trainer*, Houston, Gulf Publishing Company.

Forsyth, P. (1992) *Running an Effective Training Session*, London, Gower.

Honey, P. and Mumford, A. (1982) *Manual of Learning Styles*, London, P. Honey.

Kolb, D. (1984) *Experiential Learning*, New Jersey, Prentice Hall.

Leigh, D. (1991) *A Practical Approach to Group Training*, London, Kogan Page.

Mager, R. (2000) *What Every Manager Should Know about Training*, Chalford, Management Books.

Megginson, D. and Pedler, M. (1992) *Self-Development: A facilitator's guide*, London, McGraw-Hill.

Rogers, C. (1969) *Freedom to Learn*, Columbus, Charles E Merrill.

A

concluding case points

What was well done and worked in the delivery:

- The audience were initially engaged and involved; it worked
- Issues were being exposed by the use of theatre
- People had the opportunity to reflect on the problems of certain ways of behaving in confrontations
- People had the opportunity to discuss with their peers the realities of equal opportunities
- People could develop some ideas of their own about how their behaviour might be changed to avoid the problems witnessed

What problems were there:

- The environment shifted from being engaging to being threatening to at least some people
- Issues that could have been explored, for example, the power that heads of department do or do not have, were raised but not investigated
- It was not clear to some participants how they should be learning, what their role was
- The problem of dealing with a bad culture was raised, but not explored
- There was incomplete attention to tasks in small groups
- The facilitator felt hostility, but could not confront it, what it meant and how it might be related to helping the participants learn
- There was not enough time to review at the end what this all meant for people as managers in practice

What could be done differently:

- The **balance** was wrong; there was too much emotionally charged engagement and not enough opportunity for structured reflection and review. The **contrast** was striking; the contrast between the initial discussion with the characters, then seeing them both lose their temper in action, and then trying to quiz them afterwards.

concluding case points continued

- **Direction**. People were led through this experience according to the theatrical model, of conflict between characters providing a parallel universe that they could observe. That direction was clear. The other aspect of direction though, where they going with their discussions as a group, was not clear to some.

- **Economy**. In one sense the message was clear: managing equal opportunities involves dealing with complex and emotional situations where perceptions and behaviours matter as much as the letter of policy. In another sense the message was lost in extraneous discussions of what certain words meant, what actual policies were.

- **Emphasis**. The emphasis was meant to be on people's behaviour and its impact on others. But the emphasis taken by the men was a moral one: Philip had behaved wrongly, and Angela had been wrong to lose her temper with him. The emphasis taken by the women was about culture: that culture determines people's behaviour, and changing cultures is important. Understanding that if a work culture supports problematic behaviour then the culture itself is problematic and needs to be challenged is a fair objective, but was not the area that was meant to be emphasised.

- **Rhythm**. There was great rhythm in the theatre itself. There was a lack of rhythm in the broader learning experience: it stopped and started, got revved up then suddenly the brakes went on, went smoothly for a while then stuttered.

- **Unity**. The event was well received, it seemed, by at least some people. In that sense it can be claimed that a degree of unity existed. In principle the form (theatre) and the content (management training on equal opportunities) and the goals (encourage insights into people's own behaviours) are in a positive relationship. In practice, though, unity depends on what happens in delivery, and that depends on the facilitation on the day.

In conclusion, part of the improvements needed hinge on the quality of facilitation. Better facilitation, for example, would involve responding to hostility (why are people hostile, what is happening here and how do I deal with it?) in order to keep a safe learning environment. Another example of better facilitation would be to ask whether there were real differences between the men and women in their perceptions of what mattered about this incident and, if so, how they could be raised and reflected upon.

Part of the problem hinges on structure: there was a lot of activity, not enough time to go into detail on matters being raised, and not enough time for review at the end. The rhythm, economy, direction, emphasis and balance of the theatre, which was clearly extremely well done, was not matched by rhythm, economy, direction, emphasis and balance overall.

The actors involved appreciated that things had not gone as planned, and had not worked as well as previous events. Reflecting on these 'mistakes' is the source of new learning to improve the use of these kinds of method, to attain the great benefits they may bring.

HRD quality: reviewing and evaluating

learning
objectives

By the end of this chapter you will be able to:

□ describe the methodologies commonly used to support quality management in HRD;
□ analyse the main themes and challenges of evaluation in HRD;
□ critically evaluate the use of cost–benefit analysis in the HRD evaluation context;
□ design and construct valid and reliable ways of evaluating HRD activities.

resources

5.1	A quote from practice

'The real world is characterised by imperfections, probabilities, and approximations. It runs on inference, deduction, and implication, not on absolute irrefutable hard-wiring. Yet we are constantly asked to measure and report on this fuzzy multi-dimensional world we live in as if it were a cartoon or comic book, reducing all of its complexity and ambiguity to hard financial "data." … Putting a monetary value on training's impact on business is fraught with estimation, negotiation, and assumption – and putting a monetary value on the cost of learning is often even less precise. Yet when was the last time you saw an ROI [return on investment] figure presented as anything other than an unqualified absolute? If you tried for statistical accuracy and said something like, "this project will produce 90% of the desired ROI, 95% of the time with a 4% error margin," you'd be thrown out of the boardroom.'

Source http://www.trainingzone.co.uk/item/143544, accessed 4 September 2006

Introduction

Evaluation is the ultimate phase of the learning process. Evaluation is defined as the activities involved in determining the merit, worth or value of HRD in the workplace. It fulfils a number of functions for a number of stakeholders. This closing phase may involve determining the extent to which needs have been met, whether aims, objectives and targets have been achieved, and how the delivery of HRD has gone in practice (Hamblin 1974, Newby 1992). Yet there seems to be a general malaise around evaluation, as if it is something that is done more as a ritual than an integral part of the HRD process. Phillips (1991) describes some of the common 'myths' that help sustain this malaise (see Strategic View Box 5.1).

The myths and challenges of evaluation and quality-awareness exist across all areas of management and work, so there are general issues here which are relevant to the accurate evaluation of all aspects of organisational life. In the context of workplace HRD we are looking at the big picture of the apparent shift and conversion from basic recipes to a more robust system of quality-awareness in HRD. There are wider issues involved in this that have to be appreciated to understand HRD evaluation. Within the general HRD context the main concerns are the specific methods and challenges of evaluating HRD in relation to performance management in work organisations. Here the barriers to evaluation are attributable to the desire of those being evaluated – learners, trainers and others – to control and direct evaluation, and its costs and risks if at all possible.

Having an effective system of evaluation has always been seen in HRD to be a big concern. From the use of end-of-course evaluation surveys, often called 'happy sheets', to formulas for calculating costs and benefits, the domain has its well-established frameworks. Evaluation is also of greater concern than just reflection on the previous stages of a specific instance of learning. Assuring and improving the quality of HRD, while controlling and reducing the costs of different workplace learning systems, is the biggest and most challenging issue, and is one of the most often debated and discussed.

A common language for discussing evaluation and its connections with quality is given in Theory & Research Box 5.1 (McGhee 2003).

The importance of quality as well as conventional evaluation is being increasingly highlighted. The OECD (2003), for example, has emphasised that the economic arguments for people to engage with learning does not often win over people or organisations. People and organisations are often not attracted to HRD even by free access, or having potential economic gains in the longer term spelt out for them. They need to be persuaded that learning is appropriate for them in the 'here and now'. And central to that is having good, even great, experiences of learning when they encounter it. The concern to ensure good HRD and improve it to 'great' is central for sustaining and expanding the impact of HRD in the workplace. There are then multiple functions of exploring quality and evaluation (Scriven 1991) which are given in Strategic View Box 5.2.

5.1 | *Quality terms*

Quality: the effectiveness of a programme of learning, given the needs of the learner in the context of defined learning outcomes.

Quality assurance (QA): writing down what HRD is aiming to do and checking periodically that this is being done.

Quality enhancement (QE): finding out what those who have an interest in and use HRD systems say about them, and amending systems accordingly. This has four different functions:
- to shape or implement strategic policy;
- to meet regulatory requirements;
- to develop services and provisions based on learning from external sources;
- to develop services and provisions based on learning from internal sources;

Quality audit: keeping records to prove that QA and QE are being managed well.

5.2 | *Functions of evaluation*

□ Pragmatic functions	Identifying the 'bad', eliminating costs and waste, resource concerns
□ Ethical functions	Ensuring good service, fairness and justice for those involved in HRD
□ Intellectual functions	Providing useful information via valid tools and avoiding bias and prejudice
□ Social and business functions	Directing limited resource and effort where it is most needed, costs and benefits
□ Personal functions	Providing a basis for those offering HRD to have self-esteem; knowing that what they do works

---

Looking first at the systems in common use for managing quality in learning reveals a very mixed picture of robust basic frameworks but limited delivery across all these functions. The first step is to evaluate the delivery of the HRD experience and the planning and design process (see Figure 5.1). Have the specific objectives been met? Did the HRD happen according to plan? Was that the right plan? These all seem straightforward matters, and depending on the evidence either the HRD intervention may be judged a success or the intervention may have to be re-run in order to deal with any shortfalls or continuing gaps.

Beyond this basic 'final phase' of 'process checking' there is a long-standing and well-known framework of levels of evaluation in HRD (see Resources Box 5.2). There are plenty of conventional problems of quantifying and evaluating quality in this standard approach. It remains popular, although a more robust, more sophisticated, system for evaluating workplace HRD is the Holy Grail in this area. To get beyond the levels of evaluation frameworks' simplicity or stranglehold, there is a continuing need to engage with thinking and debates over evaluation and quality methodologies, and theories about evaluating the quality of HRD (Wang and Spitzer 2005).

5.2	*Levels of HRD evaluation*

Evaluation level	Focus and concerns
Reactions	What are the learners' reactions to the HRD they have experienced; in their estimation was the learning experience helpful and useful? This generally involves post-course or intervention feedback to the developers.
Learning	To what extent have the objectives of the HRD intervention been met? What have the learners learned? This can involve tests and assessments of knowledge, skill and abilities.
Performance	To what extent has the performance gap been closed? This is generally seen as the extent to which learning is or is not transferred to the workplace or is manifest in improved performance.
Organisational	What were the costs and benefits of the HRD? Is it confirmed that the HRD has provided value for money?
Ultimate value	What are the overall tangible and intangible outcomes of having provided HRD? Are staff more committed, are they more flexible? Is the organisation better placed to realise its strategy, to compete successfully?

Source: Based on the ideas of Kirkpatrick and Phillips

The most evident activity in workplace evaluation is at the 'learner' level, with the end-of-course or event evaluation form. This is, at least, done as a ritual and possibly with more serious intent, although the design and use of such surveys, for they are a form or survey, is not of much focal interest. However, beyond the conventional use of learner evaluation forms, there are underlying and deeper concerns ongaging with the other functions of evaluation. As the final stage in the HRD process, evaluation can be expected to fulfil at least one, and often several, of these functions. That requires much more than asking learners to complete an end-of-course evaluation form. To determine the value of HRD in these contexts we need some form of evidence, and measurement and judgement of the achievement of objectives, to confirm that the initially defined HRD need has been met.

Evaluation is often suspected to be the hardest phase to do well, and often makes for the weakest link in the whole HRD process. This is not surprising given the multiple functions it may be required to achieve. Because of its difficulty, it is the step most likely to be neglected in practice or be least satisfactorily accomplished. All the other phases have to be at least attempted, but it is possible to neglect or avoid evaluation without apparent consequence. The failure to think about needs would show when people contemplated participating but did not because what was on offer did not interest them. To fail to design would show as the absence of a balanced set of objectives. To fail to deliver would show as people turning up to an empty room! But to fail to evaluate would not necessarily show at all. Over time it would have a cumulative and powerful impact, but not immediately or evidently in the short term.

Evaluation is a challenge to both the theory and practice of HRD. In theory terms, the main framework for debate, which encompassed a wide range of concerns, was that its key failing in practice was evaluation in the context of meeting business needs.

It has been a long-established concern that most organisations find it difficult to evaluate their HRD in clear cost–benefit terms (Russ-eft and Preskill 2005). This concern still exists, but there are also problems of quality in HRD, and its evaluation. In practical terms, having invested time and effort in the earlier phases of the process, it is not clear why evaluation is neglected. Completion of the delivery of an HRD experience may, in itself, feel like the end; but, without evidence that a gap has been closed, that impression is misleading. If we do not know whether the previous phases of the HRD process have been successful, then the final outcome – improved performance – may not be secured.

As has been emphasised for each phase of the HRD process, evaluation is not just about using tools and techniques to determine how effectively the HRD process is managed; it is also about working in a broader management and political context, here about review and quality. Arguably, nowadays the significance of properly evaluating HRD at work in the organisational context is being better appreciated.

Evaluation in the HRD context

In the HRD context, evaluation is an umbrella term, one that covers a wide range of activities with various purposes. It includes:

- *obtaining information about learners*: testing them to evaluate their cognitive capacities, their capabilities and their behaviours;
- *obtaining information from learners*: how they rate their HRD experiences, and how much they feel they have learned or developed;
- *reviewing* whether the right objectives and targets have been met, and whether the overall benefits of doing that warrant the costs that have been incurred.

These various activities all seek to address the same basic questions: was the HRD that was identified as necessary planned, designed and delivered effectively, and was it worth doing?

In the evaluation of HRD at work, there is an interesting contradiction. On the one hand, basic methods have been formulated and widely used for some time (Kirkpatrick 1975). These methods are still in use today, and provide reference points that structure HRD evaluation in theory and in practice. The main method is one that defines and explores set levels of evaluation for HRD at work (see Figure 5.1). The continuing influence of methods embedded in the popular 'levels of evaluation' model is also seen in recent major surveys on training in Europe, where the information on and analysis of evaluation of quality is based on data on the levels of employee satisfaction, test results, certification, transfer to the workplace, and impact on performance. These are different ways of conceiving the same old levels.

On the other hand, there is no single, agreed, standard, universal system in use. Greater concern with quality in the present and the future, driven by forces from various contexts, has put a spotlight on the evaluation phase of HRD. These forces include strategic policy and funding reviews, regulatory organisation concerns, developmental agencies' concerns, and research for quality enhancement. As a spotlight has settled over the analysis of systems for managing quality in workplace HRD, the most noticeable feature of the newly-revealed landscape is diversity. What is measured, how it is measured, and who measures it appear to vary greatly among countries, contexts of learning, and different kinds of learner (see Theory & Research Box 5.2).

In most countries, different systems and agencies are involved in aspects of workplace HRD evaluation; for colleges, universities and work-based learning, adult learning, community learning and independent, private and commercial colleges and training organisations. Agencies vary, and the approach adopted may be based on a method such as total quality management, or just be concerned with the outcomes of a specific programme. We can accept this diversity, and simply continue to use a variety of different approaches to managing quality in HRD, or we can seek to remove diversity by developing standardised systems of best practice that can be used across different contexts.

theory & research

5.2 | *Learner concerns*

One survey (LSC 2004) of learner satisfaction showed that the quality of teaching/training accounts for the most deeply-held views of satisfaction or dissatisfaction: one in ten learners have made complaints about their course or their experience. The aspects of teaching and training that fall into the priorities for action, according to this survey, are:

- making the subject interesting or enjoyable for the learner;
- understanding the learner and how they like to learn;
- the support they give the learner, for example in improving their study techniques or time management;
- planning their lessons;
- setting clear targets to help the learner improve;
- providing prompt and regular feedback on progress;
- managing the group of learners.

The concern to bring order to this diversity and identify and measure learners' and HRD providers' success has prompted one government to seek data on the indicators of quality outlined in Resources Box 5.3.

resources

5.3 | *Potential indicators of quality to measure*

Measures of learners' success

- Successful completion of qualifications
- Value added and distance travelled
- Extended existing value-added measurement
- Non-accredited learning
- Equality and diversity and a framework for analysis of measures

Measures of providers' success

- Learner satisfaction at provider level
- Learners' destinations at provider level
- Measuring the capability of providers' staff
- Measures of employer engagement
- Giving value for money

The abiding popularity of the 'levels of evaluation' framework should not preclude deeper and broader diversity in evaluation. At present, evaluation is perceived to be stuck with what amounts to little more than a basic recipe for evaluation (the levels of evaluation model) with no more fully developed quality standards or models emerging. Seeking more rigorous and mature systems of evaluation is a major concern (see Scriven op cit, Figure 5.1).

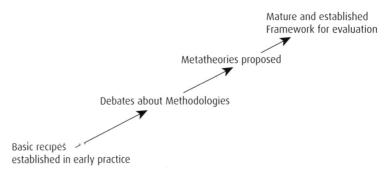

Figure 5.1 Maturity of evaluation systems
Source Scriven 1991

The search for more sophisticated and robust models of quality triggers debate about methodologies of evaluation. Methodologies are coherent frameworks for guiding the identification, collection and analysis of data and sense-making. There are several methodologies available, ranging from those which embody positivist principles about collecting and investigating 'hard' facts to those embodying 'verstehen' principles about collecting 'stories' and cases whose interpretation underlies effective sense-making in an area. This is where HRD appears to be presently. One example is offered by McGhee (2003). He suggested a review of quality management in learning that offered a general framework for taking analysis beyond a 'basic recipe' into debates about methodologies, and metatheories. In going beyond basic levels of 'evaluation as inspection', McGhee further suggested that there should be a conscious attempt to encourage a culture for quality in the way that HRD is evaluated. McGhee identifies five important features which are common to good learning cultures, and contends that if these features are all present and dealt with effectively then a good culture for quality will exist (see Strategic View Box 5.3).

strategic view

5.3 | *McGhee's culture of quality factors*

1. The **foundations**: basic systems for gathering and using information about learning quality.
2. **Cognitive**: generating and nurturing ideas for innovation and change in quality.
3. **Emotional**: that people involved in learning are able to discuss and deal with sensitive issues raised by openly exploring quality.
4. **Interpersonal**: there exist open and inclusive relations among all those concerned with evaluating quality.
5. **Organisational**: there are clear roles and a project management approach to quality.

This moves away from making evaluation something ritually rooted in asking learners to complete an end-of-course evaluation form. It is about opening up debates around methods for evolving a quality-aware culture supporting HRD. Instead of just collecting data on how training courses have gone, new concerns emerge. Such a quality-aware evaluation culture for HRD could have powerful effects on the effectiveness of HRD as a whole. It could act to reinforce change by legitimising new capacities, capabilities and behaviours among those who have changed, and by identifying effectively those who have not changed. It could also act to ensure that all other stages of the HRD process – from needs through design and delivery – are protected, sustained and enhanced. In promoting such a quality-aware culture the assumptions and perceptions of stakeholders about HRD may be clarified. Managers who do not really commit to supporting HRD, or employees who are reluctant to participate/succeed in HRD, or even HRD professionals used to the 'old ways' and systems who are averse to changing, will be more clearly visible.

This is how an apparently straightforward process of seeking to collect information to enable more quality-awareness about HRD systems and its contribution to improving performance can lead to much more interesting and challenging things. Because many stakeholders may be aware of this, one consequence can be that advocating and promoting a more quality-aware evaluation of HRD is resisted – either actively opposed or 'passively' sabotaged. In the worst case, effective HRD review and evaluation can more or less entirely break down in an organisation.

This approach connects interest in evaluation with the higher maturity metatheories level suggested by Scriven (see Figure 5.1).

Methodologies of evaluation

In the absence of mature frameworks for evaluation and quality analysis, it is still possible to look in some detail at how HRD evaluation may fulfil the evaluation functions. Whether evaluating reactions, learning, transfer or ultimate costs and benefits, instruments can be developed. They need to be practicable: easy to administer, not burdensome, and they should be simple, brief and economical, taking into account the costs of design, development or purchase, and the time taken to use them and analyse the data.

Basic questions are:

- How will the data be used? Should the instrument be tested?
- How will data be analysed? Is there a standard instrument?
- Who will use the data? What are the consequences of errors?
- What facts are needed?

This produces a toolkit, including things such as the typical end-of-training-course 'happy sheet', rationales for standard tests, models of how to analyse training costs and so on. But these are only a basic and not very sophisticated means of evaluation. In the area of HRD, some have argued that the levels of evaluation model has not provided organisations with a means for attaining robust evaluations. Organisations using these methods often still do not know what they were getting for their money. In part this is because some aspects of the evaluation recipe are being ignored or done in an unprofessional manner. HRD is still seen essentially as an act of faith, as its outcomes cannot be properly evaluated. It is not easy to identify HRD costs and benefits properly. And, in the final analysis, few really care; it is not a big issue.

To move on from this situation of only paying lip service to the recipe, there are two possible paths, reflecting a choice in beliefs and methodology – quasi-scientific or humanistic – which lead to different methodologies of HRD evaluation.

5.1   Evaluation instruments – the questionnaire

Questionnaires are the most common evaluation tool at the level of 'reactions'. They are easy to design, develop and administer. They are familiar to most people, and provide data that can be summarised easily.

1. Determine the information needed

2. Select question type:

   - open ended
   - checklist
   - two-way question
   - multiple-choice
   - ranking scales

3. Develop the questions

4. Test the question for understanding

5. Develop the completed questionnaire

6. Prepare a data summary sheet

5.2   Tests

Pre-course and post-course tests are used to evaluate the 'learning' level – to evaluate changes in knowledge, skill or ability. Tests can be classified in a number of ways, but the main divisions are by media and design:

1. By media

   - written, paper and pencil tests
   - simulations or actual performance
   - computer-based tests

2. By design

   - essays and exams: the most common in formal education
   - objective tests: specific and precise answers in relation to programme objectives
   - norm-referenced tests: compare participants with each other or other groups, rather than attainment of objectives
   - criterion-referenced tests: an objective test with a predetermined cut-off score for a minimum standard
   - performance tests: to exhibit a skill, whether manual, verbal or analytical

1. Interviews
   □ To secure data not available through other means, and probe to uncover stories useful for evaluation.

2. Focus groups
   □ If other quantitative methods are not adequate, to get at judgements about 'quality'.

3. Observations
   □ Before, during or after an HRD event. Need to be prepared and trained, be systematic, know how to interpret and report what they see, and their influence should be minimised. Use behaviour checklists, coded records, video recording or delayed report.

In a narrow way these methodologies are about the process of measuring how far objectives and targets have been achieved. Beyond accumulating and presenting facts about the achievement of HRD objectives in cognitive capacities, capabilities and behaviour to make judgments, there is also evidence relating to standards and changes in organisational performance as a whole. If it is challenging to identify and use objective standards to identify performance gaps which warrant HRD in the first place, then evaluation mirrors this challenge at this stage; the extent to which performance gaps have been closed is a challenge at the other end of the process. Quantitative information (see Resources Box 5.4) provides 'quick and dirty' data about the kinds of areas that are measurable in the immediate period after HRD experiences. Other, more robust and 'clean' assessments of cognitive capacity, capability and behavioural change can be more difficult to collect and analyse.

The feature of one methodology is that quantitative and objective standards provide a means of gauging what has been of value. The determination of objective standards may mean a range of things. Is it defined in terms of return on investment (ROI) (Flynn 1998) or some other description of expectations about what HRD can achieve or some other way of defining results or outcomes? Cost–benefit analysis (CBA) has

5.4	*Quantitative information available after HRD*
□ Cost savings	Doing more and/or better cheaply; unit costs, overhead
□ Time savings	Doing more and/or better quickly; order response, overtime
□ Work habits	Output of work; doing more; productivity, new accounts, absenteeism, rules violations
□ New skills	Improved quality of work; performing better; less defects and accidents
□ Work climate	Turnover, grievances, commitment, satisfaction
□ Initiative	New ideas, accomplishments

One definition of cost–benefit analysis is:

> A procedure by which the higher is reduced to the level of the lower, and the priceless is given a price. It can never therefore serve to clarify the situation and lead to an enlightened decision. All it can do is lead to self-deception and the deception of others. (Boyle 2001)

This is a sceptic's definition, of course. Those who agree with it argue that the concern should be with analysing the qualitative benefits – the 'higher' things – but this gets driven out by concerns with quantitative benefits. The number-crunching of exam pass-rates preoccupies the compilers of school league tables, for example, but it is the quality of development that really matters, and that is not easy to quantify.

This measurement obsession is more to do with standardisation and control (and with establishing control given a lack of trust among the people involved in HRD at work). Some managers and functional specialists insist on measuring others every step of the way because they believe that the more rigorously people are observed against impersonal 'objective' criteria the better they will behave.

To believe that perfect, objective, non-political decisions can be reached through number-crunching and that human prejudice and error can be eliminated, is the hope. Yet a fixation with quantification embroils people in a paralysis of analysis. Instead of pursuing pseudo-scientific precision – the impression of dealing objectively with things – people should measure less. Instead of analysing HRD costs and benefits why not trust HRD professionals to identify needs, design activities, and deliver them professionally?

been proposed as a means of structuring the evaluation of HRD. The costs are known in advance, but the benefits can only be estimated; they cannot be fully known. In a business and management context the common sense underlying such estimation is widely used, so why should it not be applied to HRD? One good reason is set out in Strategic View Box 5.4. It concerns the 'tyranny of numbers' when applied to intangible assets and benefits.

The idea of ROI is at the heart of this methodology, the pursuit of an absolute number, a neat package that shows the exact value returned for an exact value invested in training. This is a seductive idea as calculating the ROI of HRD can be simple and objective, and fits into the business context. However, it can also be complex and would never displace the role of more subjective judgments (Flynn 1998). Sometimes it is seen as the Holy Grail for many involved in HRD in order to prove their worth; and some are willing to go to great lengths to do so. Sometimes it is not worth the effort.

If it is a possibility in some form, the first question is 'Is it worth doing?'. Before embarking on any ROI quest, it is wise to estimate the ROI for calculating an ROI. Will it be worth the time and money that it will take? The answer depends more on the type of HRD that is planned than the cost as such. The type of training best suited to calculating ROI is one-time training on a specific skill; for example, in customer-service staff training on a new software tool. This is a discrete module in which few other factors will affect the outcome, and in which the outcome can be readily tested in a before-and-after scenario. This is the easiest and most clear-cut way to calculate an ROI. In other circumstances – although HRD potentially may have a greater effect on the company – its effects will be more difficult to quantify. It's hard to do a before-and-after test, for example, on leadership skills training, as other factors will come to play in managers' performance.

5.4 | ROI – how is it done?

1. To measure ROI, start by isolating the impact of training as much as possible. To do this it is necessary to have a control group. Train one group several months ahead of another, so that you have a control group to test against. Alternatively, narrowly focus the training so that a before-and-after comparison can be made.

2. Decide the impact the training should have. If learning a computer program is expected to shorten each customer-service inquiry, then attach a cost to that extra productivity.

3. The bottom line is: calculate the productivity effect. For instance, will each customer-service person be able to handle 10 more phone calls a day? Calculate the money associated with that: say each phone call represents £6 of the employee's time. Get a final value, for example that 20 employees each save an average of £60 a day: therefore £1200 per day, multiplied by 280 annual days. Divide that by the cost of the training.

   The result is the ROI.

In more complicated scenarios the focus is better placed on value and results than on a number-based ROI. Once the move away from an objective 'x more bolts sold' scenario into more vague managerial skills, it is necessary to use more subjective judgements to determine the effectiveness of the training. This involves making assumptions which can be difficult to defend; that there is a connection between spending on leadership training and the impact of leadership on performance. But bear in mind that HRD is not unique in this, and anxieties about ROI weaknesses may show over-sensitivity. For in other areas of management, such as advertising expenditure or internal auditing practices, these kinds of issues also exist; assumptions are also made about the impact of resources expended on advertising and audit, and these are not usually challenged. It is assumed to be worth spending money on advertising, it is assumed to be worth spending money on internal auditing; so why not make the same assumption for HRD instead of expecting those concerned with the least ROI-friendly domain to come up with an ROI case?.

An alternative proposal for calculating return on investments is to measure return on expectations instead. In this kind of approach, those who are involved decide what they expect to achieve from the HRD. This set of expectations becomes the baseline for determining success. After the HRD is complete, the stakeholders review their agreed expectations. They then decide whether the results are in line with them. This approach allows for more anecdotal and less arithmetic analysis. For example, where a group of managers complete a communications training course, stakeholders can discuss the ways they feel communication has or has not improved. This provides a more realistic picture than if HR staff were forced to place a convoluted financial figure on the value of improved communications. It is 'softer', but it is not false rigour.

Another concern which can lead to ROI calculation being sidelined is a conscious decision to focus on the long-term value of HRD rather than a simple ROI for individual events. HRD is to be seen as an investment, and all investments have risks associated with them. A company may not find a direct correlation between specific costs and helping their workforce to develop, but the company can treat HRD as one key piece in an overall business strategy.

5.1 | *Cost–benefit analysis*

In each of the following cases based on examples given in Flynn (1998) identify:

a. whether you would or would not use cost–benefit analysis (CBA)

and

b. if you were to use CBA analysis, what would be involved.

or

c. if you were not to use CBA analysis, what else you would evaluate and how.

Case 1. A manufacturer of office and school supplies, with products ranging from paper clips to binders and computer-related supplies, intends to provide training for new hires to its production lines.

Case 2. A company with 7000 employees intends to spend a multi-million amount on a programme to give staff a one-week course on the company's new computer desktop environment.

Case 3. A group of managers is to be trained on a course about communication skills to help cross-functional teams communicate and work with each other better.

Case 4. A photocopier manufacturer aims to shift to multifunctional products, where its copiers are no longer just copiers but also scanners, printers and fax machines, and its dealers need to be retrained.

Given the pressures to adopt this broad methodology – to quantify and 'speak the language' of ROI in organisations – it is a methodology challenge to shift the focus from an ROI obsession in the field of HRD. As the old saying has it, many things that count in quality HRD can't be easily counted, and many things that can be counted don't count. The change in attitude can be achieved by demonstrating that these demands aren't as much for a clear ROI as they are about making providers of HRD more accountable, and for HRD to be more applicable to jobs and organisational needs. Recognising and meeting these demands by showing some form of cause and effect for HRD can be good enough. It is, though, the case that the fewer hard-and-fast ROI numbers there are to work with, the more anecdotal information will be needed. This kind of information can be a better means of communicating with line managers about HRD because the managers may see workforce changes from HRD, thus giving credibility to HRD without an ROI.

Methodologies, such the quantitative and objective one associated with ROI, aspire to use scientific or at least quasi-scientific principles to evaluate HRD objectively. They evaluate as if they were looking 'from the outside in'. The concern is to keep a methodology of evaluation 'results-oriented', with methods that enable and speak about that. Courses should be results-oriented, and investment in them can be measured by financial returns, with senior and line managers' involvement and concern. If the ultimate level of evaluation is to compare the financial benefits with the costs of the HRD then some (Phillips 1991) conclude that HRD should be managed in organisations by converting training departments to 'profit centres' to ensure that they are contributing effectively to the organisation.

Critics of the quasi-scientific approach argue that this kind of conclusion is more ideological than practical. As an alternative methodology they offer a more marketing-oriented or even humanistic approach (Talbot 1995). This attempts to manage better subjective evaluations of HRD 'from the inside out'. This means that learners are to be involved in the evaluation process rather than subjecting them and their learning to the evaluations of others through the use of quantitative measures. In practice it means seeking to manage user surveys and focus groups, to investigate learner satisfaction, customer attitudes, job impacts, attitudes, and manager perceptions. These methods can produce great insights and save money and time. This makes sense because the problems with attempting to foresee and calculate returns in advance of actually investing in HRD are immense. No amount of ROI analysis can determine whether or not it is right to invest in HRD at work, and indeed it can distract from focusing on what can be done to establish and improve HRD contributions to performance.

The logic of this methodology is to see HRD as 'profit centre', running as a small business inside the organisation. This aligns with the thinking of those using financial lenses to make sense of HRD activity in the organisation. The alternative is to be wean the organisations themselves away from seeing HRD through these financial lenses and convert the organisations into learning organisations. In learning organisations even the 'softest' of 'soft skills' and informal kinds of development can be valued as much as specific investment in training for specific results. HRD is to be seen as an integral part of working life, not confined to what happens in a separate activity called 'training' managed by a few training professionals in the organisation. If a learning-organisation philosophy is followed, then its results cannot be separated out and discretely measured; it is an organic part of the whole organisation and its performance. The point can be illustrated by analogy with a decision, on the basis of a person's low blood pressure, that the heart was not working efficiently and that, if it were cut out, the removal of a poorly performing part would allow the rest of the body to work better. Of course it is a step to make things look better according to one measure that would kill! So with evaluating HRD; if signs indicate that it is not contributing to ROI as might be expected, then it ought to be stopped – though that too could 'kill' the organisation, but it would be logical enough.

theory &
research

| 5.3 | *Interpersonal skills* |

As an example of the potential relevance of a humanistic methodology of evaluation, consider the provision and evaluation of interpersonal skills training. HRD on interpersonal skills will often entail interventions with variable content: the same course – say on communication, or on handling conflict – will be experienced differently by different groups. This is because each course will evolve differently and flexibly as it is experienced. There is also great resistance from learners to formal assessment in areas such as interpersonal skills: people may want to be given feedback, but in no proper sense do they want to be tested and judged on their interpersonal skills. Quantified evaluation of such HRD is then neither possible nor desirable. Talbot (1995) suggests that the best that can be done is some form of joint evaluation, with collaborations between the learners and the trainers to explore what has been learned and what might remain to be done.

Metatheories

Debates about and rivalries between different methodologies of evaluation are often a symptom of more basic and deeper differences about theories which need to be considered and dealt with. For effective evaluation to be achievable, these theoretical matters and rivalries can be clarified. Scriven's term 'metatheories' implies that, although there may be many theories or answers to basic questions about how and why to value an area like HRD, these can be clustered together into a few 'higher order' explanations. It is these metatheories that can be seen to offer coherent, comprehensive explanations of evaluation, and to be rivals in this.

The idea of higher-order metatheories in HRD is easy to apply in one sense, as these may simply be taken to be the theories of the constituent human science disciplines in use in HRM: economics, psychology, and sociology. These theories will be explored in more detail in the next chapter. Here, when developing or drawing upon metatheories to evaluate HRD and its value, the higher-order theories of economics, psychology and sociology can provide the frameworks for investigating and explaining what is of value and merit (Theory & Research Boxes 5.4 and 5.5). In HRD the current state of play is that these metatheories all have a role: psychological theories shape individual evaluations, sociological theories shape social policy evaluations, and economic theories inform cost and benefit evaluations.

There is some interplay among different kinds of theory in HRD evaluation. This may be seen as healthy and productive because there is both rivalry between and synthesis of theories that makes the evaluation of HRD more robust and balanced than if it were governed by one discipline, either economics, or psychology or social theory. However, others take issue with the adoption of such an unproblematic view of drawing upon these human science theories in evaluating HRD. They argue that, even though these different domains of theory differ in their backgrounds, their dominant forms share a common philosophy that is based on a realist perspective.

The realist perspective as a paradigm can be seen to dominate across the disciplines. A paradigm can be defined as a traditional body of coherent theoretical and methodological belief that guides research and action. Paradigms can be, and frequently

---

5.4 | *Psychology and the characteristics of effective evaluation instruments*

Effective evaluation instruments for learning experiences need to be, in the constructs of psychology, both valid and reliable. A valid instrument measures what it claims to measure. Validity is defined with respect to four aspects, here illustrated with reference to a student taking an exam.

Content validity: does the instrument represent the content of the learning? The evaluation instrument should test a sample of what has been covered. All key items should be covered, with no imbalance. For example, does an exam cover all of the course, with equal weighting for equal parts of the material covered?

Construct validity: does the instrument represent the construct it purports to measure? In this case, is the good exam answer a reflection of all of the student's abilities, skills, or knowledge in performance? These are generally defined and defended by citing expert opinion or correlation with other constructs. For example, here, does a good exam answer actually measure the real differences in people's capacities?

Concurrent validity: does the instrument agree with the results of other similar instruments at approximately the same time? If assignments or other tests are done, do they provide the same results as the exam? Are the other exams a person is taking consistent with results in the exam in question?

Predictive validity: does the instrument help predict future behaviours and performance? For example, does performance in the exam predict anything about that person's abilities in professional practice?

5.5 | Reliability

A reliable instrument is one that gives consistent measures. There are various sources of error with reliability in any instrument:

- fluctuations in the alertness of the participants;
- variations in conditions of administering;
- random effects caused by participant motivation;
- the length of the instrument;
- differences in interpreting the results of the instrument.

For example, learners often complete post-course evaluation questionnaires, or 'happy sheets'. YBut are these reliable instruments for evaluating that course? Each of the factors in Theory & Research Box 5.4 can create errors, leading to an inaccurate evaluation, whether that be favourable or unfavourable. With some learners focused on the course and others thinking about getting home quickly, with some evaluations completed there and then and others taken away and perhaps never returned, with some learners who did not care about the course and others who cared deeply, the results of such happy sheets can be unreliable. And, even if not, when trainers pore over them thereafter, they can interpret selectively what has been measured and said. Some may see them as just a 'beauty' contest ranking, and take some pride in rationalising away any bad evaluations as representing the learners' inadequacies in failing to engage with a 'complex and difficult' subject.

are, challenged. Whether they are defended, reformed or replaced can alter the way that valid evaluation is seen and practised. Stewart (1999) takes issue with what he argues is the dominant realist paradigm. But, as Stewart's critique and alternative conceptions illustrate, it is largely practitioners alone who subscribe while academics disagree with it. It is arguable that a paradigm of any kind, whether of this quasi-scientific or other variety, may never be established (see Theory & Research Box 5.6). If that is so, then the evaluation of HRD will remain beset by the inadequacies of basic recipes and be subject to cycles of debate and rivalries without progress.

5.6 | The never-ending search for results

Mazlish (1998) characterises all the human sciences as uncertain. The promise of predictive and certain scientific knowledge to solve problems has not been fulfilled: either in regard to individual behaviour, social relations, or economic development. Mazlish concludes that:

Common sense tells us that a result emerges from people's passionate and political actions, not from predictive scientific knowledge. Many, if not most, problems are too delicate and disturbing to the actors involved to resolve clearly and rationally, even if a solution is available.

An example might be the allocation of resources, where the attempt to impose a rational plan often leads to a violent conflict of interests or to an unacceptable authoritarianism ... what solves social problems is social interaction ... rather than a science that pretends to deal with social interaction. Actions, in turn, constitute a never-ending sequence of solutions that create new problems.

If, in general, what solves problems is social interaction, and people taking actions that in their turn create new problems that others have to solve, then why should HRD be any different?

Rather than seeking a rational science of HRD evaluation, it is the realities of people's passions for or against HRD that will determine what happens and what the results are.

Source Mazlish 1998.

It looks as if there is an impasse at the level of metatheory in the evaluation of HRD. This means that the final and highest phase of the evolution of evaluation in HRD is far from being achieved. For Scriven the mature phase would be an evaluation system with which it was possible and scientifically practicable to deal with primary value claims. If this is true, and if such an evaluation system is required to validate claims about what is, in fact, meritorious and valuable in a scientific and rigorous way, then the conclusion is that the evaluation of HRD is far from being the robust activity that many want it to be, and which different groups claim to be able to achieve. Until there is an agreed metatheory or paradigm within which people concerned with evaluating HRD can work and communicate, the prospects for improving the evaluation of HRD are poor.

Conclusion

Review and evaluation constitute the final phase in the whole HRD process. This phase has often been seen as a problem area and a challenge in HRD at work. Recent improvements are evident, but the debates and concerns are still very much active. HRD evaluation is now done more widely than ever before, at the most basic level possible, with a preference for using the basic recipes of levels of evaluation. Evaluation can fulfil several functions, and this makes it complex. In practice there are popular and common models: the levels of evaluation relating evaluation to the different aspects of the HRD process itself, to learners and the resolution of performance gaps. But the prospect of producing more quality-aware HRD cultures or scientifically valid analyses of claims about HRD remains a matter of debate and argument. Becoming more 'quality aware' is probably the current major focus for improvement in this area.

Debates are taking shape around the use of either quantitative or qualitative measures, and how the major metatheory influences of psychology, sociology or economics impact on sense-making in HRD evaluation. In the end, the formulas and techniques for evaluations of HRD have to balance the demands of scientific rigour with the practicalities of professional practice. And the theoretical demands of 'truth seeking' have to be reconciled with the practical goals of 'pragmatic management'. To apply only the standards of scientific rigour and truth-seeking to the evaluation of HRD would be to invest so much in evaluation that there would be little time for action. To only trust in the expertise of professional practitioners in the name of pragmatic management would be to leave the evaluation stage of HRD, acknowledged as a critical phase and a weakest link, as a weak link in the process.

Multiple-choice questions

5.1 Which of the following lists the functions of evaluation in the correct order of priority?
A. Pragmatic, Ethical, Intellectual, Social, Personal
B. Ethical, Personal, Pragmatic, Intellectual, Social
C. Personal, Pragmatic, Ethical, Intellectual, Social
D. None of the above.

5.2 Which of the following definitions are correct?
  A. Content validity means that the method of evaluation does test a sample of what has been covered in a learning event.
  B. Content validity means that different results in completing the method of evaluation (e.g. a test) does actually measure real differences in ability.
  C. Predictive validity means that the method of evaluation will distinguish those who will from those who will not succeed in the future.
  D. Predictive validity means that the method of evaluation used will agree with the results of other kinds of test.

References

Axtell, C. (1997), 'Predicting immediate and longer term transfer of training', *Personnel Review*, vol. 26, no. 3.

Briggs, L.J., Gustafson, D.L. and Tillman, M.H. (1990), *Instructional Design: Principles and Applications*, Englewood Cliffs, NJ: Educational Technology Publications.

Boyle, D. (2001) *The Tyranny of Numbers: Why counting can't make us happy*, London: HarperCollins.

Canell, M. and Harrison, R. (1997) 'What makes training pay?', *Management Development Review*, vol. 10, no. 6.

Flynn, G. (1998) 'The nuts and bolts of valuing training', *Workforce*, vol. 77, no. 11, 80–5.

Hamblin, A. (1974) *Evaluation and Control of Training*, London, McGraw-Hill.

Kirkpatrick, D. (ed.) (1975) *Evaluating Training Programs: The four levels*, New York, Berett-Koehler.

Kirkpatrick, D.L. (1978) 'Evaluating in-house training programs', *Training and Development Journal*, September.

LSC (2004) *National Learner Satisfaction Survey*, London, Learning and Skills Council.

Mazlish, B. (1998) *The Uncertain Sciences*, New Haven, CT, Yale University Press

McGhee, P. (2003) *The Academic Quality Handbook. Enhancing higher education in universities and further education colleges*, London, Kogan Page.

Newby, T. (1992) *Training Evaluation Handbook*, London, Gower.

OECD (2003) *Adult learning*, Paris, OECD.

Phillips, J. (1991) *Handbook of Training Evaluation and Measurement Methods*, Houston, TX: Gulf Publishing.

Russ-eft, D. and Preskill, H. (2005) 'In search of the Holy Grail: Return on investment evaluation in human resource development', *Advances in Developing Human Resources*, vol.7, no. 1, pp. 71–86.

Scriven, M. (1991) *Evaluation Thesaurus*, Newbury Park, CA, Sage.

Stewart, J. (1999) *Employee Development*, Financial Times/Pitman, London.

Talbot, C. (1995) 'Evaluation and validation; a mixed approach', *Journal of European Industrial Training*, vol. 16, no. 5, pp. 26–31.

Wang, G. and Spitzer, G. (2005) 'Human resource development measurement and evaluation: Looking back and moving forward', *Advances in Developing Human Resources*, vol. 7, no. 1, pp. 5–15.

| case study | *Learndirect – the pledge to learners* |

Read the following case study, which describes the espoused framework of a 'pledge to learners' adopted by several case study learning centres. Compare and contrast how the various learning centres seem to look at and respond to quality issues in HRD.

Introduction

Learndirect Org is the brand name through which a national 'University for Industry' operates to promote and deliver lifelong learning in a country. It was established to help the country's businesses access training for their workforce. The key aim was simply to help employers to understand, source and access the training needed to take their business forward. Learndirect aims to engage more people in learning, while attaining a wide geographical coverage and dealing with specific sectors and issues, by the establishment of a network of learning centres.

The benefits for a learning centre of joining the network were highlighted to attract centres to accreditation. Being part of the network meant access to all of learndirect's resources, as well as access to capital funding for upgrading equipment and facilities. Centres would then benefit from the national marketing and promotion of the 'learndirect org' brand, of which they would be a part. The key benefit was that the quality of learner support would be the distinguishing feature of a learndirect learning centre. At the heart of the development, implementation and evolution of the network was a concern with quality. The 'pledge to learners' identified the following requirements:

- **Flexibility**. Offer the time, place, pace and style of learning that most closely meets the learner's needs.
- **Information** for learners to make the best personal choices and maintain their control.
- **Materials**. Provide learning materials that are relevant to learners' own personal and work interests, and have practical examples, exercises and experiences.
- **Progress**. Enable learners to monitor their progress and record their achievements as they go, not just at the end of a complete programme.
- **Support**. Provide learners with access to specialist support when they need it.
- **Learn to learn**. Work with learners to develop the skills that help them to learn and stay learning.
- **Relate**. Give learners the chance to relate their learning to longer-term ambitions.
- **Community**. Help learners to feel part of a wider learning community and put them in touch with other people studying the same things.
- **Connections**. Link their learning to key areas of learners' lives such as work, family, citizenship and their own personal development
- **Value**. Encourage learners to value learning and to see it add value to their lives.

After 3 years learndirect Org had achieved much, including the development of a network of over 450 learning centres. They were running regular campaigns to sign up new learners. They were looking at issues about further evolving and sustaining their network.

A series of visits to learning centres in different areas which were considered to be exemplary and representative of different kinds of centre was done. Exploring four cases we can consider three specific questions:

1. what the centres were doing prior to learndirect;
2. what had the connection with learndirect involved;
3. what were the issues currently for these learning centres as part of a network.

In considering these questions the role of the pledge to learners was being investigated. Four cases are outlined. In each case a description of the background to the organisation is given, and the context in which it acts as a learning provider is outlined. The link with learndirect, and its impact, is then explained. Finally, some conclusions about the pledge to learners and the quality of learning are presented, with different examples cited for each case, depending on what arose in the course of the visits.

Case 1 Regeneration Action Group (RAG)

RAG was founded in the late 1980s by a group of community activists in a former coalfield area. Initially RAG focused on providing 'hands-on' training for diversification for local people previously employed in mining. The project is run by a small group of core staff, with a volunteer board of directors, generates a turnover of approximately £2m and has created and sustained 150 jobs. It is the lead agency in community-based development in the area. At present RAG offers:

- a range of community-based learning opportunities;
- a school for social entrepreneurs
- an internet café with over 400 members, half aged under 18;
- a business centre hosting community enterprises;
- two 'Gateway to Work' contracts to deliver two-week intensive training programmes.

The project values include being accountable to the local community, being open friendly and approachable, and providing good value by working in partnership. Notwithstanding the achievements of RAG the area remains one of high unemployment, multiple deprivation and disadvantage. The major problems still remain: low income, poor access to childcare, lack of self confidence and esteem, poor educational attainment, poor transport.

RAG's learning centre was officially branded by learndirect in March 2001. Their provision of tailored learning opportunities was seen to meet the pledge to learners standard. They offer courses leading to the European Computer Driving Licence (ECDL) and vocational qualifications in information technology. Their learners are mainly drawn from the harder-to-reach groups and socially excluded needing extra support. Gaining the learndirect accreditation demonstrated that RAG was delivering a quality and valued service. They also secured £49k to improve ICT equipment, and now have 35 high specification computers, data projectors, portable equipment and a modern internet café.

The quality of what happens at RAG can be illustrated by two different examples: an individual person and the development of the School for Social Entrepreneurship (SSE).

The personal example is that of Frankie. He is an ex-student of the centre who won an individual community learning prize and ultimately won a national Learners' Award. These were achievements enough, but more so considering Frankie's background, which included losing his job, his house being repossessed, and a spell in prison. As a single parent caring for a teenage son, he had walked into RAG intending only to do a crash course in computing. He has since joined the School for Social Entrepreneurs and is developing an environmental business.

The development of the SSE is happening because of a concern that neither government programmes nor voluntary sector initiatives ever properly get to grips with social regeneration. They create a culture of dependency, they lack dynamism, and have no appetite to innovate. A movement of social entrepreneurs can overcome these deficiencies. This involves promoting leadership at grassroots level, motivating local people, being practically focused and renewing self-belief. Learndirect supports this. It was welcomed as a source of funds. But people come to them through word of mouth, not via learndirect's marketing. The accreditation of courses is a demonstration of their quality. But the main funders are European sources, local authorities and government programmes. What drives a concern with quality is their commitment to the social agenda.

Case 2 The Lime Centre (LC)

LC is a specialist training centre for building conservation, traditional building skills and environmentally conscious building. Traditional buildings are both a part of the character of the country, and also an economic resource; their loss and replacement is an unnecessary expense. The LC was established in 1994 in a small town outside Edinburgh. It has remained a small organisation, with the two main functions of training and consultancy employing around 11 people. The consultancy service provides for cost recovery and income

continued overleaf

| case study continued |

generation. They ran 15 one-day courses in their first year, but now have a portfolio of classes including 1-day masterclasses, 3-day classes, 5-day industry training and commissioned courses.

The bulk of training is courses commissioned by contractors, estate owners, and a government agency concerned with heritage. An emphasis on ecological building practice is also evident. There was a niche and gap to address. The point is that heritage is served, not that money is made. In their tenth year the LC is still subsidising training out of other income. In short, even though the government wants training in this, it won't pay for it. The LC is in an industry– construction – where there is a poor culture of learning as well.

The interest in learndirect was that the more quality marks the better. Access to small grants for learners, Individual Learning Accountss (ILAs), was also important, as this meant people would be subsidised, thus increasing the market. People could only spend ILAs at learndirect approved centres. The LC got a capital grant that was spent on new workshops, computers, TV, DVD, projector, furniture, and help with developing a new website.

Being accredited did not change the way the LC did things. Since accreditation there have been no new learners or different people because of learndirect's efforts. All learndirect advertising seems to be centred on technology or 'learning bytes' campaigns which are not relevant and have no impact there. The LC offers 3 national units, not a full vocational qualification. They wrote these units themselves and they can assess them. The staff here are building professionals or postgraduates and they all contribute to training. Staff have to have accreditation to act as trainers. They are hoping to appoint an education development manager, through the lottery heritage fund, to deal with quality issues. They also plan to set up a masonry training squad to fund a building contractor with an output of trainees. They would be doing work of benefit to, for example, National Trust properties or townscape initiatives, such as laying traditional stone paving. The centre gets income from being paid to do jobs, and the client gets the output of trained trainees. The LC acts as an employer. It has been a sub-contractor in projects with fellowship students who, at end of 2 years, work on a funded project. Keeping the training going is still the issue, not seeking to become another construction firm – the squad is a training tool.

There is a lot going on at the moment for this company. They are seeking to expand the training, range and number of training days and learners. There is nothing learndirect could do that would help this. Business Learning Accounts might help the construction industry spend more on conservation-related skills. The LC is connected with two postgraduate courses in Scotland. In the past they have given lectures and demonstrations free of charge or at reduced rates, but now one college wants threee one-day workshops for free. There is no way the LC can do this for already-funded colleges. Colleges are not interested in paying as they are really only interested in new build, not heritage. They are looking at related areas of architecture and heritage beyond Lime. Whether this means changing their identity is an issue. They would not want to be swallowed up by anyone else, and they are not 'attractive' enough for that anyway.

Case 3 Open Opportunities Project (OOP)

OOP was set up in 1995 for the residents of a local area to gain access to training and employment opportunities. In 2003 it won the learndirect 'learning centre of the year' award. OOP was established as a local council-run project. The areas around the small town in which it was based had a high rate of unemployment. The nearest large town with colleges and offices providing training and employment services was several miles away. As well as giving help with services such as CV preparation, interview skills and careers guidance, OOP was a 'mini college' acting as an accredited centre which organised classes in subjects like soft furnishing, hairdressing, tourism, and IT. It was meant to support vocational aims, but it was actually more used for recreational goals by local people. The perception of the public was poor; not much was seen to be going on.

A change in personnel and policy altered this. They decided not to carry on offering all courses but to be more customer-led in a vocational context. That meant, for example, organising classes in warehousing, electronics and administration, which were areas of employment in the locality. They could still only run short courses, on a part-time basis, so that learners were not losing benefits, and could have childcare paid for. Tutors were provided by the local college. OOP got students, told the college what they wanted, then their tutors delivered and assessed the training locally. The problem then and now is that there are few employment opportunities locally.

Learners were lacking in self esteem, having been out of learning a long time, and did not want to go out of the local area to learn. OOP's main role was getting them started: attracting learners, then contracting with the college. There were only three staff.

The local college also opened an annex in 1999, again raising the question of what OOP should do. There was a political dimension to this: the college wanted to deliver courses, and could run full-time classes. So what did OOP do? People still wanted the basic IT stuff so they concentrated on that – 'computing for the terrified'. Other people were doing other things, and OOP would not get involved.

There was some special funding available as this was an area affected by the decline of the fishing industry, but that was administered by the council. It was hardly worth applying for European funding because it was so difficult to get your head round and keep records for; OOP did a lot for a small sum. Small numbers were the problem; in rural areas, with low populations, there was not enough demand to make up a class so colleges were not interested. But, being local, OOP could get people involved because they knew them; and what they wanted. They could be confident that there would be demand. People did not see them as a learning centre; they saw OOP as somewhere to help you get a job.

OOP was conscious of having been criticised by people in the education department of the local council. While they were accredited to run ECDL and other qualifications they were also keen to introduce quality systems to prove that they were really doing well. This was for the good of the project and a message to the sceptics and critics. They saw the pledge to learners as ideal for that because it was exactly what they felt they were already doing. They work in old buildings, with limited staff numbers, and limited budgets. They did not set out to get capital funding; but they did get some. They needed modern software and received £14,000 for that and other equipment. Their facilities are very up-to-date, and look good. Online learning has been pushed, but that is not the be-all and end-all. In the OOP area, which is rural, e-learning was good, but people wanted personal contact. Roadshows for providers were organised, but learndirect was not listening to the centres; they were slow to respond, and put too much emphasis on online learning. Sharing knowledge with others was useful. This could be better facilitated by learndirect. OOP had a sense that learndirect preferred to deal with and focus on the new rather than consolidating what they already had.

Advantages of learndirect for OOP were that, having small budgets, getting access to material from the network was very useful. Campaigns did not generate business for them; but gives them resources they could not afford themselves. Only one person has found them through learndirect. In the future that might be different, they might get extra business from working with businesses rather than individuals. Tourism in this area is mainly bed and breakfast establishments. People in those can be better trained but do not have computers or internet connections. They have to come in to OOP for facilities.

OOP started with a social and economic agenda and grew bigger, on the one hand, but strayed from its purpose as well. This was addressed and a larger unit associated with a college was opened. OOP had proven to the college that there was a market and gave people the confidence to go to college. The college would never have run the short introductory courses that OOP was offering. They continue to offer ECDL level courses even with a small budget, and they need to be creative. Ultimate success for them is looking at learning being accessible to all, and doing that by encouraging people to come to a comfortable place. Community learning plans mean that, for organisations like OOP, regional links are important because planning and politics occur at a regional level so projects like OOP are always nested in layers of policy-making. Each level has a purpose, and cannot be excised. If there is some overlap or dislocation between the local (for example, relations with the college), the regional (community development most broadly) and the national (learndirect) that is to be expected and accepted; it has to be lived with.

continued overleaf

Q

| case study continued |

Case 4 Private Training Co (PT Co)

PT Co is private sector partnership providing training, HR and business services in a small town. The partnership is run by two women with an extensive background in training who set up the company after leaving another local company. The company has recently won a National Training Award for the quality of its own in-house training for staff. It is a member of associations such as FSB (Federation of Small Businesses) and runs a recruitment business too.

The company does not rely on one area in particular for business, but have diversified so as to have something to fall back on if government-funded programmes are threatened. That includes being a recruitment agency, supplying temporary, contract and permanent placements. They also offer a wide range of business services for companies and clients: events management, preparing materials, telephone services, facilities, etc. Other services under development include general HR services on policy and practice in contracts, discipline and other areas affected by employment law. They are also developing series of seminars on a range of topics.

PT Co feel that their attitude towards quality is to care very much about learning and development, and not the more laid-back attitude of the public sector. Small companies have to be like that. The key to success is quality, and being small is a part of that. They know the area very well, and people know them. That personal knowledge is essential. They are approachable, and people are comfortable with them at this level. They are very well networked at a local level, participating in bodies, such as the local Chamber of Commerce, that have a concern with business and learning. These local associations matter more than national links.

They are an accredited centre for many agencies as well as learndirect. They offer S/NVQs in administration, management, customer service, IT, business start-up, business development, learning and development, text processing, audio and speed tests. They also provide advice and guidance for CV preparation, job search and interview techniques and deliver government-funded programmes for businesses recruiting new employees or training current staff. They offer flexible training in groups, one-to-one, daytime or evening classes by arrangement, in-house or on company premises. They also provide much IT training, and are accredited to offer the ECDL computer literacy qualifications and business technology classes. Their own premises have a fully fitted and networked computer suite and seminar room.

PT Co had three of its learners acknowledged as Champion Learners by learndirect. They have been able to increase the number of learners on IT side because they are associated with learndirect. *Byte sized* learning campaigns have mattered to them; they registered 45 new learners who completed a minimum amount of learning by the end of the year. That was their set limit. In fact they were so in demand they ended up with 90 potential learners, and were able to accommodate some more of these. Another recent campaign has produced more new contacts, regarding a free Health and Safety course. Being private and small, it is a great advantage to get the marketing, advertising, and promotion that learndirect offers. They do their own mailshots, but the learndirect mailings help a lot.

The market is very local, in the immediate town and county area. The company is involved in training and assessing, but in a nice warm office. They are passionate about gettin people back into learning. They have attended a learndirect development day, meeting other centres in the local area for networking. There is some competition locally; with the colleges, for example, but also with other private companies. They are involved in some private–public partnerships, but not in any private–private joint ventures.

A

| case analysis |

These learning centres were all already in existence, and already had good foundations for quality, in practice. The pledge to learners only helped them articulate what these foundations were. This validated them and their practices. New ideas and innovation are evident in all these organisations, but these are not driven by the learndirect partnership; other sources for the cognitive dimension and innovation are important. It seems also

case analysis continued

that there was already a supportive and nurturing environment, on the emotional side, for dealing with quality issues. This seems due in part to the small size of the organisations, with only a few staff members. The 'emotional' impact of the larger organisation was not initially helpful, but has been better facilitated since by local development officers. The link with learndirect does not impact one way or another on this emotional dimension; making it nether better nor worse. Team and interpersonal relations were a strength of all these small organisations prior to accreditation, and the connection with a larger unit, through learndirect, has again, it seems, not impacted upon that one way or another. The limited networking these people have encountered has been useful, but regional rather than national networks seem uppermost in their concerns. The issue of organisational coherence is less important in many ways for these small organisations due to their size. But in another sense it is vital, given the diversity of activities they are all engaged in and have to manage alongside managing learning. These issues existed prior to learndirect links and matter more as learndirect national projects are developed and promoted.

They show areas not normally explored using old 'levels of evaluation' models, and direct attention away from the kinds of quantitative data conventionally associated with evaluating learning, and towards analysis of quality in its broader and deeper senses. Having concluded that, it is also evident that, while the 'pledge for learners' experience has been a good articulation of managing quality in learning, it seems to have made minimal impact in most respects on the learning centres investigated. Being small, diversified and entrepreneurial centres in such circumstances they do not seek or need more quality-enhancement drivers. In that respect the role of a body like learndirect may be reconceived.

These learning centres all continue to face tremendous challenges in achieving their goals to contribute to lifelong learning. They need both further support, and further challenges. Two bigger issues come to the fore, however. The first is the broad issue of business strategy and organisational development of training providers like these small centres: what strategies should they follow, and how can they evolve to continue playing a role in lifelong learning? These learning centres are an important and integral part of many communities and local economies. Second, what about the institutions that learners move on to, whether further or higher education or employing organisations. To what extent can these other institutions continue to deliver to learners who are used to the standards of the pledge for learners? What would an analysis of the cognitive, emotional, interpersonal and organisational management of a quality culture reveal about those advanced contexts?

chapter

6

HRD and theory

- identify and discuss how theories can be used to understand the HRD process;
- describe and evaluate the relevance of psychological, sociological and economic theories in managing HRD at work;
- solve problems and reflect on issues in HRD practice using theoretical frameworks

resources

6.1 Theory and solutions?

"On the high ground, management problems lend themselves to solution through the application of research based theory and technique. In the swampy lowland, messy confusing problems defy technical solution." (Schon 1987, p. 3)

---

introductory case **Learning styles**

It has long been argued that, in planning the design and development of HRD experiences, learning styles should be understood and accommodated. Learning styles were discussed in chapter 4. They are defined as different personal preferences for processing. In theory they provide an automatic way of responding to information and situations, favourably or unfavourably. Various ways of characterising learning styles exist (see Figures 6.1 and 6.2.).

Question   Do you find it more useful and valid to think about yourself as a learner using learning styles version 1 or learning styles version 2? Which version offers a keener insight into the preferences you have and the things you find enjoyable or frustrating about learning experiences?

Introduction

Theories are the torches we inherit from science or keep fuelled to enlighten ourselves and our work. In HRD we seek enlightenment on understanding how and why the HRD process works well or brilliantly, or encounters problems and difficulties, and to provide a spur and questions that lead people to propose and explore theories of HRD. Decision-making that is based on principles and theory is assumed to be preferable

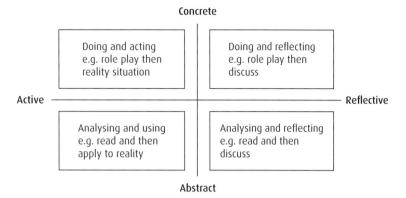

Concrete perceivers prefer to learn from direct experience by doing, acting, sensing and feeling
Abstract percivers prefer to learn from analysis, observation and thinking
Active processors prefer to learn from making sense of an experience by immediately using the new information
Refective processors prefer to learn from having an experience then reflecting on and thinking about it.

Figure 6.1 Learning styles version 1

Source Riding 1996

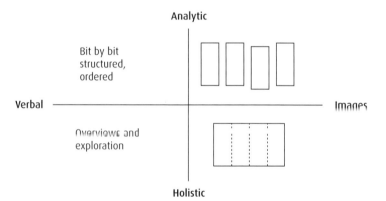

Analytic verbalisers like to learn from a bit-by-bit structure with headings and paragraphs, having a good verbal memory
Analytic-imagers like to learn from a bit-by-bit structure with diagrams and illustrations, having a good picture memory
Holistic-verbals like to learn from overviews and the explorations, with a preference for textual and verbal communication
Holistic-imagers like to learn from overviews and the explanations, with a preference for diagrams and illustrations

Figure 6.2 Learning styles version 2

Source Riding 1996

to that which is based on ignorance, guesswork or myth and doctrine. The usefulness of theory is its relevance, validity, truth and impact in contexts where doctrine or myth might otherwise intercede. Relevance, validity, truth, and impact are therefore the criteria with which to identify, consider and evaluate the contribution of theory to HRD (see Strategic View Box 6.1). These are uncontroversial ideas, but exploring theory in HRD proves tricky and challenging.

6.1 | *The role of theory*

Research both contributes knowledge to a scientific discipline and aims to apply that knowledge to advance practice. It is useful to consider how theorist–practitioner interactions fall into four critical areas:

(a) formulating the problem;
(b) developing alternative theories;
(c) collecting evidence;
(d) applying findings.

When theorists and practitioners interact at these four critical theory-building stages, the theory has the highest potential to meet the dual purpose of advancing knowledge and guiding practice.

Problem formulation consists of developing a concrete description of the symptoms, conditions, or anomalies as they exist in the real world on a topic or issue. All the unorganised perceptions or facts pertaining to a topic or issue belong here. Recognition of these perceptions or facts is acquired through experience, observation, or judgments of a problem, opportunity, or issue existing in a realistic situation. This the selection of a research question and the body of knowledge that is relevant to the research problem.

Conceptualisation: A conceptual model is the mental image or framework that an investigator brings to bear on the research problem. Selecting the conceptual model is perhaps the most strategic choice that an investigator makes, for it significantly influences the research questions to ask, and the kind of propositions and hypotheses that will be set forth to answer these questions.

Theory building consists of developing clear statements of relationships or comparisons between two or more constructs that are expected to hold within a set of assumptions or boundary conditions. A theory consists of propositions at a middle range of abstraction, and it consists of hypotheses at an operational level of concreteness.

Research design connects a theory with empirical evidence. It involves the selection and execution of operational procedures for bringing valid scientific evidence to bear in examining a theory that addresses the research question about the problem or issue as it exists in reality.

The problem as generated from reality must be relevant, the concepts of the theory must be valid, the research must verify the truthfulness of the concepts, and the research must have an impact on the science and profession of HRD. Thus relevance, validity, truth, and impact are the criteria on which to evaluate theory-building research.

Source Storberg-Walker 2003.

This is because exploring theory involves making explicit underlying assumptions and gathering evidence to test and refine them, explaining what works for whom, in what circumstances, in what respects and how in order to influence sense-making and shifts in thinking (Pawson et al 2004). As such, the desire for theory can be said to begin in the heads of researchers, policy-makers and others, and to pass into the hands of practitioners and managers and, sometimes, into the hearts and minds of users and participants (see Theory & Research Box 6.1). Both HRD practitioners and researchers have common interests in influencing sense-making and helping to make shifts in thinking. Useful theories can be the levers that help that process, so they have a common interest.

The versions of learning styles in the introductory case can be used as an example (see Figures 6.1 and 6.2). Instead of seeking to measure 'what works' and concluding

6.1 | *Theory and learning styles*

The example of the theory of learning styles is illustrative. The theory is that there is diversity in and systematic patterns among the ways that people prefer to learn. This theory began 'in the heads' of people studying experiential learning and cognition. These people hoped to encourage better learning by explaining how people learned so that trainers, teachers and learners would become aware of the strengths and weaknesses of preferences and the repertoire of preferences. It has passed into the hands of practitioners in the form of various measuring instruments, one of which has already been introduced.

There are indeed many of these kinds of instruments available. One study (Coffield et al 2004) identified 71 as widely used. The study concluded that a reliable and valid instrument which measures learning styles could be used as a tool to encourage self-development, not only diagnosing how people learn, but showing them how to enhance their learning. And learning styles can provide trainers and learners with a 'lexicon of learning' – a language with which to discuss their own learning preferences and those of others, how people learn or fail to learn, and how trainers and others can facilitate or hinder these processes.

Reprise on Good Psychometric Instrument Criteria

- **Internal consistency** (reliability): the degree to which the items in a test measure the same thing, measured by the average correlation between each item and the other items;
- **Test–retest reliability**: the stability of test scores as indicated by retesting the same group and calculating a correlation coefficient using the two sets of scores;
- **Construct validity**: how far test scores can be interpreted as measuring only what they are intended to measure;
- **Predictive validity**: the extent to which a set of scores predicts an expected outcome or criterion.

The review, however, also drew attention to a set of problems which continue to beset learning styles. Research into learning styles can be characterised as small-scale, non-cumulative, uncritical and inward-looking. There is a proliferation of concepts, instruments and pedagogical strategies. This proliferation is a clear symptom of the current conceptual confusion, a serious failure of accumulated theoretical coherence and the absence of well-grounded findings tested through replication. Moreover, most of the 13 models Coffield et al studied closely exhibited serious psychometric weaknesses. Any instrument should demonstrate *both* internal consistency and test–retest reliability *and* construct and predictive validity. These are the minimum standards for any instrument which is to be used to redesign pedagogy. Three of the thirteen most popular models met none of these criteria, four met one, four met two, one met three and only one met all four.

Despite these serious weaknesses, these instruments are currently being used very widely. Yet some of the best-known and widely-used instruments have such low reliability, poor validity and negligible impact on pedagogy that Coffield et al recommend that their use in research and in practice should be discontinued.

that one model or an intervention works 'to some extent' or 'sometimes', there is another option. There are those for whom encountering theory in the course of study is, at best, a diversion into interesting academic debates, but which, at worst, can be a descent into abstractions in which they become lost, confused and alienated. They see no connection with the demands of practice and professional development. There are others for whom the study of theory is the highest level, where encountering ideas and considering their truthfulness is the most exciting thing; they will happily trace past and present arguments about ideas in depth and detail. The former will approach the analysis of learning styles with a view to figuring out quickly how they can use it, or not; the latter will want to explore the validity of psychometrics and the underlying models behind different style frameworks. Between these two extremes are the majority who enjoy some aspects of theory and endure the rest.

In part this divergence of attitudes reflects the status that theory bestows. In the world of the practitioner the advantages of knowing and advancing theory are few; the demands are pragmatic ones, getting things done. The use of theory can seem to be an overly intellectual foundation among the peer group. If there is a learning styles instrument they can use, then good – they will use it. Detail on the theory behind it is superfluous; it has low status for them. In the world of the academic the advantages of knowing and advancing theory are many and manifest in the marking schemes and comments of assessors; not using theory can seem to be the worst sin in discussions and assignments. An academic assessor would not care if a student could administer and interpret a learning style instrument, only that they understood its psychometric strengths and weaknesses. Theory is of the highest status.

Workplace HRD is a domain of applied performance which has boundaries with several fields of theory. It thus has the best and worst of both worlds in terms of theoretical grounding. It is possible to perform well in practice without being aware of any theory; and indeed many HRD practitioners have no formal qualifications. They may use and can administer learning styles instruments freely. But the fields of psychology, social sciences and economics have well-developed forms of theory which all claim to offer some kind of scientific foundation for understanding and practising HRD. There is scope for an interdisciplinary foundation for HRD, making it a more demanding, professional domain.

It is important to define terms clearly. Theories are systems of ideas intended to explain something, based on general principles. Such systems of ideas and principles may also be the basis for practice, but not necessarily. Alternatively such systems of ideas may be the subject of speculation and interest in themselves, outside of any practical application. Exploring theory may then be both a means of managing practice and a means of understanding debates about the nature and merits of systems of ideas. The value of each of these is strongly defended by its advocates, those for action or those for critical reflection. In exploring theory it is necessary to keep this duality in mind. A synthesis of concerns, recognising the demands of practice but valuing the exercise and role of questioning and critique, is sensible.

Making explicit underlying assumptions through exploring theories can be about exploring traditions, like those associated with economics, psychology and sociology, through other people's ideas. But to consider theory is also about making explicit your own assumptions, other writers' assumptions, and organisations' assumptions. In gathering evidence to test and refine theory, you will read articles in which others have gathered evidence to test and refine their theories, so you also need to be able to deconstruct these and make use of them. Explaining what works for whom, in what circumstances, in what respects, and how is to adopt an exploratory rather than a judgmental approach in which a theory (that you get from elsewhere or your own) is modified rather than simply deemed to fail or pass the 'test of truth'. In order to influence sense-making and shifts in thinking, ultimately the goodness of a theory is its success in shifting other people's thinking; academics articulate, test and refine theories to do that, and others need to do so as well.

Theory then has to help answer the question, 'what is it that works for whom in what circumstances?'. This is crucial in HRD at work because the 'same' thing is never repeated in an identical manner or in an identical setting. No course is ever delivered exactly the same, no programme is ever repeated in exactly the same kind of organisation, and so on. What 'works' in one situation once is no guide to what will work in a different situation at another time. The concern is then, not to help us decide between the true or false and pass or fail verdicts on a technique or practice, but to help us when we seek to:

- Clarify the reasons for needing a theory – basically who is interested in defining a problem, and why;
- Map out the broad conceptual territory in the literature by searching for existing studies;
- Search data and evidence to populate a theory, in an iterative process, changing direction and the focus of searching;
- Synthesise theory and evidence to explain ways in which things work contingently.

In doing all this, appreciating diversity in 'context' will be critical; how do certain contexts and circumstances either amplify or mute the successful and unsuccessful method or practice? Looking at particular settings and social interventions is essential, as is understanding that they always involve the actions and reasoning of actual people. That this reasoning is frequently not linear, but involves negotiation and feedback embedded in social systems, is often critical for understanding what is done and why it is done. Even the most authoritative theory is open to modification in implementation as actual people make use of it (see Strategic View Box 6.2).

Exploring theory

Theory is needed to organise understanding about a subject and communicate 'using a statement of relations among concepts within a set of boundary assumptions and constraints' (Bacharach 1989). For advocates of theory they are developed to answer 'why' questions and to explore the assumptions we operate with. These theories start as guides, then become verifiable or falsifiable altered views. They are desired to:

- Advance knowledge in a discipline;
- Guide research towards important questions;
- Enlighten the professionals.

| 6.2 | *Theory grounded or pragmatics?* |

The status of theory in HRD at work is mixed. On the one hand are those who argue that the foundation of professional practice in HRD has to be grounded in an appreciation of valid and robust theory, and this ought to be the major framework for sense-making in HRD at work. Alternatively there are those who adopt a pragmatic approach, arguing that managing HRD at work requires familiarity with an accumulated body of knowledge around best practice, not to any theory; this is the surest framework for sense-making.

This mirrors the more general debate between these positions in management as a whole. The proponents of theory question how the 'normative' and prescriptive biases of the pragmatists distort knowledge and understanding about learning, leading to poorly realised processes, hit-or-miss practices, and a chronic lack of research and evidence to inform practice. For them, theory is a disciplined way of acquiring truth about cause and effect. The proponents of pragmatism question the usefulness of devoting time to getting to grips with sets of theories which are diverse and contested, seeing the agents of theorising as detached from the real world concerns of practitioners and sceptical that research and evidence can ever provide knowledge, clarity and certainty great enough to warrant requiring substantial appreciation of theory. For them theory is an abstract concern for intellectuals to argue about and students to be bamboozled by.

There are also three major rationales for being interested in a particular theory;

- **Theory integrity** – does it work as predicted?
- **Theory adjudication** – which theory seems to fit best?
- **Comparison** – how does a theory work with different groups in different settings?

Theory may be expressed either in statements or graphically, using boxes and arrows to indicate relationships. In statement form theories will be logically deduced propositions which link their key terms, concepts and constructs. In graphic form, boxes will indicate all the factors comprehensively and parsimoniously and the arrows will indicate how they are related. Either form of expression can produce hypotheses, which are propositions that are measurable. To be measurable they have to be associated with variables that have observable values. For example 'performance' is a concept, whereas 'sales made' is a measurable variable.

In some academic areas there will be one dominant theory that is accepted by all who operate in that area. In other areas there will be divergence between different theories, a plurality. In these areas the issue is often how and why one theory is better than another in general. It may be on the grounds of technical standards, related to evidence; one is deemed true and another false. It may be circumstantial; one may have clarity, expression, impact, and relevance while another may lack these. How do we recognise the best theory? How do we improve those current theories which are seen to be valid? We can alter the boxes or arrows or assumptions. Or we are just stuck with these assumptions, and a pluralism of tribes and territories plying theory games? Some become concerned with micro-validation, ignoring the big picture, while others can accept paradoxes and tensions in theory and use them. How do we build new theories? There are espoused methods for doing this and 'in use' methods showing how it is actually done (Van de Ven 1989). The main espoused method is the realist one: empirical events are observed, particular circumstances are understood, and laws of causality are identified. But the critique of this is that studies are merely co-relational and empirical, and provide no scope for identifying any substantial kind of causality or truth. The questions that need to be asked and answered, beyond the empirical are:

- What's new?
- So what? This changes what?
- Why so? What is the logic and assumptions?
- Is it complete and thorough?
- Is it well-written in terms of flow, accessibility, standards?
- Why now?
- Who cares, both narrowly and broadly?

In some fields of study, theory is generated within an agreed paradigm, a shared and agreed set of assumptions about the field of study. In others, theory is generated by multiple paradigms providing various interpretations of the field of study. HRD appears to belong to the latter kind of field. Entwistle et al (1992) noted that there is not even agreement on the most basic term we are using – the construct of learning does not mean the same thing to all people at all times. The subject of HRD theory can therefore vary greatly depending on exactly what meaning of 'learning' we adopt.

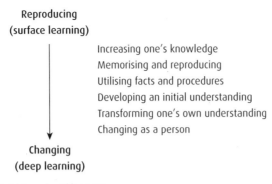

Figure 6.3 A hierarchy of learning

Source Adapted from Entwistle et al 1992

The hierarchy of meanings that Entwistle et al identified is depicted in Figure 6.3. The meanings range from learning as 'increasing one's knowledge' to learning as 'changing as a person' on a continuum from surface learning to deep learning.

So HRD theories – sets of ideas formulated by reasoning about the facts involved in a range of experiences – range from increasing a person's knowledge to changing them as a person. Such a framework also helps define process problem areas; the central problem in learning theory is normally seen as surface learning rather than deep learning, both at work and elsewhere. Surface learning is defined as superficial packing of the short-term memory; it is transient and fades away. Deep learning is real assimilation and change; it is transformative and permanent. Many learning experiences seem to achieve surface learning, not deep learning.

The pursuit of deep rather than surface learning will determine the way that process problems are perceived and solutions are sought. How can we support effective deep learning? The main goal of learning theory is to find answers to such questions. For some, the starting point will be the extent to which processes are consistent with principles suggested by various psychological theories. For others, process problems may be attributed to problems in the social context – of relationships and institutions involved in learning. They might want to explore what makes learning processes dysfunctional. And for others, the process problem might be seen as an integral part of the operation of market forces, and how these stimulate or fail to provide support for effective HRD processes.

Approaches to investigating theory in HRD

Two ways of describing and investigating theory in HRD are offered here. The first is to consider the four main contexts of theory that illuminate how and why process problems around workplace learning and HRD arise and can be dealt with. Each of these can provide insights into the 'how' and the 'why' of managing and improving learning at work. These are the fields of 'wisdom' theory, psychology, social theory and economic theory. This approach certainly helps to map out the broad fields which are relevant in workplace HRD. The second approach is to consider theory in terms of their underlying philosophies. These cut across the disciplines, ranging from the positivist to the phenomenological. This will also be considered, briefly. First, the four main contexts of theory are reviewed.

The pragmatist's context: wisdom theory and literature

The first context for theory is one that appears at first sight to be 'atheoretical' because it is derived from and applied around the experience of practitioners. This kind of theory is not uncommon in management in general, and in HRM in particular. It can be found in the wisdom literature that practitioners of HRD write and disseminate. HRM is replete with wisdom literature, work written by and for practitioners. It encompasses texts on 'how to do it' and the latest best-sellers of management gurus and popular writers on learning. This kind of theory is a popular resource, among other practitioners and often with students too, but it has weaknesses as a resource for exploring HRD process concerns at work.

The major issue is that the theory is rarely based on robust research, evidence and valid argumentation. It tends to express prescriptions about what has worked, based on one person's experience. Such reflections on personal experience, resulting in prescriptions for good practice, can provide useful and stimulating insights into practice. Reading the wisdom literature offers checklists of what to do. The literature tends to suggest that problems with learning at work are a consequence of ill-prepared and unprofessional trainers and managers. Reflecting on the experience of trainers and others, this stream provides admonitions, recipes, tips and techniques for supporting effective learning.

The implication, sometimes expressed explicitly, is that theorising based on studies and evidence, gets in the way of good practice. What is required is a clearer and better prescriptive account of the best practice, not an engagement with the mess of purer theorising. This may be seen as theory-in-practice or theory-in-action (Argyris 1994, Schon 1987). These ideas from practitioner practice are likely to be important elements of theory-building within applied disciplines but should not be confused with competent researchers who produce relevant, robust theory.

The strength of this resource on HRD at work, and the sense-making it involves, is that those who have experience are often the best-placed to explain and discuss what does and does not work. The weakness of the wisdom literature is that the research base is not rigorously collated or presented. Indeed, many practitioners seek to make a virtue out of being atheoretical, claiming to offer ideas about getting results in practice rather than 'debating' abstract and academic issues. Yet every commentator has a theory, there is not an atheoretical option. It may not be their concern to evaluate different theories, but in prescribing the best way and 'getting results' they are agents of theory; the question is only whether they are doing it consciously or unconsciously.

It is also possible to read the wisdom literature for analyses and evaluations of the theories that are being used. Mager (2000) provides a good illustration of a writer providing a practitioner's wisdom about the field of HRD. His text is aimed at managers involved in HRD, rather than being for specialist trainers or student learners. He agrees that knowledge of learning theory will not in itself make a person into a good instructor. But he still concludes that it is important to be able to describe the relevant characteristics of adult learners and know the key principles of supporting effective learning. He is critical of much training as 'a fraud' or 'an extravagance', about which managers have rightly been sceptical in the past. He claims to explain the how and why of HRD at work from a personal wisdom based on experience.

Mager argues that effective HRD can provide performance improvements through instructions in skill and can help develop employee self-efficacy, but it is up to managers to provide the opportunity and support that translate instruction in skills into improved performance. There are often other, non-training, means to the same end. These prescriptions could be adopted as an eclectic package, but what Mager is articulating is a version of the theory of behaviourism. Both these aspects of theory – theories of how adults learn best, and general principles for supporting learning – are presented by Mager as simply being 'common-sense' guides. His arguments are not based on citing studies or evidence; these wisdom theories come from knowing reality and being experienced.

| 6.1 | *Principles and methods for supporting adult learning* |

Principles
- Need independence and choice
- Need intrinsic motivators and curiosity
- Need feedback with time for reflection
- Need active involvement in real-world tasks
- Concern with higher-order abilities (e.g. critical thinking, problem-solving)
- Concern with high challenge–low threat environments
- Concern with practice and reinforcement

Methods
- Collaborative learning
- Cooperative learning
- Problem-based learning
- Case method teaching
- Peer-based methods
- Research-based learning

Principles and methods for supporting adult learning are given in Operations Box 6.1. If we try to understand the HRD process at work by understanding these principles and methods, we are likely to advance effective adult learning. Doing that in a more formally structured theoretical way takes analysis into psychology, social theory and economics.

The psychology theory context

Beyond the wisdom theories and literature the first discipline that is most associated with the theoretical exploration of learning is psychology. HRD at work appears to have much of its proper theoretical underpinnings in applied psychology. The fields and associated theories of the psychological literature provide for understanding the principles and problems of HRD at work. In this human science there are theories from the various schools of psychology providing different and diverging explanations of the principles and problems of learning.

Hardingham (2000) provides a good example of the bridge between the wisdom literature and theory-based psychology around learning. Psychology for her is a 'frame of mind' that can help to establish a learning partnership, it is not a complete recipe for success. Hardingham touches on many significant and useful points about the HRD process and concerns with processes working and not working, emphasising delivery with aspects of design and evaluation also considered. Design is about getting information across and ensuring the transfer of learning. Delivery involves understanding things that cause stress to trainees and trainers, how to build rapport and establish credibility, work in groups and handle conflicts. That is a frame of mind which is sensitive to a set of assumptions and debates.

6.2 | The psychological frame of mind, assumptions and debates

Popular assumptions about people and learning	Debates in people and learning
Learning involves an exercise of personal freedom, motives and control matter and can be influenced to promote learning	The extent to which determinism exists, and factors beyond the control of the person have a big impact on learning
Situational contexts matter, environment can have a big impact for good in advancing learning	The extent to which 'innateness' is the heart of capability, with inborn characteristics setting the boundaries on what is possible
People are unique and therefore have different development pathways which need to be facilitated	The extent to which 'universality' applies, with most people following the same or similar development pathways over a lifespan
Being proactive, taking the initiative, shapes learning positively	To what extent being reactive, driven by external stimuli, shapes learning for most people most of the time
Optimism is warranted about learning; significant change is possible for all	To what extent is pessimism about learning warranted because most people tend to be stable and unchanging, not open to learning

6.2 | From a key thinker to diagnosing performance problems

HRD theorising can be stimulated by reviewing key thinkers on positive regard like Rogers (1969) people have a drive to grow and achieve, and a secure sense of self supported by others' positive regard is central to that. Such growing involves both pleasure and pain, as people become aware of what they can and cannot do; sustained positive regard whatever happens is a highly desirable environment for growth.

As people grow up, how others have defined them and treated them – their positive regard or its absence – has a big influence on development. People's experiences in HRD are implicated in this, being both fulfilling and an arena which may contain disappointment. Problems often arise in later life when people as adults may continue to feel they have to deny a part of themselves to get positive regard; for example, to sacrifice expression of their true self.

This may interfere with learning. It may alienate people from participating in learning at all by blocking off aspects of learning dependent on improving personal awareness. Blocks can be removed if secure, and unconditional, positive regard is offered. Then change and growth will happen, driven by the person themselves, as they work things out for themselves.

Successful learning and development needs, in essence, a 'space' for a person to feel good in rather than a system of rewards and punishments. This in turn connects to the wider field of 'systems thinking'; for any individual change may be hard to sustain if the broader system that inhibited it stays the same. As people belong to many systems outside any particular learning experience this will impact on the extent to which they change.

Learning is about involving people in processes rather than transmitting data to them. Hardingham argues that in many cases the information required to underpin performance and learning can be condensed to a single A4 sheet, and most time in learning is spent on activity and discussion. This is not a waste of time; it all aids perception, attention and short-term memory and helps because people learn best when they are active, free to engage in activities, with lots of variety and challenge.

The two dominant families of theory in psychology are those formed, broadly, around the behaviourist and cognitive perspectives (Meier 2000). For behaviourists the principles and problems of HRD at work are the principles and problems of conditioning and reinforcing desired behaviours. Learning fails if the conditioning is not secured and transferred from the learning experience to subsequent behaviour. For those adopting a cognitive perspective, the principles and problems of HRD at work are those of managing and leading sense-making and information processing (Pinker 1997). Learning fails if it is not constructed to best fit with people's natural learning styles and harness their natural learning abilities.

Cognitive science attracts the most current attention, with books and research into the brain seeming the most productive and constructive basis for exploring learning. Cognitive science, the interdisciplinary scientific study of the mind, has been boosted by technologies that allow brain scanning, revealing aspects of the operation

---

6.3 | *Should learners take memory-enhancing pills?*

Repetition is 'the mother of all learning' as the brain must undergo a physical change in order to form the neural connections that create a structural basis for whatever people remember. Memory construction takes work. Researchers have identified a protein that helps nerve cells in the brain do this work, and store memories. Increase in the activity levels of the protein sends the memory making process into overdrive and makes long-lasting storage structures immediately, without the slow work of repetition.

This was first discovered while working with fruit flies. Researchers created two new, genetically altered strains of fruit fly: one with extremely high levels of memory protein and one with almost none of it. Then they conditioned the flies by placing them in tubes and blowing in scented air currents. One scent was like smelly shoes; the other smelled like liquorice and was accompanied by a small electric shock. A fly that is zapped every time it smells liquorice should eventually build a set of neural connections that says, 'Avoid liquorice!' The question was: How much repetition does it take for that long-term memory to form?

Researchers tested the flies by placing them in the middle of a double-ended tube and blowing smelly shoe scent in one end and liquorice scent in the other. Flies with normal levels of the memory protein needed to be zapped 10 times before they stopped moving toward the liquorice scent. The flies with an overabundance of memory protein formed long-term memory instantly. After only one trial, they knew to avoid liquorice for the rest of their lives.

The flies haven't got smarter; extra memory protein simply accelerates the pace of memorisation by eliminating the need for repetition. The pharmaceutical challenge is to find a compact chemical that can infiltrate neurons, stimulate an overproduction of the protein, and thereby give the human brain a hurry-up, neural-connection construction crew. This pop-a-pill enhancement is expected to last only a few hours before memory protein levels return to normal, but while levels are up, people would be like the one-zap flies, with supercharged memory-making.

But perhaps the reason evolution made repetition the mother of learning is that repetition ensures that you remember only what you try to remember. With these pills the minutiae that flitted lightly once through your short-term memory might lodge in your brain for ever, like it or not.

Source Weed 2000.

of the brain which permit analysis. More broadly though, cognitive science practice and knowledge derive from those of the primary contributing disciplines, which are computer science, linguistics, neuroscience, psychology, cognitive neuropsychology and philosophy (Thagrad 1996). Cognitive scientists aim to construct causal accounts by linking three levels: behavioural, cognitive and biological.

To study HRD is to encounter, if only briefly and superficially, an analysis of the biology of the brain and mind and brain-friendly learning (see Resources Box 6.3). The rationale of cognitive science is that the human brain, the seat of learning, can best be understood in terms of representational structures in the brain and the computational procedures that operate on those structures. The brain is a machine for creating and using representational structures in the form of logical propositions, rules, concepts, images and analogies. It uses procedures on these such as deduction, search, matching, rotating and retrieval. The cells of the brain, the neurons, embody these representations and enable such computation.

6.3 | Brain-friendly learning

- The brain is 'plastic' across its lifespan; people are naturally able to learn and re-learn.
- Learning is achieved best with all five senses engaged.
- Learning takes time, as it involves a balance of input and accommodation/assimilation (reflecting on feedback) and output (practice).
- Emotional well-being is essential for learning; high challenge stimulates learning, but high anxiety impedes it.

Cognitive archaeology (Mithen 1996) uses the evidence of artefacts to explore what was going on in the minds of early humans. The critical point is the change from hunter-gatherer to people capable of producing the sudden burst of art, technology and religion that occurred around 30 000 years ago. The archaeological record shows an increase in brain size, but it is not just about the brain getting bigger. It is not the increase in brain size that explains the change. The brain behaves like a parallel processor, doing many things simultaneously. But critics of cognitive science have gone further and have questioned the whole notion that the human mind, consciousness and sentience can be explained and mapped in terms of the representation and computation functions of the brain. They argue that cognitive science neglects the role of emotion in human consciousness, and makes the functioning of the brain, and therefore the learning associated with it, something cold and calculated. Cognitive science disregards the 'messiness' of human consciousness, and the way that what people think and feel are always enacted in social contexts. Indeed some argue that the origins of the human lie in the demands being made on social intelligence because of living in large groups, and an increase in brain size and the development of the mind enabled cunning and alliances, deceptions and friendships to be managed consciously. These were the foundations of the modern mind.

We can accommodate such concerns in our thinking and theorising about the brain and its properties by viewing cognitive functions, including learning, in the context of evolution. This involves drawing upon explanations of the brain and its properties that are couched in terms of evolutionary psychology. It proposes that people's propensities and abilities, including the ability to learn, evolved to solve the problems of our hunter-gatherer ancestors. This approach allows for a role for emotion in such an analysis, an area previously excluded from thinking about learning.

This is important, as thoughts on emotional intelligence, which we discussed in chapter 3, suggest that the emotions are the executive governors of the brain and mind; that reason is the 'slave of the passions'. There are diverse theories of emotion, but here we are interested in cognitive accounts of how the mind works. These combine the two big theories – the computational theory of the functioning of the brain and evolutionary theory of the behaviour of the species – to provide an account of why emotion features in so many aspects of human behaviour.

The recent capacity to scan and view brain activity has opened up the exploration of brain structure and function. The brain is viewed as a precision instrument that allows people to use information to solve the problems presented by their lifestyle: it is this cognition machine that underpins human success at the top of the evolutionary ladder. The human brain is large in comparison with those of all other animals. It is not just bigger; specific areas of the brain are highly developed and specialised for specific cognitive tasks, but seem to act in unison on even the simplest of tasks.

Exploiting information to sustain the 'camping trip that never ended' was the challenge of the lifestyle of all our original ancestor foragers. Early humans could use the fast, effective processing of information to outsmart competitors who might endanger them, and to work out how to exploit nature for their own ends. This meant that human populations could grow and prosper.

The heart of the analysis is the importance and value of information, and therefore the value of developing symbol systems to capture and use information. The value of information is that its possession helps with making a choice among the gambles involved in each and every move a person makes. The more and the better information people have, the less the risk they will have to take. If this is true, then it is worth 'paying' for information, and being able to handle symbols and meaning that enable quick and complex information processing, to lessen these risks and reduce the gamble. The benefits for the organism outweigh the costs.

The costs of this information-processing capacity for the organism are the resources needed to develop and maintain the sense system it requires and the need to learn symbol systems – the resources required for the brain and consciousness. These costs are varied and considerable. They include females having to cope with long pregnancies, and the risks of giving birth to babies with large skulls. They also include the young being exposed to a prolonged period of dependence in development through to maturity and competence. The mechanics of data representation in people's heads takes the form of visual, phonological and grammatical data transformed into modes of inscription in the neural networks of the brain. Neural networks act to enable cognition based on set symbols being manipulated by basic rules and procedures.

The empiricist model of the brain asserts that nurturing determines what is imprinted on the blank slate of the brain; thus culture is the most powerful force in forming the mind. This kind of computational theory asserts, rather, that there is hard wiring in the brain selected, through evolution, for obtaining and handling information. The brain is not an empty slate. This hard-wiring was formed from people's evolution of stereoscopic vision, bipedal walking (which freed the hands for using tools), group living, and hunting (which required coalitions and reciprocity among the group). The view that the brain is pre-wired and not a blank slate is a classic rationalist view. In the contemporary human environment, with the lifestyle challenges and risks it involves, the original hard-wired elements of the human brain that determine its functions and structures remain the same, but the context and the goals of intelligent behaviour are now different. Evolutionary theory implies that the brain and mind, and the use of learning in their operations, are ultimately to be judged in terms of how they help in the survival and replication of the species.

For analysts, the analogy of hard-wiring leads to the conclusion that the emotions are mechanisms that set the brain's highest-level goals. Exploring emotions, scientifically, as drives to deploy the intellect in pursuit of certain goals brackets any judgements about whether they are good or bad. They have the function of keeping people in tune with their environment, and the risks and opportunities it presents, at all times. Most evidently this is seen to be true at critical points of fight, flight and reproduction. In a scientific sense their function is to help people secure the cooperation of others in all these contexts while pursuing their individual interests and goals.

The social theory context

The dominance of psychological theory, in behaviourist or cognitivist form, can often seem to be the beginning and end of theory in HRD. But other streams of theory do exist which are equally important for appreciating and analysing HRD challenges and issues at work (Brown et al 1989, Lave and Wenger 1991, Boud and Garrick 1999, Hager 1999). There is a considerable amount of social science theory related to and relevant for understanding learning and HRD at work. This is not surprising, given that the natural way in which HRD at work has been organised for most of human history has not been in the form of professional mediated systems grounded in psychological, validated methods and models of the brain. It has been in the context of human relationships and cultures, predominantly forms of apprenticeship. What worked or did not work was embedded in the success or otherwise of these relations and their institutional features. The key features of apprenticeship in the age of more organic social relations, with stable close ties in small communities, was that it involved an individual in a community system. The learner was totally immersed in learning with a master and mentor. The context for the HRD process which this entailed – for a master to structure and supervise learning constantly and then require the person to make their own way as their own master – is an archetypal one. Much modern HRD has displaced this system or rendered it obsolete. Or it may only be that it has rendered it less visible. In the age of large employers and industrial organisation and institutional systems, the apprenticeship altered and changed. With the decline of that manufacturing-based context, in many areas the apprenticeship systems changed again. With changing work and organisation profiles, learning is still often 'situated' in social contexts, in financial, creative and service contexts as well as manufacturing. It provides a context and role for social theory and theorising to investigate how and why HRD at work succeeds or produces discontents.

The archetypal social system of apprenticeships has been largely replaced by a system based on distinctive and sustained periods and kinds of formal schooling and higher and further education. That entails one form of social context. Alongside this, occupational development and much of HRD still occurred in the workplace. The learning that happened outside the classroom and formal learning involves learning in these social contexts. In that latter context learning from and learning in what can be called communities of practice (CoPs) is central. CoPs will be explored in more detail in chapter 13. Briefly, the role of CoPs is to manage learning that existing practitioners possess, which enables them to achieve their performance outcomes. Often this is not codified or clearly articulated (Brown and Duguid 1991). It is not found in textbooks, and might not even be found in formal preparatory training; it is knowledge only found 'on the job'. CoPs are the networks of people in an occupation or an organisation who are consciously sharing and supporting each other's learning through experience.

Entry to such communities of practice, and the learning in the workplace that they can provide, is neither automatic nor easy. It may involve rites of entry to attain a status of 'belonging' at the equivalent of an 'apprenticeship' level. This enables what has been termed legitimate peripheral participation: in other words, a learner has earned the right to be among practitioners and learn from them. For many students, getting work placements is a form of legitimate peripheral participation. Once a person is a member of such a community of practice they need to be alert to the way that learning is shared; situated learning is managed through personal relationships, and through people telling and sharing stories. It is this, rather than reading textbooks, that is the key to HRD at work.

Understanding the principles and problems of making sense of and managing HRD is therefore bound up with theory about social relationships and the institutional contexts of learning, both formal and informal. The adoption of social science theory in HRD is necessary to illuminate and explore this. The social theory stream highlights that people and their behaviour are the products of social situations and contexts. For learning, people may need to be immersed in social relations that they may find amenable or may be alienated from even approaching. They may be involved in or excluded from communities of practice. The principles and problems of HRD are those of having effective relationships in formal learning settings or within those communities of practice, whether they be found in work or within special education and training institutions. The quality of access to, and relationships within, a community of practice can determine how effective learning will be. To be excluded from these communities of practice is to be excluded from effective HRD. To be part of a thriving community of practice is to access the best HRD possible.

Economic theory context

As well as the psychology and the social relations concerns there are also forms of economic theory which can be drawn upon to understand and make sense of HRD (Chapman 1993, Machin and Vignoles 2001). Here the problems and decisions associated with HRD at work are investigated within a context of economic models and theories. There is, for example, the problem that there can be shortfalls in training provision, resulting in skills shortages which in turn affect economic performance and growth. One recent case, widely reported, was a situation in train-operating companies which had arisen because many people wanted to be managers and few wanted to be train drivers. Consequently any managerial job in a train-operating company received many applicants, but there were not enough staff to actually run the trains. This represents a problem in labour market relations, and can be theorised as such. Such skill shortages represent a form of market failure. How these market failures can be addressed by governments, firms and individuals will depend on the theoretical position adopted, the answer to 'why' is this failure occurring?

There is often a primary concern in economic sense-making about HRD with large-scale policy implications, and with arguments over interventions by governments, to help make HRD pay The possible economic benefits of HRD are threefold:

- to the individual in terms of higher wages and better job prospects;
- to the firm in terms of increased productivity and profitability;
- to the economy as a whole in terms of higher economic growth and other benefits to society.

However, there is a lack of data and evidence to back up claims that 'HRD pays' from an economist's perspective in any of these respects. One important gap in the literature currently is that little is known about the cost side of the HRD equation. Information on identifying the benefits of training is merely the first step in calculating the overall private (and social) return from training investment. The research community is interested in obtaining better measures of training. For instance, data must differentiate more effectively between the different types of employer-provided training. Such primary research should be able to say considerably more than just 'training pays'. It should be possible to tell individuals, firms and policy-makers which types of training yield what levels of private and social returns. This area of HRD will be discussed in more detail in chapter 12 on government policy. For firms these conceptual and theoretical concerns increasingly involve a discussion of human and intellectual capital (see Strategic View Box 6.3).

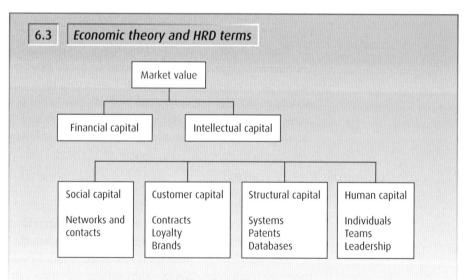

6.3 *Economic theory and HRD terms*

New models of enterprises and how they create value raise the concept of 'intellectual capital'. Instead of seeking to define value in terms of short-term profits, and identifying gaps between balance-sheet values and market valuations, there is a concern with the 'intangible assets'. Traditional accounting systems are challenged to find ways of describing ands valuing intellectual capital as an asset of the organisation. Increasing intellectual capital, through learning rather than cost cutting or the introduction of new technologies, becomes a strategic imperative. The growth of intellectual capital, in theory, depends upon HRD in practice.

Source Based on Mayo 2000

New models of enterprises and how they create value have led to the development of the idea of intellectual capital. Instead of defining value in terms of short-term profits, and seeking to identify gaps between balance-sheet values and market valuation, there is a concern with the intangible assets. Traditional accounting systems are challenged to find ways of describing and valuing intellectual capital as an asset of the organisation.

Some argue that, to date, HRD at work has received relatively little attention from economists, and what attention there was has been subsumed in general discussions of broader industrial policy or industrial relations. There are different economic approaches to analysing HRD at work that could be better explored as the bases for policy. The first is the market failure approach, explaining shortfalls in training provision and highlighting several areas of fact, for example, the participation of young people. There has been an increase in some forms of training (such as job-related in the 1980s), but there is a bias to academic achievement not vocational training, as seen in the expansion of higher education. Large numbers of people receive no training, or only enough for low-level qualifications.

The lack of training happens because, at existing costs, individuals cannot afford training they would otherwise undertake. There is also the 'free rider' problem: firms fail to train because they fear poaching. There are contract restrictions: employers and employees ideally need continual re-contracting to reflect changes in value, but this works against the advantages of fixed wages. Market failure as a consequence of these factors explains the dominant fact – the under-provision of HRD. It implies that interventions in markets will be the remedy, and cooperation among various stakeholders is required for such a solution.

Another economic theory that has influenced theory framework is human capital theory, developed in the 1960s. Earnings follow a lifecycle pattern, first rising to a maximum and then declining. This is because wages are determined by human capital, which depends on education, training and job experience as attainment in these leads to higher productivity. Individuals with higher skill levels may be rewarded with higher wages in recognition of their superior productivity. So human capital acquisition through training and education is an investment decision. In the 1960s this purported to explain why the nations defeated in the Second World War recovered so spectacularly; the significant factor was human capital, not physical capital. It also explained the developing countries' trap: they need human capital aid, not physical aid, and, in addition, it explained lifecycles of earnings: low for the young, increasing, and then declining.

The concept of human capital also emerged around an argument that individuals and firms can be seen as wealth maximisers who calculate the value of different training options and believe that whoever benefits from training should pay for it. In this context, training is to be defined as either 'general and portable' or 'specific and non-transferable'. In general and portable training there is an increase in trained persons' marginal productivity by the same amount for any firm. This benefits workers, through higher earnings for them as more skilled and productive people. Because they benefit, they should pay for the training. With specific and non-transferable training there is a productivity increase of use only to the host firm. The firm acquires the gains from the training, so it should meet the costs.

One implication of this approach was that externalities impeded the operation of a rational system in HRD. Individuals could not get the resources to increase their human capital as capital markets did not give credit for training. Further, inter-firm factors applied. Using the prisoners' dilemma model and game theory, a situation could be seen where firms should invest in training to increase human capital, but fear doing so. They think they will lose that investment as people move out of the organisation. They, as firms, therefore pursue sub-optimal strategies, collectively losing out.

Finally, the institutional school of economic theory sees differences in HRD being explained by the emphasis on external or internal labour market forces: HRD will be carried out within the firm where recruitment is limited to certain ports of entry. For occupational labour markets, wages are set by market supply and demand, so wages will be equalised across firms because of mobility. But, once hired, the internal labour market becomes paramount: progress to different skill levels, and inter-firm differences in this respect, mean that wages vary, reducing mobility. Firms seek to buy in cheap at certain levels, develop specific skills through learning by doing, and then protect their internal market against poaching.

A deeper approach for organising theory in HRD

There are a number of ways of organising ideas about theory in social science generally and the study of management in particular. One approach is to distinguish between positivist forms, phenomenological forms and reflexive forms (Gill and Johnson 1991, Easterby-Smith et al 1992, Hammersley and Atkinson 1992) (see Theory & Research Box 6.4).

In a positivist approach, theory is prospective; it is established a priori, and determines the ultimate outcome with hypotheses and theory either being confirmed or disconfirmed. The status of any hypothesis or theory is linked to the confidence with which procedures have been followed, and the degree to which results stand up to further testing/retesting. A good prospective theory is one that enables testing and leads to a causal evaluation of a body of data.

6.4 *Approaches to theory building*	Positivist theory building	Phenomenonological theory building	Reflexive theory building
Origins in relation to research practice	A priori hypotheses	Final stage explanations	Developed throughout
Typical form	Causal statements based on quantified data	Case studies	Necessary core and reasons for variations Variety of data sources
Status	Procedures and testing determine validity and reliability	Fidelity to the subject in its natural setting determines validity and reliability	Fidelity and testing
Approaches	Positivism	Naturalism/ Phenomenology	Analytical induction Action research

| 6.5 | Scope and generality theory |

		SCOPE	
		Micro	**Macro**
GENERALITY	**Formal**	Micro-formal General forms of social organisation (e.g. Goffman, presentation of self)	Macro-formal Structure, function and development of workplace HRD in general
	Substantive	Micro-substantive Study of organisations or situations (e.g. Trainer–learner interaction)	Macro-substantive Study of particular workplaces

Source Based on Hammersley and Atkinson, pp. 204–6.

In a naturalist approach, theory is retrospective; it is established through research, and is only complete when the research process is complete. Theory gives an explanation of the qualitative data collected. The status of any theory here is linked to the plausibility with which it offers a plausible account of such data. A good retrospective theory is one that exhausts the data collected and leads to an accomplished account of actors' subjectivity.

The third option is reflexive theory, which is neither purely prospective or retrospective. That means it is neither solely produced prior to nor after data collection; it develops as data is collected. Its status is neither linked solely to procedures or the 'completeness' of the analysis of qualitative data; it can be evaluated in relation to the logic of the experiment, observations and tests, but deals with qualitative data. A good reflexive theory will not struggle to justify itself in terms of how detached the researcher has been from the data. Such an approach can be associated historically with 'analytical induction' explored by Hammersley and Atkinson (op cit).

Reflexivity makes sense if it is accepted that researchers are part of the social world they study, and that no ontologically privileged stance is available in any research tradition. Researchers rely on working with common sense knowledge, and methods are simply a refinement of everyday human skills and capacities. Their research has an impact on their subjects.

There are also influences on theory at different levels of generality and scope (see Theory & Research Box 6.5), informing theory, emerging from different conceptions of the purpose of HRD at work and the focus of learning. Yang (2004) identifies both a spectrum of purpose for adult learning, ranging from a concern with performance to a concern with human potential and a spectrum of focus for adult learning ranging from an individual focus to a social focus. This allows him to map the following kinds of philosophical approaches to understanding learning and learning theory:

Performance purpose/Individual focus	=	Behaviourism
Performance purpose/Social focus	=	Human capitalism
Human potential purpose/Individual focus	=	Humanism
Human potential purpose/Social focus	=	Radicalism

There are also versions of philosophical approaches with implications for learning which he calls 'liberalism' and 'progressivism'. These are more centred, and less at the extremes of purpose of focus.

For Yang (2004) behaviourism assumes that the purpose of learning and development is to produce behavioural change in the desired direction in order to increase performance. Humanism assumes the purpose of learning and development are to facilitate a self-actualised, autonomous person. Liberalism values learning and development centred on knowledge gained in and from official institutions and sources such as texts and universities, while progressivism favours learning and development grounded in experience and unofficial sources because this is linked ultimately to social well-being. Human capitalism assumes that learning and development are required to increase returns on investments, improving organisational performance. Radicalism sees learning and development as potentially challenging the status quo, and critiques learning and development practices reinforcing the status quo and constraining the development of people's potential. The radicalist approach sees that existing systems tend to privilege a few, and over-value performance concerns at the expense of social responsibility (Yang 2004).

The various ways of sense-making exist and coalesce around these concepts because they are a 'package' of answers to fundamental questions which would otherwise preoccupy people:

- **Ontology**: what is the basic nature of reality? In the case of HRD, for example, what exactly are the material bases of cognitive capacities, capabilities and the affective side?
- **Epistemology**: how do I know what is true? In the case of HRD, for example, how do we determine which of many competing interpretations of what constitutes effective learning do we invest in?
- **Ethics**: what should I do? In the case of HRD, for example, what is right and what is wrong, what is considerate and responsible, when it comes to investing in and managing HRD?

We cannot choose to avoid these kinds of question, either because of the desire to be atheoretical or the desire to be scientific. Given the breadth of theory available around HRD processes there is, in some respects, an embarrassment of riches, or a bewildering array of theories to take into account. Theories can offer a wider spectrum view on these questions, making issues visible around effective adult learning because they use methods consistent with the principles needed to engage people with and achieve deep learning. These learning theories can be of use for exploring and explaining all aspects of HRD at work, from developing standard knowledge, based on insights from brain-friendly learning, to helping manage the change of the whole person in the context of occupation and performance. They can inform the design of learning systems and interventions. They can provide insights and guidance on issues of motivation and environment: how to diagnose problems to get results, and how to analyse problems with learning transfer. These theories are all ways of exploring how people learn that can be related to the better management of learning, either by informing the work of specialists supporting learning, or by providing insights for learners into what they can do to learn how to learn.

Conclusion

Theories are like torches for enlightenment, but too much illumination can itself interfere with seeing clearly or even be blinding. This overview has sought to avoid that. We began by considering how and why the HRD process can be investigated and shown to work well in principle, or face problems. HRD decision-making that is based on principles and theory can be better than that which is based on myth or doctrine. We proceeded to look at different contexts for theory, and the wisdom, psychology, social studies and economic literature all offer something in the study of learning. We moved beyond these to a deeper level of underlying philosophies that can inform sense-making in and about HRD theory. When exploring learning we are involved in some way in expressing and working with these philosophies. And when researchers from various social sciences are drawn to study HRD at work, and attempt to apply their theories to exploring topics in HRD at work, they too are expressing and working with them.

Learning about theories of HRD is then not only about knowing the different things that different schools of psychology say about learning and how that can be applied to practice. It is about developing a frame of mind for thinking about the HRD process and the practices it generates and supports; the purposes and the focus of learning. Insights from psychology, social studies and economics can help, as indeed can the wisdom literature. They matter for effectiveness in designing HRD interventions that draw upon appropriate learning methods with an understanding of their strengths and weaknesses. They matter for managers when diagnosing problems with implementing HRD systems in organisations. And they matter for government and others when it is necessary to critically evaluate the application of innovative solutions to HRD demands, such as introducing e-learning.

Multiple-choice questions

6.1 Which of the following are acceptable theories of learning?
  A. Music can be used in classrooms to create environments that enable more effective learning.
  B. There is a memory protein that can be increased and which will result in a reduction of the repetitions needed to embed learning through memorisation.
  C. Most kinds of informal learning partnership between people at work can be considered as kinds of mentoring.
  D. Gender can have a significant influence on a person's participation in learning activities.

6.2 Which of the following are concerns in learning theory?
  A. To examine the reasons why people who appear to be capable fail to engage with learning.
  B. To provide insights from a range of social science disciplines that can help to influence practice.
  C. To critically evaluate the claims of proponents of learning systems and products.
  D. To influence government spending on education and training.

References

Argyris, C. (1994) *On Organizational Learning*, Cambridge, MA, Blackwell.

Bacharach, S.B. (1989) 'Organizational theories; some criteria for evaluation', *Academy of Management*, vol.14 , no. 4, pp. 496–515.

Boud, D. and Garrick, J. (1999) *Understanding Learning At Work*, London, Routledge.

Brown, J.S., Collins, A. and Duguid, P. (1989) 'Situated cognition and the culture of learning', *Education Researcher*, vol. 8, no. 1, 32–42.

Brown, J. and Duguid, P. (1991) 'Organizational learning and communities-of-practice: Towards a unified view of working, learning, and innovation', http://www2.parc.com/ops/members/brown/papers/orglearning.html

Chapman, P. (1993) *The Economics of Training*, London, Harvester Wheatsheaf.

Coffield, F., Moseley, D., Hall, E. and Ecclestone, K. (2004) *Should We Be Using Learning Styles? What Research Has to Say to Practice*, London: Learning and Skills Research Centre.

Easterby-Smith, M. et al (1992) *Management Research*, London, Sage.

Entwistle, N., Thompson, S. and Tait, H. (1992) *Guidelines for Promoting Effective Learning in Higher Education*, Edinburgh, Centre for Research on Learning and Instruction.

Gill, J. and Johnson, P. (1991) *Research Methods For Managers*, Paul Chapman Publishing.

Garger, E. (1999) 'Goodbye Training, Hello Learning', *Workforce*, vol. 78 , no. 11.

Hager, P. (1999) 'Finding a good theory of workplace learning', in D. Boud and J. Garrick (1999) *Understanding Learning At Work*, London, Routledge.

Hardingham, A. (2000) *Psychology For Trainers*, London, CIPD.

Hammersley, M. and Atkinson, P. (1992) *Ethnography: Principles In Practice*, London, Routledge.

Lave, J. and Wenger, E. (1991) *Situated Learning: Legitimate peripheral participation*, Cambridge, Cambridge University Press.

Machin, S. and Vignoles, A. (2001) *The Economic Benefits of Training to the Individual, the Firm and the Economy: The key issues*, Centre for the Economics of Education, London School of Economics.

Mager, R. (2000) *What every Manager Should Know about Training*, Chalford, Management Books.

Mayo, A. (2000) 'The role of employee development in the growth of intellectual capital', *Personnel Review*, vol. 29, no. 4, pp. 521–33.

Meier, D. (2000) *The Accelerated Learning Handbook*, New York, McGraw-Hill.

Mithen, S. (1996) *The Prehistory of Mind*, London, Thames & Hudson.

Norman, D. (1982) *Learning And Memory*, San Francisco, W.H. Freeman.

Pawson, R., Greenhalgh, T., Harvey, G. and Walshe, K. (2004) 'Realist Synthesis: An introduction, ESRC Research Methods Programme', RMP Methods Paper 2/2004.

Pinker, S. (1997) *How The Mind Works*, London, Penguin.

Riding, R. (1996) *Learning Styles and Technology Based Training*, London, DfEE.

Rogers, C. (1969) *Freedom to Learn*, Columbus, Charles E Merrill.

Schon, D.A. (1987) *Educating the Reflective Practitioner*, San Francisco: Jossey-Bass.

Storberg-Walker, J. (2003) 'Comparison of the Dubin, Lynham, and Van de Ven Theory-Building Research Methods and Implications for HRD', *Human Resource Development Review*, vol. 2, no. 2, pp. 211–22.

Thagrad, P. (1996) *Mind: Introduction to cognitive science*, Cambridge, MA, MIT Press.

Weed, W. (2000) 'How about a little Viagra for your memory?', *Discover*, June, p. 82.

Van de Ven, A.H. (1989) 'Nothing is quite so practical as a good theory', *Academy of Management*, vol. 14 , no. 4, pp 486–9.

Yang, B. (2004) 'Can adult learning theory provide a foundation for human resource development?', *Advances in Developing Human Resources*, vol. 6, no. 2, pp. 129–45.

Q

Read the following case and the 14 focal areas that were the heart of the HRD provided. First, considering those 14 tips, identify which form of wisdom, psychological, social or economic theory might have justified the inclusion of the focal areas in the accompanying grid (Case Figure 1). And what is the underlying 'philosophy' you can see, in Yang's terms, at work here? My analysis is given for comparison as Case Figure 2.

Case

A leading retailer, RetailCo, was continuing to experience difficulties in competing to retain its leading position. It decided to use some HRD on sending up to 56,000 staff on a £10 million initiative in retail motivation training. This is a day-long training session run by a motivational guru. Staff from stores attend the event, which is held at a major exhibition venue, in groups of 5000. Each store group is led by team leaders, and the stores should vie with each other to show team spirit at the event. They are advised that they can dress unusually, or in football strips, and take mascots with them representing their store and part of the country.

Each day session will begin with a psychological self assessment; starting with assessing people's good points (fun to be around, brave and determined) and then their bad points (don't care attitude, moody and negative). This is followed by tips on how to treat customers. Successful sales people operate in a 'can do' circle, and avoid the circle of apathy and indecision. They are given other advice like 'when a customer approaches disengage courteously if talking with a colleague'. The staff then leave with a list of reminders, including a fake dollar bill with 'Don't pass the buck – take ownership and responsibility', a gold starfish and an ace of spades card; along with a pocket-sized plastic card reminding them of key slogans. The top 14 tips they were given during their HRD were:

1. Life can be thought about in three concentric circles (see Figure 6.4); an inner circle is what you can control; the next is what you can influence but cannot control; the third is what is outside your control. Work on things in circles one and two which you can do and control or influence.

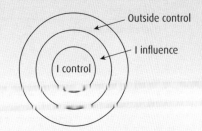

Figure 6.4 The concentric circles of influence model

2. Even in situations where you have no control over events you can still choose your reaction.
3. Communicate what can be done in an upbeat, courteous, confident language – you and the customer will feel better.
4. It's natural to bitch and complain and feel sorry for yourself. The key is how quickly you snap out of it.
5. Be a 'can do', solution-oriented person.
6. Good attitudes involve listening deeply, being gracious and empathetic, communicating clearly and being assertive.
7. Bad attitudes are being problem-oriented, interrupting, rude, vague, passive or aggressive, defensive and withdrawn.
8. A compelling vision, mission or sense of purpose is a vital first step to ensuring motivation to achieve goals.
9. If a mission is overly complex and without spirit it will just be ignored.
10. People do not leave organisations, they leave managers.
11. Customer service is about people helping people competently, genuinely and enthusiastically.
12. Be optimistic rather than resigned and pessimistic. Optimism fuels motivation, stamina and creativity.
13. Adopt an open and positive stance towards criticism. See it as a gateway to improved relationships.
14. Look after your self esteem, it provides you with the confidence and desire to make the difference.

continued overleaf

concluding case continued

Focus for HRD	Psychology, social, economic concerns	Theory issues
Know concentric circles		
Choose reactions		
Be upbeat		
'Snap out of it'		
Can do outlook		
Good attitudes to be supported		
Bad attitudes to be eliminated		
Vision		
Keep it simple		
People leave managers		
Helping is good		
Optimistic		
Take feedback		
Self esteem		
Overall conclusions		

Case Figure 1 14 case study focal areas and tips assessment grid

concluding case answer

Focus for HRD	Psychology, social, economic concerns	Theory issues
Know concentric circles	Cognitivist	Visualise a map of the world, and share it through a powerful image
Choose reactions	Behaviourist	You are in control of conditioning yourself – behave that way and it will be so
Be upbeat	Humanist	'Feeling better' is an intention or purpose that a humanist would endorse
'Snap out of it'	Behaviourist?	To be the idealised, always smiling clone?
Can do outlook	All	This is a combination of them all: we condone such behaviour, we name it with this cliché, we encourage it is a mental map goal (change from 'no can do'), and seek for all to work to a culture based on this
Good attitudes to be supported Bad attitudes to be eliminated	Cognitivist	Diagnosis of issues as being rooted in attitudes, and some dissonance needed so that prevailing structures are upset and a new shift to the positive is encouraged (which might open up onto some humanist issues)
Vision	Cognitivist	Highlighting of context of understanding, not just routine behaviours
Keep it simple	Cognitivist	Basic and a humanist (spirit) twist
People leave managers	Social	Social context and relations matters
Helping is good	Humanist	Issue is authenticity, leading to humanist ideals and connecting with those
Optimistic	Cognitivist	A state of mind as the foundation of behaviour
Take feedback	Cognitivist	Getting and using maximum information, not just responding to rewards and punishments
Self esteem	Cognitivist/Humanist	The Holy Grail of the cognitivist/humanist enterprise is high and secure self esteem, on which all else depends

The way I have perceived this is to emphasise its psychological principles, rooted in cognitive science, with some blending of behaviourism and a touch of the social; with an avowed humanistic philosophical tone and spirit to it. Of course this is being done for pragmatic and economic reasons, to drive up sales, but the design and delivery illustrates how theories can be seen to be behind, and perhaps explicitly informing, the management of this HRD.

Case Figure 2 Completed focal areas assessment grid

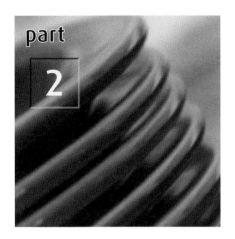

part

2

Practices

A practice is simply a form in which HRD at work is actually managed, the methods and activities that people in organisations develop and use to make workplace HRD happen. A comprehensive review of each and every practice, method and activity involved in HRD is not the purpose of this section; that would give breadth, but little depth. Instead, to structure the discussion of HRD practice in contemporary organisations, the approach taken here is to describe and review a representative range of practices. This allows for coverage of contemporary content, what is done in practice. It also allows for an exploration of themes, what questions and issues arise in contemporary organisations in practice. These are not the only areas of practice involved in HRD at work. They are areas which can be emphasised to provide an introduction to contemporary practice. The four areas of practice covered here are:

HRD strategies	Organisations can and do use different strategies, different kinds of policy for achieving major goals, in managing HRD. These are described and analysed.
HRD partnerships	An important feature of HRD for many organisations is nurturing partnerships with coaches and mentors.
Working with groups	Along with partnerships the challenges of working with groups provides a key environment for practice.
Information and communication technologies	The evolution of e-learning, and the impact this is having on HRD practice, provides some of the greatest challenges facing HRD at work now and in the future.
HRDPOs	The growth of specialist organisations and institutions dedicated to providing HRD at work creates a fascinating area to explore.

This section aims to give a balanced review of what is involved in practice, and illustrate how practices can be analysed to explore their strengths and weaknesses.

HRD strategies:
systems, roles and outcomes

learning objectives

By the end of this chapter you will be able to:

- define what an HRD strategy is;
- describe three different HRD strategies – systematic training, performance oriented and continuous eevelopment;
- analyse the HRD process in the context of these strategies with reference to key systems, agents and outcomes;
- evaluate the strengths and weakness of these different HRD strategies;
- create an HRD strategy for an organisation.

Introductory case	Corporate universities

Many employers have established or are setting up corporate universities (CUs). These take a variety of forms. Some may be little more than revamped training departments, but others represent ambitions to coordinate learning and share knowledge across organisations in 'continuous development'. They are using the terminology of academia to describe and raise the status of corporate training and development. From the first instance in the UK of Unipart in 1993 there are now around 200 CUs in the UK. The uses of technology in learning and the 'war for talent' are cited as factors. One study estimated that there are over 1500 CUs worldwide. For some observers they are merely revamped training departments using academic terminology to raise status of HRD; to others they are attempts to coordinate learning and share knowledge.

Advocates of CUs characterise the typical training department as reactionary, fragmented, and decentralised, designed to serve a wide audience with an array of open enrolment programmes. The typical CU is intended, in contrast, to pull together all learning in an organisation by managing education as a business project. It has a senior head – either a dean or a chief learning officer – and clear goals, objectives, and long-term strategic plans. It shapes corporate culture by fostering leadership, creative thinking, and problem-solving. 'Strategic' is the key word. The CU provides strategically relevant learning solutions for each job family within a corporation. It aspires to create a strategic learning organisation that functions as the umbrella for a company's total education requirements – for all employees and the entire value chain, including customers and suppliers. With a corporate university, employees build individual and organisational competences, thereby improving the company's overall performance. These aspirations and intentions will be subject to much critical scrutiny in the future.

continued overleaf

A bank was considering setting up a corporate university, and undertook a study into its feasibility. It was felt that this would help mould the disparate training and development activities into a coherent programme. A corporate university would have to include all training and development platforms, including significant use of technology. To measure the success of this the bank wanted to move away from metrics based on the number of 'training days' delivered. A corporate university was a way of re-branding training and development activities, which were based on budget spend.

As companies cannot award their own qualifications, corporate universities often still link up with 'real' universities. The companies are involved more in HRD design and delivery, with the academics providing assessment. These relationships provide revenues for universities. But there are tensions – between the performance-driven learning imperatives of corporations, and the independence of thought and critical thinking required in academic communities. In the future will undergraduate and postgraduate programmes come to be influenced by organisations and their ways of providing HRD? Would standards increase or decrease if there was more corporate influence in this way? And will a reliance on these partnerships for revenue lead to problems of viability for universities, given the uncertainties of business development, where mergers or business failures might eliminate these sources of revenue?

Introduction

The ways in which organisations set about organizing their HRD is not a case of one form or size fits all (Allen 1994, Lynton and Pareek 2000). The diverse ways in which phenomena like CUs grow suggests that there are a number of factors at work, shaping how developments arise. Practices in HRD, the activities and actions associated with it, emerge from both formal planning and a culture which can be at a level of maturity (see Figure 7.1). The maturity levels range from formal planning and a culture which is, to all intents and purposes, apparently missing to HRD being a subject in the organisation which is in clear focus and which has a definite strategy associated with it. A strategy is a policy for action to achieve the overall and long term-vision and performance goals that the organisation has in the area, in this case in HRD.

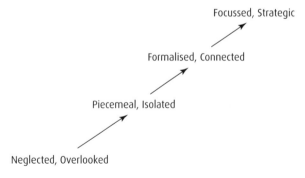

Figure 7.1 Maturity levels for an HRD strategy

Organisations and their practices can be located and analysed along this maturity continuum. The immature situation is one of neglect, sometimes found in smaller organisations or in units or parts of the workforce in larger organisations. Attending to

HRD leads to a higher level of maturity, with HRD eventually becoming an area of clear and strong focus.

The journey to being focused and having a clear strategy is motivated by a number of factors. First, in any organisation at any time there will be a wealth of both formal and/or informal practices and activities, occurring naturally or in managed ways. Strategic View Box 7.1 gives a spectrum of activities from the formal to the informal. In seeking to manage the many and myriad formal and informal practices that may be used for HRD in organisations there appear to be patterns of usage. These can be outlined and explored as different features of HRD strategy. Knowing these and what they involve can help to frame the theoretical and practical challenges of promoting and evolving successful HRD in organisations.

7.1	*Formal–informal learning continuum*
Informal ↑	Unanticipated experiences and encounters that result in learning as an incidental byproduct, which may or may not be consciously recognised
	New job assignments and participation in teams, or other job-related challenges that are used for learning and self-development
	Self-initiated and self-planned experiences – including the use of media (print, etc), seeking out a tutor, coach or mentor, attending conferences, travel, consulting
	Total quality groups/action learning or other vehicles designed to promote continuous learning for continuous improvement
	Planning a framework for learning which is often associated with career plans, training and development plans or performance evaluations
	Combination of less organised experiences with structured opportunities, which may be facilitated, to examine and learn from those experiences
	Designed programmes of mentoring and/or coaching or on-the-job training
	Just-in-time courses, delivered as classes or through self-learning packages, with or without the use of technology
	Formal training courses
Formal ↓	Formal programmes leading to some official qualification

Source Stern and Sommerlad 1999

The desire to have a mature strategic focus must accommodate a range of practices together. Policies for achieving HRD at work may embody the same intention to professionally manage the process, but take different forms in practice.

Second, Mayo proposes a framework to move beyond a narrow view of HRD strategy (see Figure 7.2). This suggests that as well appreciating the formal-informal spectrum, what being 'focused and strategic' about HRD means will involve variation in three kinds of factor; the organisations core competencies, values and mission. Appreciating variations in these can help clarify and articulate issues about the purpose of an HRD strategy, for various audiences. These communication purposes may be around planning, consulting, communicating or prioritising options for HRD practices in the organisation. The audiences of interest may be strategic (senior managers), operational (line managers and users of HRD) or external (regulatory and other agencies).

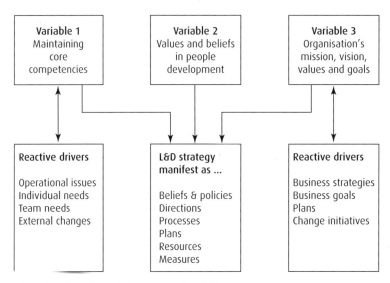

Figure 7.2 Adapted version of Mayo's framework of variables
Source Mayo 2001

Following the Mayo framework a standard format for working up an HRD strategy in an organisation can be suggested:

- Articulate a commitment to people development;
- Identify how organisational goals link to HRD;
- Have goals for HRD itself;
- Identify priority activities;
- Define roles and responsibilities;
- Define measurements of success and performance.

It is common for an integrated policy and practices document to exist in an organisation outlining these matters. It is a useful resource for identifying and exploring HRD strategy. However, there is more to exploring strategy than adopting such generic good practice in defining a strategy. As in the world of strategy as a whole, it is possible to identify and pursue distinctive value propositions and specific strategies. Supermarkets, for example, compete on the basis of different value propositions: from the cheapest with discounts and limited lines to the higher end, expensive, with prestigious brands. Their templates for strategy development might be similar, but the content of their strategies is very different. So it can be with HRD; organisations may talk about the same general areas, but the content can follow different patterns in many cases. Producing an HRD strategy does not, or should not, lead to an 'identi-kit' statement and policy.

In part the difference will be a consequence of variations, as Mayo notes, in core competence, values and mission in organisations. In part it may also reflect how stakeholders, including HRD professionals, identify with different perceptions of their roles. Strategic View Box 7.2 gives a sixfold classification of underlying value propositions and purpose.

It would be misleading to rank or otherwise judge these different identity value propositions. The point is to understand that they can shape the way HRD strategy

---

7.2 | *Identity and value propositions in HRD strategy*

- **Building learning systems** where HRD is focused on transforming or building organisations into learning systems in order to learn and apply that learning more quickly, thereby helping with change processes
- **Establishing meaningful work** where HRD is focused on helping individuals to create work that is meaningful to a sense of self and spiritually energising, fulfilling important 'inner needs'
- **Providing individual learning** is a focus on individual learning experiences that build work-related expertise, increasing work skills and behaviour
- **Building socially responsible organisations** is focused on building organisations which are socially responsible and contributing to the good of the community, contributing to a larger social and ecological good beyond organisational goals
- **Improving organisational performance** has its focus on meeting organisational goals and objectives
- **Improving individual job performance** focuses on work-related performance among individuals to meet or exceed demands at work

---

is voiced and developed in an organisation, and so used to explore the patterns arising and how they influence strategies. Working with a distinctive identity and value proposition may provide some coherence for a strategy that otherwise appears to be a complex 'mess' of practice and activity.

A final factor is to appreciate how HRD strategy is located within the broader business strategy. This involves important concepts and issues which merit detailed treatment in chapter 15 on strategic human resource development (SHRD). It is only necessary here to note that there are those who question if HRD is, or can be, a strategic-level issue in the purest sense; that is, an area of policy that requires consideration and decision-making by the most senior executives of an organisation. For some HRD is to be considered more as an ad hoc, contingent and 'downstream' activity in business, one which is of very little concern to an organisation's senior management team. That is why it does not often feature as a constituent part of business-level strategies. The activity of compiling annual training plans can be a focus for some senior team discussion about performance issues and HRD initiatives, but such training plans do not in themselves amount to developing strategic HRD. Some take a more positive view, arguing that HRD is as important an area of decision-making in the organisation as any other. Accordingly HRD plans should be developed reciprocally with business plans.

The options then for further elaboration are of seeing patterns in use arising from the demands of capturing the formal and informal at a good 'maturity level', producing clear statements and embodying definite identity and value proposition. The approach adopted here is to consider how these factors tend to cohere around three ideal types of HRD strategy, each of which involves more than just planning for the purposes of setting and managing budgets for HRD.

HRD strategies

The patterns seen in HRD strategies in this sense reflect the presence of and preferences for certain ways of approaching the activities of HRD. They will be described and analysed here as three different kinds of vision and value-based frameworks for problem-solving and decision-making. They have their foundations in distinctive approaches to basic features, including the kinds of analysis preferred, the particular agents involved, and the particular kinds of preferred outcome. They are:

- Systematic Training Strategy (STS)
- Performance Orientation Strategy (POS)
- Continuous Development Strategy (CDS)

These HRD strategies need to be appreciated and approached in context. One context is to view them as an evolutionary, chronological sequence with STS the first, POS following on and CDS more recently. The impetus for a new form of HRD strategy is disenchantment with a prevailing and dominant 'prescription' for HRD, and the problems that it seems to create with the quality and quantity of HRD in organisations. Often this takes the form of a crisis, usually attributed to insufficient investment in HRD, and concerns with its quality which prompt fresh thinking. There is an element of truth to this view. However if strategy evolution were primarily one of historical change we would expect to see the earlier forms of HRD strategy fading away: from STS to POS to CDS. This is not the case, as there is no clear or definitive replacement of one kind of strategy by another. The best comparative approach is to consider how they embody different preferences for the foundation on which HRD is to be based, the systemic things to which most attention is given, and the main agents (Operations Box 7.1).

operations

| 7.1 | **Comparative features of HRD strategies** |

HRD strategy	Foundation for HRD is...	Systemic things to get right are...	The main agents involved are...
Systematic Training Strategy	Job analysis	Formal course	Training professionals
Performance Orientation Strategy	Organisational objectives and performance	Incidents arising in performance	Managers
Continuous Development Strategy	Self-directed needs analysis	Coaching and mentoring	Learners themselves

Systematic Training Strategy

A Systematic Training Strategy (STS) is a coherent HRD strategy that can be identified and discussed. It is often still the option which is most striking in many contemporary organisations. The emphasis here is on attaining a high maturity level by being focused on being systematic rather than ad hoc and fragmented. In one sense, this is simply adopting a common-sense view. Yet it also reflects and is grounded in a broader outlook; of a scientific view of management and organisation. In essence this outlook assumes that there are right ways and wrong ways to manage practices, and these can be identified and directly controlled by expert authorities. This results in a control strategy in which the HRD practices are to be managed systematically by dedicated professionals. Just as management itself emerged to keep control of work in the hands of specially-trained expert managers, so HRD emerges as an area where control of learning is in the hands of specially-trained trainers.

This kind of strategy will also include being systematic, thorough and detailed in the formal assessment of needs by the an HRD expert. It will be most visible in the planning and organisation of formal on-job training and off-job courses by HRD experts. Off-job courses may be run either inside the organisation or by outside providers, but in either case the emphasis is on professional trainers and developers taking the leading role. Such courses are to be designed and delivered by training specialists. Training is to be formally evaluated by professionals or experts. The typical outcomes are validated by testing, and this is often recognised or accredited, leading to certification and the award of qualifications.

This approach to HRD strategy is commonplace and taken for granted. Its underlying assumptions and distinctiveness as a strategy are not often noticed. Critiques of it make this more apparent. They highlight how control through STS can encourage a bureaucratic approach to HRD that may produce a proliferation of substantial, formal training programmes, particularly off-job training programmes. Professionalism and expertise in HRD become professionalism and expertise in training course design and delivery. This emphasis on specialists designing and implementing training programmes and evaluating these programmes means that the whole HRD process is 'owned and controlled' by specialist trainers. This can become a concern, and a source of weakness, for dedicated and expert trainers are often not best placed to identify performance issues, and deliver and evaluate HRD in the context of understanding those issues.

Use and support for STS is greatest during periods of clearly identified skills shortages which need to be assessed by large-scale interventions. This is true both historically, and structurally; STS is prominent at times and in industry sectors where skill shortages require large-scale interventions. In the UK, for example, the most recent re-organisations of Sector Skills Councils (SSCs) and skills academies for manufacturing is a classic example of the re-discovery of STS. The viability of STS depends upon the commitment among employers to organising the analysis, programmes and HRD staff needed. It also depends upon a willingness among individuals in or seeking employment to participate in formal training programmes. To manage this the HRD profession has to be seen as systematic, as a specialist training function.

Performance Orientation Strategy

Developing and investing in generic courses and initiatives for HRD to reduce skill shortages or to close skill gaps can be, or can become, detached from the evolution of a business and a sector. A lot of HRD might be systematically delivered, but it might not necessarily be keeping in touch with the ultimate ends of improved organisational performance. In periods and industry sectors where dissatisfaction with STS arises there usually emerges a call for a more performance-oriented strategy (POS) to be adopted. Catalysts for this may come from concerns around the effectiveness of learning in the 'classroom', either in the workplace or elsewhere. There may also be complaints about the costs and time taken to sort out high volumes of 'sheep-dip' training, which is training where every member of staff has to have their period of 'immersion' in the same course, along with the cost of the bureaucracy that it entails.

Alternatives that provide better ways of delivering HRD are sought in order to impact directly and quickly on the development and performance of the business. The POS is the option that emerges. The language used to define it can vary from national culture and organisational culture and from time to time. In essence it entails the location and embedding of HRD practices more firmly in the critical performance imperatives faced by organisations and at the heart of their objectives. This means a much greater emphasis on managerial involvement in HRD.

Such a strategy offers an alternative rational and common-sense position. The POS is, nonetheless, a partial and limited way of perceiving and managing the practices of HRD at work. It is partial because the demands arising in 'performance' as the managers of the day understand them, are not the only force that can drive investments in HRD. Other demands on the workforce – longer-term trends – may be emerging. If HRD is mainly focused on the organisation 'here and now' it may fail to evolve to keep up with that longer-term context. For example, it may be of no interest to a particular individual organisation that their workforce is improving its IT skills 'here and now'. But that factor might become critical over the longer term for a society. It is also limited because it may be that, in emphasising business needs, other stakeholder needs which are equally legitimate and significant are neglected or ignored. It may not be of much interest to an employer in the 'here and now' to support their workforce's engagement in learning beyond their current job roles; but it may be very desirable socially, and ultimately economically, for that to be happening.

A POS way of thinking about HRD strategy and practices can become part of the problem and not part of the solution. Its existence and popularity reflects a particular balance of power among stakeholders in employment, not evidence about the best way to promote HRD at work. That is a balance in favour of the employers rather than a partnership between them and employee representatives. Were there true partnership between employers, employees and government there might be less pure POS and perhaps more effective and efficient HRD. This is because POS decontextualises HRD issues; it considers them only with reference to the existing workplaces within which learning and development occurs, in isolation from the broader social, educational and economic context. One area of contention that often arises from this decontextualisation is the idea that HRD for work ought to be dealt with more centrally in basic education rather than academic learning. The conclusion, especially from business interests, is that to change an education system to accommodate employers' needs for skills is sensible and desirable. Yet, as critics will argue, this is to overturn the rationale and direction of educational development for young people as requiring general academic development.

More importantly for other critics, the popularity of POS raises issues about integrating investment in learning and development, and skill formation, with concerns about how that learning and development then gets used. Beyond debates about education and workforce development, there are concerns around changing work organisation, job design, industrial relations and participation in decision-making, and other aspects of formal and informal people management systems. These should form a natural part of discussions about how HRD is managed, not a solely business-oriented view of how it is created and then used and renewed.

The point is that POS ignores or overlooks interests in and links between HRD, citizenship and life outside work. For example, mention may be made of education for adult life, for lifelong learning. In comparison with perceived leaders in HRD, such as the Scandinavian countries, and their development of the notion of the learning society, the reality for many seems to be that education and training to enhance citizenship, voluntary activities, parenthood, or political, social and cultural life, have limited appeal to those only concerned with workplace learning. For most, it is a business-oriented strategy that prevails.

Continuous Development Strategy

The conclusion can be drawn, then, that a POS may be a limited and even distorting way to think about HRD practices. This is particularly relevant when observing and thinking about adults whose jobs demand limited skills, and for whom other sources of motivation to engage or re-engage with opportunities for learning might be more fruitful than an agenda dominated by a POS. This is one reason why, alongside STS and POS HRD strategies, Continuous Development Strategy (CDS) has developed. The concern of CDS is on how to work with the informal and less structured ways in which learning occurs in everyday situations, rather than organising formal, structured HRD in special learning environments. The emphasis in the workplace changes from sending staff on courses to equipping employees with new skills through workplace-based problems and action learning as an ongoing process. Much of the recent proliferation of research in and books about workplace learning represents a 'discovery' of CDS via strong values propositions incorporating humanistic values and aspirations. This culminates in the new, received wisdom that HRD does not necessarily have to mean formal training, linked or otherwise to existing business needs. Instead, most of us are engaged in a naturally occurring process of continuous learning and development for which we can take greater personal responsibility, supported by coaches and mentors.

One implication of CDS is that it places an emphasis on individuals and their managers organising ongoing development in the course of normal work, and making use of options such as on-job coaching rather than drawing upon the help of professional trainers in classrooms. If development is an ongoing process then observations about HRD needs are an integral part of work, and planning for meeting those needs should be integrated with work. If this is so then it is limiting to depend on sending staff on courses now and then to achieve development; delivery must be integrated with work as well. In practice this meant the growth of new kinds of HRD strategy.

While investment in structures for competence-based HRD was proceeding apace in many countries, a quite different basis for HRD strategy was also evolving: self-development. Two principles inform the self-development strategy. The first is that almost any form of HRD is good in and of itself because it involves embracing the new, and changing skills and capabilities. This has led to the development of initiatives such as Employee Development and Assistance Programmes (EDAPs). The second principle is that the HRD that has the most potency to achieve change is that chosen and specified by the learners themselves. This has led to learners being given the central responsibility for managing the whole HRD process which, in practice, is often centred on establishing Personal Development Plans (PDPs). Problems that arise with this HRD strategy include the need for individuals to perceive that their ambitions can be satisfied by HRD, rather than by spending time 'politicking' their way up the career ladder; that people need 'space' to grow through HRD at work; and that it is critical to manage the way people learn from their own mistakes in the course of self-development.

EDAPs encourage personal development in addition to work-related learning, and often have their origins in philanthropic and paternalistic companies such as Cadburys and, more recently, the Ford Motor Company. There were estimated to be 1500 EDAP schemes in the UK at one point. They are employer-led, but may involve employee groups. They provide funding for external courses or in-house learning facilities for all staff. Simple schemes offer, in effect, annual budgets for further education. More complex schemes include internal provisions – counselling as well as off-site support. They are supported by a cadre of convinced firms to raise skill levels, encourage commitment and encourage learning. They believe that their employees:

- handle change more effectively;
- encourage a learning culture;
- contribute to productivity;
- enhance confidence and morale;
- help communications in the workplace.

Critics of these EDAPs point out that they have peaked and are now in decline. They also question the relevance of the kinds of people who take the opportunity on the grounds of business needs, as they tend to be limited to certain sectors, with few in key low-skill areas such as tourism, hotels, communications and construction.

The challenges for PDPs can be seen from a study by Antonacopoulou (2000) which looked at self-development initiatives in three retail banks. It found that moves to PDP were accompanied by tensions and contradictions, based on encouraging choice and self-direction in learning among individuals. The essence of a PDP system is development of the whole person, willing and indeed determined to commit to actions on their own part for their own reasons. But is this of benefit to the organisation? Do banks actually require lots of people exercising individual initiative? PDP enhances individual confidence and abilities that can be directly integrated with better work performance. Development *of* self and development *by* self go together, and are unified in the workplace. Changing organisations need changing people, and self-development is the way to support and achieve this. Although mutual benefits can be seen, the process is nevertheless one that requires much negotiation; the organisation is dependent on individuals growing and changing, but individuals are also dependent on the organisation supporting their growth and change. Balance and synthesis between these interests and priorities are far from easy to manage, but the problems of this are the issues that HRM practitioners need to confront and deal with.

Organisational cultures and the attitudes of top managers affect the way initiatives take shape and have effect. If an organisation does not allow mistakes, does not welcome ambition, and does not create space to grow, then self-development cannot take root. If people are blamed when things go wrong, if there is no scope for promotion, and if there is no empathy with concepts of personal growth in the workplace, then self-development will fail, even though it might have seemed attractive as a way of managing HRD. There are problems for the individual as well as for the organisation. If individuals either are unwilling to follow, or actively resist, the self-development philosophy, then it will fail as a basis for HRD and HRD will fail. Learners often rely on the organisation to manage development for them; they may have neither the interest, the will nor the skills to handle self-development. They could be developed so that they had the ability and the inclination; but the suspicion is often that this is a way to put the burden for development onto the individual, and for the organisation to avoid responsibility. Employees may then resist self-development-based HRD.

Conclusion

Companies may seek to encourage or require people to attend training, but they cannot make them learn. To explore how and why HRD in practice is done well, or how and why there are challenges in context, different kinds of forces on and features of strategies for HRD at work have been identified and discussed. It is possible to identify three common and persisting HRD strategies in practice, three major frameworks for achieving the main goals of HRD at work. Each has its strengths and weaknesses. For example, STS training is based on a system that involves professionals and experts conducting thorough analysis of needs, job analysis and performance appraisal processes. Other elements of the organisation's strategy have to be consistent with this. In practice this kind and degree of thorough and complete analysis is too time-consuming and complex, and may not be done. In this case, other aspects of the system will not support the strategy.

One clear conclusion is the need to manage each strategy well where it is in use, as befits its activities, main agents and outcomes. There are no intrinsic reasons for preferring one kind of HRD strategy to another; each one has some potential to deal with aspects of the contemporary HRD agenda. Another challenge is that multiple and combined strategies may exist and be adopted as the organisation aspires to evolve and improve its HRD practices. Then the challenge is how to manage these multiple and combined strategies in a balanced way, how to address all these different aspects of managing and organising HRD in practice. Finally organisations may use different strategies to deal with different groups. For example, for many employees HRD may be managed through STS, whereas for managers it will be managed through a CDS route. Resources Box 7.1 provides a matrix for analysing the presence of different strategies in organisations, indicating features of needs analysis, design, delivery and evaluation that would be associated with each. It is not that one or another will be present and the exclusive shaper of HRD, but that they can exist and interact, and what each requires in order to be done well needs to be appreciated (see Figure 7.3).

Figure 7.3 Interaction of HRD strategies

7.1 | *Matrix for analysing HRD strategies in organisations*

Rank the items in the following four sections from 1 (most often your experience in HRD in this area) then 2 (next experienced) and 3 (least experienced in HRD in this area)

	1	2	3
Identifying Needs			
(Systematic Training Strategy) I get regular opportunities to express formal training needs in this organisation	☐	☐	☐
(Performance Orientation Strategy) My learning needs are mainly identified whenever major business performance concerns are experienced	☐	☐	☐
(Continuous Development Strategy) I am the person with greatest responsibility for identifying my own development needs	☐	☐	☐
Design of HRD Experiences			
(Systematic Training) The aims and objectives of the training I get have usually been carefully designed by a training expert.	☐	☐	☐
(Performance Orientation Strategy) The aims and objectives of my learning are mainly concerned with specific performance issues and situations that my managers have identified as being important	☐	☐	☐
(Continuous Development Strategy) The aims and objectives of my learning are usually identified and agreed by me, and are personal to me	☐	☐	☐
Delivery of HRD			
(Systematic Training Strategy) Courses mainly involve instruction for groups of people in the organisation	☐	☐	☐
(Performance Orientation Strategy) Learning is usually delivered around performance aids and handbooks to complement them	☐	☐	☐
(Continuous Development Strategy) Learning and development is mainly guided, encouraged and supported by managers and colleagues coaching and mentoring people	☐	☐	☐
Evaluation of HRD			
(Systematic Training Strategy) Learners and trainers judge the value and quality according to how well the training was professionally organised	☐	☐	☐
(Performance Orientation Strategy) Managers and staff judges the value of learning according to the extent that it contributes to improving performance	☐	☐	☐
(Continuous Development Strategy) I judge the value of my learning to the extent that both my individual capability improves and I contribute to sustaining a learning culture	☐	☐	☐

Multiple-choice questions

8.1 Which of the following definitions of an organisational HRD strategy are correct?

    A. Organisational HRD strategies are essentially just the plans an organisation has for its HRD activities.

    B. Real-world organisational HRD strategies will be versions of STS, POS and CDS.

    C. There is only one 'best practice' approach to HRD strategy.

    D. There has been an evolution over time of various kinds of strategy in HRD, resulting in a situation where several different HRD strategies may be described and analysed.

8.2 Which of the following definitions of a POS strategy are correct?

    A. Lots of classroom training courses, which all the workforce has to attend.

    B. An organisational culture that promotes informal and unstructured learning in the course of everyday activities.

    C. The use of competence-based frameworks for appraisal systems.

    D. Ensuring that any HRD activities are tightly linked with core business goals.

References

Allen, R. (1994) 'The need for diversity in corporate training: one size doesn't really fit', *Industrial and Commercial Training*, vol. 26 , no. 10.

Antonacopoulou, E. (2000) 'Employee development through self-development in three retail banks', *Personnel Review*, vol. 29, no. 3, pp. 491–508.

Bates, R. and Chen, Hsih-Chih (2004) 'Human resource development value orientations: a construct validation study', *Human Resource Development International*, vol. 7, no. 3, September, pp. 351–70.

Lynton, R. and Pareek, U. (2000) *Training for Organisational Transformation: Part 1 for policy makers and change managers*, London, Sage.

Mayo, A. (2001) *Creating a Training and Development Strategy*, CIPD, London.

Miller, L., Rankin, N. and Neathey, F. (2001) *Competency Frameworks in Organisations*. London: Chartered Institute of Personnel and Development.

Stern, E. and Sommerlad, E. (1999) *Workplace Learning, Culture and Performance*, London: Institute of Personnel and Development.

Q

| HRD case | BankCo |

The following case outlines the basic business and HR context for a large banking group, BankCo. It also provides contemporary insights into the HRD themes and issues facing those responsible for HRD in the organisation. These have been sourced from a recent conference held to discuss the future 'architecture' of HRD in the business, and the initiatives to be taken to advance HRD in the organisation.

    As you read the case you should consider the questions in the matrix overleaf.

continued overleaf

| HRD case continued | | | | |

	STS	POS	CDS	Other
What is the HRD vision? Examples				
What is the alignment with strategy? Examples				
What do the activities, agents and outcomes indicate in terms of HRD strategy? Examples				

1. Company Overview

BankCo has grown from being a large national bank to a major international group with a market capitalisation equivalent to the GDP of a small country. BankCo has acquired businesses. BankCo has grown organically. And BankCo has done it all with speed, insight and action. BankCo entered US banking with the acquisition of USBankCo and now it's a top-ten US commercial banking business. BankCo completed the biggest takeover in its national context and now has the largest retail network in the country.

BankCo is the national number one for corporate and commercial banking. Within global banking and markets, BankCo has been recognised as the Global Best Project Finance House of the Year (Euromoney Awards 2006), the Best Securitisation House (Credit Awards 2006) and the Leveraged Finance House of the Decade (Financial News Awards 2006). Now, following its partnership with the Bank of China, BankCo is becoming a major player in the world's fastest growing economy. With more than 40 leading brands, over 30 million customers and some 137,000 staff across four continents, this is a business with 'ambition' with a capital 'A'.

By the end of 2002, BankCo was the second largest bank in Europe and the fifth largest in the world by market capitalisation.

2. Some Key Facts

- Nearly 30% of the profits come from North America
- BankCo has the largest retail banking network in the national context
- BankCo contributed £56.2 million to the community in 2005
- BankCo employs more people than Microsoft®, Nike® and Heinz® combined
- BankCo sponsors tennis player Andrew Murray and has done since 2000
- BankCo will recruit over 350 graduates this year
- In 2004, BankCo committed £5 million to the Prince's Trust for the following five years
- BankCo is the second-largest general insurer in the national context

| HRD case continued |

3.   The Business and HR: Making it happen every day

MAKE IT HAPPEN. This is the BankCo brand mark. It epitomises the way BankCo works in every corner of the business. The contexts for people management priorities of large groups like BankCo are not hard to work out. They include:

- *Growing income* in a retail organisation where the competitive service proposition is of excellent customer service means getting the best employees, and training them is critical.
- *Improving efficiency*: where people constitute a major part of the costs of an organisation, and in BankCo that may be around 55%, the place where efficiency savings will be sought is clear as day.
- *Return on equity*: enhancing returns on equity depends on talented professionals performing to the peak of their capabilities.
- *Growth* may be leveraged from the organisation's current platform, the geographical, technological and product ranges; but innovation is also needed.

All these basic features of a group like BankCo will shape a high interest in people management, and performance in that becomes of strategic concern. Because of that emphasis, those concerned with people management – HR departments and managers – are often delivered an agenda which looks something like:

- *Manage change* in all contexts and at all levels;
- *Respond to globalisation,* both the scope and scale of the challenges this brings, for collective policy rather than units 'doing their own thing';
- *Innovation* from brief and focused adaptations to major inventions;
- *Talent and succession,* seeking, growing and sustaining the best;
- *Management capability,* the evergreen need to skill and support good people managers;
- *Leadership development,* perceived to be the distinguishing feature of great organisations;
- *Employee proposition,* promising and keeping the highest standards for a diverse workforce.

Within this overall people management picture, the tactical choices that face different areas of people management need to be considered and made, around organisation design, rewards, learning, participation and so on. Of course, a legal context can frame those decisions at a threshold level, for example, the introduction of age discrimination legislation. And in an environment such as banking, where regulation is substantial, there can be an affinity with responding to regulation, playing to the rules. But to deliver on the people management takes more than responding to the rules and fulfilling such threshold standards. It takes commitment from talented managers and professionals who are also responsible for the best use of others' talent.

Managers are expected to have and to exercise knowledge and skills in the pursuit of effective HRM, to help achieve their own team's and the organisation's goals. But managers and those they manage do not experience these decisions in a vacuum. People make decisions in circumstances where aspects of the organisational culture, and power and politics will have an impact. That is why the core text and course material go beyond the theory-practice of basic processes, important as they are. They also address the opportunities and challenges that can test their people skills and leadership, particularly when change is asked for and desired.

4. Working for the Group

In attracting staff the bank highlights the following:

Salary and benefits: BankCo is recognised as having one of the most innovative and flexible reward schemes in the financial services sector. BankCo believes that its approach really differentiates it from its competitors. Called Total Reward, the approach focuses on the overall content and value of the pay and benefits package and how this supports the needs of the staff and the Group as a whole. Put another way, it's the value of everything staff get in return for working for BankCo.

continued overleaf

HRD case continued

Work–life balance: BankCo recognises that there is no one standard flexible working policy that will suit every individual and, as a result, BankCo has developed a comprehensive package of flexible working options including: part-time working, job-sharing, compressed working hours, term-time working, home-working, short- and long-term employment breaks.

Learning and development: the Group recognises that individual and Group success requires individuals to continue to develop themselves. In support of this, the Group offers, or provides access to, a wide range of learning and development opportunities. Recognising that people learn in different ways a range of learning options has been created which enables individuals to decide how to study.

New graduates: Business Class is a new 3-year rotational programme that provides participants with a unique approach to building a career within corporate banking at BankCo. Business Class trainees will undertake a number of business placements and, upon satisfactory completion of the programme, will be employed in a permanent role in one of the corporate banking business areas. The programme offers individuals the chance to 'earn and learn', gaining valuable and structured work experience whilst also studying for a professional qualification – the Applied Diploma in Corporate Banking.

5. HRD: A Vision

The HR Director sees HRD as being about performance, embedded in performance management. Learning has to be seen to be about performance to validate it in the eyes of a commercial organisation's key stakeholders, senior directors, shareholders, customers and employees. Having said that, the structure of managing HRD in such a large group is challenging: people in different parts of the organisation cannot be left to do their own thing, there has to central governance but that has to allow for diversity in organisational cultures and goals as well. The HR Director identified the following issues in evolving a HRD strategy to contribute to the business.

- There is limited cost control; they do not know exactly how much they spend on HRD, but most of the key stakeholders are quite relaxed about this and feel no need to be 'forensic' about accounting for HRD spend. The issue is to be clear and focused, not convince people it is a 'good thing' to spend on HRD. Removing duplication is an issue though, for example, moving to one learning management system (LMS).
- Over 700 HRD specialists are involved in making HRD happen: building a learning community among these people is a big task across the group.
- Leveraging untapped resources: units innovate and do new things which others can then take advantage of.
- Banking is a highly regulated business, and there are risks in too much independence in HRD for business units.
- Systems can be put in place, for example, performance management, but then it is another thing altogether to have capable managers to make them work. Actually doing it right needs support and resource.
- While a lot of attention is being given to e-learning, given the potential of these facilities across such a large group there are important debates. Is it about rationalising a LMS or is it about empowering learners to use blogs, etc? While use may be made of podcasts the fact is that bandwidth constraints limit what can be done using the IT infrastructure, so are there other ways to deliver it (MP3 players or at home)? And is promoting experiential learning in real relationships, working with actual business problems, more relevant than simulated, digital resources?

6. Current Big Issues

The new vision is of an HRD function which is validated by being seen to be about performance, delivered by a group of professionals adopting a 'hub and spoke' approach. The hub is the central resource connected through spokes with multiple business units. At the hub the following responsibilities will be important:

- **Governance**
  - setting standards;
  - evaluating HRD;
  - overseeing content management;
  - managing suppliers.

HRD case continued

- Rationalise e-learning
  - Do a strategic platform review and move to one platform;
  - Promote the philosophy of build once, use many times; de-duplication;
  - Promote the 'platinum' concept – showcasing leading examples of content in the group;
  - promote the Corporate Social Responsibility Agenda (CSR) around community involvement.

- Build the learning community
  - share knowledge;
  - build expertise in HRD;
  - create opportunities for action;
  - deliver the vision;
  - optimise spending.

7. Tools Available to Business Units

The tools available to business units have been developed to help individual employees to choose the most appropriate learning method for them. These include:

- *Access2Learning*: Access2Learning (A2L) is the Group's online learning portal, which provides employees with access to their training and personal learning information.

  A2L allows users from within the Group access to learning that supports technical, personal, and professional development. It allows employees to select materials which best support their preferred learning methods, development aims and location. Learning options include BankCo-based training courses, access to workshops and classes, books, videos, CD-ROMS and distance learning courses.
- *Professional qualifications*: Bespoke education programmes include a Diploma in Customer Relationship Management and an Applied Diploma in Corporate Banking.
- *Secondments and placements*: In support of the BankCo Group's secondment policy, individual business unit managers may consider secondments for individuals wishing to develop their career within the Group, particularly where the exposure to new environments, cultures and situations will bring the greatest benefits back into the business and the individual's personal development.
- *MBA sponsorship*: The Group may offer sponsorship to those staff who meet the criteria for MBA programmes. Decisions to offer sponsorship are made at Managing Director level within the business.
- *Work-based learning*: The BankCo Group is willing, where appropriate, to support the achievement of Vocational Qualifications (VQs). VQs offer benefits to employers and employees alike in providing comprehensive training to the highest sector requirements, and equipping staff with the skills, knowledge and understanding they need to deliver new services across new channels.
- *Professional Development website*: The Professional Development website provides employees with educational guidance and support for all aspects of internal and external lifelong learning and the development aspects of corporate citizenship. The Professional Development team is custodian of the Group Education Sponsorship Policy, Community Learning, which includes charitable work and other regulatory requirements.
- *Group Education Sponsorship Policy*: BankCo is able, via its businesses, to provide financial assistance to support staff undertaking professional or vocational qualifications, where these can be seen to provide a clear business benefit to BankCo through the improved performance of the member of staff.
- *Performance management cycle*: Every employee at BankCo should have at least one formal review during the year. During this review, employees will discuss and agree their objectives for the year, and identify the tools and processes that will help them to achieve these objectives. During the year employees' performance should be developed and measured against these objectives.

Development partnerships: coaching and mentoring

| By the end of this chapter you will be able to: |

- Describe practices associated with HRD partnerships;
- Explore the use of coaching and mentoring as HRD practices;
- Compare and contrast coaching and mentoring, sharing some common characteristics and distinctive functions;
- Reflect on the theoretical and practical trends affecting the use of development partnerships in workplaces.

| introductory case | *Coaching in RetailCo* |

Origins of coaching

RetailCo is a high street retailer with many stores in its chain. It prides itself on having weathered some hard times recently to regain a prominent position as a prestigious retailer of fashion, food and other lines. As a part of attempts to improve customer service it has implemented a coaching programme in conjunction with a new pay structure, which was introduced at the beginning of the financial year. Previously, there were over 200 different pay levels within the company as a result of performance-related pay. The company decided to try and dramatically reduce this number to 6 pay levels:

- Trainee;
- Customer assistant;
- Coach;
- Section coordinator;
- Trainee section manager;
- Section manager.

The role of coach has been implemented as a natural progression from customer assistant, offering increased responsibility and a revised pay level. The company aims to have 15% of the workforce in each store at coach level. The process is voluntary so employees who are interested volunteer to begin the training process.

Implementation

In preparation for their role as coaches, employees are sent on a two-day training programme with prospective coaches from other stores. This programme is aimed at providing them with ideas and incentives to implement this way of working, supporting and teaching within their role. The employees learn new skills by discussion, role play and presentations. They are given a folder containing each component part of the course, allowing them to view what they will have achieved at the end of the programme.

The employees are firstly required to take part in ice-breaker tasks including an informal chat in which they ask each other questions. Each employee is then asked to give a prepared presentation to the group on any hobby or interest. This is seen as another way for the employees to get to know each other, but it is also an opportunity for the instructors to analyse their interaction and speaking skills to evaluate how well the employees present themselves and appear to others. The employees receive feedback from the group and instructors and are required to learn from this feedback and discuss how they would improve in their role as coaches.

In order to become familiar with the requirements of the role and to display the characteristics they need to be effective in the role, the employees discuss what they think a coach is and what the role entails. Following this, they take part in a role-play exercise playing both coach and coachee, and the instructors observe their behaviour. At this stage, again, the employees give and receive feedback on their performances and discuss any new skills and behaviours they regard as being important for the role. The employees have now experienced the practical side of the course and progress to the theoretical elements involved in coaching.

The programme ends with the employees reading about what they are expected to do in their role. The two-day session leaves the employees 'half accredited' as a coach. The other half of the accreditation process takes place in the store through observation of the employees by their line manager. It is the decision of the line manager whether the employee becomes fully accredited as a coach. The line manager then conducts continual assessment of the coaches in-store.

Process

Once accredited the coaches are actively involved in the training process within RetailCo, training new employees by incorporating what they have learned during the course. The new employees are regarded as 'coachees' whom the coaches train and develop at this initial stage to prepare themselves for employment with RetailCo. The coach continues to work with the new employees throughout the early stages of their employment through the ongoing training and development coaching process. The use of 'coaching cards' in RetailCo allows for a universal means of employee learning and development in addition to the support network obtained through their coach. The coaching cards allow employees to learn the services, values and functions of their role and the role of the organisation. Coachees must demonstrate learning of all elements on the coaching card before they can move on to the next card. The coach must therefore record successful completion and provide feedback to the coachee and line manager. This process enables new staff to develop their knowledge of the company and its functions. It is also an interaction process between coach and coachee, developing a working relationship that embodies support and encouragement.

Strengths and weaknesses of introducing coaching

As a process, coaching enables all employees to be involved in the organisation and interact with fellow colleagues. It gives new employees a good support network from the moment they enter the organisation, one that does not end once the initial training stage is over. The continuous training and development process means that new employees do not have to partake in on-the-job learning by themselves, but can learn at the beginning and as they go along with someone to support and encourage their learning. The process also allows experienced employees to give back to the organisation some of the knowledge and expertise they have gained during their time with the company. The role also gives employees the opportunity for career progression through a large established company, an opportunity which may not be experienced frequently. The role requires time and energy from the coaches and one weakness is the increased time that needs to be allocated to the process so that it can be carried out more effectively. The process can be time-consuming, and management need to recognise this fact. The process has not been fully accepted by the workforce, due to resistance to change incorporating aspects of age and experience. It is a commonly-known problem that older employees who have worked in an organisation for a long time are resistant to changes that may benefit

continued overleaf

Introduction

The RetailCo case illustrates how development partnerships like coaching are being
integrated into working life in leading organisations. This is a trend which emerges
from recognising an important feature of HRD practice: that formal training can account for less than 10% of employee learning (Tannenbaum 1997). Much HRD in the
other 90% is apparently being practised in the context of development interactions
and partnerships. Capability and expertise is acquired through development partnerships. Developmental partnerships can be defined as:

> "Interactions between two individuals with the intent of enhancing personal de-
> velopment or growth. They may address a variety of personal or professional top-
> ics, such as career advice, work-life support, and job or task." (Eddy et al 2006,
> p. 60)

Common topics discussed in development interactions may be classified as career
advice, work-life support and job/task development. Career issues may range from
discussing specific assignments to networking support. Work-life and psychosocial
support may encompass a broad range of subjects. Job and task development is about
getting guidance and instruction. There can be a long list of different kinds of development partnerships in the workplace. One study on a range of developmental interactions (D'Abate et al 2003) mapped 13 types (see Theory & Research Box 8.1).
These developmental interactions typically describe different forms of coaching and/
or mentoring. Often these are roles which managers in organisations are expected
to fulfil. Research shows that the quality of manager–employee relations may be the

theory & research

| 8.1 | *An initial list of development partnerships* |

- Action learning
- Apprenticeship
- Coaching
- Distance mentoring
- Executive coaching
- Formal mentoring
- Group mentoring

- Informal mentoring
- Multiple mentors
- Peer coaching.
- Peer mentoring
- Traditional mentoring
- Tutoring

biggest factor in employees leaving their jobs, where moves are not related to a person's lack of satisfaction with pay but to a lack of satisfaction with how their skills and talents are being developed (Hay 2002). Here we can look at what makes the different roles of coaching and mentoring distinctive, the skills they involve and when they should be used in their various forms. This represents a substantial and growing theoretical and practical area of analysis in workplace learning. In this chapter we will analyse the conceptual issues around these different kinds of development interaction; look in detail at the core aspects of coaching and mentoring; identify some key characteristics of effective and ineffective developmental interactions; and conclude by mapping core development interactions against a set of competences and indicators.

Conceptual concerns

The D'Abate et al study (op cit) highlighted some issues with research on developmental interaction constructs. To begin with, there are significant variations across authors' use of the terms of 'coaching' and 'mentoring'. Conceptual confusion exists about these constructs. It is not possible to depend on authors meaning the same things by the same terms across different studies. Eddy et al sought to seek some clarity on this by mapping existing uses of these terms in the literature, using a nomological network approach. A nomological network approach seeks to relate theoretical constructs to each other, and to relate theoretical constructs to observable measures, and observable measures to each other. Defining a theoretical construct, such as different kinds of development interaction, is then a matter of elaborating the nomological network in which it occurs.

This kind of analysis shows how constructs are conceptually and empirically related. At the same time, such an analysis may 'net' ties that help to define these constructs in terms of key construct variables. It is then possible that constructs which appeared to be qualitatively very different, as kinds of coaching and mentoring often are, may come to be seen as 'overlapping' or indeed to be, in effect, measuring the same thing. The nomological network approach in this instance entailed distinguishing and considering measures of developmental relationships given in Theory & Research Box 8.2, with Theory & Research Box 8.3 showing the category 'behaviours' expanded.

D'Abate et al produced matrices which showed the percentage of articles citing one of the 13 named constructs they began with, using any of these items as a defining characteristic of the developmental interaction. There were four possible categories for any defining characteristics to be found in the literature:

A   cited in 76–100% of the articles
B   cited in 51–75% of the articles
C   cited in 26–50 % of the articles
D   cited in 1–25% of the articles

The main finding was that there are inconsistencies in the use of variables to define these development roles. There are very few indicators in the A and B categories, most being in the C and D categories. There were, for example, no 'A' ratings (76–100%) for literature discussing 'mentoring' at all. This strongly suggests that there is indeed inconsistency and wide variation in the use of these development partnership terms. There are even contradictions, with experts citing opposite characteristics for mentoring or coaching. With this level of disagreement, it is impossible to summarise and build on knowledge from existing studies.

8.2	**Key variables in distinguishing different kinds of development interaction**

- Demographics –age, experience, career
- Interactions – Duration, medium, span
- Distance/directed – direction, reporting, location
- Purpose – object, time, beneficiaries
- Structure – formality, choice, matching, procedures
- Behaviours – learning, emotional, career progression

8.3	**Expanded variables in development interactions in the 'behaviour' domain**

Learning	Emotional	Career
Collaborating	Affirming	Advocating
Directing	Befriending	Introducing
Goal setting	Aiding	Sheltering
Assignments	Calming	Socialising
Modelling	Confidence building	
Observing	Counselling	
Problem-solving	Encouraging	
Practical application	Supporting	
Sharing information		
Teaching		

However, it was also possible to see certain characteristics that were more in the spotlight overall than others. Eight characteristics dominate out of the 23 that were analysed, including span, object and time, formality and behaviours. The tight focus in the current literature on these factors may be helpful. Or it may mean that other characteristics are being overlooked, or not thought about at all. In subsequent work

8.4	**Factors potentially involved in successful or unsuccessful development partnerships**

Personal factors	Demographics: gender, age, ethnicity Adviser style: directive...self-discovery Adviser focus: own needs or advisee's needs Adviser expertise: in development area
Relationship factors	Initiation Choice in participation: voluntary or not Frequency and duration: time known Source of relationship: superior, friend, peer
Communication factors	Location: face-to-face or distance Primary mode: medium used

(Eddy et al 2006) investigated other factors that may help us to differentiate between effective and ineffective developmental interactions. These factors include personal, relationship and communication factors (see Theory & Research Box 8.4).

Eddy et al (op cit) conclude that for effective development interactions it is important for advisers (providing development), advisees (learners) and organisations to behave in certain ways (see Operations Box 8.1).

operations

8.1 | *Behaviour for partnerships*

Advisers
- Have a goal of self-discovery: advisers should encourage advisee self-discovery rather than being highly directive
- Frame interactions as voluntary and mutually initiated
- Focus on advisee's needs, not mediating the organisation's needs
- Be accessible for multiple conversations over time, not one quick-fix

Advisees (Learners)
- Seek advisers with relevant experience, not just those already known and convenient
- Actively seek out people to get advice and feedback
- Do not rely on one-off interactions

Organisations
- It is not safe to assume development interactions can be handled without some preparation
- Meetings with direct supervisors are the hardest, most likely to be ineffective
- Prepare supervisors for job/task-related development interactions: uncover needs and promote self-discovery

---

Having considered the basics of what might be common factors in 'good practice' for development partnerships in general, important questions about different kinds of development interactions, and their uses in the workplace, are raised. Central to these, and illustrative of the themes that emerge, is the comparison and contrast of mentoring and coaching. This central area of study and debate will be explored in more depth.

Mentoring

Mentoring can be defined as;

> "a learning and developmental relationship between two people. It depends on essential human qualities such as commitment, authenticity, trust, integrity and honesty. It involves the skills of listening, questioning, challenge and support."
>
> (Garvey and Garrett-Harris 2005, p 9)

Diverse kinds of relations and activities are included under the generic construct of mentoring. Mentoring is 'close to hand' in a number of contexts, and thereby comes to feature in diverse discussions. Different types of people, in different types of relationships, in different organisational circumstances, are all 'doing' mentoring. Thus mentoring appears to occur, for example, between:

masters	and	apprentices
senior managers	and	middle managers
managers	and	employees
teachers	and	students
senior students	and	juniors
professionals	and	aspirants

Mentoring first grew to contemporary prominence in the USA as a result of two main catalysts. The first was the influence of developmental psychology (Levinson 1978), which 'discovered' and highlighted mentoring as a natural, ubiquitous, and highly beneficial relationship for men. It was a relationship formed between adults in their 'mid-life' stage and young adults. The former were searching for a constructive role in the lives of others and the latter were trying to 'realise their dreams'. Mutual benefits could arise from forming and having a mentoring relationship.

This framework struck a number of chords. It related to the problems faced in 'mid-life' and late career by older adults; the search for purpose given the passing of previous purposes such as attaining career success for themselves. It spoke to the problems of socialising/inducting young (increasingly independent) adults into the adult world of work and family responsibility. Was it coincidence that these concerns were becoming prominent as an age of change and uncertainty in career and life success was about to be experienced? Was the concern with mentoring an early indicator of what was to come?

Secondly there was the influence of studies (e.g. Roche 1979) which claimed to show that 'everyone who makes it has a mentor'. People who had attained the most senior positions in their organisations attributed at least a part of that success to having had a mentor. Mentoring was then a specific and necessary condition of ultimate career success. This articulation of mentoring as a variable in the achievement of ultimate career success clearly stimulated both the individuals concerned with such ultimate career success and organisations seeking to manage the development of future leaders to explore the possibilities of mentoring in the context of growing and developing senior managers.

There was also a third environmental factor in the USA which helped to promote the growth of contemporary mentoring – the rise of active policies on equal opportunities (Shapiro et al 1978). It was argued that one key form of support for positive action in enabling women and ethnic minorities to progress up the career ladder, particularly in professions and management, was mentoring. This led to a growth of formal mentoring schemes.

Mentoring continued to ride upon a number of powerful waves of change in the USA through the 1980s, some practical and others cultural. Practically, an increasing concern with HRD as an essential part of HRM meant that innovations like mentoring were looked upon favourably and embraced. Culturally, mentoring made sense in circumstances where people believed in the possibilities of close personal relationships as a means to an end, the achievement of power. Mentoring attracted a lot of attention and provided a concrete instance of the exercise of power in organisations. In this cultural context, given the type of relationship involved, it was inevitable that equal opportunity issues would not only help to generate interest in mentoring; they would also provide a research focus in themselves. Thus there was concern about whether mentoring between men and women could be as effective as same-gender relations, or whether it invariably involved sexual tensions/issues. There was the issue of whether people of different ethnic backgrounds could develop effective mentoring relationships.

Finally there was a debate about the strengths and weaknesses of organising mentoring in formal schemes. Some saw the formalising of mentoring, through organised schemes, as essential (Zey 1991). This may be to ensure an effective scheme actually exists, or to ensure that there was equal opportunity to access mentoring. Others argued that mentoring could not be effectively organised through formal schemes, it could only emerge from broader Organisational Development (OD) initiatives which promoted an environment in which mentoring relationships would 'naturally' arise (Clawson 1985, Kram 1985b).

By the time that mentoring became an issue in other contexts in the 1980s, there was then a well-developed agenda of concerns. These can be summarised as:

- The contribution of mentoring to career success;
- The nature of mentoring as a 'significant' relationship;
- The equal opportunities debate;
- The costs and benefits of formally organising mentoring.

To an extent, mentoring, as it grew elsewhere, developed as a mirror of the agenda set in the USA with some modifications.

- Rather than simply focusing just on career success for those at the 'top' there was a broader concern with developing talent (Clutterbuck 2004). It was not just about those who 'made it'; everyone needed a mentor.
- The focus on mentoring as a non line manager activity was stressed. The problem of being entangled in conventional command and control relations was to be circumvented rather than confronted.

While there had been some interest in Britain since the early 1980s (Storey 1989, Mumford and Gold 2004) it was only really in the 1990s that there was a significant profile for mentoring. During the early part of the 21st century that growing interest has accelerated, with a dramatic increase in the number of publications, institutions and qualifications concerned with mentoring.

The growth of mentoring does not occur in isolation; it has been part of the growth of other formal and organised systems, for example:

- Structured 'Personal Development Plans' derived from experiences at assessment centres;
- Performance management systems being introduced or reformed;
- Workplace learning qualification systems being developed;
- Continuous Professional Development (CPD) initiatives;
- Revised degree and postgraduate programmes in higher education.

It has taken the development of these initiatives to create the conditions in which mentoring becomes a more central activity in Britain. One effect of these kinds of contextual trends was that the context seemed to be one in which mentoring was becoming more prevalent in formal and organised schemes (see Operations Box 8.2).

One of the underlying problems of a formally organised approach to mentoring is that it requires a degree of policy-making, instruction for participants and evaluation which involves a clearly prescriptive view of what mentoring is. To develop policy it is necessary to spell out what mentoring is. To train mentors and advise mentees on a large scale it becomes convenient to spell out what mentoring is. To evaluate mentoring it is, according to convention, necessary to set objectives, requiring a close definition, up front, of what mentoring is.

8.2 | *Conditions for success in mentoring schemes*

When devising a scheme it is essential to agree the scope and purpose of the mentoring and identify the factors that will support mentoring and those that will inhibit. The range of issues that need to be considered are:

Voluntarism – Mentoring is essentially a voluntary activity. The degree of voluntarism will depend on the situation and the circumstances.

Training – Both the mentor and the mentee will need some orientation towards the scheme. This may involve a skills training programme for both mentors and mentees. Sometimes this can be done with them together in the same programme.

Ongoing support – Mentors often need support. This may take the form of a mentor support group or one-to-one mentoring supervision – a mentor to the mentor.

Matching – It is important to have a clear matching process to which the participants subscribe. It is also important to establish a 'no fault divorce clause' after, say, the first 3 meetings.

Establishing reviewable ground rules – It is important to clarify the boundaries of the relationship at the start.

Ongoing review –The most important factor in successful outcomes to mentoring is regular feedback and review within the relationship about the relationship. Establishing ground rules at the start can facilitate this process.

Whose agenda? – Mentoring is for the mentee. The research suggests that attempts to impose the agenda on the mentee result in manipulation and social engineering. The benefits of mentoring to all stakeholders result from broadly following the mentee's agenda.

Evaluation and monitoring – Ongoing evaluation of the scheme is important also. There is little point in evaluating the scheme after say, two years, to unearth problems which could have been resolved at the time they became problems.

Source Garvey and Garrett-Harris 2005.

Mentoring in an organisation has been critiqued for being an institutional process of standardisation rather than encouraging and enabling people to develop a diverse set of activities in an organisation which may all be thought about as 'mentoring'. One framework for conceptualising and standardising mentoring sees it as serving a set of vocational and psychosocial functions (see Strategic View Box 8.1). A relationship that serves these functions is mentoring, whatever it may actually be called. If it does not serve these functions, then it is not mentoring.

The phases of a partnership are also important in the conception of mentoring and the issues it raises (see Strategic View Box 8.2). These phases – in what many would consider 'real' mentoring – will occur over a period of years whereas in formal workplace schemes they may occur over a period of months. The key point is that mentoring involves both career and psychosocial functions. Though mutuality is necessary for effective mentoring to take place, the mentor's openness to serve as such must be made known to prospective protégés. A dual commitment, both to the individual's growth and to learning in the workplace, is at the core of mentoring relationships.

| 8.1 | *The functions of mentoring* |

Vocational functions

- **Sponsorship**: A senior individual's public support is critical for advancement.
- **Coaching**: Enhancing a person's knowledge and understanding of how to effectively navigate in the environment.
- **Protection**: Shielding the protégé from untimely or potentially damaging contact with other senior officials. Taking credit and blame.
- **Challenging assignments**: building of critical technical skills leading towards greater responsibility.

Psychosocial functions

- **Role modelling**: Senior person's attitudes, values, and behavior become model to emulate. Desirable example-setting; mutually beneficial.
- **Acceptance and confirmation**: Validation of the individual' self-worth. Appreciation and support.
- **Counselling**: Enables an individual to explore personal concerns with mentor. Sounding board.
- **Friendship**: mutual liking, understanding. Enjoyable informal exchanges about work/non-work.

Source Kram 1985.

| 8.2 | *Mentoring phases* |

Initiation: a potential mentor is admired and respected by the protégé. The protégé is seen as someone with potential, interest in work, easy to work with. Mutual benefits are perceived.

Cultivation: generally, career functions emerge as the first focus then psychosocial functions emerge. There are wide variations around the nature of functions, depending on individuals' needs.

Separation: an outcome as a function of change in one or both individuals' confidence. Involves both psychological and structural aspects, which can be stressful, but also exciting. This allows the protégé to demonstrate mastery of skills without support.

Redefinition: the relationship, where one continues, often manifests itself as friendship. It may involve counsel and coaching from a distance. This can be uncomfortable as the protégé becomes peer and the mentor may view this development as threatening.

Source Kram 1985a.

Effective mentoring will involve some vulnerability and discomfort. It involves commitment on both individuals' parts. It involves not only supporting but also challenging one's protégé.

The underlying process in mentoring has been characterised as one of individuation. Individuation is about becoming your own person, making choices at different stages and transitions. It arises as a big issue in making particularly significant choices, such as those about occupation, career and relationships like marriage (Levinson et al 1978). Levinson et al were specifically concerned with the choices that men make and then have to build upon – living within them, or enhancing them, or moving to make new choices at times of change and crisis. Within this context mentoring features strongly as a role that older men can play with younger men. The choices being made by the younger man relate to identifying and establishing their own personal dream: the mentor is, most crucially, there to support and facilitate the realisation of the dream. Subsequent work applied the same kind of analysis to women, looking at the development pathway concerns they share with men but also their distinctive individuation issues.

For either men or women in early adult life, individuation involves working through dependences on others. Mentors are ambiguous figures here; they are people on whom the young adult will depend, but their primary role is to help the young adult overcome such dependences. Combining the concept of individuation and the hypothesised stages of adult development as they saw it in the course of their research, Levinson et al arrived at a view of the mentoring process as a key, if highly problematic, resource for young men, and as a fulfilling role for older men. Thus they saw the mentoring process as highly significant for both parties, and crucial to effective adult development by facilitating continuing individuation for both parties. They stressed that the mentoring process may be either difficult or highly problematic in its eventual outcomes for both parties. This was not a rosy view of a perfect, mutually beneficial partnership; it was a realistic appraisal of a partnership that, like all partnerships, can be fraught with difficulties and challenges.

This focus on being person-centred rather than the giver of advice/wise counsel assumes that, for people to become happy, they need to understand themselves. Faced with pressures at work and home, problems with work–life balance, and uncertainties in terms of personal and career goals, this need seems to be real, meaningful and pressing in modern society. The mentoring process is no longer about a wise figure giving counsel to heroes, or even necessarily a master in any field developing an apprentice. The legacy of this view of the mentoring process is that, to the constellation of family, peers, formal educators and superiors, we must add the mentor as someone who provides a person-centred counselling and supporting role for an adult.

Recent growth has been evident in formal mentoring schemes, but that has not stopped a persistent questioning of the value of institutionalising mentoring in organisations. It may, in theory, be more attractive to argue for broader organisation development initiatives to support mentoring rather than developing a formal scheme. But, in practice, the development of a formal scheme is an essential first step.

The qualities of mentors are listed by Clutterbuck and Megginson (2000) as: wisdom, experience, questioning, listening, patience, networking, being oneself, balancing process and content, dependable. The relations with a mentor may be triggered by a crisis, though they will require long-term trust, the ability to overcome isolation, chemistry, respect bases, ability to both plan and prepare. Organisation issues involve aligning the mentoring process with change management, CEO support, and internal and external relations. Issues around the learner often include acknowledging a need for help, isolation at the top, not accepting they can be told, little scope for role modelling.

The duality of career and /or psychosocial functions or purposes are often given as defining terms here. The controversy is about the duality of career or psychosocial development, and the role of mentoring is often interpreted in terms of North American versus a European views of work and human relations. However, it is possible to discern a different kind of division in debates on this aspect of mentoring; a duality between liberal and conservative values and conceptions of mentoring. Liberal values emphasise its progressive and modernist functions; the utility of mentoring in opening up careers for disadvantaged groups and promoting humanistic ideals through improved psychosocial development. Conservative values emphasise its contribution to the continuity of the status quo and its utility in legitimising and replicating patterns of behaviour; control through the influence of the 'old guard' on the career and psychosocial development of new generations (see Figure 8.1).

Conservative values

Mentoring is a poor substitute for natural relationships At best these are fake relations	Mentoring is the best method of ensuring continuity and the status quo; the way things are
Mentoring is not potent enough; need other reforms to open up careers and/or psychosocial development	Mentoring is very potent; key to opening up careers and/or achieving associated psychosocial development

Against   For

Liberal values

Figure 8.1 Lenses on mentoring

Viewing debates through the lenses of these archetypal conceptions of value provides one way to explore discussions about mentoring as exemplifying the broader dynamics of intellectual controversy, which follows and extends a complex history (see Theory & Research Box 8.5).

theory &
research

8.5 Historical contexts for mentoring

Context	Process and role	Process in context	HRD themes	HRD legacy
Classical mythology	Development interactions as a role in the drama of the patriot-warrior	Heroes on quests and adventures The archetypes and symbols of the wise, the young, the villains	From timidity to resourcefulness Good vs evil	The role of wise 'counsel' The ascension to power
Craft guilds	Development interactions as the lynchpins in the economics and society of small, independent businesses	Communities in emerging towns Masters–Apprentices	Craft regulation The community ethos	The role of masters The correlation with community
Humanist psychology	Mentors supporting the development of the individual	Development throughout adulthood Counselling	Transitions in adulthood Helping 'processes'	Self-development issues for adults Human relations

Coaching

While mentoring has had much of the spotlight in development interactions and partnerships, it seems that attention is now turning to coaching. Reference to a recent survey in the UK by the CIPD illustrates the general growth and interest in coaching at work (CIPD 2006):

- 90% of organizations use coaching by line managers;
- 64% of organizations use coaching by external coaches;
- 74% of organizations expect to increase their use of coaching.

| 8.3 | *The attractions of coaching* |

The popularity of coaching is apparently fuelled by:

□ The features of modern organisations: flatter, faster pace of change
□ Employee demand for training
□ Lifelong learning
□ Targeted and just-in-time development
□ Focus on performance (larger leaps in new roles)
□ Individual responsibility for development

Coaching is used for improving individual performance, productivity and skills. Coaching is about working with and alongside people and their teams in complex, sensitive and changing workplace environments to support leadership and talent management. It is about looking to support problem- and solution-focused thinking, strategic insight and personal development. That means using a combination of skill, knowledge and attributes to develop and make an impact, mainly one-to-one, with limited peer support and feedback (see Resources Box 8.1). Coaching has emerged strongly in an era of talent management challenges and demands. The classic client-coach scenario – entering into a relationship which is used for the benefit of the client and the organisation – is evolving. Coaching gives the client an opportunity to explore, discover and clarify ways of leading and developing resourcefully and effectively.

| 8.1 | *A coaching capability framework* |

□ Initiating the coaching relationship
□ Developing the coaching relationship
□ Managing self
□ Working with an ethical code
□ Communicating

□ Working with a set of beliefs
□ Focusing on goals
□ Striving for excellence
□ Having a flexible approach
□ Thinking and understanding

We can locate development of capability in executive coaching firmly in the midst of management and management research:

• Aim to be helpful and supportive for learners in developing their talents;
• Take human sciences perspectives on deepening awareness of relationships in organisations;
• Reflect on and investigate trends and demands in talent management in organisations;
• Respectfully and rigorously work with paradigms, tensions and conflicts to generate understanding about clients and coaching.

In the past the similarities between psychotherapy, counselling and coaching, leading to an interest in psychology, have been foremost. But the relational view of talent management and coaching is one among many. There is much in effective executive coaching that is about addressing core beliefs about self and abilities, and

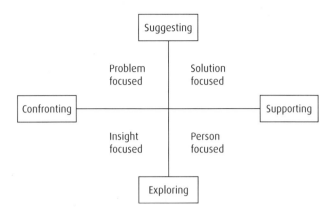

Person focused: exploring and supporting, encouraging understanding; warm and understanding (humanistic, listening and accepting some time spent 'shifting inwards')

Insight focused: exploring and confronting at a distance; looking at what is being left out, being more objective (psychodynamic and analytic, organisation coach or ladder method)

Problem focused: suggesting and confronting, looking at new frameworks to the problems, giving ideas and recommendations (directive, from the outside, GROW model and others)

Solution focused: helping with opinions and feedback; positive and constructive trains of thought (directive, looking to the future when the problem has gone, positive plans and challenges)

Figure 8.2 Coaching foci

Source Based on de Haan 2005

experimenting with new ways of being. But there is also much in other human and management research contributions; broader themes and change in society, organisation and debates informed by developments in strategy and management research.

Figure 8.2 illustrates the foci of coaching: whether to follow the person's thinking or comment and introduce other lines of thought – to follow or to lead; whether the coach is reinforcing strengths or overcoming weaknesses.

The rapid rise of coaching and the flurry of excitement that its apparent growth has brought has another side to it. Many await the faltering of the manic optimism surrounding the initiative. Critics can, indeed, find ammunition. Finding high-quality external coaches is a problem. Much of the research base for coaching is in sports and education, not the business context. Coach-training tends to focus on specific tools and techniques. There are 'cowboy' trainers and a lack of regulation, and, in response to that, emerges infighting in 'professional' bodies. In essence, asking and answering questions about the theoretical foundations is part of countering the criticisms.

On the more positive side it is expected that the interest in coaching will be sustained because there is a shortage of skilled leaders and the use of coaching in leadership development is expected to increase. The main area of growth – managers as coaches – will keep interest high. Organisations need to organise and integrate coaching internally; to develop coherent strategies for doing that. There is a belief in benefits but little formal evaluation – there is great scope to reveal the value in coaching.

There are currently no publicly available surveys on the demand and supply dynamics relating specifically to coaching.

Development partnerships: differences or common factors

Those who see a difference between mentoring and coaching are represented by Clutterbuck and Megginson (2000, p. 3) who advance a concept of mentoring as "Off-line help by one person to another in making significant transitions in knowledge, work or thinking". They contrast it with coaching, as shown in Table 8.1.

	Mentoring	Coaching
Source	Internal	External
Foci	Diverse	Behaviour
Structure	Less structured	Structured
Centre	Person centred	Performance
Duration	Lengthy	Short

Table 8.1 Mentoring executives
Source Clutterbuck and Megginson (2000)

Mentoring is for whole-person development and periods of rapid change and big challenges, whereas coaching is an activity to help people along 'level ground' in a short-term relationship concerned with skills. Mentoring, in the specific context of leadership development for executives, is growing with increasing pressures at the top, emphasis on the balance and quality of life, continuing need to learn and transitions involving radical change. Executives need a reflective mentor for an intensive and holistic relationship that is akin to looking in the mirror with someone else; an experience in which an emotional release of energy may also occur. Indeed this creation of 'Personal Reflective Space' (PRS) is the 'power' of mentoring. It is not a stark science or technique-driven, but a role whose essence is ideal for executives. This is because executives are not a law unto themselves in a self-contained world; they operate in teams, cannot 'know it all' and need to keep learning. What they are often missing is PRS and '[a]n opportunity to develop personal insight through uninterrupted and purposeful reflective activity' (Clutterbuck and Megginson 2000, p. 8).

The typical relationship goes through recognisable phases in which initial concerns to problem-solve or make a decision are suspended in order to consider deeper questions about purpose and behaviour; leading them to reframe their understanding of themselves and others and thereafter make a choice. Executives experience three potential kinds of challenge warranting such mentoring. These are given in Strategic View Box 8.4.

In addition to coaching and mentoring, several other kinds of development partnership can be mapped against a set of features for executives or other kinds of staff (see Resources Box 8.2). Each role profiles in a distinctive way against the features. What is common in organisations, whatever the specific role, are supply-side quality issues. Coach and mentor development is often based on respecting and encouraging diversity in approaches, yet organisations invariably prefer to standardise, especially with costly methods like coaching and mentoring. Inconsistent implementation and inconsistent returns are the organisational challenge. This challenge is also the key to developing in professional executive coaching and mentoring: addressing basic issues on organisation needs, the alignment of coaching with these, and due process in contracting and working.

8.4 | *Executive mentoring challenges*

Curtain Raisers
- Get noticed
- Get experience and understanding
- Manage politics and projects
- Develop networks

Once in an Executive Position
- Continue to learn and grow
- Stimulate challenge from others
- Manage performance and stress
- Influence rather than command, credibility

If also a Director
- Distinguish roles, develop skills
- Know what, and strategic thinking
- Collaborative independence
- What about my career now?

In seeking to engage with development partnerships, like coaching and mentoring, practitioners' organisations encounter much information and many options. Currently, they seem to value word-of-mouth, past experience and personal referral rather than a coach's or mentor's reputation. Yet the trustworthiness of a referrer or reputation is no guarantee of coach or mentor effectiveness. From the competent coach's or mentor's point of view, there may be an absence of clear selection criteria, and a lack of comparison of service offerings, among organisations seeking to use coaches and mentors. Background factors favouring contracts seem to be experience, along with a qualification in a relevant discipline or coaching/mentoring qualifications.

For coaches and mentors having gained an appointment, the next concern may be unfocused engagements. These tend to be signalled by a concern in the organisation with 'level', rather than on business need alignment – the level of the top leadership team, emerging executive talent, senior managers. Prioritising questions can be asked to address this potential issue:

- How critical is the business need?
- How critical is the individual?
- Is coaching suitable for the general change desired?
- Is coaching needed for that individual?

Poor matching usually occurs where 'surface' variables are considered and gut decisions are being made around availability, location and seniority. To avoid that, attention can be given to sensitivity, expertise, background, experience, personality, style, and humour.

A further risk is disconnection from the organisation, which can occur if agendas diverge from business needs under the mask of confidentiality. Managers of those being coached or mentored may be prevented from setting goals. Peers may be prevented from giving feedback on behaviour change. HR in the organisation may be unable to

8.2 | Development roles mapped against common elements

Core elements	Coaching One-to-one focus on performance	Mentoring Vocational and psychosocial funcions	Training	Consulting Providing expert advice	Therapy Helping to overcome emotional distress
Problem solving	High		High		High
Examining changes	High		Low		High
Behavioural change	High				High
Politics	High	High	Low		Low
Resistance	High	Low	Low		High
Giving information	High	High	High	High	
Support	High	High	Low		High
Reinforcement	High		Low	Low	High
Personal growth	High		Low	Low	High
Goal setting	High		Low	High	High
Action planning	High		Low	High	
Transfer of learning	High		Low	Low	High
Providing resources		High	High	High	High
Expert role	Low	High	High	High	High
Teaching			High	High	
Challenging	High		Low	Low	
Strategic planning			Low	High	Low
Exploring beliefs	High		Low	Low	High
Evaluation		Low	Low		Low
Confidentiality	High		Low		High
Data collection		Low	Low	High	
Individually tailored	High	High	Low		High
Research-based		Low			High
Giving solutions		High	High	High	Low
Advising	Low	High	High	High	Low
Transformational possibilities	High		Low	Low	High

Source: Based on Skiffington and Zeus 2005

monitor progress. Mentors or others working with the coachee may be unable to provide associated guidance. Consequently there may be non-value-adding coaching or mentoring and problems with the reinforcement of coaching or mentoring goals.

Inconsistent delivery and quality is the underlying challenge. For successful engagements it would appear that duration is not the key to either getting on, getting by or going nowhere. A successful engagement may be short, and a long engagement may be pleasant, but coasting and empty. A stalled engagement is one that is going nowhere. Options to avoid these potential problems are:

- Standardise objectives;
- Define timelines for progress;
- Have an evaluative framework;
- Conduct peer benchmarking among other coaches.

A developing professional development partnership, like coaching or mentoring, meets these common core challenges:

- **Suitability**: becoming a 'best fit' coach or mentor;
- **Focusing**: addressing the tougher questions in contracting for development;
- **Matching**: addressing the deeper issues of a partnership early on;
- **Connection**: also managing senior manager/others interest and participation;
- **Quality standard**: high standards, validity and reliability for the approach adopted.

Finally, development partnerships emerge from and help to extend networks. One model suggests there are five dimensions of networking (Cross et al 2004). These can be analysed to review how complete and well-balanced a person's network, including coaches and mentors, is. These five dimensions are:

- **Vertical dispersion**: connections with those having more experience, at the same level and less experience than you;
- **Horizontal dispersion**: relations inside and outside your 'home' network;
- **Experiential proxemics**: how close in terms of background you are;
- **Intentional interactions**: time outside routine scheduling of interactions with them;
- **Time known**: balance of well-known and newer.

Vertical dispersion

More experience
Same experience
Less experience

Horizontal dispersion

In network
Other coaching network
Another network

You

Time known

Less than 1 year
1–3 years
3–5 years
5–10 years
More than 10 years

Experiential proxemics

Same
Similar
Different
Very different

Intentional interaction

Daily
Weekly
Monthly
Irregular

Figure 8.3 Professional development network analysis

Q

concluding exercise

This exercise allows you to map your own existing network against the five dimensions given in the chapter. First you need to identify the five key people you see as forming the heart of your current personal coaching and mentoring network for professional development. If you cannot identify five people list as many as you can. Then you need to map these people against the criteria given in the network analysis table (Table 8.2) and transfer the data in summary form to the table.

Next, identify what a re-balancing of your network would look like. To do that, produce the profiles in Table 8.3 that fill the gaps you can see in your current network. For example, if you know a lot of people in the same unit and see them daily then you might want to develop links with people in other countries you see only infrequently. Once you have identified these profiles you are in a position to search for people who fit them. Understanding these profiles, and thinking about you might use them in an organisation, is one practical way to promote your professional development.

Existing development network and partnerships					
Name of person (coach, mentor, other)	Vertical dispersion 1 = more experienced 2 = equal 3 = less experienced	Horizontal dispersion 1= your 'core' coaching network 2= another coaching network 3= another non-coaching network	Experience proxemics 1 = same background 2 = similar background 3 = different background 4 = very different background	Intentional interaction on professional development (structured into your job/role) 1 = irregular 2 = monthly 3=weekly 4= daily	Time known 1 = less than 1 yr 2 = 1–3 yrs 3 = 3–5 yrs 4 = 5–10 yrs 5 = 10+ yrs

Table 8.2 Mapping existing network

Prospective development network: development options					
Vertical dispersion 1 = more experienced 2 = equal 3 = less experienced	Horizontal dispersion 1= your 'core' coaching network 2= another coaching network 3= another non-coaching network	Experience proxemics 1 = same background 2 = similar background 3 = different background 4 = very different background	Intentional interaction on professional development (structured into your job/role) 1 = irregular 2 = monthly 3=weekly 4= daily	Time known 1 = less than 1 yr 2 = 1–3 yrs 3 = 3–5 yrs 4 = 5–10 yrs 5 = 10+ yrs	Person

Table 8.3 Mapping network development

Multiple-choice questions

8.1 Which of the following statements about the mentoring are true?
 A. Mentoring has 5 vocational functions and 3 psychosocial functions.
 B. Mentoring involves supporting rather than challenging the learner.
 C. Most kinds of informal learning partnership between people at work can be considered as kinds of mentoring.
 D. Mentoring is a newly identified and promoted technique of developing people.
 E. None of the statements is true.

8.2 When introducing a formal mentoring scheme, which of the following statements are correct?
 A. Don't spend much time on selecting who will be mentors, as most people in the workforce are capable of fulfilling the role.
 B. Training mentors is a process that requires lengthy and intensive time in the classroom to produce professional mentors.
 C. Make it clear that mentoring is really just a form of confidential counselling support for special people.
 D. Identify the specific goals the scheme will address, and adopt a system to suit those.

References

Allen, R. (1994) 'The need for diversity in corporate training: one size doesn't really fit', *Industrial and Commercial Training*, vol. 26, no. 10, pp. 15–17.

CIPD (2006) *Annual Survey on Learning and Development*, London, CIPD.

Clawson, J.G. (1985) 'Is mentoring necessary?' *Training and Development Journal*, April, pp. 36–9

Clutterbuck, D. (2004) *Everyone Needs a Mentor*, London, IPM.

Clutterbuck, D. and Megginson, D. (2000) *Mentoring Executives and Directors*, Oxford, Elsevier Butterworth Heinemann.

Cross, R., Abrams, L. and Parker, A. (2004) 'A relational view of learning: how who you know affects what you know', in M.L. Connor and J.G. Clawson, *Creating a Learning Culture*, Cambridge, Cambridge University Press.

D'Abate, P., Eddy, E. and Tannenbaum, S. (2003) 'What's in a name? A literature-based approach to understanding mentoring, coaching, and other constructs that describe developmental interactions, *Human Resource Development Review*, vol. 2, no. 4, pp. 360–84.

De Haan, E. (2005) 'A new vintage: Old wine maturing in new bottles', *Training Journal*, November, pp. 20–4

Eddy, E., D'Abate, C., Tannenbaum, S., Givens-Skeaton, S., Robinson, G. (2006) 'Key Characteristics of Effective and Ineffective Developmental Interactions', *Human Resource Development Quarterly*, vol. 17, no. 1, pp. 59–84.

Garvey, B. and Garrett-Harris, R. (2005) The Benefits of Mentoring: a literature review, The Mentoring and Coaching Research Unit, Sheffield Hallam University

Gibb, S. (1999) 'The Usefulness of Theory: A Case Study in Evaluating Formal Mentoring Schemes', *Human Relations*, vol. 52 , no. 8, pp. 1055–75.

Hay, M. (2002) 'Strategies for survival in the war for talent', *Career Development International*, vol. 7, no. 1.

Homer (trans E.V. Rieu) (1946) *The Odyssey*, Harmondsworth, Penguin.

Kram, K. (1985a) *Mentoring at Work: Developmental relationships in organizational life*, Glenview, IL, Scott Foresman & Co.

Kram. K. (1985b) 'Improving The Mentoring Process', *Training and Development Journal,* April.

Levinson, D. et al (1978) *The Seasons of A Man's Life,* New York, Alfred Knopf.

Lynton, R.P. and Pareek, U. (2000) *Training for Organizational Transformation, Part 1 Policy makers and change managers,* New Delhi, Sage.

Mumford, A. and Gold, J. (2004) *Management Development,* 4th edn, London, CIPD.

Roche, G. (1979) 'Much ado about mentors', *Harvard Business Review,* January–February.

Shapiro, E.C. et al (1978) 'Moving up: Role models, mentors, and the "Patron System"', *Sloan Management Review,* Spring.

Skiffington, S. and Zeus, P. (2005) *Behavioral Coaching: How to build sustainable personal and organizational strength,* Sydney, McGraw-Hill.

Storey, J. (1989) 'Management development: A literature review and implications for research, Part 1, Conceptualisations and practices', *Personnel Review,* vol. 18 , no. 6.

Tabbron, A. et al (1997) 'Making mentoring work', *Training for Quality,* vol. 5 , no. 1, pp. 6–9.

Tannenbaum, S. I. (1997) 'Enhancing continuous learning: diagnostic findings from multiple companies', *Human Resource Management,* vol. 36, no. 4, pp. 437–52.

Thomas, D. (1993) 'Racial dynamics in cross race developmental relationships', *Administrative Science Quarterly,* no. 38, pp. 169 94

Zey, M. (1991) *The Mentor Connection,* New Brunswick, Transaction.

Q

exercise

What factors for and against increasing the role of line managers in HRD can you identify from the discussion of development partnerships?

A

answer to exercise

Introduction

Increasing line manager involvement in HRD at work is one important part of the broader changing relations between line managers and HRM. The advantages of increasing line manager involvement in HRD at work are frequently highlighted. However there are challenges as well which raise questions about the overall impact on HRD at work. Evidence about the practice of HRD at work depending on line manager involvement is limited. Instead of having an evidence base to evaluate there is only scope to reflect on the significance of the trend to line manger involvement in HRD at work in context. Two principal interpretations are possible: one that the trend is of minimal significance, the other that it is of much greater significance. For the latter, increasing line manager involvement in HRD at work is both part of the means of attaining, and also one of the ends of, broader changes in work, organisation and HRM. Even so there are legitimate concerns about increasing line manager involvement in HRD at work, where that prejudices the provision and use of specialist HRD at work resources. However, these concerns are outweighed by the greater concern to re-align work, organisation and management for an era in which knowledge management is predominant. The issue of line manager involvement in HRD at work will continue to be an important part of the corporate agenda.

Line manager involvement in HRD at work

Mapping of clusters of research themes in HRD in Europe highlighted 10 key themes. One of these explicitly identifies the role of managers in HRD at work, suggesting the issue is of some importance, most of the others also have implications for line managers' involvement with HRD at work. The concern with integrating learning and work, for example, must have implications for the role of line managers. This mapping of research clusters emphasises the specific and general interest in the role of line managers in HRD at work, in contrast with past perceptions where the focus was on HRD specialists.

Some emphasise the need to include line managers in planning for HRD, and to 'hand over primary responsibility to the line'. But there is most contemporary interest in the more general way that, in the name of changes in work, management, organisation, and HRM, greater involvement of managers with HRD has been proposed. For example, Hay (2002) argues that the reason most people leave their jobs and move is not related to a lack of satisfaction with pay, but a lack of satisfaction with how their skills and talents are being developed. HRD at work is always an aspect of the whole HRM of an organisation, not an isolated, stand-alone activity. The strategies and policies that organisations have for attracting and retaining staff and the ways that stakeholders define their different and common interests at work can have a great impact on how HRD at work is managed. However, the question here is to consider HRD at work and the involvement of line managers in it.

Evidently in many conceptualisations of changes in work, organisation and HRM in theory – and in many companies in practice – there are perceived to be advantages in making greater use of line managers as developers of people, as a part of one or a combination of these kinds of initiatives. The advantages of greater line management involvement in helping others to learn can be related to four main areas: the quantity of HRD at work, the quality of HRD at work, the value for management in the organisation, and the re-alignment of HRD activities with human relations changes in an organisation as a whole.

Advantages of greater line manager involvement in HRD

First, it is believed that there will be more development for a wide range of people if line managers are more involved in HRD at work. Long-standing criticisms of what have been called the 'sheep-dip' and 'injection' models of HRD at work have existed (Lynton & Pareek 2000). The idea that employees would, at regular intervals, be given doses of HRD had become institutionalised in organisational systems and workplace training practices. But the workplace now requires the promotion of positive attitudes towards continuous and lifelong learning. HRD at work is not something that happens periodically in formal classroom-based settings. It needs to be an integral feature of working life. To get a job, to retain a job or to develop a career people need to become more involved more often with HRD. This prescription applies to people in all situations. It applies to those who have no qualifications, and who may lack basic skills. It applies to those who have either academic or vocational qualifications, but not a balanced skill/knowledge base. It also applies to those who are highly trained professionals in occupations where keeping pace with new knowledge and skills has always been desirable but is now even more essential. To help promote such lifelong learning those currently in the workforce, rather than those in formal education, need to be reached and changed. There would seem to be a key role here for line managers to become more proactive about development. Line managers should expect and help to support the efforts of employees to learn and develop.

The second argument is that there will be a better quality of HRD at work for organisations and individuals if line managers are more directly involved. Criticisms of the quality of organisational learning interventions, such as classroom-based courses and traditional instructions/facilitation have stressed problems with the operation of the systematic training cycle (Allen 1994). The gap between organisational performance needs and individual performance can be closed where those who are familiar with both the organisational need and the individual play a greater role. That means line managers rather than training specialists who may neither understand the organisational need or the individual's needs or, indeed, fail to understand them both.

The third argument is that requiring line managers to be more involved in the HRD of employees will lead to a transformation of managers themselves. The need for such a transformation is justified by a critical estimation of line managers' generic people-management skills. The belief is that by taking developmental responsibilities on board line managers will have to change more generally, ultimately becoming more competent in

continued overleaf

interpersonal interactions in work teams. There are then benefits to line managers as they become more competent at managing people because they have to take responsibility for their development. These benefits help to enhance management in the organisation as a whole.

The final advantage, that is often identified, is that enlisting line managers as developers of people can contribute to broader organisational change and transformation of human relations at work. Broader change and transformation of human relations at work can be characterised at many levels. It may be focused on human relations being aligned with being more quality oriented, or with being more innovative, or with being more efficient and giving greater value for money. However it is characterised, the contribution of HRM-skilled line managers, and the enhanced interpersonal relationships that are thought to develop with HRD partnerships, is considered to be significant. People will be more inclined to and more able to talk to each other, to trust each other and to work together in periods of change.

Challenges in greater line manager involvement in HRD

The criticisms of greater line management involvement in helping others to learn at work can also be considered in relation to each of the claimed benefits. First there is a belief that there will be less development for many if line managers are made more responsible for staff development. Current learning at work systems are based in some way on systematically enabling people to participate in learning, despite pressures in the working environment to focus on productivity by continuously being busy working rather than away learning. If this element of the system is weakened, or indeed is done away with, then HRD might be neglected. Other pressures in the workplace, principally the need to deal with immediate tasks and short-term priorities, will take precedence. Without the option of taking time out to go and learn, learning will decline. Even if time is still set aside for learning it may be that, in the absence of well structured training plans and courses, employees will not get a complete and coherent package of HRD at work.

Second, there is no reason to believe that line managers can be better skilled developers than specialists trained in HRD at work, no matter how much development they receive as 'coaches' or 'trainers'. Inevitably most line managers will not be able to organise and evaluate HRD processes and practices of as high a quality as specialists. Line managers will not be as accurate as others can be in objectively determining HRD needs. Line managers will not be as good at instructing, coaching or facilitating development as specialists. And line managers will not be as adept at evaluating HRD in order to validate it, and/or highlight further HRD needs.

Thirdly, depending on line managers to fulfil these roles may mean marginalising specialists in HRD at work. Some argue that the specialist role will become transformed as line managers take more responsibility, rather than being marginalised; with specialists evolving to act in roles like an internal consultant or change agent, and being advisors to the line manager. In practice others fear it will often mean the actual or practical exclusion of specialists from the HRD process; as they and their facilities – whether those be humble training rooms or grand training centres – disappear from the scene. If relatively powerful HRD specialists are an important factor in ensuring that HRD is taken seriously then making managers more responsible may be a backward step. Outsourcing HRD facilities, requiring consultants to be bought in to provide HRD products and services, may prejudice effective HRD support.

Finally, many would argue it is naive to assume that relationships between line managers and staff can be the key relationship that guides an employee's development (Lynton and Pareek 2000). While managers need to evaluate performance and help out where they can, the responsibility for an employee's development should lie in part with a neutral third party. This is because the line manager–employee relationship may involve clashes of interests that the manager may not be in a position to resolve effectively. Lynton and Pareek characterise line managers' responses to being 'learning partners' as ranging from hostility and reluctance, through being critical and sceptical, to being supportive but little involved. That range of responses can be mirrored on the part of employees. In many organisations the traditional problems of managing career and personal development are compounded by the pace and scale of change, workforce restructuring and harsher

answer to exercise continued

internal labour-market regimes. Surviving in such a tough climate is a problem for everyone. What happens to the line manager as developer when, for example, the managers are asked to make decisions about the development needs of staff who might in a few months be competing for that line manager's job?

To summarise, in the absence of substantive evidence, a balanced view about these questions would be that there are clear links between using line managers for HRD and broader changes in HRM on the one hand, while on the other there are justifiable reservations about a greater role for line managers in this area of HRM. The question is perhaps better conceived as being about evaluating the implications of increasing the line manager role in HRD at work, rather than just contrasting it with a displacement or takeover of the conventional HRD specialist's role.

Learning in groups

> **By the end of this chapter you will be able to:**
>
> ▫ Identify the features supporting effective learning in groups;
> ▫ Analyse the challenges of managing interference in learning groups;
> ◻ Design systems for managing interference in learning in groups.

| introductory case | *An ensemble orchestra as an HRD provider* |

An ensemble orchestra (EO), a long established group of professional musicians, was contemplating developing a side-line in providing HRD. As they had recently lost some sponsorship income they were looking for new sources of income. The EO, usually numbering around 14 musicians, played a variety of string instruments; violins, violas and cellos. They were renowned for working without a conductor, both in rehearsal and performance, being led, instead, by the principal violinist. They had been performing music at concert venues throughout Europe, and had also been involved in educational projects in schools and communities.

The EO members thought they could offer products and services for the corporate HRD market. They got some support and worked with an HRD consultant to develop their core product: a one-day workshop event for team-building and development. The EO training day event is structured as a series of facilitated sessions:

Morning	Knowledge and Understanding
Session 1	Learners observe an EO performance
Session 2	Learners observe a rehearsal session for a new piece
Session 3	Learners discuss the rehearsal as an example of teamwork in small groups
Session 4	Learners continue their discussion on teamwork with the EO members

Afternoon	Practice and Experience
Session 5	Learners form groups to produce their own musical piece (called 'ready-steady-compose')
Session 6	Learners work in a team to rehearse their own musical performance
Session 7	Teams are modified and changed prior to performing for each other
Session 8	The learners perform their rehearsed pieces
Session 9	The training ends with tutor-led learner reflections on teams and communication

The EO members thought this workshop approach offered three things with direct connections to work organisations:

Teamworking	This is a world class team which comes together and learns new music pieces many times a year without a conductor.
Communication	Effective communication in rehearsals is the basis of the world-class team.
Speed	The team is able to attain world-class standards with less rehearsal time than other orchestras.

Introduction – context

Alongside the importance of the environment of development partnerships there is the environment of the group. Much formal and informal learning and development happens within groups. The group environment can range from being an informal collection of peers meeting occasionally and sharing experiences to sustained and intensive groups meeting regularly over years. In these latter forms members form a temporary community with the aim of learning about a subject or issue. In the introductory case the group environment is working with experienced musicians who provide a learning environment for reflecting on teamwork itself.

A group can be defined as consisting of at least two individuals, who:

- interact with each other;
- are psychologically aware of each other;
- perceive themselves as a group;
- are recognised as a group by at least one other group.

All four conditions must be met for an aggregation of individuals to be considered as a group (Tuckman 1965, Tuckman and Jensen, 1977). Group dynamics refers to the psychological processes within the group, and is concerned with the social interaction and the social forces among group members – how groups form, their structure and processes, how they function and how they affect individual members, other groups and the organisation

In this chapter we will look at how norms, roles and stages of formation can impact on learning groups. There will also be discussion of the importance of characteristics such as group size, cohesiveness, groupthink, social loafing and team qualities on learning in groups. Finally we look at some more challenging thinking about group formation and working, and the authority relations between learners and instructors and facilitators.

Group norms – role and formation stages

Groups impose norms and roles on their members. Group norms serve four main purposes:

- they express the central values of the group so they can inspire group members and project the nature of the group to others;
- they simplify and make more predictable the behaviour of individual group members;

- they prevent situations where group members may be offended or emotionally hurt;
- they increase the likelihood of group survival (e.g. by rejection of deviant behaviour that poses a threat to the existence of the group) and group success.

Roles are sets of tasks that group members are expected to complete to justify their group membership. In learning groups these will encompass the obvious roles of trainer and learner. But there can be different kinds of formal trainer and different kinds of formal learner role.

Group members have informal as well as formal roles. These roles vary widely and relate to the way a member interacts with other group members and the benefits he/she brings to the group. Belbin a well-known researcher and practitioner in the psychology of group behaviour has listed the informal roles that individuals tend to assume within groups (1996) including:

- the shaper, an aggressive achiever who helps drive the team in action;
- the plant, the innovator who provides creative ideas to the group;
- the monitor-evaluator, the critical thinker who queries the feasibility of plans;
- the implementer, hard working member who takes practical and efficient action to achieve group goals;
- the coordinator, who facilitates and organises the efforts of others;
- the completer-finisher, who pays attention to detail and ties up loose ends;
- the resource investigator, who liaises with others outside the group;
- the specialist, the technical expert who supplies the group with specialised knowledge.

Having individuals who will assume complementary informal roles within the group can dramatically improve group performance, as well as the satisfaction of group members. It is, for example, much better for a group to include a plant, a monitor-evaluator, an implementer and a specialist rather than four plants or four monitor-evaluators. The trainers and the learners can be aware of this and act accordingly.

Formal and informal groups in learning situations are never totally independent, and it is a mistake to think of formal and informal groups as distinct entities. The formal organisation is connected with, and largely determines, the informal one. Every formal organisation has informal groups and many informal organisations eventually evolve some semblance of formal groups. Learning situations are the same.

Formal and informal groups both naturally progress through a series of stages. The way in which a group does so will largely determine the extent to which it will succeed in its tasks. In the case of learning groups' learning tasks, these stages include forming, storming, norming, performing, and adjourning (Tuckman and Jensen 1977) – see Theory & Research Box 9.1.

If groups fail to progress successfully through one or more of these stages they may be dysfunctional; groups that do not deliver their objectives and/or impose psychological stress on some or all of their members. Although steps can be taken to improve the likelihood of successful progression through the group formation stages, internal group problems will always occur and dysfunctional groups in learning may always exist in organisations. The ideas of Bion can be used to explore features of dysfunctional groups in more detail.

| 9.1 | *Group formation stages* |

Forming. Group members get to know one another and understand their roles, as well as defining goals and expectations and developing procedures for task accomplishment. Group members tend to be reserved at this stage, in which case there may be uncertainty and even confusion. The use of 'ice-breaker' and introductory activities eases this.

Storming. Resolution of issues – such as methods for task accomplishment, definition and allocation of tasks, goal prioritisation, and leadership – often involves conflict and confrontation, which may cause member withdrawal or isolation. Clashes and disagreements over fundamental issues (goals, performance standards, roles) may hamper the group. Not resolving this will decrease the likelihood of the group succeeding in its mission, and progression through subsequent stages will also suffer.

Norming. The stage in which group norms are established, including intended or acceptable performance standards. Cooperation among group members is a dominant issue during this stage and ideally a sense of shared responsibility should develop, with high cohesion, shared group identity, and camaraderie. However, sub-optimal norms may be established in groups that have not successfully progressed from the previous stage.

Performing. The stage where the group reaches the peak of effectiveness and efficiency in task accomplishment, with the work roles of individual members, trainers and learners, accepted and understood. The persistence of covert conflict between group members from the storming stage will inhibit group performance. Performance can also be affected by members' pre-occupation with their individual performance and goals, the degree of functionality of norms, and the quality of leadership.

Adjourning. Once the group has achieved its intended objective (e.g. the learning is complete) it may be adjourned, and social relations are terminated. Adjourning can be 'natural' or timed to happen at the appropriate point, as with the planned break-up of a formal group after accomplishing its role. Untimed adjournment represents a sub-optimal case. In certain ongoing, permanent groups this last stage will never be reached.

Characteristics of effective groups

The characteristics of effective groups in general have been studied, and the conclusions from these studies can also be applied to thinking about learning in groups. The size of the group is a factor. When groups rely on direct relationships between their members, size plays an important role in performance. The functional size for a group ranges from three to twelve members, and optimal performance seems to occur with a membership of seven to nine. Researchers have found that increasing group size above nine has negative effects on verbal participation of group members, quality of decision-making, speed of communication, and satisfaction of group members. At twelve, interaction between members becomes difficult and the group 'naturally' splits into smaller sub-groups.

The cohesiveness of the group is a second factor. Cohesiveness refers to the strength and quality of interpersonal ties among group members. It depends on the frequency and quality of contact between group members, the degree of interdependence of members' roles, and the demographic and ideological (attitudinal/value) similarity of the group members. Group cohesiveness is strengthened when group members perceive external threats and the group has a history of success. Cohesiveness is a highly desirable quality for group performance. It serves as a motivator for the group, or the team, to work towards the advancement of the common objectives. Cohesiveness functions as a form of implicit control on group members in their activities, so these activities are compatible with the interests of the group. In most cases, cohesive groups will outperform their less cohesive counterparts. More cohesive groups are likely to perform better than their less cohesive counterparts (Evans and Dion 1991).

A history of success for the group builds cohesiveness. However, this can lead to complacency, with negative consequences for the quality of group decisions and group performance. This is because past performance creates the 'illusion of invulnerability', which impairs future decision-making. Group cohesiveness is one of the antecedents of the well-known phenomenon called 'groupthink' (Janis 1982). 'Groupthink' is defined as a deterioration of mental efficiency, reality testing and moral judgment that results from in-group pressures on individual members to conform and reach consensus.

Measures to counter groupthink include allowing free expression and even encouraging minority sub-groups and legitimising unpopular viewpoints. Clearly, it can be difficult to establish a climate of healthy debate and even conflict among group members, while at the same time aiming for a strong focus on learning around a consensus-based curriculum. Firms that operate in simple and relatively stable markets should benefit most from consensus while firms that operate in diversified and uncertain markets will benefit most if they encourage dissent and healthy conflict (Cosier and Schwenk 1990). So learning groups in simple and stable domains benefit from consensus, those in diverse and uncertain domains require dissent and healthy conflict.

'Social loafing' refers to the apparent reduction in the effort that individuals exhibit when they are required to accomplish a task as members of a group. However, although social loafing and coordination problems are obstacles in learning group performance it is still possible for a group to produce more than the cumulative productivity of its members. This is achieved when we instil coherence and purpose into the group. Coherence and purpose lead to a 'process gain' in a group situation. The implication is that the arrangement of work around groups, or teams, can have beneficial effects on performance, provided that there is appropriate planning and implementation.

A team can be distinguished as an evolution of the group; a group with some additional characteristics. A simple way to distinguish a team from a group is by defining a team as 'a group with a high performance ethic' (Katzenbach and Smith 1993). Hence, teams are groups whose norms include high performance standards. Other differences identified by some organisational scientists include:

- shared leadership in the team, rather than a clearly focused leader in the group; team members have complementary roles and shared objectives, so different members are able to assume leadership roles depending on the circumstances;
- mutual accountability of team members for team outcomes, in contrast to individual accountability of group members;
- the products of a team are collective, and cannot be produced by individuals alone, while the products of a group are accumulations of individual rather than synergetic work;
- team meetings are active and focus on resolving problems and producing innovative ideas, while group meetings simply focus on efficiency;

- performance measures for teams are direct, that is, they assess the collective products of the team, while performance measures for groups are indirect, that is, they focus on overall organisational or departmental performance.

Inter-team competition can be a major threat to the success of teamworking in organisations (Mohrman, Cohen and Mohrman 1995) because it promotes interest in and commitment to the team rather than to the organisation. In learning situations teams that compete with each other may withhold vital information from other teams or be unwilling to provide them with specialist help and support.

Group formation, working and authority

The preceding ideas outline the most common ideas about groups in current thinking around cohesiveness and themes like social loafing. The importance of factors interfering with group relations and their impact on learning is often still underplayed in the study and professional development of trainers and educators. People mostly learn through experience about the group environment for learning. But better performance in handling instruction and facilitation groups, particularly the latter which are increasing in use, requires deeper analysis. To be able to facilitate learning in groups effectively requires an understanding of the nature and challenges of group formation and group working. Practically, the aim is to nurture an environment demonstrating positive signs of being a good environment for learning, without the negative features that can indicate an environment for learning is absent (see Operations Box 9.1)

operations

9.1	*Positive and negative signs for a learning group environment*

Positive signs	Negative signs
Relaxed and friendly	Tense and stressed
Open exchange of information	Lack of exchange
Providing suggestions and solutions	No suggestions or solutions given
Willing to participate	Unwilling to participate
Staying focused on learning	Not focused on learning
Feeling of comfort and enjoyment	Uncomfortable
Working with the instructor/facilitator	Conflict with the instructor/facilitator

Source Derived from Hardingham 2000.

The leadership and authority demands on those seeking to act as instructors or facilitators of learning groups in formal adult education settings can be explored in more depth. The group and social context of most adult learning and education has attracted some 'method'-oriented analysis, with tips and techniques for facilitating groups. Adult learning has tended to stick around a prescriptive approach to facilitated learning that favours a menu of participative methods and action learning-like techniques. The learning contexts vary widely, from large lecture theatres through groups of around 30 learners and down to small teams of 3 or 4 learners. Accordingly the leadership and authority issues vary. Many professionals will have encountered a range of stresses and problems in seeking to fulfil the role of facilitator of a group in many different situations. There have been few theoretical advances, making some of the original thinking on group environments in this field by people like Bion (1977) of continuing significance.

Bion was a pioneer in applying ideas and concepts from psychodynamic theory about individuals and their problems to groups and their dynamics. His original motivation was to establish better therapy systems, based on people experiencing analysis in groups. Since he discussed and outlined his thinking, his ideas have migrated in various ways to thinking more generally about group processes and group relations in other contexts. For Bion a healthy group had certain characteristics (see Theory & Research Box 9.2.) For these healthy characteristics to be present and be sustained in a group, whether supporting therapeutic tasks or other tasks, required leader–follower relations to nurture them. This was easy to describe and prescribe, but often presented immense difficulty in practice. For Bion this was attributable to a fundamental ambiguity about being in a group. While people need to be in groups to satisfy various individual needs, they also find them a stress. Each of the positive characteristics signalling a good environment can be undermined and interfered with as the natural stresses are worked out. Alongside the potential of any group to satisfy an individual is the potential of group membership to present challenges to each person. People in a group may have diverse purposes, they may not recognise the same boundaries to the group as others, they may not respond well to losing old members or absorbing new ones, they may evolve sub-groups, they may devalue some members and they may be unable to confront discontent in the group. Each of these possible problems emerges organically and naturally from the group experience. They are not attributable to error on the part of a facilitator or leader. Central to the way that these problems may be encountered is how people form an idea of how they are being 'perceived' by the group, via a sense of its collective 'group mentality'. That may seriously jar with the individual's own sense of self.

theory & research

9.2 | Healthy group characteristics

- A common purpose
- Common recognition by members of the boundaries
- Able to absorb new members and lose old ones
- Freedom from internal sub-groups with exclusive boundaries
- Individuals all valued and with free movement
- Able to recognise and cope with discontent

Leadership and authority in groups then involves appreciating the existence and role of dynamics emerging around these potentially unhealthy characteristics and perceptions of group mentality. Managing a learning environment is like managing a leader–follower relationship that aims for the ideals and avoids drift (see Operations Box 9.2); people achieving things, cooperatively, using skills, with purposeful activity and cognitive processing engaging with reality. Tensions around group mentality and the individuals' sense of self applies equally to the leader, the facilitator, as well as the followers.

Any group of adults assembled to learn will be subject to these kinds of dynamics under the leadership and authority of a group instructor or facilitator. How group

9.2	Ideals, signs of drift and interference factors

Ideal group	Signs of drift	Learning interference
A common purpose	Different purposes	Competing purposes
Recognition of boundaries	Confusion of boundaries	Conflict on boundaries
Absorb new/lose old	Tensions on new/old	Disruption of new/old
No sub-groups	Elements of sub-groups	Definite sub-groups
Individuals valued/free	Most valued/free	Few valued/free
Discontent managed	Discontent ignored	Discontent erupting

relations might be best managed can be considered by following Bion's thinking about the leadership issues that present problems for groups, and thinking about what might be encountered in learning settings. The questions that a facilitator needs to be aware of and answer to support the positive and avoid the negative are:

- What are the group's needs?
- What are the danger signs?
- How to keep the negative group dynamics at bay?
- How detached from the group should I be?

Group needs

When people come together to participate in learning they typically face a set of inter-personal issues which they need to work through, address and resolve:

- **Inclusion needs**: the facilitator of learning needs to give them a place and accept their identity in the beginning, during the experience, and in concluding it.
- **Control needs**: the people in the group seek to understand who is in control, what their responsibilities are, and how others will be exerting their control? There are power issues, as control may lie with different people at different times. As learning experiences are unfolding people in the group may be divided and re-composed into sub-groups. It is important to avoid trainer–trainee power confrontations, and defuse trainee–trainee conflicts in group work.
- **Affection needs**: in any kind of group people have affection needs, served by open-ness and closeness, with personal worth being validated.

For instructors or facilitators a concern is to satisfy their own needs in these areas while maintaining some detachment, because the instructor or facilitator is not part of the learning group. They are in the learning environment, but they belong to other groups which are not present; for example, to external groups such as the HRD de-partment or their professional group. The instructor or facilitator seeks conformity with positive norms and values, and model behaviours.

Functional signs and interference signs

Bion provides a framework for thinking about why and how negative group dynamics can arise, despite the best efforts of a skilled instructor or facilitator. He argued that groups aspired to be functional work groups, but that underlying 'basic assumptions' might emerge and interfere with that. A functional work group would be one that is getting on with the tasks in hand; in the case of learning, the learning tasks. A 'basic assumption' is a form of group mentality that expresses a primitive emotion about what the group exists to do. As an assumption it is often never consciously perceived by people in the group, but can be traced and seen in behaviours. A group with interference from a 'basic assumption' would not be a functional work group. They would be subject to interference and be 'losing the plot'. It would be spending time and energy on things other than the functional task (see Theory & Research Box 9.3).

theory & research

9.3 Functional group vs interference effects

Signs of a functional work group	Signs of a basic assumption interfering
Clear about what needs to be done	Lose focus, or too intense and rigid
Output high	Low standards
Ready to disband at the appropriate time	Time wasted on relations not working
Open to the outside	Hostile to outside
Reviews itself and improves	Sees feedback as a threat
Acknowledges failure and analyses it	Denies failure, ignores it
Tolerates differences	Unspoken rules, in-jokes, covert activity

resources

9.1 Functional group vs basic assumption interference

Examples of the differences between a functional group and one experiencing interference are plentiful. Much 'reality television' is based on showing groups experiencing such interference for entertainment. Some to think about would be:

Functional group	Basic assumption interference
Football team in a challenging game	Same team in the pub after, disparaging their opposition
Yacht crew sailing a stormy sea	The yacht crew arguing about who is to cook dinner
Management team discussing budgets	The same management team paralysed in contemplation of a changing world
A learning syndicate group brainstorming	A learning syndicate group just having a gossip

In learning groups, as in groups generally, the foundation is that people ought to be given relevant and interesting work that is achievable. The instructor or facilitator ought to keep groups organised and structured. Even then groups may experience basic assumptions and interference. The first signs may be:

- coming to depend excessively and unrealistically on the instructor or facilitator;
- seeing the instructor or facilitator as an 'enemy' in some way;
- looking to members of the group to ally with and/or take over from the instructor or facilitator.

Underlying these signs and behaviours the following may be active issues to deal with:

- **Transference**: where negative feelings about a significant person or people in authority are being transferred from the original source into the current relationship. The instructor or facilitator is an innocent agent on the end of negative feelings in a group.
  - In learning groups these may occur in straightforward ways as people consider the instructor or facilitator to be like an archetypal authority figure such as a 'teacher' or 'parent' and respond accordingly.
  - Response – clear up any contamination of transference from other experiences.
- **Projection**: learning group members can have sensitive or negative traits or beliefs that they are uncomfortable with and anxious about. They may come to see these sensitive or negative traits and beliefs in others, recognising they exist but keeping a clean and positive view of themselves as 'good' people. This helps them to avoid owning the 'bad' traits themselves. Instead they can be seen to appear as qualities in others, allowing the members of the learning group to release tension about the sensitive or negative trait or belief.
  - In learning groups projection may occur around being assessed. People are subjective in their reactions to this but like to think they are being objective, while the assessor is seen to be subjective if they do not get a brilliant mark.
  - Response – clear up misunderstandings.
- **Splitting**: under stress people tend to perceive things in black-and-white terms; they adopt extreme positions, being either for or against ideas, suggestions, etc.
  - Learning can be stressful if the demands it makes exceed the capabilities of the learners and if, instead of reviewing that accordingly, the stress builds discussions can become polarised and the instructor or facilitator and group members may end up in extreme positions.
  - Response – reduce stress, bring learning back within capabilities.

Conclusion

Managing learning in groups is an environment for much workplace learning and development. There is much prescriptive 'best practice' on this for instruction and facilitation. This is useful, but limited. When there are difficulties with a learning group the underlying sources of that can be very complex and challenging. One framework for exploring this is an analysis of the basic assumptions, derived from Bion, that may interfere with the functioning of a group. To keep on, or get back on, track to a positive learning climate and attaining group ideals to achieve learning means understanding these basic assumptions and their dynamics as they emerge in mild forms, or even 'erupt' very strongly.

Interference from these basic assumptions can be hard to work through. One reason for that is that they may provide a rationale for the group to feel fulfilled even when the members are not actually learning. At the other extreme, the group may produce situations that make the group punishing for at least some individuals, including the leader, the instructor or facilitator. This reverses the satisfactions of group membership, and produces dis-satisfaction. While this is to be seen as something to avoid it is also an organic part of group experience, and cannot be excised. Such dis-satisfactions are never going to be eradicated as long as people continue to be ambivalent about being in groups. The more realistic aim is that people will still want to continue in membership rather than leave a learning group.

The 'solution' is not for the leader of the learning group to eradicate the prospect of interference. It is for the group to work with and through interference and strive to sustain the environment of a healthy group, which, to reprise, is:

- A common purpose;
- Common recognition by members of the boundaries;
- Capacity to absorb new members and lose old ones;
- Freedom from internal sub-groups with exclusive boundaries;
- Individuals all valued and with 'free movement';
- Able to face and cope with discontent.

9.2 Healthy group and keys to instruction and facilitation		
	Instruction	**Facilitation**
Common purpose	Obtaining information	Engaging and participating in experiences
Recognise boundaries	Limits of instructor's role, limits of learner role	Dealing with other learners, respecting perspectives
Absorb new, lose old	Who joins (new instructors, new learners)	Who joins and what occurs in group work
No exclusive sub-groups	Managing natural networks among different levels of ability in the whole group	Keeping control of syndicate groups and smaller groupings in the larger whole
All valued	No one lost, no one starring	No one lost, no one 'starring'
Cope with discontent	Misunderstanding, pace, puzzlement	More emotional responses, anxieties about roles and participating, self-knowledge and reflection

Multiple-choice questions

9.1 Which of the following is not one of Belbin's team roles?

A the shaper, an aggressive achiever to help drive the team in action.

B the critic, an insightful member who takes issue with and confronts beliefs and assumptions.

C the monitor-evaluator, the critical thinker to query feasibility of plans.

D the plant, the innovator who provides creative ideas to the group.

9.2. Wilfred Bion was

A. A pioneer in applying ideas and concepts from psychodynamic theory .

B. The person who suggested the group stages of forming-storming-norming-performing.

C A researcher who added to Belbin's team role descriptions.

D A renowned expert in adult learning and HRD.

References

Belbin R.M. (1996) *Management Teams: Why they succeed or fail*, Oxford, Butterworth-Heinemann.

Bion, W.R. (1977) *Experiences in Groups*, London, Tavistock.

Cosier, R.A. and Schwenk, C.R. (1990) 'Agreement and thinking alike: Ingredients for poor decisions', *Academy of Management Executive*, vol. 4, no. 1, pp. 69–74.

Evans, C. and Dion, K. (1991) 'Group cohesion and performance: a meta-analysis, *Small Group Research*, vol. 22, no. 2, pp. 175–86.

Hardingham, A. (2000) *Psychology for Trainers*, London, CIPD.

Janis, I. (1982) *Groupthink*, 2nd edn, Boston, MA, Houghton-Mifflin

Katzenbach, J.R. and Smith, D.K. (1993) 'The discipline of teams', *Harvard Business Review*, no. 71 (March–April), pp. 111–46.

Mohrman, S.A., Cohen, S.A. and Mohrman, A. (1995) *Designing Team-based Organizations*, San Francisco, CA, Jossey Bass.

Tuckman, B.W. (1965) 'Developmental sequences in small groups', *Psychological Bulletin*, no. 63, pp. 384–99.

Tuckman, B.W. and Jensen, M.A.C. (1977) 'Stages of small group development revisited', *Group and Organizational Studies*, no. 2, pp. 419–27.

Q

concluding short case question | *ensemble orchestra case*

Read the introductory case for this chapter again and consider:

How might the specialist HRD provider be advised to develop the product in order to ensure the learning environment of the group will work effectively?

You can also make reference to how aspects of HRD strategy, e-learning, the advantages of specialists providers and the use of developmental relations (like coaching and mentoring) might be relevant here as well.

A

concluding short case model answer

This question requires you to demonstrate achievement of objectives which are about analysing the practices associated with HRD group environments in work and organisations.

This is an example of Arts-Based Training (ABT), that is, training and development which is designed and delivered by artists using arts practices, such as theatre, music and creative writing. By using those arts and learning from people with skills from the worlds of theatre, music and the visual arts, it is believed that a workforce can be stimulated in groups to think in new ways. Proponents of ABT also argue that the arts engage groups of people's hearts and minds with unique immediacy, that there is an 'X' factor at work. Businesses have employed artist-trainers to unlock the creativity of their staff, help build effective teams, enhance leadership and personal impact skills, boost confidence, improve external and internal communication, develop future scenarios and instigate and maintain change programmes.

On one level the ensemble experience clearly represents a creative and imaginative approach to learning in groups. It is an entertaining means to a serious end. Hearing, seeing and playing music, being in the presence of world-class musicians is indeed a great pleasure, for music lovers especially. There is evident pleasure among the participants and good levels of informal interaction between them and the musicians. Using this as a means of learning and developing workplace skills related to teams, communication and speed is a version of the

continued overleaf

| concluding short case model answer continued |

same kind of design found in the adoption of outdoor activity-based training. This is fun and play, but with a purpose. This also fits with a number of trends:

- in organisations for team-based, high-performance concerns;
- in work, for knowledge workers, professionals, creative people, the changing gender composition of workforce;
- in learning design, for more creative and imaginative methods.

The first consideration is how norms, roles and stages of formation can impact on learning groups. The norms of the group would be established early around active participation with the musicians. The roles for learners would be observers initially, with the large group of musicians being 'demonstrators' of communication in teams. The roles would shift in the morning to have the learners more active as questioners and discussants, with the musicians also acting as discussants, engaging in conversations. The opportunity for all to contribute at this stage, or for some to dominate proceedings, would need some one to act as an overall facilitator. There would perhaps be a lack of 'storming' early on as the learners would be passive, and that storming might emerge in this later discussion stage. In the afternoon the roles alter considerably as the learners have to become active in doing something, creating and performing. Each sub-group which is involved with this would go through its own stages of formation to be able to get to the performing stage. The facilitator at this stage might take a more teacher-like role and, given the roles being fulfilled, there is scope for learners to slip into a 'child'-like role with the basic percussion instruments in use.

Next is the importance of characteristics such as group size, cohesiveness, groupthink, social loafing and team qualities on learning in groups. This will initially be a very large group, with the musicians and an equal or greater number of learners. At various stages there will be work in smaller groups, to make participation possible for all. The cohesiveness of the musicians as a training group would be expected to be high, and they might be expected to demonstrate cohesiveness – but learning might also emerge from seeing differences in thinking in the group, and conflict being generated and managed as they rehearse. Perhaps being observed will influence the musicians to behave in ways they would not normally in rehearsals. Groupthink is not a major concern here, but the possibility for people to be pulled into an uncritical perception of the musicians as they perform – always an impressive experience this close up among such talented people – might interfere with learning about teamwork rather than aid it. Social loafing is possible in the morning and the afternoon. In the morning people might just sit through it all, enjoying the demonstration and listening to others talking. In the afternoon people might let high contributors take over the music preparation exercise.

Finally, there is more challenging thinking about group formation and working, and the authority relations between learners and instructors and facilitators. In groups like this there seems to be scope for the deeper aspects of group environment in learning to emerge around the facilitating role in the morning and instruction in the afternoon.

	Morning facilitation	Afternoon instruction
A common purpose	Learning about teamwork, but underneath that there can be different agendas.	Preparation and performance, but differential levels of ability and interest might surface.
Recognise boundaries	The musicians need to have boundaries about what they are doing and will discuss. The learners also have boundaries as they enter each session and end them.Also they have to deal with other learners, and respect different perspectives.	The limits of the instructor's role in such exercises is important; do they step in to help move on struggling groups, or leave them to work through the dynamics of a struggling group?

concluding short case model answer continued		
	Morning facilitation	**Afternoon instruction**
Absorb new, lose old	The group would form at the beginning as a whole, uniting the musicians and the learners. It would split into sub-groups for some discussions. Who joined which group and what occurred in group work would be of note.	As teams are modified in the afternoon, some people move from one group to another. This is intended to show how issues about gaining and losing group members can influence performance.
No exclusive sub-groups	Keeping control of syndicate groups and smaller groupings in the larger whole will be an issue in the morning. Orchestras themselves have organised sub-groups, of course.	In the afternoon the whole group is split, so that needs to be managed. On what basis are the teams formed for this? Do they reflect some formal controlled creation by a facilitator, or informal sub-groups who like to work together? Should the latter option be encouraged or avoided?
All valued – no one lost, no one 'starring'	The musicians are the 'stars'.	Can be attained as long as all are recognised, accepting differential performance outcomes.
Cope with discontent – misunderstanding, pace, puzzlement	Emotional responses are elicited by music. There can also be anxieties about roles in communicating with talented people.	What people encounter as they try to practise might frustrate them, and they can be anxious about the eventual performance to end the day.

Other connections to HRD with this kind of learning and learning environment would be the following.

Understanding HRD strategies

Does this fit with the kinds of strategy favoured by organisations? There are ways in which the EO workshop might be marketed as a combination of HRD strategies. It is systematic training as it is offered as a one-day workshop with clearly defined objectives – but it is not delivered by professional trainers. It is business-oriented, for businesses where team development and communication issues equivalent to those facing the EO are a challenge. Those would be professional organisations, knowledge and high skill organisations, but it is not business-oriented because it is based on an arts experience not business world activity. It is not aligned, as a structured workshop, with continuous development practices embedded in the workplace, nor is it consistent with self-development practices.

The EO is trying to appeal to a wide range of 'real teams', groups of people in workplaces, when maybe their target audience for this kind of activity could be sharper:

- reasonable teams that need to shift up and become world-class;
- senior management leadership development awareness of world-class team issues;
- teams required to work creatively and innovatively.

EO members are using elements of the language of 'competence' around team roles and communication, but they might perhaps make more this. The ensemble is explicitly identifying these as areas of need where organisations may wish to adopt creative and imaginative approaches to learning. Constituent 'skills' that can be emphasised as underpinning their achievement of world class standards quickly are:

- motivation;
- decision-making;
- role clarity;
- goal setting;
- working under pressure;
- communication.

continued overleaf

| concluding short case model answer continued |

ABT may be particularly appealing in circumstances where there is a strategic commitment to move from 'providing training' to 'managing learning'. Experiences other than orthodox classroom-based training are appropriate for organisations in which staff are expected to be learning continuously, often within a structure of personal plans and core competences. This creates a climate favourable to innovations such as arts-based learning in general and the ensemble in particular.

Using e-learning

Could some or all of this all be transferred to an e-learning environment? There might, for example, be video clips of the EO playing and rehearsing, so that the first part of the day could be accessed by learners at their own convenience, and there would be no need to have the whole EO present at a training event. But might that reduce the enjoyment and impact of the experience as a whole? The later elements based on making music could done virtually over networks, sharing samples of sounds or creating music using software rather than the somewhat childish percussion instruments they are using in the practical part of the workshop. But aqain, unless the learners are used to working in virtual teams this would not reflect their normal working environment.

Mentoring

There is no apparent scope for mentoring roles in this HRD. Some coaching will occur in the course of the 'making music' practical exercise in the afternoon, but there is no personal, one-to-one relationship in the core areas of being in a team and communicating. This aspect of HRD might be aligned with learners' other relations rather than expecting the external HRD provider to fulfil that role.

Specialist HRD providers

The EO should appreciate the concerns arising when organisations use specialist HRD providers. These are about ensuring that joint ventures are clearly established, with explicit responsibilities and expectations fulfilled in the manner expected by both parties. The underlying challenge for the EO in using ABT is that the arts are not natural partners with business. Organisations can be uncertain about the quality of normal HRD providers, but in this case each partner also has distinct values and identity. Work organisations produce or provide services in circumstances where efficiency and effectiveness are critical. Creative and performing arts groups perform in circumstances where aesthetics are critical. It is possible to find a 'fit' between people with the values of arts and people with the values of work organisations, but it is not a seamless match.

In conclusion, the EO needs to give more thought to:

- how the workshop can be differentiated from other group learning practices designed to provide learning for the needs considered relevant (e.g. outdoor activit- based team development);
- how the shift in corporate context from providing training to managing learning can be fulfilled by using things like ABT;
- how perceptions of their professionalism as trainers is an important part of their credibility, not their reputation as musicians.

That is to say that all aspects of practices covered in the module are of relevance and significance, even if they are not all fulfilled (e.g. no mentoring as part of this event, but maybe mentoring is needed as a follow-on/ additional support for team roles and communication skills).

10

Technology change and HRD

By the end of this chapter you will be able to:

- describe the evolution of e-learning technologies in use in HRD;
- discuss the strengths and weaknesses of various uses of e-learning in HRD;
- analyse the cost, quality and other features of e-learning in HRD;
- critically evaluate the changes and challenges involved in integrating e-learning within HRD.

10.1 Technology is stuff that doesn't work yet

"It's when people stop thinking of something as a piece of technology that the thing starts to have its biggest impact...the wheel, the book, the alphabet were all once wonders of the world...now they are everywhere."

John Lancaster (2006) 'A bigger bang', *Guardian Magazine*, 4 November, p. 20.

introductory case study   *e-learning in context*

A large pharmaceuticals organisation was going through a period of major change, introducing new ways of working. The purchasing function in the organisation, which bought supplies and materials, was to be changed. It was to shift from having 'do it all' purchasing units based on each of the company's several sites to being organised into units dealing with discrete categories of expenditure for all sites. This purchasing function involved 500 people in 41 different countries. The goal for the company as a whole was to make better decisions and cost savings. The business objective for the purchasing function was to make it the 'best in class' for the industry. To achieve this it needed to develop core competences in new ways of working and in technical skills. Without this HRD the organisation believed it faced a mass exodus of staff, with the implications that entailed for more recruitment and induction training.

The first step the company took was to develop a new competence framework, based on the changed organisation, in which several levels of management had been stripped out and many people's jobs had been changed. This also required a clear career map showing how individuals could progress in the different roles of buyers, budget-holders and senior managers. Technical competences, such as negotiating skills and financial analysis, had priority during this stage.

continued overleaf

The organisation used courses, on-the-job development and 'development zones'. The last of these were delivered by self-contained multimedia modules and intranet-based materials. The organisation developed an online career and development planning tool. This enabled staff to identify their own competence requirements and gaps. There were also links to development activity suggestions, from courses to self-study modules. This was a flexible way of providing HRD across the globe for all the staff. However, they faced a number of problems with:

- different technology infrastructures in different parts of the company;
- variations in bandwidth capacity in different countries, causing problems with accessing internet materials;
- variations in levels of computer literacy among staff;
- building in effective HRD: existing instruction material could not just be transferred online, interaction had to be built in;
- costs: it took around 300 hours of development to create 1 hour of content, at a developer's fee of £100 an hour. This meant a cost of £30 000 per hour of learning material.

Introduction

Along with the social context, the development partnerships and group environments, technologies have been incorporated into learning in the workplace. Technologies are the practical applications of science, the equipment used to support learning. Just as social practices have evolved and been adapted for workplace learning so have technologies. Sometimes it appears that technological developments can drive wholesale changes in HRD, and challenge the social systems it previously was built around.

In the contemporary context HRD is evolving to facilitate the digital economy, organisations based on extensive networked telecommunications and computing power. HRD is just one area of organisational practice among many changed by the onset and rise of the digital era. For some, the potential net effects on HRD of developments in information and communication technologies (ICT) and the development of the internet are of an order that could mean the wholesale transformation of learning in the workplace. This is because the use of ICT and the internet promise to make learning more accessible, more enjoyable and better aligned, with self-directed, more realistic work-based learning systems, which could result in greater learner and memory retention rates – and all at less cost. The technical platform for such a change exists now, and continues to evolve at a rate which reduces its costs considerably.

But the widespread use of ICT, other communications media and internet-based and multimedia training is still far from being the norm. It appears that only a minority of organisations use any kind of ICT for HRD in any significant way at all. Surveys also suggest that those with access to these technologies would prefer to use older technologies such as paper- and person-based versions of learning materials, because these are easier to use or provide more detail. The early heralding of the advent of e-learning as the new platform for HRD at work seems to have been more hype than substance.

Why this might have been so leads to looking at unclear thinking about how and what HRD practices can be enhanced by technologies, and which are better kept apart from technical change. It also means recognising that HRD is indeed embedded in a socio-technical system. Certain sets of social relations emerge to fit the use of a certain kind of technology; trainers and instruction in classrooms, for example. If the technologies change they may disrupt these existing social relations. That might usher in a period of transition and change to new social relations, or it might just lead to confusion and poorer performance or even degeneration of the system as a whole. Now as technologies evolve far quicker than the social relations around them can, managing to adapt roles and change relations becomes a bigger and bigger challenge for the providers and consumers of learning.

Quality issues have always been raised about the impact of technologies. In the UK, for example, a University for Industry (UfI) was established as a clearinghouse for providing e-learning resources to companies. Learning packages from over 700 organisations were submitted as samples of work for inclusion as resources. But no more than a quarter of these were deemed to have achieved appropriate quality standards during the first stage of assessment by a panel of experts. The main reason for this

---

10.1 | *Customer contact centre*

Many organisations are faced with the need to train staff while maintaining service levels to customers. This includes organisations in the 'contact centre' sector. Contactco operated over 200 branches and employed 7500 people in the UK, France and Italy. It provided a banking service across multichannels including telephone, internet, interactive TV and wireless telephony. Its main open-plan contact centre had 450 agents who serviced over one million customers. Contactco was faced with the challenge of training 250 contact centre staff, independently from the live customer relationship management (CRM) system, while maintaining service levels. It chose a fully interactive training solution that could run in parallel with live operations.

The company identified the need to improve the overall quality of contact centre agents. Ultimately, it wanted to create improved customer quality, reduce call centre staff turnover, and improve servicing techniques. The company installed an interactive call centre agent CRM system training solution. This was based on real customer scenarios, with a simulated system environment that could be delivered to the contact centre agents at their desks as case studies. One of the main reasons for selecting such a solution was to avoid the constant interruptions the company had experienced with the previous training environment. No inductions or training could be run while the system was being upgraded, and upgrades required approximately 4 weeks to make the changes, including preparation, system downtime and testing. Upgrades may be required every 3–4 months, but with the CBT system the company can continue training during the upgrades.

Phase 1 of the project involved training 250 new employees at the call centre with the customised CRM training solution. The course focused on handling 20 key customer scenarios. PC skills training was addressed first, to ensure that the agents' PC skills were to the standard required for CRM training. It was important to work with the live CRM application as early as possible in the induction period to get the agents comfortable with the system. The solution provides the trainee with a simulation of the live CRM application in its up-to-date configuration. The training application is on a learning management system (LMS) that will allow both the user and the training manager to navigate around the learning materials easily and intuitively. The LMS will also provide information management to the training team about the progress of the individual.

When the agent has passed the 4-week induction period, more customer-facing skills are introduced, such as customer management skills, dealing with difficult customers, and advanced communication techniques. The company now has a training environment that mirrors the live environment. There are benefits in terms of being able to duplicate the most frequent call types in a scenario format, and in ensuring that delegates are aware of and can use the relevant systems.

The reaction from agents to the e-CRM training solutions has been positive. Trainees are very enthusiastic. They all agree that it is a good confidence-builder, and it is a good way to become familiar with the system. For the training function, the issue is the need to tailor the induction schedule continuously so that CBT is conducted in such a way that new trainees always find the scenarios interesting.

failure seemed to be a tendency to use presentational spin rather than informed learning design, producing e-learning materials that were strong on glossy presentation but weak on pedagogy.

To understand what has been happening, and what the changes and challenges of e-learning entail, it is necessary first to look back at the history of technologies in HRD. It is important to keep in mind three related issues here: the technology, the pedagogy and the social dimensions of technologies in learning. The technology component is the most volatile element of the three. With the latest changes in digital technologies there is continuing rapid change in web-based and other platforms. With higher bandwidth, smaller 'screens', mobile access, and innovation in multimedia communication there is much that can and will change almost daily. The pedagogy element is more constant; technological change has revealed nothing 'new' regarding adult learning or approaches to understanding how to manage learning. Ideas about managing learning can be helix-like, though: they circle in and out of fashion, and can be differently combined or formulated as they come around again. The evolution of the third strand – social relations – is about how changes in employment and workplaces also alter how social relations in organisations' look and feel as the knowledge economy emerges. This can impact on managing learning in an era where the old model of an 'expert trainer' controlling the learning of 'deficit learners' is receding into history, to be replaced by a model of partnership based on strengths and more positive beliefs and assumptions.

A brief history of HRD technologies

For much of human history, learning has not been mediated by any specialist technology. By 'specialist technology' is meant a set of materials, infrastructure and system that involve channels of communication other than direct exchange between a master and a learner. For most of human history, and across most human cultures, learning has been embedded in a personal and direct social relationship; between members of a family or a community, or in guilds with masters and apprentices. The intimate and personal expert–learner relationship has been based on direct communication between these individuals, in the context of their domestic, community and work experience on real-life tasks. There were no learning technologies as such; there were just the technologies of work that had to be learned, the mysteries of a craft. These were typically learned through experience; working and learning were directly interconnected, and were usually embedded in family and community relations.

The core of social relationships changed with urbanisation and industrialisation and, partly because of this, there were consequent developments in learning technologies. The medium of publishing and the 'classroom' and specialist institutions dedicated to education, provided the first changes and challenges to the age-old recipe. Now these technologies were mediating learning and work: learning involved engaging with being able to read and write, and was experienced in environments with formally designated specialists, such as teachers in a classroom. The value of this kind of technology was its ability to deliver standardised, mass education, training and instruction. For learners, access to the institutions and systems of learning meant access to careers and social progress. The institutions of education and training would become battlegrounds for the newly forming social classes just as much as the sites of production in factories would be.

But there was also an important and well recognised cost, much remarked on at the time: learning became divorced from work. Romantics, such as the renowned philosopher Rousseau, lamented this separation. The social context for learning changed from the workplace to the institutions of learning and the technologies used by the 'school' system to provide mass education, training and instruction. The technologies and systems of 'schooled learning' were based on providing more effective large-scale instruction. The technology of learning has changed little since the advent of the schooled learning system, with instruction remaining the core method of delivery. The changes that have occurred have been from the blackboard to the whiteboard, from the spoken lecture to the use of LCD projectors, and from the rote memorising of core texts to the use of learning projects, perhaps involving internet research. But the essential technical system remains one of instruction and schooled learning.

Many learners seemed so disaffected by their experiences of learning in institutions that they would not complete their studies or begin new courses of study. And even if they were not disaffected, the usefulness of what was being learned was increasingly questioned: learners could pass academic tests, but were they prepared for the future demands of working life?

These kinds of criticism have motivated an interest in the use of alternative technical systems to support learning, and HRD at work. This has meant that as new technologies arise, their application to support HRD is explored, often avidly to begin with. The first modern technology to offer something apparently different for learning in this respect was the medium of **film**. This was perceived as a medium that could provide structured, stimulating communication, enabling consistent messages and instruction to be delivered economically to huge numbers of people in locations throughout the world. The US military were pioneers in this, both before and during the Second World War, developing the widespread use of army training films. They used film for HRD that ranged from instructions on weapons maintenance to the promotion of personal hygiene. Thereafter commercial film providers were established, focusing mainly on learning materials for the mass market for school-based education. The modern HRD industry has many companies producing video- and CD/DVD-based learning materials, continuing this tradition of film, but, although the use of such materials is now commonplace, it is not the foundation of learning.

Next came the development of **broadcasting**, first with radio and then with television. As radio and television became mainstream features of people's lives their educational as well entertainment applications were explored. Indeed, in some countries a system of public control of broadcasting existed that explicitly incorporated a mission to educate, including the BBC in the UK. In other countries, such as the USA, the competition between private firms to run broadcasting to reach high ratings and big audiences meant that educational interests were a low priority. The broadcasters' main concerns were marketing campaigns – a different form of influencing knowledge and attitudes.

Radio and TV broadcasts were cheaper and quicker to produce than film-based productions, and they could be communicated to vast audiences simultaneously. In education there were forecasts of the demise of teachers in classrooms and their replacement with the 'teacher on a screen'. These visions have, of course, failed to materialise. In some countries, however, there have been significant developments in broadcasting. In the UK, for example, the most sophisticated incarnation of this vision was the development of the Open University (OU) in the 1960s. The OU continues to provide much programming for learning support in all kinds of subject. The 'cheap and cheerful' production values of the early days have been superseded by professional and sophisticated products. Early programme makers, of course, did not have much experience in how to make 'learning' programmes well; they produced material that was too often boring, with no scope for interaction with learners or feedback. Teachers in classrooms and trainers in their training facilities were still safe. Even when quality improved, the impact of broadcasting has not been as conceived by the more fervent visionaries. This is attributable to both economic and social challenges, as there was neither enough money to make good educational programmes economically nor the staff to make them. And the interests of many learners in experiencing direct contact regularly with teachers or trainers in local relations persisted.

The 1980s saw the development of **computer-based training** (CBT). This promised more interactivity, getting over the problems of the passive learner in broadcasting and film. This was possible because CBT enabled personal involvement and participation. With the development of powerful personal computers the prospects for this seemed even better. The use of multimedia – text, graphics, animation, film and audio mixed together to provide information and enable interaction – was heralded as a way to 'turbocharge' learning. But in practice there were problems with these developments. First, there were technical issues associated with diverse kinds of platform and operating system, not only those provided by vendors but also those found within the user organisations. Second, the material that was created was, in the view of many, deadly dull. The content comprised textbooks on screen, but more difficult to read, and interaction that was restricted to unstimulating drill and practice exercises. Third, there was the problem of content stability. This refers to the inherent dating of material: high content stability material does not change quickly; low content stability material has a short shelf-life. CBT cost a lot to develop, but often its content was quickly rendered obsolete. This fact alone curtailed interest and investments, regardless of the technical and quality problems. It was only any good as a medium in circumstances where many people needed instructing in a short time in a subject that had a short shelf-life.

The current question is whether the evolution of e-learning, and especially developments around Web2, is replicating this pattern – the cycle of hype, fad, failure, and eventual integration – or will this media be genuinely different, with a different and high impact transformation of HRD at work because it fundamentally challenges the socio-technical system? Some believe it changes and challenges the classroom, the trainer and conceptions of what being a learner means from root to branch. For others the uptake of Web2 through the characteristic ICT simply replicates the benefits and problems of distance learning systems. Distance learning has been used for a long time, but there has been no transformational change. For others the use of ICT and

operations

10.2	*Organisational resources*

- ▢ Course catalogues
- ▢ Registration system
- ▢ Up-front competency assessment
- ▢ Assessments
- ▢ Library of materials

- ▢ Point-to-knowledge resources
- ▢ Provide reports
- ▢ Support knowledge communities
- ▢ Integrate with other IS systems

‘e-learning’ is a genuine step change in the management of HRD. This is because it goes beyond improving the delivery of instruction via a trainer to establishing the ‘learner handling information’ as the core of the HRD process (see Strategic View Box 10.1 and Operations Box 10.2).

10.1 e-learning and HRD	
HRD through conventional media: instruction	**HRD through handling of information: e-learning**
Based on a diagnosis of user needs	Based on people searching for knowledge in the course of their work
Purpose and direction of learning defined by instructional designers	Purpose and direction of learning is defined by users as they experience problems in work
Focused on a defined learning outcome	Focused on providing contents that can be accessed in varying combinations
Sequenced for optimum memory retention	Sequenced for optimum reference in the ‘here and now’ then can be forgotten
Contains presentations, practice, feedback and assessment relating to learning set outcomes	Centred on effective presentation of many kinds of information relevant to performance

Exploring e-learning

The umbrella term ‘e-learning’ includes a range of technologies and uses. The technologies themselves include all of the following:

- computer and multimedia software;
- the Internet and company intranets, including their use for computer conferencing;
- video and audio tapes;
- television and radio broadcasting;
- telecommunications;
- satellite communications;
- videoconferencing;
- virtual reality.

The categories in which e-learning activities can be analysed are as follows:

- technology-based training (CBT);
- internet technologies;
- learning centres;
- task replication systems (TRS);
- virtual reality systems (VRS).

Enhanced computer-based training

Enhanced computer-based training (enhanced CBT) is still the largest single application of technology in training. This is the delivery of learning through computer-based training or multimedia, most typically as self-paced open learning. CBT seems to offer all the advantages of flexible and open learning. They include consistent presentation of material, the flexibility for the learner to work at his or her own pace, and the opportunity for the learner to study at a convenient place and time. CBT may be used as a self-study resource, with or without tutorial support and/or mentoring, for small groups or as part of a larger course or training event. Learners may study at a single CBT workstation in the workplace, in a learning centre, on the premises of an external training provider, or at home if they have the right equipment. Organisations are increasingly delivering CBT via networked computers, intranets and the internet, but these do impose some limitations.

A CBT approach may entail a significant investment. Decisions on hardware will depend on the software applications that will be used. For some applications, a standard PC will be sufficient; for others a higher-specification multimedia PC will be essential. A wide range of off-the-shelf software is available for CBT HRD. One key lesson is that buying an off-the-shelf package, if a suitable one exists, will normally be much cheaper than commissioning new material.

CBT has specific advantages over paper-based open learning. These include:

- interactivity, which can improve motivation and retention;
- immediate feedback to completed question and practice exercises;
- greater realism as a result of including graphics, photographs, sound and moving images in simulations.

CBT also has disadvantages compared with paper-based open learning. These include:

- the need for a power supply and specialist equipment, equipment that is not easily portable;
- learning material that is more costly to prepare.

The relative costs of technology-based and paper-based open learning depend on a number of factors. In general, CBT has higher origination costs, lower production and packaging costs and higher delivery costs. Advantages and disadvantages have to be recognised in the context of learning style issues as well (see Resources Box 10.2).

10.2 *For and against CBT*	
For computer-based systems	**Against computer-based systems**
Fun; mimics games	Less than inspiring systems
Multimedia presentation	Mainly text-based
Self control order of presentation	Pre-structured
Choose activities	Required activities
Pace self	Being on your own
Able to monitor and assess on your own	Celebrate success with other people
Use of simulations (experience)	Quality of 'realism'
Links to tutors or groups	Limited feedback
Access internet	Internet may not be available

Internet developments

E-learning also includes the use of internet technologies to deliver a broad array of solutions that enhance knowledge and performance. It is network-based and therefore capable of instant updating, unlike other CBT platforms. It is delivered using a computer and standard internet technology. e-learning can then be seen to involve a broader set of activities in HRD at work, not just an interest in conventional training and instruction.

It is the use of the internet and intranets that has most caught the imagination and which represents a step change in the socio-technical system. The internet is a global web of computers interconnected with each other. It enables three functions relevant to and important for effective HRD:

- many forms of communication: one to one, one to many, many to one;
- the search for resources;
- the publication of resources.

Intranets are internal networks within organisations that use web browsers and web protocols. Because they are internal networks they are faster than the internet. They are also more secure than the internet, and provide a controlled environment for communication, accessing and publishing resources. Intranets can also be more assured of standardised software/plug-ins required to access web pages. These systems not only enable new approaches to instruction, they also open up new possibilities with the provision of information to support performance improvement and knowledge management.

Videoconferencing has been seen as the least used and understood technology. It involves people in various locations being linked by a visual, audio and information channel carried through cable. It may occur with people using one-to-one connections over the internet, or using special videoconferencing facilities. One problem has been that the videoconferencing hardware is very expensive: it has therefore tended only to be used by large companies. However, providers of videoconferencing facilities now exist, and they can hire time out to anyone. As with other aspects of technology, operational standards are evolving, and some of the problems of the technology are being overcome. For some there is a lack of potential, as they see it as just a poor 'face-to-face' substitute, rather than as a source of innovative learning experiences. In the aftermath of events such as the September 11th attacks on the USA and its impact on air travel at the time, the prospects for these kinds of facilities being more widely used and seemed good. Over the longer term these impacts could be less significant. Whether that then means that HRD applications will also evolve within these facilities remains to be seen. It does highlight the way the uptake of technologies reflects a whole host of factors that are not directly concerned with learning.

There is one qualification: it is valid to emphasise this type of e-learning, but it can also be misleading. Much recent and current e-learning growth has been in the context of the development of learning centres in workplaces, not in systems networked to lone learners or to workstations as such. Among the main technical problems with e-learning are: wasting time on searches, computers crashing, poor quality of materials, and gimmicky websites.

Learning centres

To date the most visible and popular use of e-learning – the greatest new version of a revised socio-technical system for learning – has been through developing learning centres, rather than providing access to network-based systems on their own. Learning centres are physical spaces devoted to providing resources for learning in organisations, usually with PCs that have intranet and internet access. The benefits of these are:

- a good learning environment, away from the workplace;
- a secure place for often expensive materials;
- a focal point for providing learner support;
- the provision of a physical presence, for image and marketing;
- the use of existing standard hardware.

The process of developing a learning centre involves steps that will be new to the trainer in the workplace: researching what will be supplied in the centre, planning the administration of the centre, and marketing it on launch and thereafter. Retaining some of the social aspects of learning on courses can be important in the success of a learning centre (see Operations Box10.3).

| 10.3 | *Social aspects of learning centres* |

- A welcoming environment
- Suitable opening hours
- A distraction-free study environment
- Equipment and materials which would be uneconomic to provide for one individual
- Access to a range of high quality open learning materials
- Access to a range of other learning services (e.g. conventional courses)
- Access to information and communication technology

- Advice and guidance
- Information about learning opportunities
- General and specific support
- Mentoring
- Communication with other learners to share experience and gain peer support
- Loan of materials to facilitate home or workplace learning
- Loan of computers and other equipment
- Accreditation

Small learning centres are essentially information points which provide access to information about learning opportunities, taster materials and advice. A Standard centre usually provides computer facilities linked to the internet, a range of courses and general learning support. A Major learning centre is a substantial centre which provides substantial computer facilities with multiple links to the internet, access to a library of open learning materials, e-mail and/or face-to-face access to advice and guidance service. A Virtual centre can provide access to the service from home or public locations.

Networks of centres have been developed in most large companies, cities and countries. Many centres do not offer a comprehensive range of services but are customised to meet the host organisation's needs. The success of a centre is clearly related to how well the centre serves the needs of its customers. Appropriate support is critical to the success of a learning centre. Support can take many forms and it is not always necessary to provide immediate face-to-face subject-specific help. A trained generalist who understands learning can provide significant assistance. The availability of expert subject support is only required occasionally and can be provided by e-mail or telephone access or the occasional tutorial. Learners may find it far easier to approach each other with questions than to contact an expert. Many students need a balance of general and individual help.

Task replication systems

Task replication systems (TRS) simulate work tasks, apparatus, systems and processes to support learning. They may involve the development of large-scale business systems, modelling the way something works, replicating operation or decision-making exercises. The benefits of such simulations are the ability to practise in a safe environment, to measure learning as it occurs, and to control situations to various degrees of difficulty. They are popular, because they can substitute for on-job training, and they involve the trainee in the learning. There have now been over three decades of experience in the design and development of learning materials for TRS. Despite guidelines for doing this there have been many problems:

- The content was not good: courses were not revised and updated to take into account changes in policy and procedures.
- Exercises were not 'authentic': people did not believe the steps they completed were realistic, and simulations were not believable.
- They were great looking but awful to use.
- Users are at the mercy of rapid changes in technology, making their technical platforms redundant.
- TRS learning packages are useless after the initial use, because they are not searchable.
- Learning was not being reinforced.
- There was no support for it within the organisation; TRS was not really cared about.
- It went against people's views of what training should involve – what 'real' training should be.
- It was plain boring.
- It was just 'shovelware', delivering old material in virtually the same way, just moving the delivery to TRS or the web.

Virtual reality systems and games

Virtual reality learning (VRS) and games are a special case of TRS. They involve people experiencing a 'fully immersive' environment. The classical example is that of the flight simulator, which is used to train and test pilots. The pilots are exposed to simulations of flights that are fully immersive because they are in a model of a cockpit, with the plane responding to their actions. The logic of this is obvious: the costs of errors using the 'real' environment are so high that the costs of developing simulators make sense. The advantages are the possibilities of controlling complex tasks, to provide situated learning and monitor learners closely as they learn.

Fully immersive simulations and environments have been developed and used for many purposes. Entertainment is probably number one, with architectural design, sales and prototyping functions also important applications. Learning environments have been low down the priority list for the application of virtual reality simulations, perhaps with the exception of the military, though the scope for the evolution of learning environments can be glimpsed.

Theory & Research Box 10.1 provides a set of options suggesting how computer game formats can be adapted or applied to work-based learning.

10.1 Digital game-based learning

Learning content	Examples	Learning activities	Possible game styles
Facts	Laws, policies, product specifications	Questions Memory Association drill	Game show competitions Flashcard games Mnemonics Action, sports games
Skills	Interviewing, selling, operating equipment, project management	Imitation, feedback, coaching, continuous practice, increasing challenge	Persistent state games Role-play games Adventure games Detective games
Judgement	Management decisions Timing, ethics, recruitment	Reviewing cases, asking questions, making choices, feedback, coaching	Role-playe games Detective games Multi-player interaction Adventure games Strategy games
Behaviours	Supervising, exercising self-control, setting examples	Imitation, feedback, coaching, practice	Role-play games
Theories	How people learn	Logic, experimentation, questioning	Open-ended simulation games Building games Construction games Reality testing games
Reasoning	Strategic and tactical thinking, quality analysis	Problems, examples	Puzzles
Process	Auditing, strategy creation	System analysis and deconstruction, practice	Strategy games Adventure games Simulation games
Procedures	Assembly, clerical	Imitation Practice	Timed games Reflex games
Creativity	Invention, design	Play, memory	Puzzles, invention games
Observation	Moods, morale, problems	Observing, feedback	Simulation games
Communication	Appropriate language, timing, movement	Imitation, Practice	Role-playing games Reflex games

Source Prensky 2000.

Performance support uses of e-learning

E-learning can help people do something better, faster, or cheaper, without having to learn it completely in the conventional way. Some roles and tasks require full and formal training, and cognitive capacities and capabilities must be internalised and kept up-to-date – for doctors and pilots, for example. But for other roles and tasks people can become 'expert' through finding and using information rather than being formally instructed and trained. For example, new managers in an organisation do not need to know all the HRM policies immediately to perform well. Performance support provides the means for supporting HRD as it is needed, in the course of accomplishing tasks, without having to learn chapter and verse. ICT job aids are either external aids to work or intrinsic aids to a computer package (see the case study in Operations

10.3 *The advantages of e-learning*		
Social system issues	**Old technical system**	**New technical system: e-advantages**
The learner as knowledge producer	Learning is controlled by the providers of training. Intellectual capital is distributed by them to passive learners.	Knowledge is constantly changing, and the training department is not equipped to cope with constant update Have staff capture, organise and disseminate knowledge Value learners as knowledge producers contributing to the organisation's intellectual capital.
Supporting performance	The problem of 'transfer' has to be managed as learning is not done in the actual performance environment	Improve performance while reducing time spent in training. Electronic performance support systems, an integrated electronic environment that is available to and easily accessible by each employee and is structured to provide immediate, individualised online access to the full range of information, software, guidance, advice and assistance, data, images, tools, and assessment and monitoring systems to permit job performance with minimal support and intervention by others.
Integrating individual and organisational learning	Not integrated as learning is targeted at individuals, not about reciprocal exchange.	Make training experiences direct contributors to the organisation's intellectual capital gain? Transform individual training events into organisational learning events. Design learning activities so that learners produce meaningful results that contribute to the organisation's knowledge base. Put less emphasis on 'instructionally designed material' and more on 'instructionally designed activities' using primary resources
Enhancing learning experiences	Unrealistic environments in which to learn.	How to provide realistic, non-threatening learning environments supporting the practice of critical skills? Use simulators
Customising learning	Not customised, mainly sheep-dip, the same for everyone	Improve the link (efficiency) between skill-gap analysis (learning needs) and learning activities. Link learning activities and resources to competence database. Provide skill-check and 360° assessment facilities.

Box 10.4). External aids require the user to stop work to get support from job aids, documents, or help desks. Intrinsic aids can be accessed while work continues: software help, wizards, or cue cards provided as part of a computer package. Summing up, Resources Box 10.3 presents the pedagogic advantages of adopting e-learning in the changed social relations of contemporary organisations., and Operations Box 10.4 gives a case study illustrating some of these.

operations

| 10.4 | *Oilco Exploration and Production* |

OILCo Exploration and Production (OEP) was concerned with global teamworking, recruitment and staff retention, competitiveness, and what the company termed 'faster time to competence'. In fashioning a formal and informal learning culture, in which the acquisition, distribution and enhancement of expertise had acquired growing business status, OEP sought to link personal career development with the concept of being a professional 'lifelong learner'.

Participation in knowledge-sharing and learning support structures was immense: with 10 000 active members on the various technical and cross-business networks regularly participating in the exchange of solutions, ideas and learning. These networks, along with a new 'guru' class of global consultant from within OEP's ranks and several designated 'centres of excellence', have helped move knowledge out of people's heads into oil field operations. Engineering and technical support staff at any one location can depend on peer assistance throughout the world, often at the touch of a button, to support and enhance their efforts locally. The personal challenge is to seek and grasp the opportunities to learn, to create knowledge and, most importantly, to apply it day to day. In this way the company can build a highly competent workforce ready to face new business challenges.

The second critical part of OEP's model for achieving 'competence faster' was lifelong learning provided through its corporate university (CU). Within 6 months of the CU's launch some 6500 students had signed up to take courses, growing to the 10 000-plus strong student body of today. The CU represents an integrated education framework comprising regional learning centres, online learning materials and libraries and a network of accreditation links to degree-validating third parties. Both internal and contractor 'students' can use this blended learning model, seeking to match various styles of learning with appropriate access channels and opportunities for self-driven personal development.

With so many complex operations running globally, the organisation sees knowledge sharing and lifelong learning not as options but as necessities to improve its competitive edge, through being able to realise a higher standard of technical and operational excellence. Being 'in the know' through learning or the transfer of knowledge clearly makes good personal, professional and corporate sense. These advantages have become mission-critical: the future depends on OEP's ability to harness the diverse talents, experience and creativity of its people, and it emphasises the capacity of its worldwide professional network to share learning and disseminate knowledge rapidly. It succeeds by being both global and local, applying the experience of worldwide operations through locally rooted organisations sensitive to the needs of its customers and communities.

A conceptual framework

With these different features of e-learning it can be challenging to develop an analysis and evaluation of advantages and disadvantages. Laurillard (2002) has provided a model of the various dimensions of learning which makes these matters more transparent. She considers effective learning to be an outcome of several kinds of experience being enabled by various methods which typically require a range of different media forms to be used (see Theory & Research Box10.2).

10.2 | *Laurillard's concepts*

Learning experience	Methods	Media forms
Attending, apprehending	Print, lecture, video/DVD	Narrative
Investigating, exploring	Library, DVD, web	Interactive
Discussing, debating	Seminar, conference	Communicative
Experimenting, practising	Lab, field trip, simulation	Adaptive
Articulating, expressing	Essay, product, model	Productive

A matrix can be derived which enables the capture and consideration of the elements of any course, and the e-learning alternatives that might be introduced (see Resources Box 10.4).

10.4 | *Re-design matrix*

Learning design factors		HRD options analysis	
Elements of learning	Importance for learner	Conventional course elements	E-learning options and alternative
Narrative	I get information	Print, lecture, video/DVD	Web base
Interactive	I explore	Library, references, DVD	Learning centre, TBT, internet
Communicative	I discuss	Seminar, conference	Videoconferencing chatrooms
Adaptive	Then I try out	Lab, field trip, simulation	TRS
Productive	I can now do...	Essay, product, model	Virtual reality immersion

10.5 | *Blank analysis grid*

Elements of learning	Conventional HRD	E-learning options	Socio-technical issues
Narrative			
Interactive			
Communicative			
Adaptive			
Productive			

The organisational context

The organisational context for adopting and applying technologies in learning can be considered from a practical perspective and a socio-technical perspective. From a practical perspective, for organisations to make use of e-learning in HRD they need reliable access to technologies and partnership with IT professionals inside or outside the organisation. They should aim to create a learning portal; a single point of access that serves as a gateway to a variety of resources (see Resources Box 10.5). They also need to consider establishing a Learning Management Systems (LMS) to manage e-learning; for example, recording who is learning what. From a socio-technical perspective it is essential to appreciate that changes in technology that might bring benefits in some ways may also disrupt the social relations that evolved to be effective with prior technology (see Theory & Research Box 10. 3). Unless attention is given to the social system of learning and how technologies impact on that the uptake of e-learning may produce disturbance and interference with learning rather than supporting it.

theory &
research

10.3	*Socio-technical aspects of technologies in learning*				
Realising an energised and productive social system around learning					
Improve HRD relations	Try new things	Expand and deepen capabilities	Inspire participation and contribution	Beyond the 'trainer' channel	Promote value and image of HRD
Cost	**Innovation**	**Execution**	**Relationships**	**Channels**	**Brand**
Blend in e-learning	Exploit existing IS platforms	Refine learning processes	Leverage networks and alliances	Internal and external resources	Active learner management
Realising an efficient and productive technical system for learning					

Source Derived from Finkelstein et al 2006

Theory & Research Box 10.3 shows that as new technical systems, like learning centres or CBT, are adopted the way they impact on aspects of the social system have to be thought through if the changes are to improve not harm learning relations:

- to encourage people to try new things rather than switch off;
- to expand learning in capabilities and not curtail it;
- to inspire more people to join in learning, not alienate them;
- to get beyond dependency on the trainer rather than reinforcing that dependency;
- to add to the reputation of HRD, not detract from it.

If the uptake and change does not consider these aspects and have positive outcomes it ought to be left alone.

The uptake of e-learning also involves a challenge to the organisation's learning culture; the beliefs and values that people have about learning, and what makes for effective learning. Organisations need to get beyond lip service about learning being a valued part of what people do, when they really see it as a waste of time. This means overcoming the perception that learning and work are different tasks, one of which is worthwhile and productive and the other is for remedial actions and at a cost.

All this raises the need for 'champions' of e-learning in HRD among senior management. But it is argued that e-learning in HRD projects is often assigned to people who 'don't have a clue'. They are given verbal support but no money. This happens because senior managers are not involved, there is a belief that HRD is really a remedial activity and managers see access to the internet as potentially disruptive to work and performance. Success will come where there is a sound business case and there are success stories. It requires a process of educating and coaching managers to change perceptions and to 'work the politics' in favour of e-learning in HRD. That means presenting communication as an integral part of changing to e-learning in HRD, more than just investing in the e-learning. To achieve such change is an exercise in change management; overcoming resistance to change, establishing the skills and abilities to engage in e-learning, and providing resources. Operations Box 10.5 provides the background for doing this.

10.5	Business concerns and e-learning
Cost	What will it cost and how can that be managed? Savings create higher profits or resources for investment. What will training cost to get or develop? e-learning is more efficient; conveys information quicker. Costs more on development, saves on the delivery, particularly opportunity costs.
Quality	Are we meeting customer expectations? Reactions: proper surveys built in. Learning: use for feedback not assessment. Performance. Results: for the business, intellectual capital.
Service	Do we respond to needs? Access and availability (24 hours a day, 7 days a week). Tailored to individuals.
Speed	How fast can we change strategy, bring in a new product, respond to customers – this is the key criterion? To get up and running. To reach everyone. Be altered due to changes.

Source Rosenberg 2001

On reviewing e-learning, it can be seen that the advantages are all the advantages of flexible/open learning: consistency, flexibility of place and time. In addition, there are the benefits of interactivity, immediate feedback and high realism. Training time, it is claimed, is reduced by 26%, excluding the gains from reduced need for travel to locations of HRD. Direct costs are dramatically reduced: premises, travel, course fees. It is more enjoyable than paper based. Checking progress is easy, as is practising in safety.

The problem is that all these kinds of e-learning-based methods have the same disadvantages as flexible/open learning: individual isolation, motivational problems, the quality of help and support. And the use of e-learning is not right for all kinds of learning and HRD. It is seen as the best option in certain circumstances (see Strategic View Boxes 10.2 and 10.3).

| 10.2 | Conditions for e-learning |

- Learners are dispersed
- Difficult to assemble at same time
- Blocks of time are hard to schedule
- A computer-related task is involved

- Consistent messages are absolutely essential
- Systematic test marking is required
- Instructors are in short supply

| 10.3 | Evaluation of e-learning in HRD |

Reactions	Learners are positive about using e-learning
Learning	The use of e-learning makes no significant difference
Costs	Lower costs at volume, so big organisations can use it but the smaller cannot
Transfer	If it is 'IT' learning itself the learning transfer to performance is high; if it is other kinds of learning transfer is still an issue
Ultimate	Organisations need to be on the wave or be left behind. It is becoming the norm to at least 'blend' e-learning into HRD at work, if not to rely on it entirely

New opportunities and challenges are presented by the changing roles which the use of e-learning in HRD creates. Trainers become purchasers/developers/facilitators of hardware and software. Providers have to shift to be online and produce multimedia materials, which takes a great deal of investment. Government has to be concerned with infrastructure development, and the extent to which it should play a role is open to question and divides different stakeholders. Users too have to change to being learners live at the screen-face. And, once again, it seems that connections with managers are removed from the HRD loop.

Evolving delivery technologies

Delivery technologies will continue to evolve, and this will have an impact on the design and delivery of e-learning. Until recently distance learning and e-learning services were available either via dial-up access to the internet or via broadcast TV. The internet is the obvious choice for hosting interactive digital courseware, but available only to those networked and with a PC. Countries leading the way with high percentages of households online have high internet 'readiness'.

There are other options, with intriguing implications for how HRD at work could evolve. Most households have a TV set, but these to date have only provided access to broadcast educational programming and limited analogue interactive educational services. Only a limited number of educational programmes is available, and no interactivity is possible without cable or satellite. The development of technologies around the TV could provide simpler and cheaper access devices. This would encourage

10.4	**An evolution**	
Maturity		**Socio-technical systems concern**
Entry level	Convert some existing provisions to CBT or purchase CBT	Experimenting
Stage 2	Develop a learning resource centre and HR website	Unifying around new relations
Stage 3	Develop network provisions and/or make use of 'e partnerships' for up to 25% of HRD needs	Expanding new relations alongside the old
Stage 4	Full integration of all elements of development between learners and managers mediated by ICT (from identifying training needs to evaluation)	Integrating HRD around the new
Stage 5	Electronic performance management; integration with other information and HR systems (appraisal, career development)	Integration of HRD in business in new ways

those who do not now have access at home to look into learning. Meanwhile the quality and reliability of internet access will evolve. Broadband technologies will provide much faster download times, and facilitate new services and applications that simply could not be supported by dial-up connections.

Other technologies may have a role, including mobile phones. The use of wireless data applications is predicted to take off when the wireless interface to the internet becomes more user-friendly and the transmission speed increases. In addition to an improved interface, other enhancements are envisaged. Mobile telecommunications will bring mobile networks significantly closer to the capabilities of fixed networks. It will provide mobile users with full interactive multimedia capabilities and make full video streaming possible, allowing people to watch 'broadcast' materials on their handsets. All these developments may provide new means to provide instant performance-support HRD for people in all kinds of work situations – or perhaps all that will happen is that people will text each other more or surf the internet for non-work related reasons!

Conclusion

E-learning's promise of greater access to and potential cost savings in HRD has generated a lot of hype – and this is big business for hardware and software suppliers and companies. But there are difficult and complex issues surrounding platforms, technologies, and the organisational realities of using e-learning. Even e-learning advocates have to counsel care rather than unbridled enthusiasm. They have sought to brand 'blended learning' as a way of accommodating the critiques of e-learning that threatened to swing the pendulum back against them. For e-learning's potential to be realised, the classic four Cs of technology evolution in HRD still matter: that is, a need for the right culture, for champions, for communication, and for change management.

At present few organisations use e-learning for HRD or have an e-learning strategy; some have websites or use courseware and other e-learning artefacts. This reflects three important factors:

1. Internet technology may be the key to a profound revolution in learning, but technology is just a tool.
2. There is an enduring and important role for classroom instruction; it is misguided to think otherwise.
3. Learning is a continuous process, not a series of events; it is not just formally organised provisions and training.

If e-learning's potential is to be realised, organisations must have an overall business- and people-centred strategy, alongside their e-learning strategy. This message is reinforced in all areas (Table 10.1).

Elements of learning	Issues and questions
Narrative	Multimedia resources available online can be great. But moving narrative elements to being computer or web-based removes face-to-face contact. Is that necessary or desirable?
Interactive	More experts may be available to more people but, again, adopting e-learning interactivity removes direct and personal contact between people.
Communicative	Discussion may be broader, and involve all kinds of people, not just those in one place at one time. But who gets to talk to who, and when, with what controls? Who has to respond to who? What about those who 'lurk' but do not contribute?
Adaptive	It is a safe environment, but good ones are expensive; are they worth it? Adopting TRS rather than using real systems may be right in some situations, but not in all.
Productive	Automated tests completed online tend to require certain kinds of response (multiple choice) that may test short-term memory rather than capability. Conventional academic exercises, like exams and essays, have their flaws – but they do test an individual learner's capabilities in a controlled way. e-learning alternatives, even if they appear more task-like to the point of replicating work, can be manipulated.

Table 10.1 Issues in adopting e-learning options

If e-learning in HRD is to flourish, then the role of the developer is crucial. The role of the developer may be rooted in market forces, special institutions and organisations, or governments. They are the potential leaders of change that becomes infrastructure driven with the fear that it all snowballs; because the delivery mode exists and it can be done, so it must be done – and e-learning takes over even if it is not wanted.

The uptake of e-learning provides an opportunity to rethink and redesign learning experiences, and resolve apparently intractable problems such as access, flexibility, quality and cost. But this still presents as many challenges as solutions (see Operations Box 10.6), and it is still the quality of basic needs analysis design, delivery and evaluation that matters. Equally, the management of implementation matters as much as, if not more than, the management of the medium itself. It is still important to retain the benefits of the 'old ways' of learning in groups and in positive personal relations. The concept of 'blended' leaning, in which e-learning offers something in addition to conventional media and methods rather than a substitute for them, goes some way to meeting these concerns.

10.6	*Learning technologies: a full costing model*
Research and development	Staff time, reports and reviews, administration, research activities, displacement costs, briefing meetings
Initial investment (non recurring)	Building or refurbishment, electrical work and cabling, furniture, fittings, hardware and peripherals
Initial investment (recurring)	Replacements for hardware, software, insurance, staff training, technology-based training development, support staff, admin support, telephone charges
Operating and support	Hardware, software, peripherals, security, rentals, materials, staff and evaluations
Disposal and salvage	Sale of hardware, disposal cost, retraining

10.4	*e-learning: areas to debate*	
Claims		**Counter claims**
New multimedia is relevant everywhere		Limited to some kinds of instruction
Lower costs		Higher initial costs
Greater access and volume		People switch off
More effective learning		No difference
Replicates situated learning		Cannot replace situated learning

Q

concluding exercises

Re-read the cases in Operations Boxes 10.1 and 10.4 and use the grid in Resources Box 10.5 (reproduced below) to describe the different aspects of e-learning being used in each case.

Elements of learning	Case 1 Customer contact	Case 2 OilCo
Narrative		
Interactive		
Communicative		
Adaptive		
Productive		

Multiple-choice questions

10.1 Which of the following describes all the key concepts Laurillard defines as relevant to analysing e-learning potential?

    A. Narrative, Interactive, Communicative, Social, Productive.

    B. Narrative, Games, Communicative, Adaptive, Productive.

    C. Computer-based, Interactive, Communicative, Adaptive, Productive.

    D. Narrative, Interactive, Communicative, Adaptive, Productive.

10.2 Which of the following circumstances favour the use of e-learning?

    A. Learners are dispersed.

    B. There is no computer-related task involved.

    C. Access and availability outside the 'normal' working day is an issue.

    D. Consistent messages are essential.

References

Finkelstein, S , Harvey, C, and Lawton, T. (2006) *Breakout Strategy: Meeting the challenge of double-digit growth*, New York, McGraw-Hill.

Hills, H. and Francis, P. (1999) 'Interaction learning', *People Management*, vol. 5, no. 14.

Hunt, M. and Clarke, A. (1997) *A Guide to the Cost Effectiveness of Technology-based Training*, London, DfEE.

Laurillard, D. (2002) *Rethinking University Teaching: A conversational framework for the effective use of learning technologies*, London, Routledge.

Prensky, M. (2000) *Digital Games Based Learning*, New York, McGraw-Hill.

Rosenberg, M. J. (ed.) (2001) *e-learning: Strategies for delivering knowledge in the digital age*, New York, McGraw-Hill.

Sadler-Smith, E. et al (2000) '"Modern" learning methods; rhetoric and reality', *Personnel Review*, vol. 9, no. 4.

Scott, A. (1997) *Learning Centres: A step-by-step guide to planning, managing and evaluating an organizational resource centre*, London, Kogan Page.

Schank, R.C. (2002) *Designing World Class e-learning*, New York, McGraw-Hill.

Q

| concluding case | E-learning at HotelCo |

Organisational background

HotelCo employs over 15,000 colleagues in 78 properties. One regional division covers 14 hotel units spread throughout a small European country. The vision of the hotel group is to be 'the preferred choice in hospitality' in that country, and this is underpinned by the company's four core values of People, Profit, Customer and Quality. Under the People value, 'talent development' is a key focus area.

As a part of talent development, the Managing Director of HotelCo had a vision to create global access to regular learning and development for all. Traditionally, talent development was based around learning in the classroom to complement on-job training. Believing traditional classroom-based instruction was, in effect, rationed, the CEO wanted a tool which put learners in control of their own development and enabled more consistent learning. The alternative, he believed, was e-learning. Resources were therefore bought in and made available over the organisation's intranet. Yet after some time of using this approach to e-learning, information came to light that raised concerns in the regional division of 14 hotels. It was found that only 13% of staff could currently access e-learning and of these only 26% were regularly doing so.

To change this situation and increase uptake, it was decided that designated 'Learning Zones' would be introduced in each hotel. Learning Zone provision should be concerned with providing designated environments

concluding case continued

with PCs with internet and intranet access. It was also recognised that the e-learning system had effectively been 'gifted' to the hotels, and was not the result of any specific learning and development needs assessment in each locality. Hotel management has been slow to embrace the new tool or actively use it to address local needs, the consequence of which has been a knock-on effect on its reception by all levels in the organisation. The introduction of designated learning zones was seen as an opportunity to change that.

Case Questions

1. What issues are top of the agenda if the introduction of designated learning zones is to succeed?
2. Provide 4 recommendations about what might be done to secure the long-term success of the initiative?
3. Should e-learning be such a prominent part of this organisation's HRD strategy?

concluding case answer

1. What issues are top of the agenda if the introduction of designated learning zones is to succeed?

As well as analysing issues relating to the use of e-learning reference should be made to the concepts of HRD strategies, learning partnerships, the use of providers and other HRD practice areas. There is no published e-learning strategy as such but the aim is to enhance the use of e-learning through the designated learning zones. Work on key targets needs to be planned to add users in front office, housekeeping and engineering roles. Further enhancements need to be planned for the HR and finance departments and the needs of very senior professionals within these disciplines

Facilities will vary with the size and kind of hotel. The best will be well-resourced spaces with appropriate seating and a library of resources as well as access to e-learning. The smaller hotels may have more limited zones, little more than a converted small space with room for a desk, PC and little else. All such zones have theoretical access for 24 hours, although usage within them is more likely to be within office hours, with the zones are unsupported outside of these times. These zones may share accommodation in general office areas, meaning that a lack of privacy would be a potential barrier.

Time commitment for employees to complete learning during working hours is an issue. By and large staff are expected to commit personal time, and at best are allowed access during 'down time' in business. In business areas like reservations call centres the scope to use such learning is much greater than elsewhere. However, most of the hotel population do not use PCs in the course of their daily roles. Whilst this may be viable with some staff – those in front office roles like receptionists can log on and dip in and out as shift demands permit – in reality it would prove difficult for a food and beverage colleague to do likewise.

Other practicalities exist around the introduction and project management of learning zones, the time to be allocated for learners to use these learning zones and the management support available. The kind of issues that can be highlighted around how best to ensure maximum value is gained in the future involve:

- transfer of statutory courses to e-learning.
- considering local training needs analysis and unit-based strategy and objectives;
- consideration of design and content together with learning styles of individuals to target users and sustain e-learning coursework;
- addressing the need for adequate time resources to support e-learning.

There has been no research to uncover employees' needs or receptiveness to this kind of e-learning. e-learning has not effectively provided additional learning resources and little, if any, displacement of traditional

continued overleaf

A

training can be seen. To date there has been no 'blending' in training provision although some is being carried out locally to link e-learning to traditional coursework.

IT literacy among the staff may also be a barrier. It is possible that in some divisions of the business, for example, housekeeping whose population is typically older than average and is less likely to have previous IT exposure, participation rates may be lower.

Of the promotional and management tools available, the following might be suggested:

- Promotion of HotelCo University at interview stage with prospective employees;
- Introduction of facilities at induction of new employees;
- Open days on the learning zones;
- Flyers, posters and internal newsletters, e-learning noticeboard facility;
- Incentives for course completion;
- Recognition ceremonies after course completion;
- Discussion of learning available at staff meetings and in formal performance reviews;
- Promotion at employee forums;
- Providing management targets for participation.

2. Provide 4 recommendations about what might be done to secure the long-term success of the initiative

Actions necessary to facilitate greater employee involvement and initiate business benefits include regional involvement in assessment of need or design of the resource. The following may therefore be recommended.

1. A unit-level training needs analysis should be carried out. This exercise would allow a more targeted approach identifying potential users rather than the current expectation that they will step forward. Unit-based strategy and objectives can then be set and measured.
2. The design and content of the tool should be considered in relation to the abilities, needs and learning style of the learner. Failure to consider the appropriateness of the learning for the individual is a weakness.
3. The introduction of learning zones should be managed using examples of successful initiatives from within the region, to provide guidance as to best practice. A planned approach is advocated, targeting management teams initially and clearly communicating objectives in order to maximise support.
4. The way in which Learning and Development is managed as a whole must be adapted to accommodate the new tool. Those responsible for this, usually HR teams, should themselves be clear about that.
5. Serious consideration should be given to addressing the issue of time allocation. In a staged approach a tacit commitment may be incorporated into the learning culture which may, in time and on realisation of benefit, be openly communicated. In order for this commitment to be realised General Managers and Heads of Departments must be influenced by HR teams demonstrating the business benefits through evaluation.
6. In the long term, the senior Learning and Development teams within the company should consider the development of certificated courses which provide the repetitive statutory training required by the industry such as Elementary Food Hygiene, Health & Safety and Fire. These courses would ensure greater use of the learning zones.

3. Should e-learning be such a prominent part of this organisations HRD strategy?

Reference can be made to the following factors in weighing the extent to which e-learning may or may not be such a major feature of HRD in this situation.

At some stage the e-learning strategy must be seen to add value to the business; increasing operational effectiveness or training cost-effectiveness and hopefully both. As the e-learning has not yet displaced any traditional training methods it is added training at added cost with an unvalued outcome.

The use of e-learning can be boosted by setting up these kinds of designated learning zones; it might be asked why this was not thought about in the first place, as part of the establishment of a Corporate University.

A

The uptake of e-learning does not appear to be wholly coherent and carefully implemented. The hope of benefits in the quantity and quality of learning available to employees has not been realised yet, but remains. Recognising that early progress has been below expectations is the initial catalyst, something that is especially obvious at the individual hotel level. Participation is currently 'free' and there are no obvious barriers, but little participation is seen.

The students should be emphasising the need to clarify the HRD strategy issue. With e-learning there is usually a shift from a traditional systematic training strategy (with 'sheep-dip' classroom-based learning complementing on-job coaching) to more continuous development strategy where learning is learner-driven, across a variety of opportunities and relations.

Partners are important in e-learning, even in an organisation as large as this one with all its internal HRD resources. There are many providers seeking to offer material and tools for e-learning and these partnerships raise issues that need to be managed. For example, a major software provider may be used as the provider of generic programmes which largely meet the needs of the company in core management skills, but other providers may be involved in niche areas. This presents a problem for a global company dealing with regional audiences. The company needs to balance customisation which is specifically HotelCo whilst still enjoying the benefits of the relatively less costly off-the-shelf package of generic courses considered valuable and relevant to personal and organisational objectives. Some issues were raised regarding the 'Americanisation' of some course content; bought-in material originating from the USA was perceived to be culturally marked and consequently a potential barrier to learning.

With regard to developmental relations, e-learning can be blended in with other development relations – with trainers, managers and those who might coach them at work. This leads on to the consideration of management support form e-learning. Managers will want to see Head of Department support and staff may want to see managers using the facilities before they will consider them to be credible. Non-participation by managers may simply reflect a need to learn by other methods, they still need to encourage their team to participate. Their apparent lack of interest and/or knowledge may have an adverse effect.

In providing recommendations for success the achievement of 'balance', 'culture change' 'support' and 'control' are paramount to success but how can these intangible, coveted conditions be realised? The management of the implementation of learning zones is a change in HRD strategy, not just about resourcing a room with computers. In such HRD strategy change lies the biggest challenge which involves a shift from systematic training to continuous development and learning. To widen access without effective promotion and system change is to risk facing great problems. Perhaps the biggest barrier is the absence of any time resource to use the zones, a sign that e-learning has failed to displace traditional training strategy and link to specific business objectives.

HRD provider organisations

> **By the end of this chapter you will be able to:**
>
> □ identify a range of HRD providers and partners;
> □ describe the opportunities and threats of using different kinds of providers and partners in HRD;
> □ analyse trends and changes in the use of providers and partners in HRD;
> □ critically evaluate the issues involved in using external providers and partner consultants for HRD.

Introduction

The practices considered thus far – development partnerships, group environments and the use of technologies – have been presented with the assumption that workplace HRD is being designed and delivered inside an organisation which has its own trainers and managers supporting staff HRD. In fact, in many instances, HRD is managed by sending people outside the organisation to a specialist HRD Provider Organisation (HRDPO) or by getting HRDPO partners to come into the organisation to provide HRD. HRDPOs are therefore an integral part of the practice of HRD at work for many organisations. As outsourcing and organisational partnership ways of managing HRD have increased, the issues involved deserve a separate and distinct examination. HRDPO partnerships may be with a range of providers, from individual consultants through to major organisations such as large management consulting firms and universities. The practice of workplace HRD cannot be understood without exploring this market for HRD and what is entailed in operating in it. HRDPO partnerships cover a large volume of HRD activity and are central to some of the most important HRD projects that organisations will pursue.

What makes an HRDPO?

HRDPOs are organisations whose business is adult and workplace HRD. The people targeted are the post-16-year-old age group. The practices they manage can involve one or a mix of the following activities associated with learning for adults: setting standards, sourcing trainees, delivering training, monitoring progress, assessing and/or certifying HRD. HRDPOs are often organisations whose rationale is to make a profit, but which may be functioning within the publicly-funded and subsidised HRD economy as well or solely. This means that, included in the HRDPO category, will be actors in the institutional networks of public, community-based, FE and HE or Non Departmental Public Bodies (NDPB) that manage learning. These organisations may on occasion, or in some units, engage with commercial income generation activities; but they are not private companies which prosper or fail according to their ability to make a profit from learning. They may either prosper or fail according to their ability to obtain and manage public funds.

HRDPOs will be defined here as:

> Organisations whose primary business is providing learning and development for employment for adults and involves one or a mix of the following activities: setting standards, sourcing trainees, delivering training, monitoring progress, assessing and certifying.

HRDPOs may be dependent on public funding, making them part of the public sector and voluntary sector. In these sectors there are HRDPO providers with a history grounded in the provision of general learning in educational institutions, as well as colleges and universities. The structures of these may vary in some respects, but they are essentially alike: governed by boards of stakeholders and involved in all aspects of learning from setting standards to assessing and certifying. Their staff are subject specialists, often professionally qualified, though not all are accredited as teachers or trainers. These are organisations staffed by people who are, or who see themselves primarily as, providing public services. They have been primarily funded by state-directed spending on programmes which implement government policies on education, social policy and economic development. The public sector in this definition includes colleges, universities, local authority funded units, and much community learning.

The introduction and influence of commercial concerns is most visible, perhaps, in units in FE/HE institutions which are revenue- or profit-generating. On the other hand, there is also scope for a role for voluntary sector organisations and trusts. Others, such as companies whose core business is publishing but who provide learning materials, can also be included as HRDPOs even though they are not directly involved in delivery, as they may partner learning providers in various ways.

| 11.1 | *HRDPOs in one national context* |

Information is available about private sector partners which are registered with Learning and Skills Councils (LSC) in England and Wales. This is a register of around 1300 private and voluntary sector work-based learning providers in England and Wales. The list includes some organisations which are not private sector and only those registered are eligible to deliver LSC-funded programmes. Together that accounts for, at most, around 2100 of the estimated 8000 private sector providers in England, or around 25%. Private sector HRDPOs have been estimated to employ around 34,000 people in the UK (LLL SSC 2003), and to constitute 29% of all learning provider organisations. They deal with more than a third of all trainees on government-funded programmes. So basic questions about private sector contributors exist, and are worth exploring as they currently play a significant role that may increase.

HRDPOs: public and private forms

The HRDPO sector deals with a set of audiences:

- Initial education for 16–19-year-olds;
- Continuing education for adults;
- Workforce development;
- Retraining;
- Community learning.

There is a need to deal with young people and others in schools, colleges and universities. HRDPO organisations are funded and governed in various ways, and 'joined up' to an extent by shared visions and frameworks. As HRDPOs, they are major institutions dealing with large volumes of learners. The management and leadership development provision in these is often criticised as patchily developed. The second and third audiences are concerned with developing those in the workforce and employment, and is, again, to an extent 'joined up' in webs of policy and frameworks of support, such as, in the UK, Investors in People (IiP). Employers are to be motivated to engage with HRDPOs and helped with initiatives and funding. Conventionally most large organisations are seen to invest fairly well and rationally in learning, while small and medium-sized enterprises (SMEs) invest less but often need it more.

The HRDPO provision in many countries is one where there have been two dominant organisational forms. In the initial education sector there have been specialist institutions of education, state-funded, planned and delivered as public services through bureaucracies directly owned and managed by the state. There may be examples of contracting the delivery of public services to private and voluntary organisations, blurring the public service nature of these. Continuing concerns to modernise public services, looking at patterns of provision and relationships, extends this. There have also always been private sector providers as well; organisations dedicated to providing training and learning for or along with government and employers, some involved in work-based training, others in distance learning or other methods.

Knowledge and understanding of these two sectors – the public and the private – including management and leadership development, is mixed. There is a gap in knowledge about private providers in the learning and skills sector. The interest is not in knowing more about HRDPOs for the sake of it, but to focus on how to create the conditions for positive learning outcomes to be achieved. This includes the following:

- Learners willing to identify with providers and engage with them, including brand and image;
- Productive learner–teacher and ancillaries relations;
- Adequate resourcing: capital investment strategy;
- Trusting relations with other agencies, inter-agency relations;
- Protecting the learner–teacher relationship from potentially damaging pressures but being open to clear signals about requirements, inspection regimes, targets, provider missions and ethos.

The growth of this private HRDPO sector is not well documented. Some of it emerges from specific contexts, such as the development of a market for learning among young adults in periods of high unemployment. However HRDPOs existed before such concern with youth unemployment in the 1970s. They were companies whose business was providing adult learners with learning which the state or enterprises did not provide, contracting with either individuals, organisations or the state to make a profit for their owners and investors. In these organisations either the sole business is learning or the company has a significant interest in learning. Their activities may vary considerably, from small companies in niche markets to those operating as arms of major multinational companies like IBM or Accenture (Harris 2003).

Exploring HRDPOs

HRDPOs are central to improving access to and the quality of training for adults. Three common concerns often underlie publicly-funded training policy and provisions for adults:

- It should be led by the needs of employers and learners.
- It should be shaped by the skill needs prioritised in each sector, region and locality.
- It should give the HRDPO maximum discretion to decide how best to respond to needs.

To achieve this governments are interested in a range of actions on: providing wider choice for employers and learners of publicly-funded providers of adult skills and training; reforming the funding system to give incentives for providers to be more responsive, while cutting bureaucracy; helping HRDPOs to build their capacity to offer a wider range of support to local employers.

The public sector providers exist to fulfil government's policies through large-scale, 'big' education, both academic and vocational. Private providers exist to fill in the 'small' gaps these large institutions cannot manage. This has meant that they exist to meet both employer needs and small and local needs. The net effect is that they operate in areas where they encounter the greatest interaction of issues around economic development and social inclusion, often with people who have backgrounds of disadvantage and poverty. Another view is that the private sector exists to fulfil the demands enterprises have for learning services for their staff because, while some organisations may have their own training staff, most use external resources at some point for some needs. HRDPOs start to meet this market, and may then seek to interact with publicly-funded programmes.

In contrast with the attention devoted to analysing employer behaviour and public sector partner behaviour less is known about the private sector in HRDPOs. Even basic questions about where they come from, who they are, how they have evolved, what their business models are, and many more are unanswered. Few providers have a market share of more than 10% nor, therefore, do any three constitute over 50% of the market. There may, however, be niche providers for particular occupational skills or types of client who deliver a significant share of particular provisions.

While staffing information about the public sector – the FE and HE institutions – is publicly available, the private sector HRDPO sector is virtually invisible. The number of colleges and universities is known, their spending is known, their staffing is known, their quality is known. This is not true of the private sector HRDPOs. The quality of what is provided by colleges and universities is well reviewed. Some private sector provision, where it involves publicly-funded programmes or links with public institutions, may be assessed using formal quality management systems (QMS) or other frameworks, but not others.

Clearly organisations in the public sector, colleges and universities, identify and seek to meet demands that arise from enterprises; often to generate income streams of their own, additional to those provided by government. Equally, many government programmes are implemented by private provider organisations, and some of these providers are entirely dependent on government programmes for their revenues. Rather than there being a split between the public and the private, then, there is some overlap, and therefore some scope for both partnership and competition.

This is often seen to require a strategy that is more joined up than in the past. To that end reviews of new policy are undertaken, and new institutional arrangements created. The question has always been about the development of a system which ensures each sector is contributing to best effect (Gospel and Foreman 2002) and that their combined efforts and activities produce the desired outcomes: effective learning for the benefit of individuals, organisations and society. The existence of problems within the UK in achieving that goal – alongside evidence that other countries with

strategic view

| 11.2 | *LLL sectors in one national context* |

The key sector for the purposes of this discussion is the establishment of a Life Long Learning (LLL) Sector Skills Council (SSC) in the UK (LLL SSC 2003). The development of a LLL SSC has highlighted five areas of LLL:

- Community-based learning
- Further education
- Higher education
- Library and information services
- Work-based learning

The LLL sector exists to provide employers with the skills they need, and support a diverse and inclusive society. The numbers employed in this sector are considerable, and given in Table 11.1.

Community-based learning and development	110 200
Further education	270 600
Higher education	413 000
Library and information services	104 300
Work-based learning	34 700
Total	932 800

Table 11. 1 Employment in the LLL SSC areas

better results in this regard do things differently – has meant that each sector and the system as a whole has been repeatedly reviewed and reformed.

It is expected, or hoped, that the number of providers will increase where existing providers are unable to meet any additional demand as a result of new strategies. However, it has been noted that dependency on government-funded programmes presents substantial problems and risks to HRDPOs. Many HRDPOs seek to diversify into other aspects of learning, non-state-funded, or into other areas of business. The danger is that effective and efficient HRDPO organisations fail to engage with government initiatives and funding as they are not sufficiently attractive to them. This leaves less effective HRDPOs serving the state-funded sector. Broadly speaking, the corporate direct sector is more lucrative, less bureaucratic and provides more motivated learners and more interesting projects. As many organisations may seek to outsource their learning (Harris 2003) the HRDPO sector may grow but not engage with government policy areas and priorities.

HRDPO functions and activities

HRDPOs may be involved in a variety of different kinds of activity:

- Setting standards;
- Sourcing learners;
- Delivering learning;
- Monitoring progress;
- Assessing;
- Certifying.

Here there is potential for three different kinds of HRDPO: single purpose agencies, multiple purpose agencies, total process agencies. Operations Box 11.1 (overleaf) shows the kinds of organisations which may be involved in independent provisions along with the activities in which they may be involved.

The market context for HRD

The market for HRD at work is part of two bigger markets: the market for management consultancy and the market for HRM provision and services. The market for management consultancy is made up of buyers and sellers of independent advice and assistance about management issues. This typically includes identifying and investigating problems and/or opportunities, recommending appropriate action, and helping to implement those recommendations.

Consultants are experts playing the role of external adviser to organisations, based on their experience and their expertise, though they may be hired for many reasons. These reasons may be broad and high level, connected with the organisation's plans and policy for achieving major goals. For example, a client company might want help in putting in a new financial system, or it might want advice on redesigning the organisation. The reasons may also be more specific and low level. For example, a client company might require an external review of its pay structures or recruitment policies, or it might need help in product design and marketing. One common perception is that

| 11.1 | *HRDPO functions and activities* |

HRD provision contexts	ACTIVITIES					
	Setting standards	Sourcing learners	Delivering learning	Monitoring	Assessment	Certifying power
Single employer	Own performance issues	Employees	Training dept	Internal	Internal	Not certified
Formal education contexts	Subject benchmarks	From schools or community	Classroom-based and other facilities	Retention and progress of learners	Methods for continuous assessment	Internal power and quality assurance
Private sector learning providers	Government-funded or commercial scheme standards	Government-funded or commercial opportunities	Own premises or employer premises	May monitor only during own training	May assess or rely on others	Arrange to certify or do own certification
Multi-employer organisations	As above	As above	As above	Employers' needs	External standards	Arrange to certify
Issues	Balance of technical and other skills and knowledge	Attractiveness of provider to targets	Quality of trainers and training	Completing, changing, succeeding	Validity and accuracy of assessments	Paperwork and esteem involved in certification

buying in consultants means that a company has inadequate internal management resources. In principle, consultants are valued because they are external resources, who can bring in knowledge of best practice.

As traditional consultancy firms have prospered and grown, other kinds of business have also started to offer consultancy services. Advertising agencies and design firms offer consultancy, as do IT companies and law firms. Many specialist management consultancies start up when redundant executives set up on their own as consultants. Today the consultancy industry is both huge and amorphous. All kinds of companies can become partners in providing HRD at work in the course of their work with organisations.

Management consultancy can also be analysed by looking at its market sectors and those who provide consultancy. The second market for HRD at work is the HRM consultancy market. This includes services and provisions in HR planning, recruitment, reward, training, development, appraisal, career development, leadership and communication. It interfaces and overlaps with two other segments of the consultancy market – corporate communications and organisation development. This market expands with the outsourcing of HR activities.

The HRD market can also be analysed by identifying the kinds of sector and organisation that use consultants. For example, in the UK the importance of the financial services sector has been rising each year, and consultancy earnings from the energy and water industries increased dramatically in the 1990s as these industries were subject to much public interest both as takeover targets and as public service providers. Public-sector work as a proportion of total consultancy revenues declined during the 1990s. In part, this was because the public sector was much smaller than it had been and, in part, because the major privatisations had been completed.

So the market for consultancy involves various kinds of provider, offering a range of different kinds of service including HR-related and HRD services, working with diverse kinds of organisation.

Partners in training

Organisations have always involved consultants in their HRD activities, as they can support the improvement of performance systems. Partners may be able to identify needs, to plan and design HRD, or to deliver a programme of HRD. But more recently, although many companies have retained and developed their in-house training function, an increasing number of organisations have cut back their internally managed provisions, and therefore have to choose a specialist HRDPO to meet their HRD requirements.

11.3   *Independent partners*

□ Technical independence	Not tied to one kind of solution
□ Financial independence	Not dependent on 'getting results' to earn fees
□ Administratively independent	Not part of the organisation
□ Politically independent	Not tied to any power grouping in the organisation
□ Emotionally independent its people	Not emotionally involved with the organisation or

strategic view

Organisations select an outside provider in order to obtain the best training available, and because the required training cannot be supplied in-house. Factors of quality and capacity combine to lead organisations into partnerships. Factors that influence the choice of partner include the training facilities available and the quality of the HRD design. A dedicated HRDPO is likely to have broad experience in designing different courses for the needs of various clients. An in-house training department is unlikely to have this breadth of knowledge and experience.

Training managers play a significant role in the selection of trainers. Although external partnerships may be required for design and delivery, companies still need internal HRD departments and HRD professionals with a knowledge of training suppliers.

Despite this apparent shift towards the use of external HRD resources, various factors still make in-house HRD both attractive and economic. The Industrial Society suggests three factors that play a crucial role in persuading companies to carry out their own training rather than use partners:

• price, as external providers can be very expensive;
• for many organisations, the need to tailor the training to their own needs – they do not want 'off-the-shelf' training from an external provider;
• the number of people being trained: the larger the number, the more likely the company is to opt for internal training to control costs.

In the HRD market

Marketplaces in the form of trade fairs exist for selling HRD products and services, and the activity there is an indication of who is in the market. Independent training organisations are probably the most important type of HRDPO. They can be public companies, private limited companies or, occasionally, charities. Most are small businesses, employing from 50 to 100 people. Most of the trainers they employ are full-time, although some training companies rely heavily on contract staff.

Colleges of further education and business schools are also important. Colleges of further education provide vocational training, whereas business schools offer general management training with an academic input, which is mainly for managers and executives. Information technology (IT) companies are expanding rapidly in the HRD market: it has become a natural additional service to their traditional products. The provision of HRD can also help to increase their customer base.

The HRD market is served by many sole practitioners. These have often developed their skills at a larger management consultancy, training organisation or business school, and then gone independent. They may have worked as training managers with specific companies, designing and managing training courses in-house. Some may have started up on their own when their former employer decided to outsource all the company's training needs. Some will work for their former employers as HRD consultants.

Partnerships with these kinds of organisation and people will involve either bringing consultants into the organisation, or sending staff out to events or courses – or a combination of both. The issues and tensions of managing this effectively are about ensuring the quality of the person coming in or the external provider. Good consultants give value for money and care about the working relationships they have with clients. Partnership is a way of working not an opportunity to 'dump' things on consultants or abdicate responsibility because a consultant has been paid to manage an aspect of HRD. If that approach is taken, disappointment is almost inevitable. Before any organisation uses a partner it should be clear about why it is using consultants, what it wants the consultant to do, and how that will be managed, and it should then be effective in choosing the right person or company.

Good HRDPOs work in a high-risk environment, and have to be commercially focused. They seek a good relationship as a partner with the client to earn their fees or their living. An effective partnership begins with a clear written brief from the client, detailing the outcomes wanted, and the scale and scope of the project, and making clear what is needed in a submission. To select an HRDPO from a written submission to a brief, the HRDPO must tell clients what they need to know about them. Clients must feel confident that they can work with the partner, and that other key stakeholders feel the same.

What is required to work with the HRDPO? This varies according to the project. If they are to be used to provide one-off courses then, once the format is agreed, they can be left to get on with it. If they are to be involved in a larger-scale project then regular meetings, and perhaps some kind of project steering group, will be appropriate. It will be more difficult to maintain a good partnership over a longer-term project, as challenges and issues may arise in the course of the project. The conclusion to any partnership should be an evaluation that mirrors the usual evaluation of HRD. What were people's reactions? What learning has occurred? What improvements in performance are there? What have the costs and benefits been?

11.2	*Questions to ask when using HRDPOs*
□ Why?	Partners are needed because of: The scale of a project; A lack of resources; A need for objectivity; A need for credibility; A lack of confidence among internal staff.
□ What?	What outcomes are being sought? How you will these be identified and measured? Agree outcomes with all the key stakeholders, including the consultants.
□ How?	Consider in detail what the project is likely to involve. Be prepared to consider ideas and options the consultants have. Keep in mind the implications of any options for budgets and other resources. Be realistic about expectations.
□ Who?	Know the HRD consultancy market, and test it by asking for tenders. Be clear about what you want from a consultant. Consider the stakeholder relationships. Be clear about the skills a consultant can offer; they are not all things to all people.

HRDPOs and HRD strategy

The overall objective of HRD strategy is to contribute towards raising productivity and competitiveness by creating a more highly skilled, more productive workforce. In this context external partners are organisations seeking to operate independently and privately, alongside the state sector and work organisations, to fulfil government policy aims. Government can direct funding into these high-priority areas. The priorities in this respect are currently:

- Skills needed for employment for social reasons, i.e. basic skills and level 2 skills;
- Areas of skill shortage, for example, level 3 technician/craft skills;
- Identified areas of deficiency such as management and leadership, maths and science.

HRDPOs will respond to these priorities and adjust the balance of current learning provision and learners. Colleges and providers will also have to develop effective marketing strategies to encourage much greater numbers of low-skilled individuals to engage in learning. This group is typically among the most difficult to engage in learning, and are least likely to be offered training by their employers. Effective engagement of both low-skilled individuals and their employers will be an important aspect of successfully delivering the strategy. There are issues involved in recruiting new tutors to deliver different provisions and in structuring the teaching workforce to ensure that skills are appropriate for the new, more relevant, provision.

One European study concluded that, of all those organisations which supply training, the highest proportion of training participation hours was accounted for by organisations which were private HRDPOs (Eurostat 2002). Yet despite that it is often the other actors who are the centre of attention for research and policy analysis. Private HRDPOs seem to be taken for granted. Yet their performance is an integral part of both corporate and public spending on training.

A Skills Strategy needs to open the door to the funded training market to new providers. This may mean some existing providers being replaced by ones of higher quality. From a quality point of view the best option, according to Table 11.1, is training provided by a single employer. However there are two major problems with seeking to rely on this or expand it further. The first problem is the recognition that there are islands of high skill in a low-skill sea; not all employers invest in training equally. The second problem is that the expense of effective training cannot be met by SMEs. Conventionally FE colleges are meant to help overcome these problems by providing for equal access and national coverage, offering cost-effective development of knowledge and skills. However there are also problems with this option. The FE colleges may be considered too remote from employers' needs, unable to provide development on their own, be somewhat out of date, and unattractive to young people.

One study (Gospel and Foreman 2002) that analysed the relative size and activity of various kinds of training provider in the UK, based on data concerning the review of government-funded programmes, particularly Modern Apprenticeships (MAs), showed that what are termed here 'private sector HRDPOs' constituted 29% of all learning providers and dealt with 38.5% of all trainees. This is substantially ahead of other specialist NDPB providers (18.2% of all trainees) and all the other three public sector types of learning provider, namely FE colleges (19.1% of trainees), local authorities (5.8% of trainees) and charities/not for profit sector (6.2% of all trainees).

Organisational form issues

The issue of organisational form in the HRDPO sector is important. Should there be more private sector providers, more public sector providers, or more original forms of HRDPO? The issue is partly about whether private is better than public, or voluntary better than either of those. Some locate the issue as part of a bigger understanding matters of organisational form in analysing the effectiveness of the learning and skills sector (Cameron and Marashi 2003). In other areas of activity debates about organisational form are prominent, including debates about developing Public Interest Companies (PICs) or foundation hospitals, or transferring social care from the public to the voluntary sector. Questions about legal form and legitimacy, and who owns, coordinates and manages resources and performance, are widely discussed in other sectors. The same is arising in HRD.

Questions about organisational form that arise in general can be applied to the learning and skills sector:

- What model of governance in an organisation is to be adopted to enable effective accountability, authority and decision-making?
- How does organisational form, whether hierarchical, professional, collegial, or consultative, affect the way that the work of learning is managed?

- How is the organisation legitimised for its users: through membership, choice, image?
- How does the organisation secure resources: fees, contracts, grants, donations, loans, equity, reserves?
- How does the organisation allocate resources: rationing, vouchers, price?
- How does the organisation protect and manage its resources: safeguard, secure borrowing, actively managed?
- How are inter-provider relationships affected by organisational form: the capacity for collaboration – joint planning, referral, joint provision, sharing resources, joint delivery?

Consequently the HRDPO sector is a complex sector, with public, private and voluntary organisational forms all represented to some degree. For some, at heart, the voluntary sector exists to deliver vocational education and second chances to those who have not gained from initial schooling. The primary partnerships are, then, between FE colleges, HRDPOs and employers.

One concern is that some contexts lack a healthy HRDPO sector. A problem may be then that there are too many 'small gaps' in learning needs. These are not met by either employers or large institutions, nor are there HRDPOs around to deal with these, or if they exist they deal with them ineffectively. Another concern may be that the sector is not operating effectively. There are not enough HRDPOs and there is an imbalance between private and public forms, with too many social justice-oriented HRDPOs embedded in public or voluntary sector models and not enough strong private HRDPOs concerned with economic returns. Alternatively, some companies may perceive that HRDPOs charge too much for what they do, while other HRDPOs struggle to remain viable going concerns. The uncertainty of short-term contracts for government work and similar problems with stability in work for employers is a factor. HRDPOs may also struggle with too many targets, an underdeveloped cadre of management and staff with limited qualifications. Solutions then are focused on long-term contracts, fewer, clearer targets based on outcomes and strengthening managerial competence.

Cameron and Marashi identify a number of interconnected policy contexts in which the question of organisational form arises. With a view to improving learning outcomes these include:

- Wanting to expand the sector but there is a high cost of entry for new providers – regulation, inspection and targets regimes are prohibitive.
- The inertia encountered given the sunk costs in certain forms of provision and existing loyalties – hard to rationalise provisions.
- The problem of transaction costs – collaborative working creates transaction costs that are easier for large organisations to bear than small organisations. This drives small providers out.
- The use of inspection as a proxy for the voice of the user – consumers cannot have a comprehensive understanding.
- Maintaining efforts at reaching the most excluded – the hard-to-serve are difficult, the easy-to-serve are demanding. Embed the interests of non-participants.
- The concept and application of the principal–agent relationship in the sector. A principal–agent relationship occurs when one person or an organisation acts on

behalf of another. If the relationship is too loose then the principal's intentions are not realised. If it is too tight then the agent has no discretion to innovate. In England the DfES is the main principal working through LEAs, LSC, UfI which then become principals themselves.

How to develop government policy on the HRDPO sector

More initiatives around HRDPOs often mean more targets, and more inspectors, so as investment goes up bureaucracy increases. Leaders in these organisations may lose motivation and become more cautious. They may begin to focus on back-watching not delivery. To influence and change government policy and practice in those circumstances, the points of leverage need to be identified:

- Treasury interests: they aim to set simple targets agreed with departments and seek to control public expenditure on education, training.
- Departments and Ministers: they like initiatives which show they are active. Targets and rules are needed to ensure expectations are clear.
- Departmentalism: with several departments involved, there is scope for inter-departmental 'turf wars'.

HRDPOs have played a part in learning and training in the past, but are now of greater interest in the context of LLL and skills strategy goals. They are of some significance, but it is conceivable that they may play a bigger role in the future. In the past they have existed to fill 'gaps' in either government provision or the corporate sector, but their quality has been questioned. Now the best HRDPOs are seen to provide better quality learning in either state-funded programmes or internal company provisions. In the future, if the increasing outsourcing of training in the corporate sector continues, then external partners may become players whose voice and interests become even stronger; to equal or indeed rival those of the state or employer organisations. Three key themes underpin this.

First, improving the quality of providers is an issue, along with innovation and creativity. The learning provider sector includes many and varied kinds of provider; ranging from the single, self-employed consultant specialising in one subject to the complex, multi-faceted modern university. The quality of learning found in these different areas is seen to be patchy. While all kinds of learning providers have their share of failures the perception is that those motivated by profit are most at risk of failure, or of exploiting learners. Why this is so, and what can be done to change that, requires research.

Second, while the level of employers' commitment to training in general is hard to gauge, it is a constant theme among many commentators that it is low and weak. For the particular group of most current concern – low-waged, low-skilled, adults in work – employer neglect of HRD remains an issue and, unless employers engage with the HRDPOs who can aid these people, this group will remain neglected.

Finally, there is the issue of work-based training. In its formal guise in the UK, for example, this is represented by initiatives like Modern Apprenticeships (MAs). In its 'informal' guises work-based learning has also come to be recognised as a major, if often hidden, contributor to skills and knowledge development. Work-based learning in both of these senses presents a continuing challenge for the role of external partners. In formal schemes the issues are those of providing effective instruction and experience rather than simply using trainees as a source of cheap unskilled labour, combining basic skills with vocational development, and ensuring that standards are maintained while trainees actually complete their training. These are not new, but are all abiding challenges. Some of the attractions of work-based training are firmly founded in sound principles of adult education; but some of the realities of work-based learning are deeply rooted in a system in which there is no parity of esteem, and academic learning is still seen to be, and funded as if it were, the best path to career development and success. This is true for both formal and informal work-based learning. One hope is that subsidised job-specific training, subsidised management training and wage compensation for the time employees spend training would help SMEs to give more attention to training.

Conclusion

Much HRD at work is supplied by HRDPOs working with an organisation, or by staff going outside the organisation into an HRDPO. This approach to HRD has always been used, but seems to be increasing for various reasons, including the greater use of outsourcing of HR services by many organisations. Effective management of HRD therefore means effective management of partnerships with HRDPOs. The nature of the market for HRD services and products is evolving, but the main sectors and providers are fairly well-established. Being able to research and access them as needed is an integral part of modern HRD at work. In developing relationships the building of positive partnerships should be the key. This requires clarity about what is wanted, and skills to ensure that the right partners are selected.

Organisations are partly dependent on what the market offers. The effectiveness of market forces as a driver of improvements in the provision and quality of HRD remains a concern for many stakeholders – for work organisations as buyers, for providers as sellers, and for the government – as they seek to evolve better HRD at work provisions over the years ahead. Changes in government policy, trends in outsourcing HRM work, and the merging of organisations in the consulting and HRM sectors will all provide impetus for change in the market for HRD at work. New forms of, or areas for, partnership may emerge and evolve.

HRDPOs represent a sector which faces challenges across all five key policy areas:

- High quality – people should demand, and providers should deliver, high quality learning: Where are the best practices among HRDPOs?
- Participation – giving people the confidence, enterprise, knowledge, creativity and skills to take part: How can HRDPOs help to achieve this? Do we need more HRDPOs, bigger HRDPOs?
- Recognition – knowledge and skill should be recognised, used and developed in the workplace: How do HRDPOs respond to an environment where this is desired?

- Information, guidance and counselling (IGC) – giving people the information, guidance and support to make decisions and transitions: What issues for HRDPOs arise from seeking to improve IGC via private sector HRDPO?
- Chances – giving people chances to learn irrespective of background or circumstances: How well do HRDPOs meet this expectation?

HRDPOs operate in the context of, and often in partnership with, the other sectors as well. Thus there are also research issues about these relations and partnerships.

Taken together, there is a set of issues relating to questions about the structure, strategies and challenges facing HRDPOs. Making these more visible in the first instance is a prerequisite of considering the extent to which the existing HRDPO sector is providing an effective contribution to achieving lifelong learning; and the extent to which support for a better understanding of structure, strategies and challenges might be of benefit to the sector itself, and those who interact with them.

Multiple-choice questions

11.1 Which of the following statements are true?
A. HRD providers tend to operate as self-employed or small independent companies.
B. Being able to offer a cheaper solution is the most often-cited reason for choosing external HRD providers.
C. Because they are market-driven, external HRD providers usually supply an independent and higher quality of product.
D. Handling a relationship with providers is simply a matter of preparing a clear brief and then letting them get on with it.
E. None of these statements is true.

11.2 Which of the following is not an area in which HRDPOs would be found to operate ?
A Workforce development
B Initial education for 14–16-year-olds
C Retraining
D Community learning

References

Cameron, H. and Marashi, M. (2003) 'Form or substance in the learning and skills sector: Does organisational form affect learning outcomes?', *Report to Learning and Skills Research Centre*.

DfES (2003) *Success for All*, London, DfES.

Eurostat (2002) 'Continuing vocational training survey (CVTS2)', European Social Statistics, Eurostat Working Paper, Luxembourg, Eurostat.

Green, F., Felstead, A., Mayhew, K. and Pack, A (2000) 'The impact of training on labour mobility: Individual and firm level evidence from Britain, *British Journal of Industrial Relations*, vol. 38, issue 2, pp. 261–75.

Gospel, H. and Foreman, J. (2002) *The Provision of Training in Britain; Case Studies of Inter-Firm Coordination*, The Centre for Economic Performance, London School of Economics and Political Science.

Harris, P. (2003) 'Outsourced learning: A new market emerges', *Training and Development*, vol. 57, no. 9, pp. 30–8

LLL SSC (2003) 'Transforming learning: expression of interest in establishing a Sectors Skill Council to support the Lifelong Learning Sector', *LLL SSC Executive Group*.

LSC (2003)' Success for all – implementation of the framework for quality and success', Learning and Skills Council *Circular 03/09*.

Scottish Executive (2003) ' The Lifelong Learning Strategy for Scotland', *Scottish Executive*.

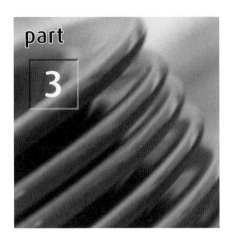

Perspectives

Perspectives are points of view. HRD at work can be explored from the different points of view that can be identified among stakeholders in workplace learning. In much of HRM, for example, a common version of this is to identify and consider both the employer and employee perspectives and, by viewing issues from these two perspectives, come to a balanced view. In a more complex picture, different points of view reflect different values, beliefs and interests about understanding and managing HRD at work. What is focused up as important and challenging about HRD at work depends on the point of view being adopted. In the case of HRD at work four major points of view provide the source of much contemporary discussion and debate.

Public policy	Government has both an economic and a social policy agenda which involve engaging with the promotion of HRD at work
Knowledge management (KM) and Communities of Practice	The rise to prominence of KM has involved both emphasising the importance of CoPs and challenging conceptions of what HRD at work should be about
Diversity	Many contemporary concerns converge on the issue of diversity, from advancing opportunity to developments in globalisation and the consequences of continuing major migrations of labour in times of tension and conflict
Strategic HRD	The nature and meaning of HRD being integrated with organisational strategy

The nature and concerns of these broad perspectives, and what they have to offer as ways of making sense of HRD at work, need to be understood. Familiarity with the debates and discussions involved within the different sense-making paradigms is to be encouraged as a way of increasing our depth of understanding.

Workforce HRD and public policy

By the end of this chapter you will be able to:

- Describe the roles of states in public policy-making for HRD
- Discuss common factors in the historical context for HRD policy in different national contexts
- Analyse the contemporary political context and its impact on HRD policy
- Critically evaluate the evolution and impact of HRD policy and practice in a specific case study context .

Q

| introductory exercise | *Themes from a public policy perspective: prioritising human capital development* |

Strategic View Box 12.1 overleaf lists twelve possible public policy concerns that can have an impact on the quality of the workforce. Rank them according to whether you believe they should be high, medium or low priorities for public policy in contributing to advancing workforce HRD. You can only use each ranking up to four times; so four priorities will be high, four medium and four low.

Introduction

One suggested set of responses to the introductory exercise can be found at the end of this chapter. When you review them you should see that they take into account the following core beliefs and values:

- Learning begets learning as there are 'dynamic complementarities'; governments have to understand this and act accordingly. The challenge is not just about employers failing to train, but also about individuals and groups in various categories not engaging with learning at key stages early on, and therefore not engaging in later stages of life either.
- Families, schools and firms can all create 'human capital'. HRD policy can be related to all of these. In other words it can be a part of policy on the most fundamental social issues, including some of the most contentious arenas of policy: for example, the quality of parenting, and what parents want for their children. Paternalistic interventions by government may be seen to be strongly warranted in early life in dysfunctional families, or they may be fiercely resisted.

12.1	*Human capital development policy and spending issues*			
		Priority status for contributing to workforce HRD?		
		High	Med	Low
Spread 'human capital' spending equally across all life stages, not mainly for investing in young adults				
Concentrate spending on the under 5-year-olds				
Intervene in dysfunctional families to protect the interests of vulnerable children				
Measure levels of IQ and target HRD spending and systems accordingly				
Spend on higher education for more people				
Increase subsidies for higher education participation among the least well off				
Promote spending on vocational, non-cognitive skills				
Reduce class sizes in education institutions				
Ensure access to good on-the-job training				
Retrain older workers				
Promote flexibility in labour markets				
Tax policies favouring individual and company spending on learning				

- There is a complex dynamic to the human capital creation and accumulation process because a multiplicity of actors and institutions are involved in determining investments. It is never possible for one central stakeholder to control all of this; a variety of powerful stakeholder interests need to be reconciled.
- Policy-making must recognise differences in abilities, and proceed with cost–benefit analyses on that basis. This realism rather than an ideology-based approach is important because, otherwise, policy-makers can skew the system badly. For example, rather than focus on higher education for the many – arguably because we are in the era of the knowledge economy but also because that appeals to key target voter groups – governments might do better to invest in improved care and education for the under-5-year-olds to produce a core productive labour force. But the latter option involves appealing to a group whose voting power is weak.
- People who benefit from HRD should pay for it.

Your beliefs and values will be different, so your priorities will be different. This illustrates how developing and implementing HRD public policy is embedded in wider policy debates and challenges. That may be helpful where these connections stimulate interest in workforce HRD and have a positive impact on it. Alternatively, it may be a challenge if these connections impede effective workforce HRD policy-making. In public policy there is no right and wrong answer. Of course those responsible for policy and its implementation seek to be 'evidence-based'; but often there is no definitive, or even very clear, evidence available. Social, political and moral factors inform and shape policy development (see Strategic View Box 12.1).

Government-produced HRD public policies and programmes are a major feature of the HRD landscape. They may range from looking at the operation of systems for early childhood development through to policy for older people, and include action on tax policy as well as outlining areas of subsidy and spending specifically in HRD. Successful policies in HRD are usually developed by government in partnership with other agencies and stakeholders, to support the development of a knowledgeable, capable, and committed workforce. The kinds of initiative that fall under the HRD policy umbrella are ever evolving. For some critics this has become part of the problem, as there is a tendency to meddle with policies before they have had a chance to settle in and make an impact. However, even through changes of government, of environment and of the various means used, the goal tends to stay the same: to ensure the existence of the necessary skills base for effective economic performance so that skills shortages are avoided and opportunities for economic development are taken.

12.2	*Wider social benefits for individuals who improve their basic skills*

- Improve their chances in the labour market;
- Suffer less from poor physical and mental health;
- Less likely to have children experiencing difficulty at school;
- More likely to be active citizens, for example in voting and expressing interest in politics;
- More liberal and less discriminatory in their attitudes.

Source Brynner et al 2001

Concerns about HRD policy are a matter of finding a balance between believers in HRD and those who are more sceptical. Those who see a role for public policy in HRD advocate various lines of action. They express a need to make better use of HRD to deal with the changing economic environment, responding to the effects of globalisation, technological innovation and a continuing high pace of change. They see a role for HRD as changes occur in the composition of the workforce, in the types of work available and in career structures and patterns, HRD needs to evolve in response. And they see a role for HRD in a changing society, with an apparent growing polarisation between those 'getting on' and those 'going nowhere' – the rich and the poor. These divisions can be manifest in polarised lifestyles, expectations and attitudes. Those who are more sceptical challenge the argument that public policy in HRD can be a response to any of these concerns; they would leave it to markets and employers to resolve the issues which emerge and confront workforce development, not government.

Such public policy issues are facing the industrialised and the developing countries. The issue is not just the rise of new technologies or globalisation and the need for new strategies to deal with these. Attention is focused on the need to develop a workforce that is able both to compete effectively in the new environment and to take advantage of the increasing opportunities arising from globalisation and technological innovation.

12.3 | *A national review: the UK*

The Leitch Review of Skills in the UK (2006) suggests there is still a long-term challenge here, despite many previous reviews since the pro-HRD Labour government was first elected in 1997. The UK has a strong economy and world-leading employment levels, but its productivity trails many key comparator nations. Poor skills are a key contributor to this problem as well as having wider impacts on social welfare.

Over the last decade, the skills profile of the working-age population in the UK has improved. For example, the proportion of adults with a degree has increased from a fifth to over a quarter of the population. Despite these improvements, the UK still does not have a world-class skills base: over a third of adults in the UK do not have a basic school-leaving qualification and five million people have no qualifications at all. One in six adults does not have the literacy skills expected of an 11-year-old and half do not have these levels of functional numeracy.

Looking ahead to 2020, global, demographic and technological change will place an even greater premium on the UK's skills profile. New analysis conducted by the 2006 Review shows that, if the Government meets its ambitious targets for improving the UK's skills, by 2020 the proportion of working-age people without any qualifications will fall to 4 per cent; and the proportion of adults holding a degree will increase from 27 per cent to 38 per cent. This will have significant benefits for the economy – increasing annual productivity growth by 0.2 per cent with a net benefit to the economy of £3 billion a year, equivalent to 0.3 per cent of GDP.

However, even if the UK can meet these challenging targets, the nation's human capital will still fail to be world-class. Considerable problems will remain; at least 4 million adults will not have the literacy skills expected of an 11-year-old and 12 million would not have numeracy skills at this level. Ambitious scenarios are needed for tackling the stock of low-skilled adults without qualifications, basic literacy and numeracy; investing more in intermediate skills; and further increasing the proportion of adults holding a degree.

Significant economic and social benefits would result from higher productivity and employment gained through improving skills. The Leitch Review argues that the UK must urgently raise its game and set itself a greater ambition to have a world-class skills base by 2020.

Source http://www.hm-treasury.gov.uk./independent_reviews/leitch_review/review_leitch_index.cfm, accessed 25 July 2006.

Themes and issues in HRD public policy

Workforce HRD policy, it is routinely argued, ought to be grounded in rigorous, hard-headed analysis of the issues. However, continuing review and change in many national contexts suggest this is not the case. Consequently, public policy in this area has not been genuinely strategic, has not had an impact on the ground, and has not engaged all the relevant government departments. Sorting out the basics is a recurring theme, with new reports concluding that there is a need to more thoroughly analyse the workforce development problem and its causes, covering the full range of demand-side and supply-side factors that determine investment in workforce development. Fresh policy options ought to better include the aspirations and capabilities of the main stakeholders. The focus would then be on developing a coherent strategy that draws together all the key initiatives and actors involved in workforce development.

- To fit workforce development into a strategic framework that is shared by the key stakeholders and grounded in a rigorous and hard-headed analysis of the issues.
  - This implies that past HRD policy has not been based on analysis and has not been shared by key stakeholders. The levers of research and the politics of stakeholder partnerships are therefore important.

- To ensure that government policy is genuinely strategic and not, as has so often been the case in the past, piecemeal, tactical, disjointed and low impact.
  - If being piecemeal and disjointed means low impact, then being genuinely strategic means having a greater impact. Strategy is about plans and policy for major goals; however, it often seems that what happens here is institutional reform, not goal change.
- To ensure that the analysis of the issues leads to real improvements in workforce development 'on the ground'.
  - This contrasts with improvements in the abstract, which produce better-looking or better-sounding policy; improvements 'on the ground' are with real people, and real companies.
- To engage fully with the different government departments with a stake in workforce development.
  - In the UK, for example, this includes at least two different departments involved in skills and dealings with business, as well as the Treasury, which leads on fiscal and other matters.

The central tension here is that HRD at work is caught between two major public policy agendas: improving productivity performance, and employability and social inclusion or social justice. This is because the available evidence suggests that there is a positive link between HRD and both private benefits for individuals and firms and social benefits for the economy and society at large.

Establishing indicators to evaluate policy in terms of HRD at work is a concern. These may include labour force participation rates, rates of participation in higher education, and levels of expenditure on HRD at work. The volume of HRD (as opposed to numbers of people participating in it) has stagnated in recent years, and much HRD tends to be job-specific. In addition, institutional weaknesses have resulted in few businesses participating in training networks that promote workforce development, or accessing and using supportive government structures.

These problems relate to productivity issues. The quality of the labour force, as measured by the skill mix, can be compared with that in other countries. Problems may exist in both the current stock of people in the workforce and those entering the workforce. An underdeveloped workforce produces less, works harder and longer for the same pay, and attracts less capital investment. For government all these HRD concerns are not isolated and distinct; they need to be addressed in the wider context of government and business strategies towards innovation, information technology and other policy areas relevant to business.

There is evidence to show that HRD can contribute to enhanced productivity. Equally there is evidence of HRD's potential contribution to employability and social inclusion. More HRD means higher earnings. But, at present, the distribution of HRD tends to reinforce social exclusion. There is a link between skill levels and deprivation. Particular groups, for example disabled people and certain ethnic minorities, are disproportionately likely to have low skills. Such low skills are correlated with poor employment prospects in the labour market. The low-skilled are less likely to receive HRD opportunities that might help to overcome their disadvantage. The HRD-rich grow richer and the HRD-poor become poorer.

This problematic state of affairs has existed within HRD for some time. Why? There are three different explanations (see Theory & Research Box 12.1).

12.1 | *Three explanations for the policy problems facing HRD*

▫ **The economic development explanation.** The premise is that HRD provisions will match the demands of economic practices, and economic practices involve low skills. Therefore there is ineffective HRD because employment as a whole, and skills and performance within that, are trapped in a 'low skills equilibrium'. It does not make economic sense for people to invest in HRD when organisational strategies and individual career success do not require it.

▫ **The flawed HRD policy system explanation.** The premise is that a coherent HRD policy system could be constructed by government, but government has not done this yet. Therefore the assessment of needs, design and delivery of HRD remain flawed. Although HRD policy is a key part of the political agenda, the system that emerges – of agencies, initiatives and policies – is inconsistent, confusing, poor-quality and provider-driven HRD policy.

▫ **The social factors explanation.** The premise is that HRD provisions can have an impact only if people are motivated, and are in a position to participate in HRD, but many people are neither motivated nor able to participate. Therefore, any otherwise relevant and effective HRD policy fails because it encounters the challenges of social exclusion, where the vulnerable and disadvantaged are alienated from and will not engage with, learning. Until HRD policy deals as effectively with social inclusion issues as with economic development concerns it will always be hampered and obstructed. The provision of opportunity has to be an engine of policy.

The background

Skills revolutions are persistently sought, as each nation or region fears that it may stall and lag behind others in changing times. It may lag behind in producing a skilled and educated workforce, particularly with young people. It may lag behind in challenging perceptions and behaviours, for example the view that academic education has higher prestige than vocational training. It may lag behind because employers and the state have an uneasy relationship in these matters, arguing about who takes the lead, and who pays. It may lag behind as there may be congestion within the field of local economic development where there is confusion, overlap, duplication and even active competition between the many agencies involved. These issues have long been debated, but they are now generally collated into one conclusion: that all these factors matter and that many countries are deficient on all of them.

To understand the current situation, we must explore the historical background to HRD policy and practice. This is important because, as the saying goes, if we don't learn from the mistakes of history we are doomed to repeat them. History informs intelligent analysis in this as in all matters. Pessimists, of course, would say that the only thing we learn from history is that we do not learn from history; we repeat the same mistakes no matter how great our historical insights are. Our rationale here is to review the distant, the recent and the immediate history of HRD in one context, that of the UK. The themes and issues that we explore can be applied in any national context. The distant past must be analysed because it influences recent concerns. Recent concerns with change and unemployment have shaped the system substantially, and have influenced what happened in the 1990s when a complex web of programmes and agencies was created.

The distant past

There is an image, partly emerging from fact and partly reflecting myth, of a pre-industrial golden era when learning was an organic part of the lives of working people in agricultural and home-based craft economy. Learning was something that happened within families or within guilds, or for the intelligentsia in institutions such as monasteries and a few medieval universities. Capabilities, knowledge and behaviour were shaped within these close, personal environments. For most people there were no schools or colleges, no exams or qualifications, no government departments or agencies. Colleges – the few that there were – were institutes linked to the medieval powers, either royal or religious, for the development of clerics through scholarship associated with the classical disciplines. People learned to be farmers, or clothmakers, or tanners, or smiths, or bakers, or masons, or fishers, as a natural and integral part of their lifestyle.

Following the rise of industrial capitalism, this 'golden era' ended and the whole approach to HRD had to be radically transformed. The reasons why, and the effects of this, are many, but two are particularly relevant to understanding the subsequent history and current state of HRD policy. The first relates to the requirements for efficiency in mechanised production in factory systems, and the large-scale bureaucracies and clerical factories required for business and government. This was a shift from a system based upon individuals completing all stages of a process, with all the HRD that required and the skills it involved, to a system based upon a division of labour with little requirement for much HRD of the individual.

This was a shift that curtailed the requirement for the complex development of independent and multi-skilled working, and the identity that went with it, and gave birth to the world of employment in unskilled 'production line'-type environments. But the accompanying social upheaval, involving the destruction of small town and country jobs and ways of life with the shift to urban and factory environments, had greater and well-documented consequences. As unemployment, poverty, health and safety, and crime provided more pressing issues for policy-makers and campaigners, and as people came to terms with the onset and evolution of industrialisation and capitalism, the questions of HRD seemed marginal. There were greater social questions about welfare and the quality of life; those also seemed strongly connected with education, opportunity and HRD. Overall, with the decline and eradication of old systems of work and development, there was a downturn in HRD.

This, however, was offset by another concomitant of industrialisation and the development of capitalism – the growth of democratic government as a force concerned with economic and social affairs. Together these formed a situation where the increase of wealth through the creation of profit-making firms required an increase in knowledge and skills, the development of new skills, and the establishment of new patterns of behaviour. This was an era where the quality of the workforce would matter as much as technological innovation, requiring greater investment in HRD. This was the age when science, and scientific research into materials, production processes and engineering, was complemented by the growth of institutions and industry in areas such as banking and finance. These pillars of industrialisation and capitalism required many literate, numerate and knowledgeable professionals. They also required armies of literate, numerate and skilled clerical and administrative staff to push all the paper that had to be processed for the engineering innovations, the factories and the institutions to work. How were these people to be developed? The answer was to be investment in mass education – in the development of technical schools, the evolution of colleges and universities, and the development of HRD at work.

Since the onset of industrialisation and capitalism there has been a tension between forces undermining and precluding investment in HRD and forces dramatically increasing the requirement for such investment. Governments, according to their ideological hue, made choices about what to do and where to invest. The skills and knowledge involved in manufacturing cloth were made redundant, when all that was required was a 'hand' to mind the machine that did the work. But the skills and knowledge required to make the machines and manage the legal, financial and operational aspects of such manufacture were now in demand. What did governments do to help manage this?

Through industrialisation, the guild system for managing HRD, where it was the responsibility of independent masters in trades and professions, was superseded by the growth of large employers. But apprenticeships in the major industries where crafts were practised the factories and shipyards, publishing and mining – became a battleground where employers and trade unions came to contest their different interests. For trade unions, controlling the time serving of apprentices was one way of guarding their existing members' interests, pay and conditions of work. For employers, there was an interest in enforcing their control of work and changes to methods of work by challenging job demarcations and the kinds and levels of skill needed for jobs.

Such tensions persisted throughout much of the 20th century in most industrialised countries. They formed the background to ongoing debates in economic and social policy, though major events tended to bring them into starker relief. The first such event, which created critical points for HRD policy in the 20th century, was the First World War in Europe, which brought an influx of unskilled people into the labour market. The problems encountered in having such an unskilled workforce, or in creating systems to develop more skills, were evident then – as was the trade unions' opposition to 'dilution', using unskilled, untrained people to do the work of skilled craftsmen.

The second event was the depression in the 1930s in the UK and Europe. The causes of this economic collapse were many, but mass unemployment was one of its greatest effects. Government policy in general, and HRD policy in particular, were important in responding to this, and in providing some foundation for moving on to recovery. The depression, and unemployment, were implicated in the growth of both fascism and communism, and in interventions in democracies elsewhere to cope with their effects. Some countries saw the development of government training centres, intervention designed (it seemed) more to get people off the streets than to fit any specific strategy for an HRD-led economic recovery.

Finally there was the period during and after the Second World War. The impact of this around the world was varied. In the UK, among other things, it meant once again the need to draw an influx of new people into work which exposed labour market deficiencies, with many of these being unskilled. This period is often best remembered for the influx of women into the workforce, proving their worth and value in a whole range of occupations for which they had never been considered suitable before. After the Second World War the demands of rebuilding after the destruction experienced in many regions and countries placed a premium on HRD, and on the resourcefulness of people.

After each of these critical events there were sustained changes, but there was also a return to the status quo in many areas. That is to say, lower priority was given to investing in HRD to improve the quality and skills of the whole labour force, or to maintaining a central role for government, or to consolidating new entrants in the workforce. But each of these issues was to be encountered again during the 1960s, when concerns about the economic consequences of performance problems in industry as a result of skills shortages attained strategic rather than fleeting significance, and arrived as subjects of real and sustained prominence. The conquered and vanquished regimes and destroyed economies of the Second World War were experiencing recovery, while those of the military victors were experiencing problems. The human capital factor was highlighted.

Recent history

In more recent times the key problems were seen to lie with intervening to make employers invest in HRD. Schemes whose purpose was to promote investment in HRD by monitoring employers' spending on training and raising a levy for investment in HRD became popular. Although this concern remained in the 1970s, the institutional context often changed, from a concern with employers' investments in training to government's role in dealing with the unemployment that accompanied economic change and the decline of traditional heavy industries. In some countries, such as the UK, this period provided the origins of the proliferation of schemes and agencies that, over the next three decades, would be set up, enlarged, reduced, re-named and re-launched almost constantly. By the 1980s, with the growth of new technologies and industries, the need to change the institutional context again was evident.

By the early 1990s, reviews deemed much HRD policy activity to have been a failure. Investment had not changed the situation significantly: there were still skill gaps, concerns about productivity, and inequalities in access and opportunity. The UK's answer was a new strategy that gave more emphasis to the role of employer-led bodies, providing local leadership rather than a national Civil Service-led system. In addition, major initiatives, such as the Investors in People (IiP) standard, were developed as an advanced and substantial attempt to upgrade and improve HRD in the workplace.

Despite these attempts to ensure that HRD was better focused as employers led the agencies that determined practices, barriers to attaining key goals still seemed to exist. In particular, the worlds of education and of training – of the academic and the vocational – seemed as far apart as ever. There were then further attempts at institutional reform to break down these barriers, with better 'joined-up' policy thinking and practice across HRD as a whole. The intention of ending the 'schism' in thinking and policy about training and education is often enshrined in separate government departments dealing with each issue. There was also a challenge in establishing a culture where all groups recognised and took responsibility for their own HRD. Finally, there was also an investment of resources, and of hope, in the era of the internet and the e-business boom – the hope that the use of these technologies could offer a new route to better HRD policy and performance.

These kinds of issue confronted all governments, whether interventionist, voluntarist or abstentionist. Versions of voluntarism predominated. This did not mean abstaining; it meant a policy of encouragement by the state but a dependence on others to fulfil expectations. If this failed to produce results, the government would set about developing or changing policy; government was then quite active. Voluntarism also does not mean that there is no state responsibility; a state role in education, and in responding to unemployment, has been constant. What it does mean is that the state will not take the primary leadership in a system where the state, employers and employee representatives will be partners. There is an uneasy dance about who should do what; who should take the lead. And there are issues where leadership rather than consensus is required. For example, the quality of higher education of professionals has always attracted much middle-class attention and seems, therefore, to receive more political attention, than deficiencies in intermediate-level development of skills. The outcome is the 'Cinderella' status of the further education sector, reflected in its low status and low levels of funding. Vocational education may be the better investment, but governments do not want to alienate the influential middle classes.

HRD policy has been caught up in the rivalry between political philosophies, in essence between laissez-faire opponents of state intervention and liberal proponents of a social agenda for HRD. This has been largely fought over interpretations of what voluntarism should involve, rather than taking issue with voluntarism itself. For the laissez-faire opponents of state intervention, HRD policy should happen 'naturally' in the interests of all, as market forces drive investments and activities, and employers have a key role as they have the greatest knowledge of and interest in HRD. Policy activity should be left free to track labour market supply and demand dynamics; wherever earnings and employment are growing there will be HRD policy. Voluntarism is preferred to its alternatives. One is greater state intervention, involving greater taxing and spending. The other is a corporatist model, such as that found in some countries, which involves a degree of assumption of control and responsibility by employers for things that employers see that the state should rightly be concerned with. The conclusion is that there is no role for intervention through legislation on HRD policy, nor the establishment of individual rights in matters of HRD policy.

Liberal proponents of voluntarism argue that markets fail, for various reasons, to provide the necessary HRD policy. Instead of a natural evolution of HRD policy, and change in it being driven by change in labour markets, there are many failures; the skills required by employers are in shortage because the HRD policy system is not developing them. Interventions by government are then needed to deal with these market failures, to shape and centrally allocate resources to the HRD policy system. Laissez-faire voluntarism does not deliver sufficient HRD policy quantity or quality. Some employers train; some do not. Some programmes are good; some are bad. There is value in the state and employers working together through institutional developments.

How far can we now see the development of a clear, coherent and comprehensive HRD policy system in most countries? This is open to debate. The muddle of different kinds of voluntarism may not be resolved, but new systems do seem to exist that are popular and well supported by employers, government and institutions in a range of areas. The 'cultural' blocks are being overcome, though there are still reservations; take-up is still low, and the performance of reformed institutions is still problematic.

More state investment and intervention in HRD might mean, for example, legislation to make training compulsory, equivalent to the requirements on employers about health and safety, and employer responsibility. Or it might mean, for example, a new form of levy – in effect a tax – to be centrally controlled and redistributed to high-quality training facilities and centres (private or public sector) which employers can then use. Does your country need more state intervention like this or less?

The contemporary agenda: lifelong learning

Regions are developing an interest in HRD policy. For example, in the past in the European area a major public policy focus was on standards in employment, together with associated matters of employee consultation and representation, but now the emphasis is firmly on learning. When the European Commission considered the direction of policy and action in the European Union (EU), it concluded that Europe had indisputably moved into the knowledge age, with all that this will imply for cultural, economic and social life. Patterns of learning, living and working are changing. This means that individuals must adapt to change, and long-established ways of doing things must change too.

The EU then highlighted a move towards lifelong learning as accompanying the successful transition to a knowledge-based economy and society. The Commission defined lifelong learning, within an overall European employment strategy, as 'all purposeful learning activity, undertaken on an ongoing basis with the aim of improving knowledge, skills and competence'. Lifelong learning is no longer just one aspect of education and training; it must become the guiding principle for provision and participation across the full spectrum of learning. All those living in Europe, without exception, should have equal opportunity to adjust to the demands of social and economic change, and to participate actively in the shaping of Europe's future. The implication is that Europe's education and training systems are at the heart of the coming changes. The Member States, the Council and the Commission within their respective areas of competence must identify coherent strategies and practical measures with a view to fostering lifelong learning for all.

A memorandum on lifelong learning was circulated to launch a Europe-wide debate on a comprehensive strategy for implementing it at individual and institutional levels, and in all spheres of public and private life. The implications of this basic change in perspectives and practices merit much debate. The Member States, which are responsible for their education and training systems, should lead this debate. The aim was to fix European guidelines and timetables for achieving specific agreed goals, establishing, where appropriate, indicators and benchmarks to compare best practice, and then regularly monitoring, evaluating and reviewing progress. This decentralised approach will be applied in line with the principle of subsidiarity, in which the Union, the Member States, the regional and local levels, and the social partners, will be actively involved using variable forms of partnership.

The EU argues that promoting active citizenship and promoting employability are equally important and interrelated aims for lifelong learning. Others may tend to emphasise competitiveness and organisational performance. Member States agree on the priority, but have been slow to take concerted action. The argument is that the scale of current economic and social change in Europe demands a fundamentally new approach to education and training. Lifelong learning is the common umbrella under which all kinds of teaching and learning should be united. To put lifelong learning into practice, everyone must work together effectively, both as individuals and in organisations. This is analysed in terms of six key messages, which offer a structured framework for an open debate on putting lifelong learning into practice with priority areas for action (see Strategic View Box 12.4).

The EU has an interest in and influence on HRD and HRD policy. The political foundations of EU-level government provide a means through which ends in both economic and social agendas can be attained. The union is not just about trade, but about managing a social dialogue between employers and employees to consider interests and resolve differences over issues such as HRD policy. The huge numbers of people involved in the elected bodies and associated institutions of the EU have considered many HRD issues and policies. The harmonisation of common systems and policies in HRD continues to be a central part of the EU project.

12.4 | *Lifelong learning: European Union aims*

The public policy aims are to:

- guarantee universal and continuing access to learning for gaining and renewing the skills needed for sustained participation in the knowledge society;
- raise visibly levels of investment in human resources in order to place priority on Europe's most important asset, its people;
- develop effective teaching and learning methods and contexts for the continuum of lifelong and life-wide learning;
- improve significantly the ways in which learning participation and outcomes are understood and appreciated, particularly non-formal and informal learning;
- ensure that everyone can easily access good-quality information and advice about learning opportunities throughout Europe and throughout their lives;
- provide lifelong learning opportunities as close to learners as possible, in their own communities and supported through ICT-based facilities wherever appropriate.

In the short term and long term these aims are central to sustaining an enlarged and competitive European Union, and so require some form of agreed and joint policy and action.

A framework of partnership is needed to mobilise resources for lifelong learning at all levels. Working together to put lifelong learning into practice is required to build an inclusive society that offers equal opportunities for access to quality learning throughout life to all people, and in which education and training provision is based on the needs and demands of individuals. This in turn means a need to adjust the ways in which education and training are provided, and the way paid working life is organised, so that people can participate in learning throughout their lives and can plan for themselves how they combine learning, working and family life. This, it is argued, will help to achieve higher overall levels of education and qualification in all sectors, to ensure high-quality provision of education and training, and at the same time to ensure that people's knowledge and skills match the changing demands of jobs and occupations, workplace organisation and working methods. Ultimately it will encourage and equip people to participate more actively in all spheres of public life, especially in social and political life at all levels of the community, including the European level.

The key to success is argued to be the same at the European level: that is, to build on a sense of shared responsibility for lifelong learning among all the key actors. These include the Member States, the European institutions, the social partners (employers and trade unions) and enterprises, regional and local authorities, those who work in education and training, voluntary organisations, associations and groupings. The shared aim should be to build a Europe in which all citizens have the opportunity to develop their potential to the full and to feel that they belong. This European agenda clearly emphasises the broader social and political aspects of better HRD at work.

12.1	*HRD in the EU and APEC*

	EU	APEC
Model	Social model	Political economy of up-skilling
Integration	Deep and wide	Narrow and superficial
Dialogue	Social partners	Narrow financial approach
Spend	Partnerships and infrastructure	Very little

This can be compared with the approach of the Asia-Pacific Economic Cooperation (APEC) region (see Operations Box 12.1).

The EU was founded, as the European Economic Community, in 1957 with the Treaty of Rome. It is not just an economic and trade unit; it has an elected Parliament, a Council with policy-making power, and a Commission which acts as the executive body. This involves tens of thousands of staff in many institutions. In the EU the HRD concerns are to raise employment skill levels (not just deal with unemployment), to enable skills development and measures, to improve the quality of working life, and to ensure social inclusion. Matters ranging from migration to qualifications are researched and discussed.

There are three key points to note regarding HRD. The first is the integration of HRD into the policy- and decision-making of the EU – it is a central part of it. The second is the open method of coordination for compliance in HRD policy: this means that the major policies are to be reviewed each year, and progress determined and reviewed. The third point is the presence of social dialogue: the European social model is to involve employers and trade unions jointly in consultations. Together this provides a mechanism for dealing with difficult and complex issues and either avoiding or managing crises. The enlargement of the EU in 2004 was seen as a threat to strategy of the social model, because of weaknesses with unemployment and unions in some new accession states.

The Asia-Pacific Economic Cooperation (APEC) was set up in 1989, out of a concern to ensure that other supranational bodies such as the EU did not come to dominate the world scene. It includes 21 economies, including the USA, China, Japan and Australia, along with some much smaller countries. Together they represent around 50 per cent of world GDP. APEC works through a downward cascade mechanism: ministers from the countries meet and propose ideas, and set up working groups. These working groups arrive at decisions through the Kuching Consensus process of consensual decision-making. Any country can veto any decision, or simply not turn up to discuss a matter. There is no imperative to act following the decision-making. This is a 'thin' organisation, run from Singapore with around 40 staff.

There are many HRD issues – improving the quality of teaching and the skills and labour force issues are central – but spanning the differences among the included economies is a huge challenge. This is not really a regional community with a political project like the EU. It has a trade and investment agenda. It is very conservative; refusing, for example, to research projects on labour migration. It adopts a technicist view that there are no politics in production. Alongside a unitarist philosophy this means that there are no discussions with social partners, and delegates are advised by business only. There may be myriad HRD projects but there is no unifying political power which presents problems with the labour market response to economic crises.

HRD is on the agenda because its importance is accepted. APEC delegates are comfortable talking about that rather than other things. Yet a fear of human capital deficit does exist, and there is more than a trade agenda to consider.

Conclusion

To understand HRD from the perspective of HRD public policy is to encounter a set of beliefs, debates, historical legacies, public policy choices and complex stakeholder preferences that need to be reconciled. In any national setting, HRD public policy development and review will face common challenges. Superficially there is a mosaic of overlapping initiatives, and an 'alphabet soup' of acronyms to be familiar with, and all of these emerging from an equally complex past. The underlying common issues are clearer: from an economic and social policy perspective, there are often major gaps in HRD workforce provisions and contentious matters of 'who pays what' to be resolved. These are long-standing and, despite many studies, initiatives and policy reviews, there is still no clear agreement on what needs to be done. This is so, notwithstanding the latest country-based studies into workforce development, such as the UK's Leitch review, and supranational bodies such as the European Commission's consultations on, and promotion of, lifelong learning.

Taking the long-term view – looking back and looking ahead – we can argue that such problems with HRD public policy are a symptom of the general problem of the complex interaction of the key partners and institutions in contemporary societies. Is it important to influence either government policy or the practices of firms in free market capitalism? Neither alone can provide the HRD at work required, but those seeking to influence either, or indeed both, find it difficult to strike the right balance of partnerships. This was true of the industrialisation era, when nation-states were pursuing national interests in conjunction with indigenous firms; it seems equally true of the post-industrial, service-based era, where regional alliances such as the EU seek to deal with the realities of governing a large region when international firms are operating in an open global economy.

Some countries' problems seem to reflect circumstances in which a commitment to a voluntarist philosophy has bound up the encouragement of investment in HRD with endless institutional reform in the hope of finally hitting the right approach to involve individuals, employers and government in an optimum way. On the one hand, there is a concern to provide a strategic, impartial and wide-ranging view of workforce development and its role, as exemplified by the more recent review in the UK. But, on the other hand, such initiatives seek to develop a strongly argued case for the benefits of workforce development, with clear links to productivity and economic performance. There is a tautology here, in that they are assuming what they seek to prove: that investment in workforce development and skills is the answer. The point is that, no matter how strong the argument for HRD, other political and economic forces and factors exist. Sustaining and directing policy support for HRD remains a challenge for all countries in the future.

A

Human capital development issues	Priorities for government intervention in HRD
Spread spending equally across all life stages Skill formation is a life-cycle process.	High
Concentrate on the under 5-year-olds The greatest returns on investments in human capital come from those investments made pre-school, under five years old; thereafter they tail off until post-school job training which provides the lowest rates of return.	High
Intervene in dysfunctional families Families are major producers of skill. Dysfunctional families produce children with lower levels of ability and motivation than functioning, healthy families. There should be paternalistic interventions in dysfunctional families in early life to alter social and motivational skills and reduce crime.	High
Promote, test and measure levels of IQ Skills are multi-dimensional in nature. Both cognitive and non-cognitive skills are important in the workplace. An emphasis on IQ or on success measured by tests is misguided.	Low
Higher education for more people The differences in skills and abilities that open up at an early age produce differences in the economic returns to schooling. Rates of return to higher education vary greatly. Higher education is not for everyone.	Low
Increase subsidies for higher education participation The middle class has a strong interest in getting the rest of society to pay the bills of its children. And under the guise of equal opportunity policy for the poor subsidies are also defended. However, those who benefit should pay.	Medium
Promote non-cognitive skills Skills differ in their malleability over the life cycle. IQ is more or less set by age of 8, and it varies greatly from person to person. Non-cognitive skills are malleable until later ages.	Medium
Reduce class sizes Changes in educational policies that receive much attention, like reducing class sizes or increasing quality, are unlikely to have dramatic effects on economic or social performance.	Low
Ensure access to good on-the-job training Post-school, on-the-job training is a productive activity with a high economic rate of return. The return is higher for the most able and so this form of investment perpetuates and even exacerbates initial disadvantage.	High
Retrain older workers Retraining younger and more able workers to higher levels of skill can be a sound investment. However, public job training programmes targeted towards older, displaced workers and the less able have a sorry record.	Low

continued overleaf

introductory exercise continued	
Human capital development issues	**Priorities for government intervention in HRD**
Promote flexibility in labour markets Wage subsidies and policies that promote flexibility in the labour market are far more likely to promote employment than job training.	Medium
Tax policy favouring spending on learning Tax policy reforms are not likely to increase human capital accumulation dramatically, although they can promote capital formation and raise wages.	Medium

The list was based on one proposed by Heckman and Masterov (2004). There are no definitive rankings of priority here; it depends on the economic and political positions adopted. Your responses may show that government ought to intervene in all these areas, or stay out of all them, or pick and choose where to intervene.

In terms of agreeing or disagreeing with the points listed there is likely to be a range of responses. Some points are not controversial: for example, that the area of HRD is a complex one with many agents involved and with government playing some kind of facilitating role. Some points are open to more evidence-based analysis and should be judged on that: for example the costs and benefits of changing class sizes in primary schools. Others, however, are more controversial and political: that resources should be taken from elite higher education and invested in the general education of under 5-year-olds, or that those who 'benefit' from education should pay for it. Agreeing or disagreeing with these is a matter of values and world-view, not common sense or research evidence. Heckman and Masterov may be world experts on developing human capital, but their conclusions reflect as much a moral as an analytical approach to analysing human capital and behaviour.

Multiple-choice questions

12.1 Who are the major stakeholders seeking to influence government HRD policy-making?
   A. Civil servants with evidence-based research about 'what works'.
   B. Employers and employer organisations who want government to spend on skills shortages.
   C. Trade unions and other employee representative bodies who want government to ensure that the state and employers invest in their people.
   D. Citizens who, in their roles as employees, parents and so on, expect government to provide them with learning opportunities over their lifespan.

12.2 Which of the following statements about National Vocational Education and Training (NVET) policy are true?
   A. NVET policy is something that national governments alone are concerned with.
   B. Most countries adopt a voluntarist approach to NVET policy.
   C. HRD policy initiatives tend to flounder and fail because governments can never produce a coherent and 'joined up' approach to HRD.
   D. Skills revolutions are only of interest to certain nations and regions.
   E. None of these statements is true.

References

Brynner, J., McIntosh, S., Vignoles, A. Dearden, L., Reed, H. and Van Reenan, J. (2001) *Improving Adult Basic Skills: Benefits to the individual and to society*, DfEE research report RR251, London, HMSO.

Cohen, S. (1994) *Human Resource Development and Utilization: Economic analysis for policy making*, Aldershot, Avebury.

DfES (2003) *21st Century Skills – Realigning our potential*, London, HMSO.

ELLD (2003) *Life Through Learning, Learning Through Life: The lifelong learning strategy for Scotland*, Enterprise and Lifelong Learning Department.

Esland, G. (1991) *Education, Training and Employment*, Volumes 1 & 2, London, Addison-Wesley.

European Commission (2003) *Choosing to Grow: Knowledge, innovation and jobs in a cohesive society*, European Commission.

Heckman, J.J. and Masterov, D.V. (2004) *Skill Policies for Scotland*. Institute for the Study of Labour, Discussion paper No. 1444.

Lange, T et al (2000) 'SMEs and barriers to skills development: A Scottish perspective', *Journal of European Industrial Training*, vol. 24.

PIU (2001) *In Demand: Adult skills in the 21st century*, Performance Innovation Unit 1.

Steedman, H. (1993) 'Do work force skills matter?', *British Journal of Industrial Relations*, vol. 31, no. 2.

Q

| concluding exercise | *Public policy options: compulsion, non-legislative approaches and doing nothing* |

Given all the above, if you were asked to justify adopting either a compulsory, non-legislative or 'do nothing' public policy' on HRD what would you choose and what factors would you say are in favour of your stance? Do this in the context of one specific national context.

A

concluding exercise answer (in the UK context)

Possible factors in favour of a compulsory approach

- There is a long history of encouraging employers and individuals to invest more in skills but the skills gap remains, i.e. the voluntary approach has not worked to date.
- Compulsion, in the form of regulation, forces the pace of change because it becomes much harder for individuals and businesses to avoid their responsibilities. It would mean everyone changing their approach at the same time.
- Could very quickly address the employer demand side, for example through a training levy, which (because of the funds this would make available) would impact directly on the provider supply side.
- Communicating a compulsory approach is potentially more straightforward. While highly desirable there is less of a premium on capturing 'hearts and minds' than required through a voluntary approach.
- Addresses social and diversity risks although this would tend to be a 'one size fits all' solution.

Factors in favour of a non-legislative approach

- Training levies in the 1970s proved overly bureaucratic (although Industrial Training Boards remain for the construction and engineering construction sectors, as does the legislation conferring the ability to raise a compulsory levy).
- Presumption against regulation given the burden placed on business.

continued overleaf

A

- Important reforms, e.g. to post-16 education, have already been made and there is much more to do to ensure that Government and its agencies are able to fully play their part. It is reasonable to exhaust all the options under a voluntary approach before considering legislation.
- The voluntary approach is very much more flexible, allowing different industry sectors/segments/geographic areas to develop approaches that meet their own needs and those of their people and to take account of time factors in implementing change.
- The voluntary approach is more reasonable in terms of addressing the demand side from the individual's perspective, i.e. why should we force people into training who do not wish to do so?
- Addresses social and diversity issues through being adaptable to the circumstances of different groups, e.g. age, ethnicity, sex, and geographic location.
- The voluntary approach gives the individual a greater sense of ownership and choice. This may lead to an improved sense of achievement and stimulate further learning and progression.

Factors in favour of doing nothing

- Many of the existing activities, strategies and approaches will be long-term in their nature. There may be arguments in favour of 'wait and see'.
- Overlaying yet further voluntary or legislation approaches might risk additional confusion as employers, providers and individuals come to grips with any new proposals.
- Change upsets the status quo, those who perceive themselves as 'losers' will complain while the 'winners' will not necessarily be clear at the outset. Doing nothing is, from that point of view, the easier route.
- Doing nothing will mean that those currently engaged in learning, or in supporting it e.g. employers, might be more likely to continue doing so. An advantage of doing nothing is that the 'winners' under existing arrangements remain.
- Doing nothing avoids any further pressure on the organisational capacity of stakeholder organisations, including providers.

In the UK context a recent review concluded that the voluntary approach is best, with one exception in respect of Industrial Training Boards (ITBs). This is more acceptable to business and individuals, enables a flexible response and delivery approach on the part of business and providers, and minimises the burden of bureaucracy. The voluntary approach would not affect existing legislation, including that for ITBs. Sectors which have ITBs (construction and engineering construction) will continue to have the ability to raise a compulsory levy. But one size does not fit all and the ITB/compulsory levy arrangement is not appropriate for all sectors. Flexibility of approach is a benefit of the voluntary option proposed. The UK Government that was elected in 2005 has a manifesto commitment that, where both sides of industry in a sector agree, it will help them set up a statutory framework for training. If a sector supports this as the best approach, the Government is willing to use *existing* powers to create a new ITB. When the opportunity arises, the Government would seek to amend the ITB legislation to provide a more flexible framework. However, the reviews of the ITBs suggest that, while this approach may suit some industries, it is unlikely to be a solution for many. They believe that the collaborative voluntary action that Sector Skills Councils (SSCs) can broker will be the appropriate route for most sectors. A key element of the proposed approach is to improve the way that resources are targeted into areas of highest priority through flexing, and in some cases relaxing, the funding rules. The priority needs are:

- skills needed for employment for social reasons, i.e. basic and level 2 skills;
- areas of skill shortage, in the early 21st century level 3 technician/craft skills;
- identified areas of deficiency such as management and leadership, maths and science.

Funding should be diverted into those high priority areas although it will mean less for other areas.

Given that the recommended approach is a voluntary one, 'enforcement' measures are not needed beyond those contained in the existing strategies and legislation. Rather, achieving the outcomes needed is about persuading individuals and their employers that skills, training and qualifications are worth the trip. They must see the benefits. A communications strategy and plan is the key to achieving this rather than sanctions.

Introduction

The Investors in People (IiP) standard can be investigated as an example of leading edge promotion and improvement of HRD which has been experienced by many and varied kinds of organisation. It is an initiative to accredit organisations which are able to meet the standards expected of an organisation in which HRD is taken seriously and is at the heart of the business.

The IiP standard was introduced in the UK by a government task force in the early 1990s to help organisations grow their businesses through developing their people. It was a major element of a revamped national strategy with the aim of improving business performance by involving employers themselves in defining what should be done to improve HRD, rather than the state forcing employers to follow a recipe made up by civil servants.

The IiP Standard

The basic framework for the IiP standard consists of 4 principles (see Case Box 12.1). These were present in the first version and in subsequent upgrades and revisions of the standard.

The changes to the original standard include a reduction in the number of indicators associated with these principles – organisations are now required to show evidence of IiP standards in the four Principle areas in 12 rather than in 23 categories, a reduction or deletion of paperwork and a simplification of the language used in the standard. The language is 'plain and simple', not jargon or 'HR speak'. The 12 indicators supporting the four key principles are given in Case Box 12.2.

The rationale behind the need for the change in the standard was to ensure that the standard was more accessible to a wide range of organisations, especially smaller firms who may not have internal HR expertise of their own. The IiP standard also had to retain the challenge for those companies already recognised.

The IiP process still works as was initially envisaged. First a company must commit to becoming an IiP. This requires exploring, internally and with others, how the company needs/wants to develop. A gap analysis is then undertaken to identify where there is a match or gap between the organisation and the IiP standard. In order to achieve the standard an organisation must have a business plan which incorporates a training plan and mechanisms by which to evaluate the training and development which takes place. Actions may be required to close those gaps. The organisation is then externally assessed by IiP. This whole process takes an average of 18 months. Organisations are then reviewed regularly for 3 years.

continued overleaf

| 12.1 | *IiP principles* |

1. **Commitment**
   Public commitment by top management to training and developing people as a core means of achieving organisational objectives

2. **Planning**
   Planning to review training and development needs in the context of the business

3. **Action**
   Assuring relevant steps are taken to meet training and development needs

4. **Evaluation**
   Measuring outcomes of training and development for individuals and the organisation

12.2 | IiP indicators

Commitment

1. The organisation is committed to supporting the development of its people
2. People are encouraged to improve their own and other people's performance
3. People believe their contribution to the organisation is recognised
4. The organisation is committed to ensuring equality of opportunity in the development of its people

Planning

5. The organisation has a plan with clear aims and objectives which are understood by everyone
6. The development of people is in line with the organisation's aims and objectives
7. People understand how they contribute to achieving the organisation's aims and objectives

Action

8. Managers are effective in supporting the development of people
9. People learn and develop effectively

Evaluation

10. The development of people improves the performance of the organisation, teams and individuals
11. People understand the impact of the development of people on the performance of the organisation, teams and individuals
12. The organisation gets better at developing its people

Q

concluding case continued

The costs involved in accrediting organisations as IiP vary. Characteristics other than company size are felt to have at least an equal impact on the level of support required. The employers' 'baseline position', the extent to which the principles of IiP are in place before they get involved with IiP, and capacity to manage change are the critical factors. The way in which IiP advisers work with employers to support them to the recognition stage varies, and subsidy and charging policies also vary considerably. In most areas SMEs, schools and the voluntary sector pay little or no costs. Overall, IiP support can be characterised as belonging to one of three models:

i. free 'unlimited' assistance: mostly free services and 'hands-on' support given to help achieve the standard. IiP advisers' time is given free;
ii. costed assistance: mostly free support given to a costed ceiling and employers are aware of the value of any services received;
iii. charged services: some charges made for most elements of support including IiP advisers' time.

Research also suggested that some 'deadweight' was associated with the delivery of IiP in that around 30% of employers would have made the changes they needed to make to become IiP accredited without any support. However, the vast majority of employers do say that they value all of the elements of support offered to help achieve IiP status.

Who Designed the IiP Standard?

The task force which designed the IiP standard looked at successful businesses and explored why they were successful. They concluded that successful organisations took care to develop their employees effectively.

concluding case continued

At the time a view that an acute skills shortage could hamper an organisation's ability to be a truly competitive player in the world economy was commonplace. Future competitiveness would increasingly be dependent on employers actively developing their people's skills and potential; but many were lagging behind.

The aim then was to establish a standard of good practice which would enable organisations to improve the quality and effectiveness of their HRD at work practices. The IiP standard links people development to strategy, organisational goals and performance. It was 'developed by business for business'. This was meant to ensure that the standard would link HRD to achieving organisational goals, rather than being a wish-list of what 'outsiders' thought businesses ought to be doing. Such an approach was entirely consistent with the era of its origin when 'employer-led' initiatives were the foundation of policy in general. This was the era when the 'business-oriented' HRD philosophy was paramount; with the strengths and weaknesses of that system. The standard was developed with the backing of most major business organisations including the Confederation of British Industry (CBI), the Trades Union Congress (TUC), the Institute of Directors (IoD), the Chartered Institute of Personnel and Development (CIPD) and all the major political parties. Yet it was still very much part of an overall government strategy. Consistent with the characteristics of the British institutional and economic context, it was part of a market-led, voluntarist strategy. There was to be no requirement for organisations to be accredited as IiP as there are with other areas of standards in HRM such as Health & Safety at Work.

Points about the Design

One other notable aspect of the IiP approach is that the rationale was that a single standard would be suitable for all sizes and sectors of organisation. According to the developers and those who promote IiP it is suitable for all sizes and sectors of industry. The headline figures of 20,000 accredited organisations and 34% of the workforce in IiP organisations since it was established seems to suggest that this initiative has been a success. However, the picture is not so good when the attainment of targets for IiP recognition is looked at.

Why these targets had not been attained requires an analysis of organisations' motivations, the standard itself and the process of being accredited. The motivation for obtaining IiP accreditation will vary from organisation to organisation. For some, it is an opportunity to review current policies and practices against a recognised standard, receiving recognition for their good practice. For others, it provides a structured way to improve the effectiveness of basic HRD activities, offering an opportunity to improve on what is being done. Others consider it can provide a framework for introducing a strategy and plan of action for HRD at work, where that has not yet been properly thought through.

Organisations tend to be motivated to obtain accreditation to get both tangible and intangible benefits. They want the kudos and status of being accredited. That may help attract and retain staff, and attract business. Organisations also seek benefits from being accredited as an IiP in terms of lower turnover, higher morale, greater motivation, ownership and understanding of the organisation, higher calibre recruits, better communications and higher productivity. These are certainly the kinds of practical benefits emphasised by those who promote IiP (see Case Box 12.3).

Criticisms of IiP

With benefits like these associated with accreditation as an IiP it seems surprising that the initiative has not yet reached the targets set. Why would organisations fail to take advantage of such a good thing? The gap between targets and achievements has raised questions about the standard itself and its role in policy overall. For some IiP is clearly a necessary and sensible promotion of HRD at work, but, for those who are already doing HRD well and want to be 'badged', it has involved little more than an 'Increase in Paperwork'.

There have also been questions about the amount of 'investing' done in the promotion of the IiP standard itself, with concerns about the resources devoted to its promotion among organisations and the quality of assessment and help given through the process of accreditation. The lack of integration with other HRM elements of concern to organisations and competition with other benchmarking tools, like more general

continued overleaf

12.3 Benefits of accreditation as an IiP

- **Improved earnings, productivity and profitability**
  Skilled and motivated people work harder and better. Productivity will improve and extra effort will be made to close sales so a positive impact will be seen on the bottom line.

- **Reduced costs and wastage**
  Skilled and motivated people constantly examine their work to contribute to reducing costs and wastage.

- **Enhanced quality**
  Investing in people significantly improves the results of quality programmes. IiP adds considerable value to BS 5750, ISO 9000 and other total quality initiatives.

- **Improved motivation**
  Motivation is improved through greater involvement, personal development and recognition of achievement. This leads to higher morale, improved retention rates, reduced absenteeism, readier acceptance of change and identification with the organisation beyond the confines of the job.

- **Customer satisfaction**
  IiP is central to helping employees become customer-focused, thus enabling the organisation to meet customer needs, effectively and at a profit.

- **Public recognition**
  IiP status brings public recognition for real achievements measured against a rigorous national standard. Being an IiP helps to attract the best quality job applicants. It may also provide a reason for customers to choose specific goods and service.

- **Competitive advantage**
  Through improved performance, IiP organisations develop a competitive edge.

Q

concluding case continued

quality standards which are of interest to many organisations, have also been discussed as problems with promoting the standard. Most critically, the lack of interest and uptake among small/medium-sized firms, where productivity and HRD issues have long been acknowledged, has raised doubts about the design and development of the IiP standard.

In the late 1990s, after consultation with organisations, stakeholders and individuals, the standard was redesigned and revamped. This was done, IiP claim, to take into account their customers' new requirements. The changes were needed for the standard to stay relevant and credible, to provide greater flexibility in its use and to make it more suitable for smaller organisations. The redesigned standard was given the 'stamp' of a newly elected government with different policies and values and was relaunched in 2000. The changes included the following:

- An 'outcomes'-based standard; accreditation was to be less concerned with evaluating what HRD organisations were doing and more concerned with what outcomes they attained from HRD.
- Equal opportunity issues in HRD at work were to be a more prominent and explicit concern.
- The paperwork previously required for accreditation was reduced or even not required; assessors would seek out materials themselves.
- Flexibility was built into the process of accreditation; it is not the same for every kind of organisation.
- Measures on subjective matters – the 'soft side' like motivation – are now seen as important, not just objective measures of the use of appraisal, for example.

concluding case continued

Others report that few employers believe that IiP status helps to boost profits or income. Companies agree that IiP has improved training and the link between training and business needs but they do not believe that this has affected profits. All those with IiP status said that achieving it had brought some benefit, but the standard – which was developed to improve business performance – is failing to do so. Statistics show that 81% of businesses surveyed thought IiP resulted in closer links between training and business needs, 52% mentioned positive publicity and 40% agreed that it had boosted staff morale.

IiP counter these criticisms by arguing that that the IiP standard is a tried and tested flexible framework which helps companies succeed and compete through improved people performance. Research among accredited organisations showed that 80% have increased customer satisfaction and that 70% have improved their competitive edge and productivity. Research among employees within recognised organisations showed that 94% are satisfied in their jobs, compared to 37% in the businesses lacking the standard.

Although the overarching view is that the original IiP standard was a successful initiative and the revised standard is a useful evolution, there remain difficulties. It is not a panacea and does not guarantee improved organisational performance, particularly for SMEs. There is much evidence to suggest that SMEs do not train and develop their workforce and, where training does occur, it is more likely to be informal, reactive and aimed at the solution of immediate problems rather than long-term development initiatives. HRD in SMEs is critical to the success of the UK economy, but SMEs frequently do not have the HRD expertise, infrastructure and general resources which larger organisations enjoy.

Research indicates that resistance to IIP focuses on issues involving time, money and resources, fear of unnecessary formality and bureaucracy, lack of clarity about the essential nature of IIP and confusion and uncertainty about the value of IiP to a small organisation.

The experience of IiP in action has seldom been investigated in detail, but quantifiable data have been collected in the form of large-scale surveys. However, now that the standard has changed these data are outdated. Even so, there are two assumptions with IiP that are largely untested. The first is that there are definable standards of 'best practice' on which to base a standard. It is not clear that is so, as illustrated by the discussions of the various HRD strategies and options in earlier chapters. Second, that if there is a direct link between HR practices and organisational performance such causality is difficult to prove.

Based on research within three companies at different stages of the IiP recognition process, one study concluded that the most effective motivation for engagement with IiP was the influence of key customers. Employers tended to be sceptical regarding the alleged benefits of IiP, but were worried about diminishing work from customers if they were seen not to be adhering to the standard. In other words the badge was important for retaining and attracting customers. Employees also stated that employers appeared to avoid and compromise the substance of the initiative, IiP procedures often being complied with in a 'minimalist fashion' in order to limit their impact on the nature of the workplace.

The types of firms committing to IiP appear to be initially unconvinced of its contribution to business performance and think the standard will have little impact on their organisation. For others, IiP may be irrelevant or inappropriate, for example, small professional service firms where deployment of knowledge and educational credentials are an essential personal asset and where informal approaches to communication and a cultural resistance to being managed influence the daily running of the business. Some studies conclude that IiP may be viewed as little more than an administrative requirement for marketing purposes, rather than an important contributor to organisational performance.

Least to change, least to gain?

It is possible to conclude that the evidence suggests that the organisations currently achieving IiP recognition are those with 'least to change and the least to gain'. They contend that, because the initiative is voluntary, the organisations with most to gain from IiP are less likely to take up the standard. Many of the organisations they surveyed already had the procedures and controls in place to gain IiP. The reasons these organisations

continued overleaf

concluding case continued

were accredited are twofold. The first is that the IiP promotion agencies were 'cherry picking' organisations that were going to achieve the standard easily. Second, that organisations were more attracted to IiP if it was relatively easy to obtain. IiP was merely 'encapsulating what organisations were already doing rather than introducing any new substantial element in training'. Significant measurable business benefits can result from the IiP process but organisations do not usually quantify them or recognise them as business benefits. Research has failed to quantify the benefit as organisations seem to lack interest in doing so and their motivation for embarking on the process does not include the achievement of such quantifiable benefits. Government policy in this area would benefit from the introduction of greater incentives to any organisation that is currently unlikely to adopt the standard.

Case References

Website: http://www.investorsinpeople.co.uk

Alberga, T. et al (1997) 'An evaluation of the Investors in People Standard', *Human Resource Management Journal*, vol. 7 , no. 2.

Down, S. and Smith, D. (1998) 'Investors in people: the search for measurable benefits', *Personnel Review*, vol. 27 , no. 2.

Hoque, K. (2003) 'All in all it's just another plaque on the wall: The incidence and impact of the Investor in People Standard', *Journal of Management Studies*, vol. 40, no. 2, pp. 543–71

Mason, D. (1997) *Achieving Investors in People*, London, Pitman.

Ram, M. (1998) 'Investors in People in small firms: case study evidence from the business services sector', *Personnel Review*, vol. 29, no. 1.

concluding case analysis

You should see several key points relating to the public policy which can be adopted to explore and understand HRD. In sum this was a product of a voluntarist policy; seeing HRD in largely economic terms, aiming to fit with the strategic concerns of organisations and in some sense addressing the social agenda linked with HRD. That is, each perspective has something to give to understanding the strengths and weaknesses of IiP.

Overall the claims that the original IiP standard was effective clearly had to be modified because of concerns among those who were accredited and those who were reluctant to get involved with IiP. To review the standard and 'continuously improve' it is, of course, quite sensible and laudable. At the time of writing the revised and revamped IiP standard is still being implemented and has yet to be fully evaluated, but it remains to be seen whether the review really got to grips with criticisms of the standard and its contribution to improving HRD in companies.

IiP is likely to remain a centrepiece of workplace learning policy as the core of a voluntarist strategy for encouraging employers to adopt good practice and improve their HRD. Further changes are planned: widening the scope of the standard and liaison with other standards in business might suggest that a 'merger' of standards, including HRD and other employment standards, is likely. For some it is not the content of the standard, but the extent to which HRD at work can be motivated entirely through 'encouragement', that is the key issue. Research investigating IiP as a means of encouraging improvements in HRD, and, through that, business development will continue to keep the statisticians busy. Whether that can convince and persuade employers who are currently outside the system to come into the fold is another matter altogether.

Knowledge management and communities of practice

> **By the end of this chapter you will be able to:**
>
> □ identify the connections between HRD, information systems, organisational learning and intellectual capital;
> □ define communities of practice;
> □ describe the theory and practice of developing communities of practice.

13.1 | *Knowing where to kick*

A motorist takes his about-to-break-down, spluttering car into the garage. The symptoms and problems are explained. The mechanic walks to the car and kicks it at a point near the front bumper. The engine revs back to normal life. He hands over a bill for £100. The customer is taken aback, '£100 for that? How do you justify that?'. The mechanic takes the bill back and amends it: 'Labour – £1.00, Knowing where to kick – £99.00'.

introductory case study | *The reps' breakfast*

A company wanted to improve the learning of its customer service representatives (reps). Their job was to install and fix photocopying machines. Customers who were having problems with their machines would contact a customer service centre, which would notify a rep, and he or she would then go out to the customer's site. The rep would diagnose the problem and follow instructions for fixing it, with the help of codes generated by the machine that reported its state and supporting documentation that showed what those codes meant. The reps were simply 'following the map' provided by the codes and documentation, and doing what it told them to do.

However, what happened in practice was quite different from this picture. Reps often succeeded in fixing the photocopiers only by departing from what the codes suggested and what the manuals prescribed. In doing this they were using knowledge gained from other sources. That knowledge had been generated by experience – by reps exploring what was wrong with a machine when the codes and documentation were not complete or were misleading. Indeed, on many occasions, if they had followed the instructions they were being given from 'the book' they would have made customers' problems worse rather than better as it would have taken longer to repair the machines.

continued overleaf

So, although reps had a formal 'map' to refer to, they frequently found it of little use and had to resort to their collective experience. The generic codes reporting problems, and the instructions for fixing them, were often inadequate. Large and complex machines made up of multiple subsystems, of different ages, with different patterns of use and in different environments behave idiosyncratically, not predictably. Reps had had to learn to repair machines for themselves – to create their own maps based on diagnosing and fixing problems with these idiosyncratic machines. The researchers exploring the reps' learning were surprised to find that the new areas mapped by the reps were common knowledge; they all seemed to know what to do with particular machines. How had reps learned what to do when they fell off the map?

The answer was that they had learned at breakfast. During breakfast with their colleagues, before starting their official work, reps shared experiences and explored the problems of idiosyncratic and difficult machines. Reps who knew the peculiarities of each machine would swap stories about what they had done to fix those problems. These brief discussions over breakfast provided their HRD, not formal training. While eating, playing cards and gossiping they talked continuously, posing each other questions, offering solutions, discussing their work and telling stories. What might appear on the surface to be time-wasting behaviour was in fact an HRD process in which the reps kept each other up to date on what they had learned and what they knew. From hearing about an individual's improvised solution to a tricky problem everyone else could learn.

Even in this apparently independent job, where the rep worked alone and the work did not seem to require any use of discretion and continuous learning, there was continuous learning. And that was embedded in a social network, one that supported learning and work among a specific group of people. The reps' breakfast was an example of what has come to be called a community of practice in action.

Introduction

The case of the continuous learning experienced during the reps' breakfast illustrates that so-called communities of practice (CoPs) can be substantial contributors to workplace HRD. CoPs are informal, self-organising networks of people dedicated to sharing knowledge in an area of common interest or expertise. The advantages and attractions of nurturing such learning groups are illustrated by the introductory case. These advantages and attractions suggest CoP as a complementary method of providing HRD functions. More than that, CoPs may be important because they fit with an era in which organisations are seeking to become more effective in knowledge management (KM). The idea of KM has come to provide a major perspective on understanding organisations as a whole, and on HRD and learning in the workplace. Here we will take 'knowledge management' to include the institutional management of knowledge as outlined in Figure 13.1. These are all part of KM in firms or sectors that are part of the knowledge economy (see Strategic View Boxes 13.1 and 13.2).

strategic view

13.1	**Kins of knowledge that may be managed**	
Codified knowledge: know what and know why	**Tacit knowledge: know how and know who**
Know what: knowledge of facts Know why: principles of why things happen Gained through education	Know how: skills gained through practice Know who: collaboration in networks Gained through experience

13.2 | *Knowledge management concerns*

Know what	Know how
To what extent is there a significant element of 'knowing what'? How do people in the occupation get to 'know the facts'? extensive education.................basic education	To what extent is there an element of 'know how' that can only be gained through practice and accumulating tacit knowledge? personal tacit knowledge.................rule books
Know why	**Know who**
To what extent is there a significant element of reflective practice? Are 'principles' or theory needed to perform in unusual/unique situations? How do people in the occupation get to appreciate the principles and theories? reflective practice....................................routine	To what extent is 'knowing others' and accessing others' tacit knowledge a significant issue in performing in the occupation? To what extent does the occupation need people collaborating in networks, with access to other experts in associated areas? need to access others' knowledge..............solo

The implication is that a key to greater current and future performance is how well knowledge workers can create and sustain knowledge-based organisations that are capable of competing in a knowledge economy (Foray 2004). One of the principal means for creating and transferring such knowledge in organisations is through developing CoPs, among other kinds of effective groups at work (see Operations Box 13.1).

13.1 | *Kinds of groups compared with CoPs*

	Purpose	Members	Cohesion	Lifecycle
Operational team	Work	Assigned	Common task	Permanent
Project team	Task	Roles in project	Project	Project goal attained
Informal network	Get and give help	Friendship basis	Personal need	Evolves with career
CoP	Create and exchange learning	Self select	Identify with learning issue	Till learning cycle is completed

Organisations are aware that they now have technologies that enable CoPs, but they need to develop systems that can help them make the most of the knowledge that has been developed and is held by their workforce, from the top to the bottom of the organisation. Indeed, the intellectual capital that an organisation possesses may represent its greatest asset, and provide the foundation for its continued existence and success.

Thus one task for HRD is how to capture and codify the evolving knowledge, capabilities and behaviours as people engage in daily work and learn. This is in addition

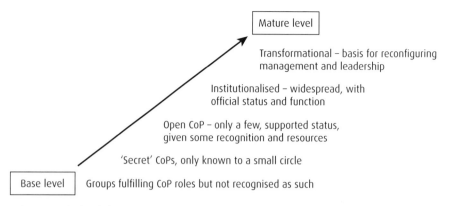

Figure 13.1 Various maturity levels for CoPs

to transferring knowledge to employees so that they can perform effectively. CoP can be seen to function to attain this newer HRD role, and to do so at various maturity levels (see Figure 13.1). These will range from groups which are informal gatherings of people exchanging knowledge and learning through telling stories to managed and directed groups under a style of leadership which nurtures a CoP in the whole organisation (see Strategic View Box 13.3).

theory & research

13.1 | The KM era

The sustained interest in 'knowledge management' has been ascribed to six causes:

- **Wealth**. This is demonstrably generated from knowledge and intangible assets. An often-cited example is Microsoft, which has been assessed as having 94 per cent of its market value based on intangible, knowledge-related assets.
- The recognition of **people** as the locus of organisational knowledge, rather than written guidelines and procedure manuals. For example, as organisations downsize and make people redundant, they soon find they have to re-hire them as consultants, because they still need their knowledge and know-how in addition to the guidelines and manuals.
- Accelerating **change**. This requires increased attention to be paid to continuous learning: the need to create, absorb and assimilate new knowledge, skills and behaviours rather than rely on existing knowledge.
- Recognition of **innovation** as the key to competitiveness, as innovation depends on managing knowledge. This involves a high degree of risk, both in managing current knowledge to innovate and in seeking the new, the untypical and the creative.
- The importance of **cross-boundary** transactions. There is a need to recognise the dependence on crossing internal organisational boundaries and on drawing upon external sources, to have more complete and full knowledge. Yet doing either of these things represents a real challenge; the walls between units, organisations and potential partners can be quite a barrier to knowledge transfer.
- The **limits of technology**. The potential of information technologies to make organisations and their businesses more effective and efficient in their basic tasks has been a major hope. Alongside the increasing use of information technologies comes the additional hope that more transparent and easier access to information might have pay-offs in other ways. For example, it could enable more knowledgeable management as all kinds of information could be easily accessed and shared. Indeed for some this is exactly what KM means. But it is **knowledge**, not information, that is the issue. And much knowledge in organisations is hard to codify, since know-how and know-who are often tacit. There are no truly effective software or hardware solutions to tap these kinds of knowledge

13.3	Traditional management functions compared with CoP requirements

Traditional management requires	Communities of practice involve
Specifying the way tasks are organised	Exploring the way tasks can be done
Establishing routine	Being spontaneous
Orchestrating work	Improvising at work
Assuming a predictable environment	Responding to a changing environment
Relying on explicit knowledge	Driven by tacit knowledge
Making knowledge structured and linear	Seeing knowledge as web-like
Top-down control of learning	Bottom-up generation of learning
Imposing systems	Responding to invention

In the more mature versions the issue is to capture and codify new knowledge from employee learning, the process has to be managed (see Figure 13.2). Phase 1 of this process is to acknowledge and recognise the existence of these, often informal, CoPs, in which new knowledge, capabilities and behaviours are produced and shared by employees as they work. Phase 2 is to capture or map such knowledge, capabilities or behaviours. In phase 3, mapped knowledge, capabilities or behaviours have to be made available to others who may need it, in the organisation and beyond. The end of this process might signify the end of the CoP. But as new issues and experiences are encountered, new off-map problems arise, once again requiring a CoP.

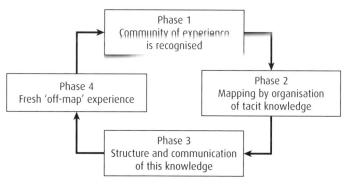

Figure 13.2 Phases of knowledge capture and conversion

The kind of learning seen during the reps' breakfast – learning from each other through sharing each other's experience – is universal, and occurs naturally in all kinds of organisation, group and job. The issue for managers is to convert this CoP learning into a structured form that fleshes out and expands the knowledge map so that all employees can perform effectively. Advocates of knowledge management suggest that the main job of senior managers in modern organisations can be reconceived as being to better help the workforce capture and use knowledge from CoPs.

Although such a view of management may be desirable and attainable, there is no doubt that the implications of supporting KM and nurturing CoPs radically alter the way that the function of HRD is seen. HRD is no longer to be thought about as a process whereby trainers or managers remove deficits in knowledge or skill; rather it is about managing and enhancing the naturally growing knowledge assets and skills emerging in practice. This increases the intellectual capital of the workforce. The challenge is that organisations can be environments which can either help or obstruct the sharing of knowledge and learning (Ipe 2003). The relevant issue is the recognition of how knowledge sharing arises in contexts where it is:

- *Mediated* by stakeholders with different perceptions and understanding of organisational goals;
- *Situated* in concrete interpersonal and group, power-based relations;
- *Contested* among the common and different interests which exist in any organisation.

As Kessels (2002) put it, 'co-operation and joined knowledge work is feasible when participants each choose their community based on reciprocal attractiveness, passion, involvement and identification with each others' expertise' (p. 51). What this needs in practice is outlined in Operations Box 13.2.

operations

13.2 CoP issues

Conditions for a CoP
- Can identify each other; co-location
- Clarify benefits for organisation
- External recognition
- Facilitated not led; negotiate and interact
- Bounded authority; does not issue guidelines
- Success and enthusiasm
- Funding

Problems
- Learning from off-map experience is important, but may not extend to all staff.
- Are people ever 'on map' if things change so quickly?
- A relaxed atmosphere encourages talk, but will that survive if it is managed?
- Will people just 'moan' in the canteen, an opportunity to gossip?
- Might a CoP even encourage employees to discuss how not to work?
- More work for managers as coaches, more work recording and sharing learning

exercise

13.1

Think about an organisation with which you are familiar. To what extent are there 'communities of experience' among employees that provide for the creation and dissemination of learning from experience, leading to new or different ways of working? Are there equivalents to the 'reps' breakfast' where employees share learning with each other, but not necessarily with managers? How might these become 'communities of practice'?

Three currents of thinking

The hope is that the extent to which organisations can perform and achieve their objectives depends on facilitating CoP better. It is groups, not individuals, that create and share know-how and sense-making. There is always a collective knowledge base.

A large organisation can be seen then not as a unified, single CoP but as several overlapping and interdependent CoPs. Smaller organisations can be seen to interact in supply chains and networks that also contain multiple CoPs.

As models of KM develop, with concerns about how to develop and manage CoPs, there have been three important currents of thinking:

- the **information systems** perspective, which emphasises the potential of information management tools for the capture, storage and retrieval of knowledge for CoP;
- the **organisational learning** perspective, which emphasises the way CoPs in organisations are embedded in and influenced by the internal organisational structure and culture;
- the **intellectual capital** perspective, which emphasises the value of IC and the worth of knowledge as embodied in patents and strategic core competences, and raises issues about ownership and control of such assets.

The example of the photocopier engineers illustrates each of these streams. The reps' learning must be captured and stored, and more widely shared. That can mean logging it all in an open database, which can be accessed and searched by others. But it is not as simple as just recording what the reps have learned and putting it on a website. The reps have a 'political' interest, as do others in the organisation, in retaining their knowledge as it is their main source of power, influence and means of gaining economic rewards. Can an organisational structure and culture be developed to overcome these problems of politics and interests among employees? This is open to question, because it would have to deal with the thorny questions of who benefits and who gets what.

The information systems (IS) perspective

For some people the IS perspective on capturing and codifying knowledge in organisations is the most important. One model suggests a tripartite structure for HRD: instruction through training, performance support through information provisions, and KM. KM can be seen as the pinnacle of a hierarchy of IS and performance management concerns, up to being concerned with creating what some term the 'intelligent enterprise'.

Resources such as job aids have always existed, and IS technologies enable an online central repository that people can access by downloading manuals and guidelines. CoP could use these to input their knowledge and operate more effectively, using access to such information-sharing systems. In addition, activities such as company suggestion schemes have always existed, seeking to tap workforce knowledge; what IS enables is more extensive and faster sharing of such knowledge. Finally, in one sense enterprise intelligence is a form of integrated enterprise resource planning (ERP) system, in which IS-enabled systems monitor and analyse the performance of all aspects of the organisation's functioning – including people. In another sense it is more that the organisation has the equivalent of a 'brain', a master governor in control of the whole. The expertise of people is embedded in this system, and it is possible to access ideas and analysis relevant to any issue. Thus IS-based KM issues and concerns in performance support range from enabling better access to existing and already-mapped knowledge in the organisation to the wider sharing of newly captured knowledge and the attainment of enterprise-wide intelligence, enabling innovation and rapid change.

Organisational learning (OL)

The essence of organisational learning (OL) is that the complex interactions that are involved in organisations must be continuously learned and re-learned for the system to survive. Learning is not a discrete function, restricted to trainers providing training. The brain of an organisation should be treated like that of an organism in which continued learning is essential for continuing existence and performance.

OL has often been a forum for applying systems thinking to HRD, for exploring the complexes of connections and feedback loops in organisations that are believed to govern and regulate human behaviour. Behaviour and performance cannot be magically improved by providing some training courses. Instead, we need to explore the whole system and the factors inhibiting or enabling the kinds and level of behaviour and performance desired. Interventions involving HRD, working on cognitive capacities, capabilities and behaviours, cannot be properly conceived or implemented without analysing these factors. Therefore a systemic rather than a systematic approach to KM and learning is appropriate.

This leads, undeniably, to a different, more elaborate and more sophisticated way of thinking about HRD and KM. It is also potentially confusing. We have got used to thinking about HRD at work as a systematic process of identifying needs, planning, delivering and evaluating, and the tasks seem to make sense: run training courses, provide on-job coaching, or design multimedia software packages. But the OL perspective plays down such activities and replaces them with another, more difficult-to-grasp set of concepts and activities: systems thinking, action research into problem-solving, trying to map and tap the knowledge of the workforce and developing CoP. OL analysis often runs into problems because it vacillates between two perspectives. On the one hand, it seeks a substitute recipe of prescriptions – a new toolkit – to help manage systemic learning; on the other, it denies that these are useful, and says that OL is more of a way of thinking in holistic and systemic terms about organisations. From our perspective, however, OL perspectives see learning as an integral part of the organisation going about its day-to-day business.

An interpretation 'industry' has grown up around the various models proposed for OL. KM has attracted experts in management from many academic disciplines, including psychology, sociology, economics, anthropology, political sciences and history, and it now provides an interdisciplinary focus for them similar to the way that strategy did during the 1980s and 1990s. This is also true for the newer fields of study (we cannot really call them disciplines) in management – information management, strategic management, change management, HRM and innovation management – that are all interested in OL. In this sense OL provides an altogether new way of thinking about management and organisations. The problem for practitioners is that these disciplines all have their own way of looking at OL, whereas what is needed is a truly trans-disciplinary perspective.

Currently we have many models, and no one has yet claimed to have identified the perfect 'learning organisation'. There are no templates equivalent, for example, to the Ford motor car production line, which exemplified a certain kind of management and organisation practice. Proponents of OL say that they can see glimpses, or suggest practices and tools. One concern, though, is that the first-generation prescriptions have not helped achieve the large-scale reform of organisational structures and cultures explicitly embraced by OL proponents. New methods have to be developed,

> ### 13.2 | *Streams of thinking in OL*
>
> The ways in which OL capacities relate to the solution of major business problems have origins in three main streams of thinking. These have all played a part in generating the concept of OL, and are emphasised to different degrees in the various models of a learning organisation.
>
> **Traditional organisational development (OD)**
> - How can we describe the processes and problems of organisational design, structure, culture and development?
> - The organisational learning idea is another metaphor of organisation: the organisation functions like a brain, to learn and regulate itself.
>
> **Innovative HRD**
> - How can the organisational/work environment be used to enable individual learning?
> - The organisational learning idea is an embodiment of continuous development in the workplace.
>
> **Humanist-inspired thinking**
> - How can work and workplaces be made better environments for the whole person, consistent with the insights of alternatives to traditional Western cultural mores and values?
> - The organisational learning idea provides transformations of workplaces and environments for personal development.

beyond conventional HRD methods such as team-building and personal development. Such 'frontier' issues represent a continuation of the constituent fields that have led to OL as a construct (see Theory & Research Box 13.2).

OL can also be seen to have emerged from classic concerns in three areas of concern to management:

1. identifying and dealing with problems while they are still small;
2. drawing on internal resources and tacit knowledge;
3. using systems thinking about snowballing and balancing feedback loops.

Identifying and dealing with minor, fragmented problems is the stuff of everyday organisational life. It happens all the time in healthy organisations, so that people hardly even notice it. From afar, the organisation appears to be a seamlessly efficient operation. Close up, the organisation is seen to be a hive of activity around large numbers of errors being noticed and dealt with.

Identifying and remedying small problems at source as a strategy for ensuring organisational effectiveness has been addressed primarily by the quality movement for over 50 years. One way of summing up this movement is to say that it represents a desire to identify and eliminate all errors that can be eliminated, by continuously improving systems and processes. The oft-acknowledged barriers to the detection of small problems are often related to human communication failures:

- managers claiming 'but nobody told us there was a problem';
- employees claiming that 'nobody listened to us when we told them';
- information available and communicated, but overshadowed by other concerns that took precedence.

Second, there is the question of making the best use of internal resources – the intelligence and knowledge of people inside the organisation. Smart people can fail to be an effective resource (Finkelstein et al 2006). The questioning of the effectiveness of professionals in modern organisations remains a contentious issue. Professionals are meant to be the solution: developing and using experts with the knowledge and skill to ensure organisational effectiveness in all kinds of areas, highly educated and specialist people. Whether it is doctors in hospitals, engineers in manufacturing or personnel managers in work organisations, they are often perceived as being less effective than they could be. One source of this ineffectiveness was thought to lie in the education of professionals, suggesting a need for reform of this education. However, researchers argued that it was the climate within organisations themselves that hindered the use of professionals. There was little point in simply reforming education for professionals; organisations needed to appreciate the ways in which they presented barriers to professionals using their knowledge and capabilities.

It was in this context that the researchers Argyris and Schon (1974) outlined and modelled two types of organisational learning. The first was what they called single-loop learning. This occurs when an organisation detects errors in performance that will compromise the achievement of its preset goals. For example, productivity may be too low to meet an important order on time. The organisation will have to adopt a new strategy to meet its goals; for example, organising extra shifts or increasing productivity. Identifying and correcting these kinds of error is single-loop learning. The organisation is acting, by analogy, like a heating system governed by a thermostat: as long as it acts to maintain the temperature set by the thermostat it is said to be single-loop learning. Many performance management systems are elaborations of this kind of learning: to set goals, to get feedback on them, and then to take corrective action to attain those goals.

But there is also another form of learning which occurs when an organisation can detect errors in its overall master goals, and respond to them. Argyris and Schon called this double-loop learning. Extending the thermostat analogy, it is the ability to determine that the preset temperature is wrong: it is no good trying to run the system to meet that set temperature, as the thermostat setting – the goal itself – must be changed. If the environment is too hot or too cold, a new temperature should be set. Following the productivity example, there is little point in increasing the productive capacity if either the market is declining or a new market is emerging in other products. The overall goal must be reviewed: new product development must be introduced. Double-loop learning does not supersede single-loop learning, it complements it.

According to Argyris and Schon, the problem with many organisations, and the problem for professionals in organisations, is that they are not at all good at this double-loop learning. They find it hard to question the appropriateness of the governing variables they have adopted – their key goals and assumptions. Hence they continue adopting new strategies to try to reach preset goals when they should be questioning the goals and assumptions themselves. Argyris and Schon went on to describe and analyse the ways in which organisations could be seen to inhibit professionals' contributions to double-loop learning. They concluded that professionals' behaviour in organisations is characterised by what they called espoused theories and theories in action. An espoused theory is the explicit reason that people give to describe their behaviour; a theory in action is a description of the beliefs that underpin their

13.2 | *Organisational learning climate issues*

	The ideal	But...	So the problem is	The solution is
When defining goals...	Collaborate with each other to set goals; review collectively as well	Act unilaterally, set own goals, or only with own group/peers; have own goals attained rather than others'	No commitment among various parties to shared goals; people are used to acting unilaterally	Build trust; maximise acting with commitment to common goals
When problem-solving...	Mutual problem-solving and adopt a win–win outlook;	People adopt a maximise winning and minimise losing position in the course of problem-solving	Playing a blame game to ensure 'winning' and avoid 'losing'	Be able to accept/explore failure without 'blame' cultures
The culture should be....	Everyone should speak up and be open	People want to minimise provoking others, eliciting negative feelings	Protecting oneself by keeping quiet, not taking the risk of aggravating others	A climate aware of and able to discuss feelings as well as ideas
Conflict should be handled...	Rationally; people in formal roles should interact rationally	People act politically; the workplace is political	Behind closed door 'politics' is seen to be necessary to succeed	Get 'politics' out from behind closed doors

Source Based on Argyris and Schon 1974.

behaviour, regardless of the 'espoused' reasons that they give. Theories in action reflect what people really think rather than what they say they think.

The net effect is that, without careful management, professionals and others behave competitively and are mistrustful. Those supposed to ensure learning and success are complicit in obstructing it. Either they are stuck in cycles of compliance with goals they do not believe in, or they find themselves pursuing goals that they know are no longer right but which they seem powerless to change. Even though people may be aware of impending disaster, they cannot use their internal resources to break free and stop it happening. There is a need for individual awareness of these dynamics and professional development to provide individuals who can manage to support double-loop learning – people who can confront its challenges with 'emotional intelligence'. This is the key to creating an environment that supports OL.

Finally, there is systems thinking. Systems thinking investigates the principles common to all complex entities by developing abstract models that can be used to describe them. Systems analysts emphasise that systems are open to, and interact with, their environments. Because of this they can acquire qualitatively new properties through emergence, resulting in continual learning. Rather than reduce an entity, for example the human body, to the properties of its parts or elements – the organs and cells – systems thinking focuses on the arrangement of and relations between the parts that connect them into a whole. The body works as more than the sum of its parts under the influence of active learning. Socio-technical work organisations can be explored as this kind of system.

Being a system implies that something other than simple cause-and-effect relations is involved. Rather than A affecting B, there is the possibility that B may also be affecting A. From the mutual interaction of the parts of a system, there arise characteristics that cannot be derived from any of the individual parts or one-way causal relations between them. The phenomenon is synergy: the whole is greater than the sum of its parts.

We can characterise systems as either closed or open. A closed system is one that does not need to interact with its environment to maintain its existence. Examples of such systems are atoms and molecules. Mechanical systems are closed systems. Open systems are organic, and must interact with their environment in order to maintain their existence. People are open systems: they must interact with their environment in order to take in food and water. An open system will interact with its environment in a growing (reinforcing) or in a balancing fashion.

Two types of loop occur within systems. The first are reinforcing loops in which the interactions are such that each action adds to the other: what happens to A adds to B and what happens to B adds to A. Any situation where action produces a result that promotes more of the same action is representative of a reinforcing loop. The 'snow-balling' metaphor represents the reinforcing loop. Typical examples of 'snowballing' reinforcing loops are population growth or decline, uncontrolled nuclear reactions, or panic runs on banks in times of financial crisis. It is, for example, what happens in a savings account. The principal sum in the savings account interacts with an interest rate and the principal is increased. This reinforcing action happens regularly, depending on the period over which the institution computes the interest.

The other form of loop is the balancing loop. This is one in which an action attempts to bring two things to 'agreement': what happens with A reduces B, and what reduces B also reduces A. As the system state gets closer to the desired state, the gap between A and B gets smaller and smaller, so the action adds less and less. Once the action has moved the current state to a point where it equals the desired state, the gap is zero and there is no more action. A typical example of a balancing loop is closing a gap in space by making a journey from location A to location B. The desired state is to be at B, the actual state is at A: the further from A, and hence the closer to B, the less action is required to get to the desired state. Another example is developing from being incapable (A) by trial and error (action) to becoming competent (B). The more that the action (trial and error) reduces A, the more it also reduces what is needed to get to B.

These effects of actions, leading to snowballing or balancing loops, can combine in many ways that result in all manner of typical situations in daily and organisational life: the escalations that run out of control, or the reaching of states of satisfying equilibrium. Sometimes snowballing is wanted; sometimes it is not. Sometimes equilibrium is wanted; sometimes it is a form of paralysis. The point of this systems perspective is that it opens up insights into the pitfalls of obvious solutions for apparent problems. Obvious solutions are those that have a short-term effect, and may improve situations temporarily, but make the situation worse in the long run. For example, safeguarding crops against insect infestations may be done by using insecticides, dealing with crime by greater levels of imprisonment, or encouraging economic growth by investing in the 'new' economy rather than the old. These obvious solutions seem to work. But these actions occur within systems, with potential snowballing loops: using insecticides may cause pollution, which makes the land useless, and insects evolve immunity; prisons become schools for criminals, who fail to rehabilitate; investment in the new economy peaks, the bubble bursts, and subsequently slows general economic growth or causes a recession.

Where obvious solutions are seen to fail, we must seek to understand the apparent 'system' in operation which has not been changed – or may even have been made worse – by the intervention.

This is the approach of Senge (1990). There are situations in organisations where systems are in balance, are stable and persist, or they are reinforcing growth and escalation, or they set limits to success and can cause decline. Senge sees organisations as needing to develop a networking culture in which everyone engages in dialogue in order to question their own assumptions and to expose and deal with these kinds of systems problem (see Resources Box 13.2).

| 13.2 | *Systems thinking and learning* |

One of the main problems in the National Health service (NHS) in the UK lay with patients who had suffered serious illness and had been hospitalised for a long time. When they were discharged they tended to yo-yo in and out of hospital. A research group examined the experience of a stroke team by talking to patients in hospital. They found that they had difficulties adapting to home life after hospitalisation; lots of professionals visited them to help after discharge –20 in 2 months in one instance – but the patients generally felt hopeless and helpless. The hospital trust concerned started cross-training to reduce the number of visitors and provide continuity of care on discharge. Patients planned with their carers what they wanted to achieve. They were then supported in specific projects relevant to them; for example the patient who was helped to use a keyboard and pen so he could start work again. They then networked with others to share their new knowledge rather than doing what they might otherwise have done, which was to write up their innovations as a report to be published. They repeated this networking until it eventually grew to the point where many people were convinced this was the strategy to adopt, and government policy came to be concerned with changing intermediate care as a whole. So here, the initial attention to detail, networking and sharing knowledge moved from looking at one stroke team and patients' stories to changing systems and then to changing policy.

Systems thinking is synthetic, expansionist and non-linear. It is synthetic and expansionist in defining problems in terms of clusters of variables, and the interactions within and between them, and not in terms of discrete variables. It is non-linear in envisaging both cyclical and mutual interactions among the elements of a system – the inputs, processes, outputs and feedback elements. The net effect is the argument that to solve problems we need a way to understand interconnections and interdependence, producing a set of interacting solution ideas simultaneously. In terms of management and organisation, HRD and performance, the key conclusions are the following:

- Human systems are 'open' systems: they involve internal and external relations with regulation. People and organisations can always be learning.
- There are both wholes and constituents: individuals, groups, organisations, societies. Trying to change one part may not work if the other parts of the system are not in favour.
- There are always clusters of problems.
- Real problems are ill-structured and ill-defined; they are 'wicked'.
- The subjects must be included in any study of a system.
- There can only ever be tentative, incomplete solutions.
- Ethical issues matter in redesigning systems.

There are many challenges with using systems thinking to explore organisations. If problems cannot be reduced so that it is possible to solve them piece by piece in order to remedy larger problems, then all problems are probably beyond the capabilities of one group of specialists to grasp. This is because, to understand the whole, it is necessary to understand every part – in other words, to possess some kind of transdisciplinary awareness. If there is a need to understand interconnections and interdependence, and produce interacting solution ideas simultaneously, then every inquiry is about systems change. Any enquiry is then potentially 'boundless'. In the context of what is practicable and pragmatic in management and organisation, there is a preference for analytical, reductionist and linear causal thinking. That is inconsistent with systemic approaches to management.

Intellectual capital and strategic management

The connections between KM, CoP and HRD have become associated also with the concept of intellectual capital (IC). This implies the idea of measurement using the infamous cliché 'bottom line'. Capital is thought of as money or other assets owned by a person or organisation that can be used to control economic activity. IC represents the development, possession, ownership, control and use of knowledge by people or organisations as a part of that economic activity for profit. This means that knowledge, as well as natural resources or technological advances, provides a basis for competing, and indeed for wealth creation and prosperity as a whole. Knowledge has always been an integral part of capitalism, and an intellectual ferment of research and development of market, products and services is a feature of its dynamism. But the concept of IC suggests something beyond that. Part of this idea was captured with the dot-com boom (and bust): investors believed that some IC, based on internet-based business, was all that was needed, as there had to be potential for growth with the uptake of internet services. In most cases this was incorrect, and substantial losses were incurred as many dot-com businesses failed to generate any money at all, never mind profit. However, there were developments, such as the human genome project, that posed questions about IC. Two groups raced to map the human genome. One sought to benefit mankind as a whole; the other sought to map the genome in order to control, and have the right to control, the use of that knowledge. The medical implications of knowledge of the human genome were immense, and the issue of IC was at the heart of the story. The 'race' and rivalry ended with a 'draw', when public and private projects joined forces.

So IC was not just a hyped element of the rise of the internet. It represents a real concern, and provides both new accounting problems and challenges for organisations, as it is less tangible than other forms of capital. As a construct, IC challenges the dominant, conventional, financial and legal modes of thinking about value in organisations and societies, and about economic activity as a whole. This opens up many debates, but what matters here is that people and organisations with IC have a market price: they can supply what is in demand. As owners of the means of knowledge rather than the means of production they can also 'walk out of the door' with their IC at any time. This problem applies to regions and nations if their knowledge workers leave to take up jobs elsewhere. There are also problems with renewing IC if people or organisations are prone to 'walking away', causing investors to be wary of investing in companies where the assets are invisible and highly mobile.

The evolution of IC ideas and practices presents challenges for organisations. These centre on the classic issues for organisations and HRD: loose–tight control and empowerment, communication, and creativity. There are also wider social issues. There is a prospect of creating a new underclass of people without capacities in or involvement with IC. There would be a boom in employment for highly knowledgeable and skilled people and organisations, who will be dispersed and mobile throughout the globe, but further unemployment and urban decay for those who are excluded from a share in IC.

How far does an era of wealth creation depend on IC and the management of tacit knowledge? This is questioned by those who point out that employment growth is often in low-skilled personal services, not high-tech and high-knowledge jobs and industries. Some believe that IC is relevant only to a minority of organisations, whereas others see it as universally relevant. In some sectors – software development and biotechnology, for example – the creation, ownership and protection of intellectual assets are central. Yet even these sectors depend on conventional physical infrastructures and explicit knowledge as much as on the tacit knowledge of their employees.

13.3 │ *Postal worker case*

Take the case of a postal worker to indicate the universal relevance of IC. A postal worker would not usually be seen to possess IC. But if he or she has developed knowledge about the best way to do a route, and about its peculiarities, then when he or she leaves, taking his or her own map of how to do the route quickly and efficiently, the organisation loses because an unexpected sum of IC disappears. For all that the era of KM appears new, the underlying issue is still an old one: how to try to quantify intangibles in the organisation and render them manageable. The capture of experience and learning, of tacit knowledge and its transformation into wealth creation and prosperity, is just a variation on the theme.

An application of IC as an element of general and strategic management is provided by Leonard-Barton (1995). Her model is broad in its concerns, but quite straightforward. She sees knowledge as the core capability of organisations. This capability is found in four forms: it is embedded in physical systems and technologies, in managerial systems, in skills and in values.

1. Core capability in the form of knowledge may be in a **physical** form. It may be, for example, in a design a company has protected by patent. This is knowledge you can see and touch; it is tangible.
2. Knowledge may be embodied in **managerial systems**. It can be embodied in learned ways of doing things most effectively.
3. Knowledge may be embodied in the explicit **skills** bases and tacit knowledge of employees: the individual competences that have been brought into the organisation or developed within it through experience.
4. Finally, knowledge is to be found embodied as **values**. These may be explicit 'big' values of the company; for example the values of a bureaucracy, which emphasise following all guidelines rigorously, or the values of an entrepreneurial firm that emphasises a bias for action. It may also be found in what Leonard-Barton terms 'little values', to do with the norms of behaviour in the workplace, or what others would call organisational culture.

Leonard-Barton's concern is to analyse how knowledge embodied in these forms can be the foundation for knowledge-inhibiting activities. Knowledge-inhibiting activities are experienced as limited problem-solving, an inability to innovate effectively, limited experimentation and the 'screening out' of new knowledge in organisations. These problems, in Leonard-Barton's terms, are caused by an over-commitment to the current knowledge base and recipe as embodied in existing physical forms, management systems, skills and values. The practical focus is on overcoming old recipes, which act as inhibitors of experimentation, problem-solving, innovation and the inclusion of new knowledge.

The purpose of this analysis of knowledge management is to emphasise that inherited knowledge is everywhere in an organisation, embodied in many different forms. To change and renew knowledge may require new physical systems, new management systems, new skills or new values. It is necessary then to understand how to ensure and enhance changes in physical systems, management systems, skills and values in order to manage knowledge effectively and maintain a core capability. Values as a form of embodied and fixed knowledge provide the form that is most difficult to change and develop. The evolution of new physical forms, products or services, facilities or technologies is inherent in market capitalism as companies seek success. The need for management systems to evolve over time is something of which most organisations are well aware. The need for new skills is also a touchstone of current thinking. The problem is often with the issue of new values.

The evolution of HRD in the CoP context

It seems straightforward enough to look at the KM and CoP implications for HRD – to learn from and with employees rather than ignore or suppress their learning. If it was this simple, then KM and CoP would imply little more than a reinvention of the kinds of activity associated with old-style staff suggestion schemes. But, as this chapter has shown, there are various dimensions and aspects of management that are challenged by the concepts of KM and CoP. In practice, managers have been criticised for being too concerned with re-engineering processes to increase efficiency using past management principles, rather than embracing the principles of working with KM and CoP to improve HRD. This continuing concern with imposing structures for HRD and work stifles knowledge capture and the HRD that emerges from that. On the other hand, for organisations, there are problems with defining managers' roles in terms of the principles consistent with encouraging KM and CoP, and having to cope with HRD constantly bubbling up and leading to changes in working practices in an almost chaotic way. In organisations there is a tension between general management and the principles of KM and CoP. It manifests itself as the dilemma of balancing the freedom of people who can learn and change while maintaining the necessary elements of structure that can fix and stabilise such learning so that it can be more widely circulated and implemented.

These tensions in capturing and codifying learning from employees partly reflect the argument that knowledge is power. Knowledge capture and codification cannot be analysed in a vacuum; they are pursued in circumstances where different groups, with different interests, contest the same ground. In the context of HRD at work those circumstances are about the structuring of, control of and returns from work.

The KM and CoP context has implications for HRD (see Operations Boxes 13.3 and 13.4) with its purpose to have processes and structures to help people create new knowledge, share their understanding, and continuously improve themselves and the results of the enterprise. CoP and KM are not just different ways of framing HRD programmes or projects, but a different kind of management philosophy.

13.3 | *What can HR managers do to support CoP?*

- Set aside time for informal meetings and/or formalise the informal
- Information mapping course, workshop on creating a learning culture
- Common areas for meeting and talking, 'greenhouses'
- Incentives and rewards, no blame culture
- Suggestion systems; ideas farm; websites to post suggestions
- Turn the tacit into the explicit via existing systems; through appraisal discussion; with knowledge transfer being discussed as an aim
- Make it in people's best interest to share knowledge
- Full and proper use of information systems

13.4 | *Traditional HRD compared with CoP/KM-influenced HRD*

Traditional HRD	CoP/KM
Employees receive skills training	All employees receive learning
Executives receive development	support and lifelong development
Training goals are based on requests by users	Learning goals are based on strategy and users needs
Primarily addresses immediate or short-term needs	Focuses on core competences and long-term needs
Needs assessments are done by trainers or managers	Needs assessments are done jointly by individuals and managers and trainers
Conducted locally or at an off-site classroom	Takes place at the workplace, job site, anywhere
Training scheduled on a periodic basis	Education given real time upon request
Approach is a delivery of knowledge	Approach is to design learning experiences as workplace interventions
Instructor-driven; programs designed by specialists	Self-directed, design process involves participants
Content is generalised, developed by specialists and often prescriptive	Content is specific and applied, developed jointly, trainees determine content
Trainers develop and deliver content, trainees are recipients	Educators facilitate process and coach learners who are joint developers

Source Adapted from McGinty Weston 1994.

Conclusion

Some roles are heavily codified and prescribed, some roles needing constant updating of specialist knowledge. Organising and transmitting established codified knowledge has always been an issue in HRD, yet performing well is rarely based on just having accumulated finite, codified pre-existing knowledge. The challenges for the organisation are:

- Accessing new 'know what' and 'know why';
- Accessing people's tacit knowledge;
- Sharing such knowledge freely and effectively.

To work for this, organisations may develop KM practices and CoP. These require:

- People who will collaborate because they trust each other (across teams, projects, departments);
- Win–Win attitudes to knowledge-creation and sharing;
- Ability to manage emotions and challenges of sharing knowledge collaboratively – speaking up, being open and honest;
- Recognising a more general human challenge; to promote innovative solutions and thinking in constrained rationality.

No exemplar models of HRD shaped by KM or CoP are evident. There are prescriptions for changing the HRD process in the context of KM and CoP in general, but there are many unanswered questions, such as an analysis of how to foster and further invention and innovation through supporting free practice and KM and CoP. For some critics, instead of progress there has been a spiralling into greater and greater complexity and obscurity. Perhaps more than any others in recent times the concepts of KM and CoP, based on developments in information systems, organisational learning and intellectual capital, have intrigued and bemused equally. The glimpses have remained vague as a result of problems with defining, modelling and providing empirical evidence for these concepts, despite well over a decade of intensive interest.

One problem in theory and practice is that the different streams involved in the area do not necessarily speak the same language. There is also a problem with the distinctiveness and separateness of regional interpretations of these concepts, particularly between European and US approaches. But none of this explains why developments in theory and practice have proved so problematic. These issues exist in many other areas of the human sciences. Why then should KM and CoP provide so many difficulties?

It seems as though developments such as KM and CoP are still detached from much in HRD practice, with its focus on more prosaic activities such as better systematic training systems, employee development and assistance programmes, and corporate universities. That leaves the concepts of KM and CoP isolated in organisational theory. Perhaps there is too much 'bundled up' in these grand synthesising concepts, and the most productive way ahead in theory and practice is to stick to promoting smaller, more specific and more discrete developments in HRD practice.

Multiple-choice questions

13.1 Which of the following correctly lists the main currents of thinking in use to examine knowledge management?

    A. Information systems, Organisational learning, Intellectual capital.

    B. Information systems, Cybernetics, Intellectual capital.

    C. Chaos theory, Organisational learning, Intellectual capital.

    D. Information systems, Organisational learning, Social exchange theory.

13.2 Which of the following statements are consistent with what Argyris and Schon propose about the conditions for 'double-loop' learning?

    A. Jointly agreeing goals is necessary to avoid people acting unilaterally to pursue their own private goals.

    B. Blame cultures are needed to ensure that people will adopt a 'win–win' outlook.

    C. People often fail to speak up when they know something because they might aggravate more powerful people.

    D. Conflict is always irrational and ought to be managed out of the organisation.

References

Argyris, C. and Schon, C. (1974) *Theory in Practice: Increasing professional effectiveness*. San Francisco, Jossey Bass.

Davenport, T. and Prusak, L. (1998), *Working Knowledge: How organizations manage what they know*, Boston, MA: Harvard Business School Press.

de Geus, A. (1999) *The Living Company: Growth, learning and longevity in business*, London, Nicholas Brealey.

Easterby-Smith, M. et al (1999) *Organizational Learning and the Learning Organization*, Cambridge, Sage.

Finkelstein, S., Harvey, C. and Lawton, T. (2006) *Breakout Strategy: Meeting the challenge of double-digit growth*, New York, McGraw-Hill.

Foray, D. (2004) *The Economics of Knowledge*, Boston, MA, MIT Press.

Garvey, B. and Williamson, B. (eds) (2002) *Beyond Knowledge Management: Dialogue, creativity and the corporate curriculum*, London, Pearson Education.

Ipe, M. (2003) 'Knowledge sharing in organizations: A conceptual framework', *Human Resource Development Review*, vol. 2, no. 4. pp. 337–59.

Kessels, J. (2002) 'Knowledge productivity', in R. Garvey and B. Williamson.

Lave, J. and Wenger, E. (1991), *Situated Learning: Legitimate peripheral participation*, Cambridge, Cambridge University Press.

Leonard-Barton, D. (1995) *Wellsprings of Knowledge*, Boston, MA: Harvard Business School Press.

Mayo, D. (2000) 'The role of employee development in the growth of intellectual capital', *Personnel Review*, vol. 29 , no. 4.

McGinty Weston, D. (1994) *Organizational Learning in Practice*, Menlo Park, CA, SRI Business Intelligence.

Pfeffer, J. and Sutton, R. (2000) *The Knowing-Doing Gap: How smart companies turn knowledge into action*, Boston, MA, Harvard Business School Press.

Seely Brown, J. and Duguid, P. (2000) 'Balancing act: How to catch knowledge without killing it', *Harvard Business Review*, May–June.

Senge, P. (1990) *The Fifth Discipline: The art and practice of the learning organisation*, London, Century.

Wenger, E., McDermott, R. and Snyder, W. (2002) *Cultivating Communities of Practice*, Boston, MA, Harvard Business School Press.

| concluding case question | *Developing creativity* |

What can experts in HRD offer to an organisation which is seeking to promote creativity among its workforce?

You should make reference to the concepts discussed in this chapter on CoP, and other subjects in the 'perspectives' section you think are relevant.

Background

Many organisations express an interest in promoting innovation and creativity throughout their workforce, believing that the benefits of this in fresh thinking and new and useful ideas will help them to be productive. Several themes and issues of relevance for HRD arise from this.

Creativity can be defined as 'imaginative activity fashioned so as to produce outcomes that are both original and of value'. The creative impulse in this sense has always been a feature of dynamic cultures and civilisations, but it seems now to feature more strongly as something that advanced economies and businesses are more dependent upon. In the context of long waves of historical change it is argued that at the economic leading edge there has been first the rise and decline of the 'working class' in the manufacturing industries then the rise and decline of the 'middle class' in the professional and service sectors and now the rise of the 'creative class'. The creative class is to be found in creative industries, services and manufacturing; and it is to be found also in certain roles inside all kinds of organisation, from marketing professionals to general managers. It is the quality of these creative people that provides the engine of economic vitality and success at the leading edge of sustainable competitiveness for advanced economies.

It seems that some kinds of localities and organization are better than others in either fostering or attracting these creative sectors and people. Places with a high proportion of creative sector businesses and 'creative class' members tend, for example, to be more 'open to diversity'. In studies on localities in the USA it is areas like San Francisco, Austin, San Diego, Boston and Seattle that are the top spots for employment and wealth creation, providing role models for other aspiring cities. The organisations and places that seem to succeed in attracting and keeping 'creative' people are ones where there are informal, 'no collar' workplaces, characterised by casual, fun and stimulating environments, and high maintenance management as the expectations they have of their occupational life, careers and lifestyle in general are high.

Creativity will then only form and develop where the amenities and environments that suit a 'creative class' exist. To attract and foster creativity and nurture the creative class it seems that the following values have to be recognised and embraced:

- Self-assurance and risk-taking – the creative class includes many people who are subversive, disruptive, rebellious;
- Variety in interests and knowledge – all forms of creativity are deeply inter-related, and 'creators' feed off of one another;
- Creativity as work – even though the process of creating may appear 'playful' and 'time-wasting' rather than productive it requires its own kind of discipline and focus to be respected rather than restricted;
- Motivation by the intrinsic rewards of successful creativity rather than material and monetary benefits.

| concluding case answer |

Answers should make reference to the roles of:

- CoPs: the challenges of developing CoPs among the creative class, to share knowledge;
- Theory: researching the issue of creativity, and how best to develop it – what it means, what works best;
- Policy: the role of government in developing initiatives from elementary schooling to workforce development that are relevant to creativity, and more broadly in diversity;
- Strategic HRD: the extent to which creativity issues are significant for different kinds of sectors and organisations.

A

Start by considering perspectives on HRD. In narrow terms HRD may be defined as being concerned with practice in and perceptions of the education, training and development of people in the employment context. Or it can be defined in broader terms as practice in and perceptions of a discipline which is the product of the union of organisational analysis and theory on the one side and HRM on the other, with connections to strategic themes and concerns. In the narrow sense, the concerns of HRD may be seen as training for creativity. In the broader sense, the concerns of HRD may be seen as an integral part of organising and the management of a workforce where creativity is a core capability. In any case, HRD involves more than running training courses, and vocational education for skills.

CoPs

Different kinds of creativity represent different kinds of challenge for promoting CoPs. The basic issue of organising a CoP is the potential to share knowledge systematically and fairly for the benefit of all. In different areas this will require different things. For example, Crafts, Architecture, and Video Game Development are sectors based on self-employment or small firms. Other areas of creativity involve large multinational firms, such as media groups, or art and antiques trading, where issues about intellectual property are more significant and may impede CoP development.

The underlying challenge of CoPs is to change from an old style of organisation and management, founded on the typical full-time, dedicated employee in a large, permanent organisation to a new style organisation and management, founded on specific teams coming together for projects then disbanding to form again in different combinations on other projects elsewhere. Learning anything – including learning how to be creative – takes place in that ever-reforming series of project groups rather than in self-perpetuating and stable groups.

Theoretical concerns

Theories provide ways of framing or reframing problems in order to guide action, helping to give general answers to important questions. In this case the context is one about framing or reframing the problem of creativity. How do we define creativity, and what have studies shown about how to nurture it? Is the way the organisation is thinking about creativity a useful and valid one, or does it need to be reframed in some way?

For example, consider the concept and theory of 'play'. Is it possible to encourage greater creativity through integrating more 'play' with work? Play is a category which can include many practices, including games, outdoor experiential learning and the use of theatre. One perceived leading edge of play, which can be explored more closely, is the use of computer games.

Government policy in HRD

As many governments now seek to promote the creative industries, the significance of the creative/cultural industries increases. Some countries have an enormously strong position in some of the world's fastest growing cultural industries. Music and computer games industries can be as large as steel and textiles. Publicly-funded cultural institutions play a role in supporting these industries, turning out film makers, animators, designers, architects, musicians, performers and visual artists. These cultural and educational institutions are a part of modern industrial and economic policy because they produce the specific and often highly technical skills that are transferable and used in the high-growth private-sector industries.

If all aspects of creativity, in the arts, science and business, work together then perhaps Government could be persuaded to fund more creative industries activities in the expectation of economic benefit. It could seek to integrate these more with schools and education at all stages, encouraging more children and young adults to be creative as well as literate, numerate and technologically capable with information technologies.

Beyond that Government may seek to foster an environment favourable to creative industries and people: fostering and promoting cultural freedom, respect for diversity, and non-conformism. The hope would be to get economic benefits from attracting and keeping the 'sunrise' industries in the creative sector. These levers

continued overleaf

| concluding case answer continued |

offered by social and cultural contexts can be a first step to attracting, or further greenhousing and expanding, creative organisations and economic sectors. For government to forego the pursuit of homogeneity, conformity and 'fitting in' is an important contextual condition for organisations to be able to attract and retain the talent.

Strategic HRD

Finally, creativity may be considered as a strategic issue in two senses. First, creativity may be seen as a trans-workforce concern, relevant to all employees in any job and at any level of the organisation, not just in jobs that are traditionally viewed as requiring some personal creativity, like marketing. If the successful workplace of the 21st century is going to be founded upon knowledge and how knowledge is used for new solutions, services and products, then creativity is strategically significant. Creativity to drive change in technologies and the increasing integration of viable knowledge in work processes and outcomes are all connected. This would also need a culture which changed in order to support more participation in creativity, questioning, feedback and experimentation. In a second sense, creativity is strategic as the dynamism underpinning economic growth, new ideas, new technology and new content are founded on dynamism in science and engineering, architecture and design, education, arts, music and entertainment. More creative professionals in these areas will be needed. And organisations will find that seeking to manage the interaction of creatives with non-creatives will present a larger and more significant task in the future.

Conclusion

If wealth is increasingly derived from generating and applying novel and distinctive ideas then it is sensible to produce more creative people. So with reference to the aspects of perspective covered in this book it can be concluded that connecting HRD with creativity means more than the provision of training courses for training in creativity. It is clear that promoting creativity has strong links with managing learning and evolving strong cultures favouring it. The HRD practitioners' role is in promoting individual, group and organisational learning. But concluding that children should be encouraged to enjoy cultural experiences, through drama, art, music-making because this contributes to economic success may be to confuse value systems. Cultural institutions and creative practices can and should widen and deepen people's growth through learning and education to help provide the context and background for creative education for its own sake.

Diversity themes and HRD

By the end of this chapter you will be able to:

- Define and analyse the nature of prejudice and discrimination;
- Identify policies and procedures for tackling discrimination;
- Relate the management of 'diversity' to achieving HRD goals;
- Define and analyse the role of 'ethics' in determining HRD actions;
- Describe four different theories of ethics;
- Reflect on the problems of acting 'ethically' in an HRD context.

| introductory case | *AROCo and developing women leaders* |

Company Background

AROCo repairs and overhauls aero engines for the commercial and military markets. At one of their plants they have 1100 employees. Most of these employees, predominantly male, are working on the engine repairs, with around 270 professional and technical support staff. Of these professional and technical staff 63 are female, some 23%.

All of these women work full-time at the factory. The majority of them are aged between 26 and 35. Many were recruited into AROCo directly from school, with a minority recruited from university or from another AROCo plant or outside companies. Most of them were recruited as trainees in professional areas, with around a third being initially recruited in secretarial or administration roles. A few had been employed as professional entrants or as managers but since been redeployed.

The lack of women in senior management roles in the company was perceived to be a weakness. The company decided to research the attitudes of their existing female workforce to explore potential points of action to change this. They had been proud that many of these women had been recruited as trainees and progressed into a professional role during their time at AROCo. Within the next ten years, the great majority of the women would like to move up in the organisation. They also found that, while these women did not perceive any barriers to career progress, only two of them saw themselves as having the potential to reach senior management positions.

None of the women believed that age or length of service would prevent someone moving on at AROCo, with only a few believing gender was a problem. Many women did feel that AROCo did not do enough to develop its employees. The main reasons they cited for lack of progression were line-managers' negative opinions, a lack of opportunities at AROCo and a person's home life. Despite these factors nearly half the women said that they personally felt no barriers to progression. However a majority did feel that restrictions

continued overleaf

on their geographical mobility and pressures in their home life did affect them, and stop them from aspiring to further their career development.

The majority of these women did not believe that women as a group required special attention regarding their development as potential senior managers. They saw themselves as being equal with men and feared that special attention would in fact mark them out as inferior in men's eyes. Those few who felt that women should receive more help thought that women needed to be brought on a par with men to get around the 'Old Boys Club' networks at AROCo. Some people made comments which suggested that there was a culture of 'favouritism' at AROCo; that is, that those who get on with current management best are the ones who progress, not those with the greatest talent. This it was felt often meant men in senior management favouring other men.

There were substantial existing HRD provisions in the company. Formal further education was available at AROCo, with many of women participating in this at one time or another to obtain qualifications. General internal training courses existed and most of the women participated in these courses. Appraisal also existed, with the majority of women taking part in this process. Many of them regarded mentoring as an important and available source of development, but only a few had actually had a mentor at any point in their career. Prime responsibility for managing development was felt by some to lie with themselves, for others with the line-manager; with some seeing it to a joint responsibilities with management.

Introduction

The perspective considered here is that workplace HRD, like all adult education, is centrally involved in the contest for knowledge and power in society (Cervero and Wilson 2001). Power relations in society influence and are influenced by the policies, programs and practices of workplace HRD. Workplace HRD can be viewed through the lenses of political and ethical agendas. Cervero and Wilson saw three possible levels to this political context:

- The political is personal: expressed as the learner-centred view of the adult learner in workplace HRD;
- The political is practical: concerned with the ability to get things done within political relationships in workplace HRD;
- The political is structural: the context of the redistribution of power through workplace HRD.

In this book the political level in the first sense was included in discussions of design and development partnerships. In the second sense it has been considered in the context of HRD strategies and the KM and CoP discussions. That leaves the final sense to be explored here, and the central focus for this is the management of diversity.

Managing diversity has emerged as a major concern in many areas of management, including HRD (Briley 1996, Kirkton and Greene 2000, Mavin and Girling 2000). It can be a critical factor in promoting good practice and achieving goals. The changing nature of the workforce is the underlying reason for this. These changes include:

- Higher levels of employment participation by women;
- A significant percentage of the workforce with dependent children or 'carer' responsibilities;
- Increased number of dual income families;

- Changes in the family structures of employees, e.g. sole parents, fewer men and women in traditional family roles;
- An ageing workforce;
- High levels of cultural diversity with substantial labour migration.

There are also some organisational factors which create greater concerns with diversity. Some of these are:

- Aspirations to alter the traditional perceptions of male and female work roles and careers;
- Changes to workforce profiles as a result of downsizing and outsourcing;
- Fewer levels of management and a reduction in 'command and control' styles of management;
- Impact of globalisation and technology on HRD practices;
- Trends toward knowledge work.

So diversity concerns arise, and have a general impact on management. In managing HRD this has included, alongside responding to equal opportunity legislation, concerns with issues of gender, race, culture, age, family/carer status, religion and disability. Organisations need to improve awareness, review their management practices and develop new and creative approaches to HRD in this diversity context. This is not just about complying with the law, it is also about clarifying and reviewing in general the 'ethical' grounds of contemporary HRD.

The aim of this chapter is to stress the need for HRD process and practices to be developed and used to be diversity-supportive. To achieve this means reviewing the core ideas and concepts relating to the management of diversity, and the role of ethics in HRD.

Why manage diversity in HRD?

Equality has been a strong theme and focus of policy in HRM as a whole. At some points in many organisations, it can become critical. Overcoming inequalities and dealing with unjust discrimination can provide a major perspective with which to make sense of many issues and problems in the workplace. The ethical case for social justice and the business case for talent management combine and can come to the fore, if sometimes uneasily, as dual drivers of change in the workplace. The outcome has been to question and change decision-making processes in selection practices and in reward systems; as well as in career management and development.

It is often only once this has happened that deeper issues appear. Following such change in decision-making processes and practices a further agenda for action emerges around promoting diversity. Two deeper concerns are often highlighted. First is a difference in strategy between liberal and radical proponents on how to pursue consolidation and momentum in advancing diversity. Liberal proponents advocate individual freedom to compete as the strategy that will secure diversity in the workplace. Critics of this strategy tend to highlight two concerns. First is that, in the short term, not much seems to change if we rely on the freedom to compete. A few people from groups experiencing discrimination compete and succeed, but not enough to deliver true diversity. The second concern is that this approach to diversity fails to challenge the biggest problem, the pre-existing templates of success. If the previous ideal, for example the 'ideal leader', is still assumed, that invariably favours those who in the past have fulfilled those ideals – previous 'ideal leaders' who were primarily male. Those who fit the ideal are still at an advantage, rather than the newer and more diverse competitors. They are then still most likely to succeed, as they are more 'suited' for the role. Until visions of, for example, leadership are reconstituted to be more diverse themselves then this will be a source of blockage to the progress of diversity. That is why some advocate more systemic change, such as forms of positive discrimination in favour of key groups among those discriminated against. This would overcome the weaknesses of the liberal strategy. The acceptability of these more radical approaches is constrained by a mix of legal and political issues, reflecting concerns among organisations and their stakeholders.

The second, deeper issue is the inertia of organisational culture. The impact of changing policy in major decision-making areas, such as selection, reward and career management, opens up a period of possible transition as new kinds of entrant or successors in senior roles – the pioneers – emerge. Given the gradual pace of this, the transition from small changes in the beginning to more fully realised change establishing a different equilibrium reflecting diversity can be a long one. If the transition is to be successful, rather than reverting to old patterns, there will need to be a culture change over the long term as much as personnel policy changes in the short term. In this context HRD has been seen as a tool of culture change, a means of supporting the evolution of equality in the organisation as a whole, supporting these pioneers.

Alongside the use of HRD as a means of achieving longer-term equality goals there have also been voices directly considering and exploring what equality means inside HRD. The diversity concern has been a touchstone of those who advocate non-traditional and distinctive approaches to adult learning. Non-traditional approaches are those which are grounded in learning relations outside the classroom, in development partnerships such as coaching, mentoring, and action learning. In this context, distinctive approaches are those emerging from exploring adult and workplace learning specifically rather than approaches derived from applying principles of psychology to adult and workplace learning needs. It has been evident to many working in this field that the standard 'expert–novice' relationship template is deeply misplaced, and is not a helpful perspective to adopt, or appropriate for supporting and sustaining diversity.

Alongside this long-standing concern there has emerged another concern, understanding organisational learning. Attention has been given to concepts of learning organisations, and on cultivating a culture of learning, putting greater responsibility for learning and shared approaches to learning with individuals, with facilitators and learners carrying out HRD activities together. Within this tradition the question of the relationship between these two groups has been mainly concerned with re-conceptualising the role of the 'trainer', and the learner has been neglected. But if in cultivating learning organisations the role of trainer changes, so too must the role of learner. One source for the concern with equality in HRD may be the humanist articulation of new structures for adult education. These were first proposed in the 1960s and progressive movements promoted adult and experiential learning in 1970s. They have become incorporated in HRD as themes around the political aspects of advocating access to learning. Providing 'freedom to learn' meant not just leaving it to the individual but an openness to hearing learners' own ideas and engaging employees as active partners in learning. But the relationship between learners and those helping them, including coaches, mentors and HRD professionals, will always be unequal in the sense that the former have a development demand and the latter have a development offer. Under-examined prescriptions about how facilitators and learner can be 'partners' in learning, and how organisational learning is to be fostered through treating each other with respect, mutuality, and trust, provide an interesting domain of research.

Prior to the greater impact of demographic forces increasing awareness about the potential 'business case' for valuing diversity, there had been a long history of political and ethical concerns about tackling prejudice and discrimination in HRM. The focus was initially one of pursuing 'equal opportunity', then more recently 'diversity'. Three kinds of reason are relevant for HRD:

- Economic reasons: get and use the best talent, globalisation and international business;
- Social reasons: changing composition of societies (e.g. migration and movements of ethnic groups) and workforces (e.g. greater participation of women) means that the 'traditional' profile of the workforce changes;
- Political reasons: legislation on equal opportunities.

Governments and companies have created initiatives to improve standards so that all kinds of decisions in employment, from selection to promotion and reward, are based on merit alone. Discrimination is both explicitly, in law, and tacitly, in cultural terms, proscribed; yet significant problems seem to persist. We still then need to consider the basics: why does unfair discrimination occur, and how might that impact on HRD? Unfair discrimination occurs when decisions or behaviour are based on prejudice. Prejudice is a negative attitude towards a particular group of people who, for cultural or social psychological reasons, are considered to be 'different'. Prejudice may be focused on a range of groups:

- Women
- Ethnic minorities
- Disabled people
- Age – young or old
- Part-time workers
- Personal (e.g. people with red hair)

Discrimination and diversity issues arise where people are treated unfairly because of their membership of a particular group. Discrimination in the world of employment was a major part of the agenda that inspired the growth of a concern with civil liberties/human rights throughout the 20th century. As the promotion of civil liberties gained ground in general, in political and social contexts, it was natural to expect change and progress in the employer–employee relationship. The highest profile area for this in the past has concerned discrimination in employment against women as a group on the grounds of their sex, and discrimination against ethnic minority groups on the grounds of their race. Race is defined here with reference to a person's colour, race, nationality, ethnic or national origin.

The concern here is not with the specifics of employment law in the field of discrimination, which are bound to national legislative systems. Rather the concern is with general principles of discrimination and diversity and their connections to HRD

	Areas of application in HRD			
	Needs	Design	Delivery	Review
Specifying what conduct leads to discrimination; considering direct and indirect discrimination				
Identifying the grounds of prohibition; which bases of discrimination will be prohibited. Four main groupings are sex, race, ideological, other				
Identifying aspects of diversity to be pursued and promoted				
How will this be implemented; who has responsibility for doing what?				

Figure 14.1 Auditing diversity management in HRD

at work (see Figure 14.1). The general principles are as follows, and each of these areas will be considered in turn:

1. Specifying what misconduct leads to discrimination; considering direct and indirect discrimination.
2. Identifying the grounds of prohibition: which bases of discrimination will be prohibited. Four major groupings are sex, race, ideological, other.
2. Specifying what exceptions are permitted to these general rules: discrimination relevant to the inherent requirements of a job, state security, special measure of protection.
4. Considering the field of application: which elements of employment will be covered e.g. pre-employment, general terms and conditions, specific issues such as pay, harassment.
5. Considering how these laws will be implemented, what agencies will be created and what competence they will have.

Defining direct and indirect discrimination

It is important to distinguish between direct and indirect discrimination. In employment we can describe direct discrimination as occurring when people are judged in terms that do not relate to their competence to do a particular job. Direct discrimination occurs when, on the grounds of someone's sex or on racial grounds, an employer treats a person less favourably than he treats or would treat a person of a different sex or racial background. If a job application is rejected or a promotion denied because the applicant is a women or a member of a specific racial group that is direct discrimination. Direct discrimination is the exercise of prejudice, either openly or masked by reasons which cannot be justified in terms of the person's ability. Rooting out such direct discrimination is the first concern of any equal opportunity policy.

One of the major problems with identifying and challenging such direct discrimination is that it can be difficult to detect. Few employers are likely to be explicit about their prejudices. It is often only when an employer's HRM procedures are analysed, following a complaint from an individual, that such direct discrimination comes to light. For example, if an employer is systematically evaluating all applicants for a job but rejecting women even where they are objectively the best applicants it would be evidence that direct discrimination is occurring. One of the positive side-effects of equal opportunity initiatives is that they often force organisations to adopt or improve basic HRM procedures so that people are only judged on their merits relative to the job.

However, even if all direct discrimination could be eliminated, it is still likely that discrimination would persist. This is because the legacy of the past is an institutional set of 'common sense' ways of thinking and practices which can lead to indirect discrimination. Indirect discrimination means that a requirement is applied equally to all, but it is not relevant to the job and disadvantages a particular group. In employment indirect discrimination may create or perpetuate inequality. Dealing with indirect discrimination is an abiding issue in many national, occupational and organisational contexts. The use of affirmative action policies to try to deal with the problems of this legacy from the past has led to much debate in the USA and other cultures which have been influenced by the 'civil rights' approach.

The grounds of prohibition

In any legal system there will be scope to specify the bases on which discrimination will be prohibited. Anyone can suffer discrimination in the context of employment. It is possible to identify four main groupings of bases for discrimination which can be prohibited: sex, race, ideology, and other reasons. The category of 'other reasons' has been taking greater form recently, with legislation around disability, sexuality and ageism being prominent. Sex and race issues remain major concerns.

There are some exceptional circumstances where discrimination is permitted on grounds that are normally prohibited. The main categories are jobs in which sex, race or some other criterion is inherent. Jobs may be specifically listed, or indications of the type of job concerned may be given. Other grounds for exception to normal anti-discrimination rules include jobs related to the security of the state.

The HRM fields of application

Wherever a human resource decision is made there is a risk of unfair discrimination. It is useful to look at HRM in terms of three areas where employment law has an impact; pre-employment, terms and conditions and other specific issues.

In pre-employment, access to training can be crucial. Without access to training there will not be an option to apply for jobs and develop careers in the area concerned. Providing positive images of role models for women or racial groups in occupations can be an essential catalyst for individuals to pursue path-breaking careers. Employment services, both public and private, can be important in ensuring that equal opportunity precepts are maintained in recruitment matters. It is also relevant to monitor advertisements and scrutinise methods such as psychometric tests for discriminatory elements. Recruitment should be based on competence only. Thus the development of job descriptions, person specifications or equivalent systematic and objective tools for helping with selection needs to be emphasised. Training in selection methods such as interviewing is also critical. Untrained interviewers are prone to making mistakes which can be discriminatory, such as seeking to confirm their initial impressions of a candidate rather than probing for relevant information.

With terms and conditions of employment any and all terms and conditions can be considered relative to equal opportunity issues. The example of promotion is illustrative; for even where direct discrimination against women has been explicitly dealt with in pre-employment terms there can still be problems inside the organisation. Even where women are recruited, for example, to management posts they may find their path to the very top of the management system is hampered. There appears to be a 'glass ceiling' which women come up against; an invisible barrier beyond which they cannot go. As the management of careers is becoming a hotter issue in general, due to organisations downsizing and the career 'ladder' seeming to disappear, such issues raise fundamental questions.

There are a number of specific HRM issues that the promotion of equal opportunities has brought to the fore. Concerns about diversity an HRD have to be seen in this context. These include equal pay, probably the most crucial 'bottom-line' issue in the field of discrimination. For individuals it can mean increased earnings, for organisations it can mean increased wage bills. Not surprisingly it is a hotly contested area of debate and analysis. The principle of equal pay for work of equal value has been promulgated at length. The validity of the concept of equal value and the practicalities of altering occupational payment structures has its advocates and its detractors. Another equal opportunities issue is sexual harassment, which can be defined as any unwanted conduct of a sexual nature or other conduct based on sex affecting the dignity of women and men at work. It includes all unwelcome sexual advances, requests for sexual favours, verbal or physical conduct of a sexual nature.

Implementation

Machinery for preventing discrimination and applying, supervising and enforcing the principle of equal opportunity is needed. This may be a direct government role, or agencies, either general or specialist, can be set up. Whatever machinery is implemented special features for dealing with complaints need to be considered. For example, complainants may be afraid of initiating proceedings as, unlike unfair dismissal proceedings, they will still be in the organisation and may feel exposed. It can also be difficult to substantiate allegations. The approach often adopted is that, if a complainant can establish a prima facie case, the burden of proof shifts to the employer.

In organisations clear commitments to equal opportunity policies, and procedures to ensure fairness and monitoring of policies in practice are all required at the organisational level (see Strategic View Box 14.1).

In practice the management of equal opportunity in this context comes down to employers striving to ensure that there is meticulous attention to systematic HRM procedures. If there is any evidence of 'bad housekeeping' in HRM procedures inferences of discrimination may be brought from that alone. It is thus vital to introduce and monitor a good equal opportunity policy.

strategic view

| 14.1 | *Dealing with discrimination* |

Companies need to:

- Have formal statements
- Stress equal opportunities in principle
- Intend to have no discrimination
- Stress employee responsibility

What else can be done to deal with discrimination?

Even with international conventions, constitutional backing or legislative support for equal opportunities there remain big challenges. Some think it is possible to go beyond such measures, and legislate for 'positive' or affirmative action The experience of the USA, and its affirmative action principles which grew out of the civil rights era, can be reflected on. The USA is a distinctive context to analyse. On the one hand it is one of the least 'regulated' labour markets in the world, with a culture that enshrines entrepreneurial zeal and organisational autonomy. On the other hand it is a society with ethnic divisions at its heart, given its social composition and history. And, as a nation, Americans are perceived to be among the most prone to pursuing litigation, as part of the 'compensation culture', when any hurt or pain is suffered. The affirmative action argument is that the law above all else can help to reshape behaviour where there are significant costs for failing to comply. Legal solutions are important as a statement of value, even if they cannot cover all the unacceptable forms of discrimination which can occur.

The alternative to affirmative action is promoting a strategic and coordinated approach to organisational practice. The following 'Ten Point Plan' suggests an outline for this:

1. Develop an equal opportunity policy
2. Set an action plan, including targets
3. Provide training for all
4. Monitor position and progress
5. Review HR procedures regularly
6. Draw up clear and justifiable job criteria
7. Offer pre-employment training and positive action training
8. Consider your organisation's image
9. Consider flexible working
10. Develop links with local community group, organisations and schools

Ethics

Whether a legislation-driven approach, such as affirmative action, or an organisational 'best practice' approach is valued, there is a deeper level of analysis that might help throw some light on the opportunities and threats of managing diversity. These are the opportunities and threats of shaping people management practices to combine a 'contribution to the business' and dealing with the 'human-ness' of the human resource. Here ethics matter. They are about making judgments concerned with moral right and wrong, here related to employment and, more specifically, HRD at work. Ethics provide the ground rules that determine how people think about what is right and wrong, and then how they act. They offer a constraint on selfishness and self-interest, and a potential basis for justifying actions. One simple, common sense list of ethical qualities is:

- Honesty
- Fairness
- Respect for others
- Promise keeping
- Trustworthiness

The management of diversity and its impact on HRD at work does not have to be based on legislation; it can be embedded in the promotion of these ethical qualities at work. There are three responses to this ethics-embedded approach. The first is to deny it wholly, arguing that work organisations are places where 'anything goes' as long as performance is high. Ethics ought to be kept out, and firms left to pursue their interests. Businesses are not white knights to rescue society from its own problems. Only in pursuing their own interests will companies recruit the best, promote the best, and so on. Thus economic imperatives determine high standards, not ethics. This extends to HRD. It is not the function of a company's training strategy to right the wrongs of prejudice and discrimination; the role of HRD is to improve performance.

The second position is that ethics are to be left to personal conscience, and work organisations cannot be expected to do anything beyond ensuring compliance with basic standards. It is society that needs to socialise people with the right norms and beliefs about diversity, not work organisations. If people take their weaknesses with them into organisations, their human fallibility, then that has to be managed but cannot be changed or eradicated. No amount of organisational action in HRD is going to change a person's conscience.

The third position is to argue that work organisations ought to lead, beyond developing codes and good practice. They can provide leadership, relating to their core values, which are meant to be consistent with high standards in diversity. The problems arise when codes remain on paper only and when the organisation gets bogged down in 'equal opportunities' for some minorities rather than valuing diversity in the workforce as whole.

The focus on monitoring and targets rather than culture changes becomes a diversion from progress on promoting diversity in these leading organisations.

theory & research

14.1 | *More sophisticated approaches to ethics*

It can be helpful to analyse issues about organisational practice and debates around them with more sophisticated models of ethics.

- **Utilitarian**: judge what is right by the consequences of actions; the greatest good for the greatest number. Possible to use people as a means to an end as long as it provides the greatest good, i.e. if unfortunate consequences only touch a minority.
- **Rawlsian**: what is good is what is agreed by consensus; consultation with stakeholders. This can be connected with those justifying practices in terms of long-term survival for the sake of the stakeholders, as long as the stakeholders participate in decisions.
- **Aristotelian**: individuals need to achieve self-actualisation within healthy communities. Can be connected to ideas of the learning organisation and similar ideals which challenge pragmatic standards.
- **Kantian**: treat all people with respect, as rational beings with individual dignity. This is easy to connect with promoting 'soft' HRM-individualism, responsible autonomy; and eschewing justification in terms of economic aims or ends.

In terms of HRD and diversity, the utilitarian would want to calculate the overall costs and benefits and take up those options for the greatest good of most; the Rawlsian would also be calculating, but seeking groups' views and a consensus; the Aristotelian would be most prescriptive and positive about individuals taking actions; the Kantian would be more concerned with collective action on standards around doing the right thing.

Multiple-choice questions

14.1 Which of the following has been identified as the root of a concern with diversity in HRD ?

A Specifying what leads to discrimination in terms of direct and indirect discrimination

B Identifying the grounds of prohibition, including sex , race, ideological, other.

C. Identifying aspects of diversity to be pursued and promoted

D The political is structural; the redistribution of power through workplace HRD

14.2 Which of the following describes a Rawlsian view of ethics ?

A Judge what is right by the consequences of actions; the greatest good for the greatest number. Possible to use people as a means to an end as long as it provides the greatest good i.e. if unfortunate consequences only touch a minority

B Individuals need to achieve self-actualisation within healthy communities. Can be connected to ideas of the learning organisation and similar ideals which challenge pragmatic standards

C Treat all people with respect, as rational beings with individual dignity. This is easy to connect with promoting 'soft' HRM-individualism, responsible autonomy; and eschewing justification in terms of economic aims or ends

D What is good is what is agreed by consensus; consultation with stakeholders. This can be connected with those justifying practices in terms of long-term survival for the sake of the stakeholders, as long as the stakeholders participate in decisions.

References

Briley, S. (ed.) (1996) *Women in the Workforce: Human resource development strategies into the next century*, Edinburgh, HMSO.

Cervero, R. and Wilson, M. (2001) *Power in Practice: Adult education and the struggle for knowledge and power in society*, San Francisco, Jossey Bass.

DfEE (1996) *Equal Opportunities Ten Point Plan*, London, DfEE

Ford, V. (1996) 'Partnership is the secret of progress', *People Management*, vol. 2 , no. 3.

Iles, P. (1995) 'Learning to work with difference', *Personnel Review*, vol. 24, no. 6, pp. 44–60.

IPD (1996) *Managing Diversity; An IPD Position Paper*, London, IPD.

Legge, K. (1997) 'Morality Bound', *People Management*, vol. 2 , no. 25.

Kirkton, G. and Greene, A.M. (2000) *The Dynamics of Managing Diversity: A critical approach*, Oxford, Buttterworth-Heinemann.

Mavin, S. and Girling, G. (2000) 'What is managing diversity and why does it matter?', *Human Resource Development International*, vol. 3, no. 4, pp. 419–33.

Wilson, E. (1996)'Managing diversity and HRD', in J. Stewart and J. McGoldrick (eds) *HRD Perspectives, Strategies and Practice*, London, Pitman.

Re-read the introductory case. Would you suggest that organising and providing a single-sex leadership training course for women would be the best way of helping more women to achieve advancement into senior management positions?

A

concluding short case model answer

This is a case requiring the demonstration of knowledge and understanding of HRD perspectives. It describes the situation of a manufacturing organisation, in which the development of women as potential senior managers has become an issue. To be more explicit that means addressing the following:

- How may effective HRD be informed by human science theories?
- How may effective HRD be connected with Government policy-making?
- How may learning can be managed in communities of practice?
- In what ways are HRD issues of substantial significance to the strategic management of an organisation?

It is becoming increasingly important to take factors such as gender into consideration in the workplace, whether formulating a training policy or any other policy with the potential to discriminate against individuals. The extent to which professional women are adequately equipped to progress through or up the organisation is the HRD issue here. There is evidence from the survey that development tools are available and are actively used by women in the organisation, but few of them recognise the more informal methods of development, such as engaging with self-directed learning and mentoring.

Leadership training schemes have been seen as one solution to the problem. Many companies feel that by encouraging women to build on their leadership abilities they will be able to move further into management and thus balance the inequality of sex that is present. Women-only training schemes are one option. These training programmes often include basic material about leadership, general management development, such as decision-making, organisational communication, coaching and providing feedback to employees, and managing conflict. However these programmes often involve examining issues that are more likely to affect women only, such as gender discrimination, sexual harassment, childcare issues and balancing work and family.

Yet these women-only training schemes imply that the main problem is that these women have a skill deficiency in the first place. Perhaps the real problem is prejudice and discrimination rather than a skill gap in comparison with their male counterparts. Rather than reducing prejudice woman-only training programmes can actually increase the prejudice. Such training could reinforce the belief that the females are not as good at their job as the men and need extra training. Such courses also place women in an artificial environment because there are no males to interact with during such activities as role-play; but it is in these situations that they need more experience in order to have greater capability.

A conclusion might be that mixed-sex leadership training would be more beneficial, as it does not label women as under-skilled. It develops women's ability to work cohesively with men and may help to dissolve prejudice. Women would still be able to work on issues that more usually affect women, such as dealing with discrimination, in other ways. This is where aspects of developing COPs might help. Establishing a women's a senior management COP, with voluntary membership, to set its own agenda and develop its own support techniques may seem a natural and logical step. Indeed some would argue that women tend to be more collaborative and inclusive than men, who tend to be more 'competitive' developers. Alternatively others might perceive establishing such a voluntary, group-directed resource as being a way of marginalising the issue, and isolating it from other mainstream development concerns and activities (like formal education or mentoring).

In any event, there should be no hope that such training programmes will act as 'testosterone injections'; that is, training women to be 'more like men' – assuming that archetypal masculine qualities are what define a good leader. Instead every person should be encouraged to develop leadership skills appropriate to their

concluding short case model answer continued

personality, and the organisation should accommodate diversity. Equally, the argument that now it is archetypal 'feminine' qualities which are proving more important in the current organisational climate should be avoided. Social, communicative and interpersonal skills are important in leadership, but are not the be-all-and-end-all.

Most leadership training schemes, although they may now include women, have been constructed by men, for men and may therefore embed and convey a male perspective on leadership values. Females on such courses are nearly always in the minority and therefore may feel alienated or excluded. As classroom environments frequently rely on the use of lectures and argumentative debates, women often express feelings of self-doubt when discussing their educational experiences. They may attribute this to their own skill deficiency and possibly conclude that they are not management material.

Mentoring is another option for developing females in order to aid their rise into senior management roles. Informal mentoring relationships have been shown to be the best at achieving this. Formal mentoring practices are more practical, whether they should be same-sex or cross-sex is open to debate.

There are general issues here, not just challenges specific to female participation in senior management. These would include:

□ Theory issues to help frame and reframe questions about discrimination and diversity;
□ The role that government can play to promote, assist and support such initiatives;
□ How such HRD activities and initiatives are of strategic significance;
□ How concerns arise around adopting single-sex leadership training.

Theories provide ways of framing or reframing problems in order to guide action, helping to give general answers to important questions. In this case the context is one about framing or reframing the problem of women in senior management where, over the past two decades, the nature of work has changed considerably. As society changes, so has the make-up of the workforce, the hours they work and the jobs they do. Women have always made up a part of the workforce, but still tend to work in different occupations from men and to be concentrated in a narrower range of occupations. Some of the questions which theories might help answer are: would women benefit from separate or combined development? would women benefit from the introduction of techniques like mentoring? how can the organisational change that seeking to promote more women into senior management represents be best understood? Drawing on theories from the 'wisdom literature' psychology and the other human sciences cannot provide definitive answers to problems such as advancing more women into senior positions, but it can help to structure thinking and subsequent actions.

Part of the context here is clearly that theory about HRD alone – about how to best provide learning and development – is not enough on its own; other policy issues around promoting equal opportunities, including practical concerns around childcare, are important. It is in areas like this that government can play a role, as well as including equal opportunities within specific HRD initiatives like IiP.

Does this issue suggest that HRD is of strategic importance or not? Does the absence of women in senior management represent an issue that can affect the long-term future of the whole organisation? If this is seen to represent a threat to creating the best possible leadership for the organisation then it would represent a strategic issue. That may be in the guise of a need to ensure that biased favouritism is not allowed to prevail, and that the most talented people are identified and promoted. If it is believed that all the career patterns of talented people and leaders, both men and women, are beginning to resemble the fragmented career patterns that women have traditionally had, then this might be a strategic issue. With more and more talented men becoming interested in career paths that include consideration of personal and family needs, there is a significant need to be considerate and adaptable in order to develop and retain such people as leaders.

If gender imbalance is seen to represent a response to social and political pressures to conform to highly valuing equal opportunity then it is unlikely to be seen as strategically important. A company which wishes to alter a status quo of apparent gender imbalance can simply examine how its HRD practices can be changed to be more positive for women. In a male dominated, technical environment like AROCo such a change will be

continued overlea

concluding short case model answer continued

slow and complex. Women limit their career choices for reasons other than their abilities and career motives. Parenting is one of the main reasons for the lower status and lower salary of women in management positions. That is followed by the influence of constraints arising from a partner's career and lifestyle.

In conclusion, in order to see HRD play a role in addressing the question of improving the succession of women into senior management roles leadership training and associated tools are relevant, but also the following can be dealt with:

□ Using theory and research to frame and reframe the problem so as to make targeted actions possible;
□ Supporting government policy to help women, and men, in caregiver roles;
□ Training to deal with the generic problems and issues facing women aspiring to senior management roles; supporting mixed-sex leadership training programmes, coupled with cross-sex mentoring schemes for new female employees, would be the most successful at promoting females to higher management levels;
□ A greater interest in monitoring gender issues would enable the organisation to evaluate its training policies.

However, any individual HRD initiatives are only effective as part of a larger organisational change. Only if and when the culture of the organisation shifts towards accepting diversity will there be sustainable equal opportunities for all within the workplace.

Strategic HRD

learning
objectives

By the end of this chapter you will be able to:

- define the concept of strategic HRD (SHRD);
- identify the key themes and issues raised by SHRD;
- analyse the functional and status factors underpinning the rise of SHRD;
- critically evaluate the theory and practice of SHRD.

---

introductory case | **PowerCo**

Organisation: business and background

PowerCo is an international energy company with annual sales of £5.2 billion, 13,800 employees and in excess of 5 million customers in the UK and western USA. It has a wide range of retail customers, including large industrial and commercial businesses and individual householders in the western USA and across the UK. Its business is electricity generation, transmission, distribution and supply services in both countries. PowerCo has a strategic aim of becoming a leading international energy company. In both the USA and the UK, their customers tell them that they are most interested in the same key issues: reliability, price and value, customer service and company reputation. In addition they are in a business that involves high profile and very sensitive technological and environmental issues as a result of their operations, including:

- Energy: how they reduce the carbon intensity of their generation emissions by investing in renewables; their customer energy efficiency programmes and how they link these to fuel poverty.
- Air quality and global climate change: how they minimise the effects of the use of fossil fuels, as well as emissions from the various forms of transport they use.
- Land and biodiversity: how they manage their impacts on land biodiversity as a result of their coal mining, hydro-electric and network activities;
- Resource management and waste: how they manage the resulting waste streams, including waste reduction programmes and recycling.

Altogether these pressures combined carry significant challenge and responsibility. PowerCo needs to strike a balance between competing imperatives, such as securing energy supply now and into the future, keeping that supply affordable and minimising its impact on the environment. It also needs to maintain the trust of key stakeholders in an age when levels of investor and public trust in corporations have declined and demand for more transparency and accountability is growing.

continued overleaf

Company basics

PowerCo is a large electricity and gas provider. It has all the usual HRD provisions you would expect of a big, multinational organisation. These include substantial management and professional development programmes and in-house training centres for manual and clerical staff. These are all managed by a large HRD department with many training staff, together with links with colleges and universities.

A special unit, PowerCo Learning, was founded in the late 1990s in partnership with trade unions in the company. It represents the company's commitment to lifelong learning for all its staff, and its belief in sharing its success and resources with the communities that support its operations. This entails a strategic framework with four areas of learning (see below).

The PowerCo Learning unit has the mission statement: 'Whoever you are, you have the power to become what you want to be.' The staff believe that everyone can transform their lives, and that learning is the ultimate transformer. Whether the person is an employee or a relative, leaving school or unemployed, looking for a new challenge or a career, they seek to put learners on track. PowerCo Learning has learning centres and partner organisations, including schools and businesses. It exists to provide access and choice; whatever the learners want can be provided. Access may be in learning centres or via the internet. The only question the staff in PowerCo learning department ask is: 'are you prepared to work for it?'.

PowerCo offers learning opportunities in four areas:

> **Learning for Life**: a broad range of personal development opportunities for employees and their families, e.g. a learning helpline and an e-mail account for internal and external learners to obtain advice and brokerage about learning opportunities.
>
> **Learning for Real**: interesting and innovative approaches to encourage young people within communities to return to learning, e.g. to support the transition of young people from socially deprived areas from school, FE or unemployment to work.
>
> **Learning for Work**: highly focused learning aligned to the specific job roles and career needs of employees, e.g. involving staff in work with young people participating in charitable trust-based learning initiatives.
>
> **Learning for You**: learning initiatives designed to help young people in the communities the company serves to take the first steps into employment, e.g. technology-driven learning link to schools with four school-based learning centres set up by PowerCo to deliver enterprise-oriented learning.

Corporate values

One reference point for managing this is to identify a set of aims that will help guide PowerCo into the future:

- Working at the highest levels of industrial safety and continuously improving health and safety performance;
- Well-earned customer loyalty – to deliver quality and value-for-money services which meet and influence its customers' needs;
- Enhanced shareholder value – to create shareholder value by building businesses and continuously seeking opportunities to gain advantage over competitors;
- Positive working environment – to seek to provide a positive working environment which inspires employees to fulfil their potential and maximise their contribution;
- Trust of communities – to maintain the respect and trust of communities through recognising and responding to the needs of both the local and the wider environment;
- Teamwork and leadership – to place continuing importance on the way PowerCo staff work together and increasing focus on developing teamworking skills.

Four key workplace issues to be expanded upon

1. Building a high-performance culture

PowerCo aims to develop the leadership skills of senior managers, to create a working environment that encourages this approach to optimising personal achievement and satisfaction.

Performance comes down to the security of energy supply; how to ensure a reliable supply of energy when and where it's needed to meet current and future demand.

1. System availability: seeking to reduce the average length of time customers are without power due to supply interruptions;
2. System reliability: seeking to reduce the average number of times customers experience supply interruptions;
3. Momentary interruptions: seeking to reduce the average number of momentary power interruptions customers experience;
4. Worst-performing assessment: seeking to improve the five worst circuits' performance;
5. Restoring supply: seeking to ensure that at least 80% of customers who experience a power interruption have their power supply restored in less than three hours.

Performance also includes price and value of energy – how to deliver affordable energy – and, of course, customer service – how to ensure all contact with the company meets or beats customer expectations of service; for example the aim is to answer 80% of telephone calls to Customer Service Centres within 20 seconds. PowerCo has not reached industry-leading status on these measures yet.

Once PowerCo meets these basic customer needs, the stakeholders tell them they have other expectations. These include providing green energy options, educating the public about safety, improving energy efficiency, serving priority-needs customers and ensuring accessibility to services for all customers.

2. Ensuring a consistent, positive working experience

PowerCo seeks to provide the kind of working experience that encourages and supports its employees in achieving their best personal performance. The company has an annual staff survey which examines the following attitudes:

I am proud of what the company is trying to achieve
I feel valued as a member of a team
My colleagues and I are able to produce high-quality work
I feel a sense of personal accomplishment in my work
I have developed my skills over the last six months
I have recently spoken to my manager about my training/development
I am able to act decisively on behalf of the company
I am clear about where I add value

3. Training and developing people

PowerCo seeks to offer training and development programmes throughout its businesses to implement their policies, procedures and business plan and to ensure that they comply with legislation and best practice standards.

Their investment in work-based training over the year amounted to a cost of over £4.8 million and involved in excess of 460,000 employee hours. PowerCo Learning has helped to train more than 6500 young people and reached 1200 in 2002/03 through joining a range of government-funded programmes. The US division announced support for a new $1 million, three-year early childhood literacy project that partners agencies in cities in their region to deliver literacy programmes.

4. Providing equal opportunities to all individuals

PowerCo aims to maintain and promote a foundation of fairness, mutual respect and understanding, recognising that all employees contribute to the success of the company and its reputation as an employer, service provider and member of the wider community.

continued overleaf

Across the PowerCo group, 72.8% of employees are male and 27.2% are female. In the UK, about 0.6% of the workforce identify themselves as minorities compared to the general minority population of 2% in Scotland and 9% in England and Wales. In the USA, 9% of the workforce identify themselves as minorities. This compares to 18% of minorities in all other companies that report to the Equal Employment Opportunities Commission in their major areas of operation.

Training and development issues

Finally, an interview with the HRD Director of PowerCo raised the following 5 training and development issues.

Issue 1

Specialist in-house HRD staff had been mainly training needs assessors, but now the organisation expected line-managers do that (with HR partners in the business). More in-house skills were needed in design and delivery and in organisation development.

Issue 2

PowerCo uses many external training suppliers; they are seeking to reduce this number, but increase the volume of training they do and reduce costs by up to 20%. PowerCo wants to make them associate trainers, coming in to deliver PowerCo's material, not just pay for 'design and development' with costs that seem excessive and variable for no good reason. And the company wants innovations that add value: the use of more e-learning material, e.g. for technical training, will save costs and fits with strategy.

Issue 3

PowerCo wants a new programme for engineers which emphasises skills in asset management at the expense of 'people skills', which are overdone and not critical to them. The engineers need to begin to have a knowledge transfer culture in which they must share what they learn. They can do new masterclasses in technical areas and support the professional accreditation of engineers. Leadership skills have been pushed until now, and professional neglected, but the company wants people to see professionals as equally valued and credible. There are gaps in engineering career management, with few apprentices and potential successors to current plant managers. This is compounded by workforce immobility in the UK; staff are happy with their lot and reluctant to move even a short distance to a new post.

Issue 4

Talent potential is currently managed at 3 levels:

> Level 1: on or potential for top tier board;
> Level 2: on or potential for MD, 2nd tier;
> Level 3: in top 250, or potential to join at 3rd tier.

The development of the 250 people in the Level 3 group is owned by the CEO, individual reviews, coaching (via the Institute of Directors) and plans. The company wants to develop partnerships with premier business schools for top-level management development, and local business schools for others. It is using executive coaching extensively for Level 1 and 2 talent.

Issue 5

PowerCo wants learning to be more learner driven. They have put in personal planning processes, but people are still dependent. They need to challenge what they see as a dependency culture.

Introduction

In this chapter, we consider the perspective of HRD as a strategic activity with its own distinct contribution to overall business success (Garavan 1991, McCracken and Wallace 2000, Garavan 2007). The brief outline of PowerCo's HRD activities represents one example of an organisation apparently seeking to link HRD with business success. In moving from practising HRD as a professional service to an activity integrated with the strategy process how do things change? Does this movement change the kind of HRD practices and services required? Does strategic focus lead to different performance improvement, core competence issues and different roles for managers? Or is it simply about creating a better climate for learning at work?

The traditional reason for dissatisfaction in HRD – that HRD was not taken seriously – appears to have subsided, new forms of discontent arise to replace the old. Much of this debate now centres on the concept of SHRD, and the issues that it raises (Grieves 2003).

Previously important HRM roles – such as smoothing employee relations, ensuring that wage rises were linked to productivity, and attempting to manage human resource flows through HR planning – would not have been thought of as strategic. Such activities reflected what could be called the equilibrium role of people management – that of maintaining a steady state. Specialist personnel managers were perceived, at best, to be responsible for implementing major decisions rather than contributing to them. At worst, personnel managers were seen to be irrelevant to the business: responsible for a bureaucratic service function that could weigh down organisations with procedures and dilute managerial prerogative.

Now that HRD concerns are more prominent, and can arise from the process of strategic analysis, and be a feature of strategic choices, HRM in general might assume greater links to strategy. Where the flexibility, quality and efficiency of human resources become major concerns of top management this leads to a greater concern both with the macro-environment that influences human resources (labour markets, education systems) and with the internal environment, where past practices need to be reviewed and changed in order to align and/or integrate HRD practices with strategic aims.

As well as this link of HRD to traditional strategic management, HRD can also be in the forefront of developments in thinking about strategic management itself where the trend is away from the use of mathematical models and planning techniques towards attempts to draw on human creativity and learning. That means a greater concern with 'vision' rather than planning, and with mobilising human resources to achieve that vision. The dominant view of strategy has shifted. It is not a preconceived and detailed set of steps for achieving a coherent package of concrete goals within a given timescale. Nor is it a rational process that is amenable to mathematical modelling. Rather it is the outcome of a process of decision-making and resource allocation that is embarked on in pursuit of a vision. Such an approach is less rational and plannable. This is the changing model of strategy into which thinking about strategic HRD needs to fit.

Thinking on strategy and HRD: three options

Here the approach is to adopt a framework which offers a way of organising and advancing thinking about how HRD can be a feature of strategy development and practice for the whole enterprise (Finkelstein et al 2006). There are three specific kinds of framework for thinking about the possible nature and evidence for a role for HRD in the strategic context. First is the modelling of special kinds of process and products associated with strategy (see Figure 15.1). These identify aspects of strategy as a series of possible processes and products constituting SHRD.

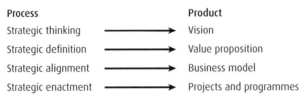

Process		Product
Strategic thinking	→	Vision
Strategic definition	→	Value proposition
Strategic alignment	→	Business model
Strategic enactment	→	Projects and programmes

Figure 15.1 Steps towards SHRD

Source Finkelstein et al 2006

For HRD to be a valid and significant part of strategy we would need to observe its contribution to vision, value propositions, business models and projects and programmes. If these are present in a case like PowerCo then the idea of SHRD has substance. One concern about the reality of SHRD is that such visions and value propositions are superficial rhetoric rather than real commitments enacted in practice.

Second we can look at a broader analysis of developments in the strategy literature. When the evolution of the strategy literature is mapped onto the management literature we can see how 5 Cs (see Figure 15.2) can be proposed, and the reasons that a concept of SHRD has emerged may be glimpsed in the links between the highest level (changing) and learning. These approaches to exploring strategy each have their major thinkers and themes over time, with HRD coming more to the heart of this as we move from the early thinkers and themes to the more recent ones. HRD is an invariable partner of change, and if change is at the heart of organisational life then so must HRD be.

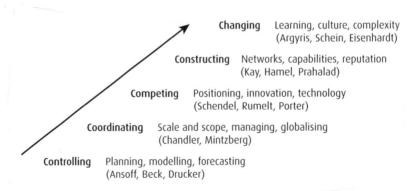

Changing   Learning, culture, complexity (Argyris, Schein, Eisenhardt)

Constructing   Networks, capabilities, reputation (Kay, Hamel, Prahalad)

Competing   Positioning, innovation, technology (Schendel, Rumelt, Porter)

Coordinating   Scale and scope, managing, globalising (Chandler, Mintzberg)

Controlling   Planning, modelling, forecasting (Ansoff, Beck, Drucker)

Figure 15.2 The 5Cs typology

Source Finkelstein et al 2006

Thirdly, we can consider how strategies result in implications for bridging between the technical and social aspects in concrete delivery (see Figure 15.3). Strategy, once defined in terms of the vision and dealing with the 5Cs, means delivering an energised and productive social system with an efficient and productive technological system.

Realising an energised and productive social system					
Improve work practices	Create protected space	Expand and deepen capabilities	Inspire trust and loyalty	Enhance knowledge and communication	Promote ideas and identity
Cost	**Innovate**	**Execution**	**Relationships**	**Channels**	**Brand**
Optimise value chain	Exploit R&D	Refine business processes	Leverage networks and alliances	Develop market access	Active customer managing
Realising an efficient and productive technical system					

Figure 15.3 Strategy delivery through a socio-technical system

Source Finkelstein et al 2006

The key dimension in this, as far as HRD is concerned, is providing the interfaces between the social and the technical systems, taking into account:

- HRD and cost
- HRD and innovation
- HRD and execution
- HRD and relationships
- HRD and communication channels
- HRD and brand

SHRD can be seen to exist where these connections are of interest and managed. The presence of SHRD is observed not simply by the existence of an explicit and special articulation of mission around and including HRD, nor just in an organisation concerned with 'changing'; it is integral to all organisations at all times. HRD is an integral part of all organisations' work around these issues and developing, managing and keeping optimal both the 'hard', technical system and the 'soft', social system.

SHRD would not then need to be thought of or represented by an explicit vision and role in top management team discussions, nor would it have to be a partner in managing change; it would exist in many forms, in organisations whose value propositions (see Strategic View Box 15.1) ranged from cost leaders (the cheapest) offering the basic functional product/service through to the premium-priced offering the most prestigious products and services. This perspective on SHRD opens up the entire range of organisational circumstances for consideration, not confining it to special and particular kinds of organisational circumstance.

Value propositions

Organisations are concerned to generate a value proposition, and they can consider six areas for doing that. In each area they can seek to locate themselves on a scale. At one end are organisations whose value proposition is that they are price leaders (cheap), basic, with acceptable quality, providing minimal support, restricted availability and with a functional reputation. At the other end of the spectrum are those organisations whose value proposition is premium pricing, original features, excellent quality, comprehensive support, universal availability and prestigious reputation. Any sector will contain organisations with value propositions at both ends and all the stages in between. For the purposes of considering SHRD the implication is that HRD would support and in some way mirror these value propositions; being a contributor to and consistent with the value proposition. So one company's strategic HRD is premium-priced, excellent and prestigious; another company's strategic HRD might be cheap, acceptable and functional. Management development in a major financial services company might fit the former, and customer-service posts in a fast-food outlet might fit the latter. Each in its own way is strategic HRD.

15.1	*Generating a value proposition as a context for SHRD*

Price	Features	Quality	Support	Availability	Reputation
Premium	Original	Excellent	Comprehensive	Universal	Prestigious
Premium/ Competitive	Original/ Customized	Excellent/ Average	Comprehensive/ Standard	Universal/ Selective	Prestigious/ respected
Competitive	Customized	Average	Standard	Selective	Respected
Competitive/ Leader	Customized/ Basic	Average/ Acceptable	Standard/ Minimal	Selective/ Restricted	Respected/ Functional
Leader	Basic	Acceptable	Minimal	Restricted	Functional

An analytical framework: contingencies and SHRD

An empirical link between HRD and organisational success – that is, the realisation of any value proposition – has yet to be demonstrated consistently and rigorously in any forensic sense. The climate appears to be one where HRD and the initiatives associated with it can still be seen as an additional cost that is vulnerable to being cut, whether that be by reducing HRD staff numbers (downsizing), by reducing the resourcing of certain critical activities (such as appraisal systems), or by trimming specific budgets (for example, training).

An underlying problem for the case for SHRD is the extent to which the visions that ostensibly frame the long term for HRD can be criticised as culturally bound, managerial 'fictions'. The knowledge bases and disciplines that underpin research and practice in employment and SHRD are just not secure enough to influence strategising substantially. They are not influential in providing a framework for thinking about the future, and consequently for including concerns about HRD at the elite level of strategising. SHRD is restricted to informing the world-views of practitioners and researchers defining and exploring human resource problems and solutions.

The tensions lie among meeting the demands of short-term problem-solving when seeking to 'play the longer game' provide major strategic challenges. Reducing the workforce, controlling pay and rewards for performance, and working a reduced workforce harder in a tough climate does not sit easily with longer-term visions of the benefits of 'win–win' HRD. The potential erosion of HRD commitments due to organisational change is an issue, with the cultural dimension seen to be the securest bedrock available. The role of culture, beliefs and values underpinning commitment to HRD is shared among individuals, organisations and societies. It ranges from individual expectations of a career, through the management of corporate cultures, to different national or regional versions of capitalism.

Alternatively it may be that HRD is shaped by the structural dimensions of employment and people management, leading some organisations to be much more concerned with SHRD than others. These differences reflect the nature of the employment environment and work organisation in different sectors and kinds of situation. The employment environment is traditionally analysed in terms of the economic, social, legal and political contexts. Changes and developments in these contexts will also affect interests in SHRD. Rational and empirical analysis of the employment environment and of work organisations provides a necessary perspective on developments in SHRD, not a universal commitment for all organisations to sign up to.

Employment, technological and social change

A standard approach to good employment was identifiable. As part of this in HRD, in enterprises and organisations there was a status quo, an equilibrium established upon key economic and social realities and standard organisational practices. Crucially, it meant a relatively secure full-time job for life, with fair wages, with full employment as an accepted aim of HRD.

Such a universal case is no longer relevant: the standard enterprise or organisation and the standard workforce employed in standard employment relationships have gone. Internally the search for efficiency and effectiveness, getting more from less, has meant change in jobs, flattened hierarchies and transformed organisations. Further flexibilities in employment practices, and changes in workforce composition, have also altered the technological and social interfaces considerably. Job security and full-time work for the many are gone, or at least threatened. More generally, the decline of old sectors and the growth of new sectors have transformed the basic infrastructure of work. Information and knowledge are now fundamental to that infrastructure

The innovations made possible by information technologies and the social changes accompanying the embracing of diversity, for example, can be seen to bolster SHRD. What was ideal and desirable in employment – what value propositions entail in terms of interface and interaction – has altered fundamentally, and this raises questions about the meaning of SHRD and the perspective it offers.

If we look at the organisation as a unit of analysis, then the universal case for SHRD can no longer be based on the structure of work and people's experience of standard or typical employment in traditional organisations. This applies to both the private and public sectors at a general level. It assumes management to be a mix of classical command-and-control functions, integrated with human relations activities and processes. In practice, SHRD centres on a number of discrete employment systems. These would include human resource planning systems, appraisal systems, reward systems, and systematic training and development.

If we consider the environment, the case for SHRD can no longer be informed by traditional approaches to the employment relationship within capitalism, albeit possibly in different forms of capitalism. Freedom to contract in labour markets meant that the contract of employment between employer and employee bound them in a standard employment relationship. People management themes and concerns reflected issues about management as a controlling function in production systems and bureaucracies. The concept of labour was analysed as a factor of production – as a commodity subject to market relationships. The role of large organisations within a national framework was predominant: enterprises concerned with profitability, and organisations providing public services.

The structural certainties have changed at the level of the organisation and at the level of the nation-state. An old equilibrium has passed, but a new stable system is yet to be determined, hence the continuing experimentation with employment and career flexibilities inside organisations and the political debates around levels of skill, wages and employee representation. As this takes shape, there are many who emphasise that HRD cannot be seen in isolation, but must be located within the power relations that affect organisations as a whole.

Employee attitudes and SHRD

Affective certainties also matter and shape how SHRD is to be defined. These are formed around two core sets of beliefs and values. One was about the employment relationship *between* employee and employer. In some cases this developed around a system of industrial relations where collective bargaining provided the main framework, whereas in other cases a more direct relationship between managers and employees was sought. The other set of beliefs was about relationships *within* employment. This can be described as the psychological contract – the unwritten expectations that individuals and organisations bring with them into employment.

It is also argued that the nature of psychological contracts is changing. Attitudes to work and working life, to what is desirable and possible, have changed. At one level this is reflected in surveys that chart the transformation of traditional frameworks such as the 'British industrial relations' system. It is also reflected in the growth of approaches to employment, where commitment rather than compliance is argued to be the primary framework. There is a degree of harmonisation within organisations, with old values being, apparently, transcended.

Employee attitudes appear to have changed as well. It is not possible to identify a single direction of change. There seems to be a polarisation. On the one hand, there are groups who expect more from work. Work provides a 'community' within which creativity and personal growth is possible. On the other hand, there is a group whose attitude to work is entirely instrumental, and where the notion of job satisfaction is not entertained at all. There is, of course, a further group of people who are, in effect, excluded from the experience of work at all: the socially excluded, including single parents, the long-term unemployed, as well as some disabled people.

Human sciences and strategising

HRD as an area of interdisciplinary study offers strategising to two areas of knowledge: economics and behavioural science. Economics encompasses both the micro and macro levels of analysis. This means that it can provide an analysis both of individual firms and of the broader reality in which those firms operate. The evolution of economic thought has encompassed people at the core of both levels, as a factor of production and as the policy field of employment. The role of HRD has therefore been a major concern in both the pursuit of profit and the realisation of broader goals such as full employment. Questions of efficiency (and productivity) go hand in hand with questions of equity (full employment, wage levels, etc) – though which of these aims gets top billing depends on political factors, as the recent development of the social dimension of the EU demonstrates.

Behavioural science includes psychology, social psychology and sociology. The roots of many developments in HRD lie in the development of fields such as industrial psychology, and experiments such as those at Hawthorn in the 1930s, through to the ideas of humanistic psychologists in the 1960s, and the insights of cognitive psychologists in the 2000s. The different frameworks of scientific or classical management and human relations management in some ways reflect the economic–social split. For classical management, people were a factor of production, motivated by money in organisations whose primary goal was profit – the pure micro-economic picture. For human relations research, people were social beings, motivated by needs for belonging and identity within organisations. Organisations were conceived of as communities with dynamics and processes of their own, beyond the entirely rational behaviour of economic man.

In the contemporary language of HRD, the economic and behavioural science disciplines are associated with the resource side (economics and efficiency, profit, the organisation as an economic system) and the human side (behavioural science and people interacting in communities/groups). At one level these may meet in a useful dialogue, providing complementary insights into an area of common focus, for example increasing productivity and group performance based on social psychology. For some, however, the future of HRD relies on behavioural science providing answers for business problems.

Cognitive certainties also matter and shape how SHRD is to be defined. These are the product of knowledge in a particular field. Cognitive certainties were a development of ideas from economics and the different fields of behavioural science, psychology, social psychology and sociology. An increasingly diverse range of themes, concepts and initiatives occupy the minds of theorists and practitioners in people management. At a superficial level this is reflected in the new language of people management. It is a world of excellence, competence, learning organisations, empowerment and strategic HRD itself.

In this context, there are two major traditions that influence thinking about SHRD: the radical and prescriptivist approaches. The radical tradition has emphasised the potential antagonisms between employer and employee in modern industrial economies, and has defined the problem of human resources as embedded in processes of exploitation and alienation. Value judgements about society and the development of modern economies were central, and, depending on a commentator's precise position, this concern might be translated into anything from radical blueprints for workers' control of work to systems for ensuring harmony within the existing order of industry and organisations. The increasing de-skilling of labour and the use of technologies in production and service systems were major focuses of concern. Much humanistic thinking from North America in the 1950s and 1960s also worked through the problem of alienation by seeking to map motivation as a positive framework for engaging with people.

The prescriptivist tradition, by contrast, has adopted a purportedly 'neutral' view. Indeed, it often characterised itself as scientific, and defined the problems of HRD in terms of efficiency and effectiveness. The classical and administration theories, as well as much thinking in industrial psychology, are historical examples of this. Training managers or personnel specialists in this 'neutral' science was the keynote of this approach. The emergence of professional HRD can be seen as one aspect of it. Contemporary approaches such as competence-based theories and systems continue to embody this 'scientific' stream of thought. The continuing arguments that range around the issue of promoting professionalism in HRM and management reflect the persistent instability of the cultural claims to neutrality, a scientific foundation and ethical rigour as the means of solving human resource problems.

SHRD thinking suffers from insularity because of its lack of connection with key contemporary thinkers. There is not enough cross-fertilisation and interdisciplinary activity in SHRD as a whole with other areas of study about people. This is not simply about the development of better models of SHRD and employment systems. It is about dealing with substantially different views of people at work, and it is about being better connected with management in practice and broader developments in knowledge more generally. Only when the knowledge base is healthy, innovative and challenging can there be an effective link between theory and practice.

Professional roles and SHRD

In any of its forms the concept of SHRD is subject to questioning. Identifying and analysing the links between strategy, HRD and effectiveness has proven to be conceptually and practically complicated. It is equally difficult to prove that HRD was not 'strategic' in the past but is 'strategic' now. Meanings, evidence and value judgements are unclear. In general there appears to have been a shift from the equilibrium model of HRD to a concern with change: and activity to redress perceived weaknesses with HRD in order to compete or improve service standards. Rather than direct attention to proof of any definite link between strategy and HRD, it is necessary to analyse both the status, functional tasks and power of HRD.

It has become commonplace to argue that 'people make the difference' in ensuring corporate and national success and company mission statements abound with the sentiment that 'people are our most important asset'. The status of people management relative to other aspects of the organisation, such as financial management or technological innovation, would seem to be high. Yet research in even an evidently heavily people-dependent sector such as the health services is ambiguous. Some conclude that people management is considered to be peripheral, whereas others claim to show that effective HRD is central to key performance, such as reducing post-operative mortality rates. Nevertheless, evidence suggests that the traditional higher-status functions of finance and marketing continue to overshadow HRM and HRD: people with an accountancy background and skill make good senior managers, whereas people with HRM/HRD backgrounds and skills do not. This echoes the findings of those who found a negative correlation between managers' concern with HRM/HRD and their career success.

In traditional approaches to HRD, there was a tendency to equate effective people management with the development of specialist personnel and HRD departments. Consequently, no great premium was put on people management skills for general managers. General managers were the decision-makers who needed to be clear about business aims and manage budgets effectively. Management development in general, and the development of 'soft' people skills in particular, were not a high priority for supervisors, middle or senior managers.

Yet the management of people is both an integral part of all managers' work and a distinctive field of professional practice. These sentiments are best expressed in the aphorism that 'managers achieve results through people', even when the reality of much managerial work would seem to contradict this. Some attention has been given in the past to the development of a specialist role for HRD practitioners, and more recent research continues to highlight the changing nature of the specialist role. There has also been a growing literature on the way that general management has changed. Here the emphasis on the quality of management generally, and the need to develop better managers, has been important. In addition, the impact of restructuring and delayering has been emphasised. The role of senior managers has been reviewed, middle management has been squeezed, and the supervisory role has been transformed.

This area of balance between specialist and line-manager responsibilities across the spectrum of HRD activities is attracting a lot of interest. The net effect seems to be that the devolution of people management responsibilities from specialists to line-managers has an impact on the number and roles of specialists, while managers need increased development to manage their new responsibilities. Specific agreements to clarify responsibilities can be made. The association of changes in this sphere of activity with new HRD approaches is often highlighted. Given the thrust of new HRD ideas, there is clearly a greater need to have managers who are able to create and develop the committed, flexible, quality workforce required for success. The feeling that personnel specialists and departments were not up to meeting and driving the changes necessary led to a reinforced emphasis on the role of managers. Although this view of personnel has been disputed, the quantity and quality of management development concerned with HRD have become major issues and a priority for many organisations.

The popularity of this delegation and devolution to line-managers is hard to gauge. Specialists may lose their jobs or core parts of their workload. Managers may see the devolution as simply added responsibilities at a time of increasing stress and work intensification, rather than an opportunity to become better managers. Resistance to change is likely to occur on the part of both specialist and manager.

In addition to the changing balance of responsibilities, there is the issue of the changing content of responsibilities. HRD has been characterised in the past by agreements and procedures that reflected a mixture of legal, social and professional best practice. Change or improvement meant revising those agreements and procedures. This often happened in an ad hoc way: an issue was dealt with as it came up.

New approaches to people management have a substantially different set of emphases. The first is the idea that the foundation of effective HRD is culture rather than procedure. Having a culture in which human resources are valued, in which commitment is expected, and where all managers are highly skilled and trained can be seen to preclude the need for collective agreements and procedures. Second, the use of levers such as teamwork is much more important. Overall, there is a concern to restructure employment patterns, jobs and organisations. In this context, training and development assume a greater role, which involves more than the level of technical training being given and extends to initiatives such as empowerment. This is a difficult construct to pin down, but it refers, at a minimum, to a significant reconceptualisation of roles by both managers and employees.

In sum, the organisation as a unit of analysis has changed and the national context as a unit of analysis has changed. As a result of these changes, the roles and activities of management and personnel specialists appear to be changing. Stable structures and systems administered by specialist staff are perhaps necessary, but they are not sufficient.

Power and SHRD

Finally, perceptions of the challenges of SHRD are affected by how power in organisations is distributed and works. Power in organisations is commonly discussed in terms of unitarist, pluralist and radical perceptions (see Theory & Research Box 15.1). SHRD may be perceived as either part of unitarist control or democratic pluralism, or as a contributor to radical change. Equally, barriers to SHRD can be associated with these theories of power: as unitarists desire control they inhibit the emergence of SHRD effective learning by regulating organisational life and alienating the workforce; as pluralists advocate involvement and participation there is a trade-off in HRD investments which compromises SHRD; the 'liberating' aspirations of radical theory fuel scepticism about its advocates and the changes they propose in the name of 'learning organisations'.

theory & research

15.1	Perspectives on power		
	Unitarist	**Pluralist**	**Radical**
Outcomes and logic	Zero sum All benefit	Non zero sum Balance over time	Non zero sum Winners and losers
Organisational norms	Harmony should exist	Conflict is natural and healthy	Conflict is evidence of deeper divisions
Task relations	Common objectives	Different interests	Opposing interests
Power bases	Power for 'legitimate' sources only; managers	Power is distributed and shared; win and lose in turn	Bases vary; there is a perpetual contest
Aim of use of power	Compliance change	Negotiation	Transformational
SHRD	Autocratic Bureaucratic	Democratic Technocratic	Liberating Contested

Conclusion: scenarios for SHRD

Strategies will, and should, be determined by contexts, rather than representing a compendium of best practice. Here the contexts of strategising for HRD, of vision, change and of business value propositions have been considered. Learning about HRD involves the identification of relevant contexts and analysis of trends within those contexts. The continuation of strategising, change and value proposition analysis at the frontiers of work and organisation invite and require further thinking about SHRD. There is a whole new world to map and explore, beyond previous certainties. SHRD is a field in which, for example, new models of competence are being developed. These can be used to profile the ideal workforce and employee and provide a framework for integrating human resource systems. A sense of reinventing people management, of discovery and opportunity with scope for progress is evident. The tone is optimistic, and the deconstruction of the old cannot happen fast enough. Creativity, innovation and progress are the hoped-for outcomes.

A more critical analysis of the new rhetoric of SHRD can be given, suggesting some old preoccupations. Despite superficial harmonisation and the rhetoric of commitment there are still the same old divisions between employer and employee. The issue of control in the workplace is still evident, whether that be in traditional sectors and industries or in new sectors and services. The problem of control at work and the consequences that has on HRD systems still applies. The gurus and consultants who market the new corporate fashions in HRD need to be exposed. The tone is more pessimistic, with a critique of the deconstruction of past strengths and scepticism about innovation.

Such critique does not begin or end with the concept of SHRD. We are in a period of uncertainty, which will not be resolved easily or quickly as new systems or simply duplicate old ones with new names. Prescribing strong and autonomous individuals and organisations who should be able to transform themselves almost at will to deal with a wide array of new situations. Our maps of HRD need to be capable of making sense of all this transformation and change; our images of ourselves, organisations and work have to alter.

Multiple-choice questions

15.1 Which of the following are concerns in strategic HRD?
   A. Having a high-status HRD director at the top of the organisation.
   B. Integrating HRD activities and aligning them with organisational strategy.
   C. Developing and realising a vision of HRD in the organisation that influences decision-making and resource allocation.
   D. Rebranding the HRD department as a corporate university.

15.2 Which of the following is not a good indicator of the presence of strategic HRD ?
   A. The existence of an explicit and special articulation of explicit mission around and including HRD
   B HRD linked with the vision, value propositions, business models and projects and programs
   C HRD linked with the 5 Cs , especially the highest level, changing, and learning
   D HRD seen to be a means of delivering an energised and productive social system with an efficient and productive technological system.

References

Finkelstein, S., Harvey, C. and Lawton, T. (2006) *Breakout Strategy: Meeting the challenge of double-digit growth*, London, McGraw-Hill.

Garavan, T. (1991) 'Strategic human resource development', *Journal of European Industrial Training*, vol. 15, no. 1, pp. 17–31.

Garavan, T. (2007) 'A strategic perspective on human resource development', *Advances in Developing Human Resources*, vol. 9, no. 1, pp. 11–30.

Grieves, J. (2003) *Strategic HRD*, London, Sage.

McCracken, M. and Wallace, M. (2000) 'Towards a redefinition of strategic HRD', *Journal of European Industrial Training*, July, no. 24–5, pp. 281–90.

concluding case question	*PowerCo revisited*

Read the introductory case again now. As you read, consider the following questions.

1. In what ways could HRD help the organisation to realise its values?
2. What HRD practices might this organisation adopt to help achieve progress on the highlighted four key workplace issues?
3. Does this organisation appear to be one which achieves 'strategic HRD', that is, the integration of HRD with the development of the whole enterprise and its competitiveness? Bear in mind the concerns raised by the HRD director when interviewed.

PowerCo case answers and analysis

1. Values and HRD

The values provide a core reference point for the HRD process, for identifying needs, designing and delivering interventions and evaluating HRD.

Continuously improving health and safety performance is the highest profile and central value. Needs here will vary with the kind of environment faced, from call centres and offices to power stations and work on live transmission lines in all kinds of conditions. Clearly mapped needs for all kinds of roles and professional training and advice about those is essential. PowerCo also needs to continue to manage the 'ABC' dynamics, so that initial and ongoing training is embedded in workplace practice. They should continue to set targets, monitor and compare their performance internally and with external benchmarks. There is always room for new initiatives and fresh approaches to keep the message in people's minds and reinforce a safety culture. An active accident investigation programme at facilities can identify actions required to prevent recurrence, and that knowledge can be communicated quickly and effectively. There could be regular communication with employees through safety bulletins, alerts and a quarterly staff newsletter. The company should not neglect broader issues of health campaigning, as well as the priority of safety in an industry with such high-risk environments.

Improving customer loyalty entails providing high standards of customer service, and that begins and continues with effective development of professional staff so that the service is secure with competent sales, administration and support staff to deal with the processes and queries accompanying service provision. It also takes talented marketing, finance and other professionals whose continuing professional development is necessary for sustaining standards.

Enhanced shareholder value – gaining advantage over competitors – is the sum of capability of everyone in the organisation, from the senior managers setting strategy to the behaviour of contact centre advisers dealing with billing queries. That capability is grounded in the basics, including the 'basic' values of reliability and honesty, and literacy/numeracy, extended into occupational capability and in these overarching values.

Positive working environment: a positive working environment here means having the opportunity to realise potential and contribute, suggesting a strong career management and development infrastructure, fair management of activities from regular performance appraisals to opportunities for growth and promotion.

Trust of communities: appreciating the impact the company has as a major business and employer can be managed through participation in initiatives to help certain groups, including disadvantaged young people, into employment and training. It may also get involved in supporting schools or active community groups in areas like the arts, or allow staff to engage in work for charities in the local community. All these activities can increase the skill of pooled people, and help raise the standards of employees' skills.

Teamwork and Leadership: direct training inputs, such as courses or using outward bound and other activities, can be used for teamworking skills development for team leaders and other managers. Continuous development of teamworking and team-leading skills will depend on ongoing support and advice, and recognition of effective teams.

PowerCo case answers and analysis

2. HRD and four key issues

Building a high-performance culture

Organisations can look to various systems to implement improvements aimed at reducing the overall level of complaints and raising customer service. Putting in place targets and processes to reduce customer complaints is important. It is sensible to work proactively when changes, such as new technology, are considered as they may impact customers.

Developing leadership capacity is critical. Articulating key behaviours and describing how the company expects senior managers to behave in carrying out their roles and responsibilities would be central; and mentoring or coaching systems to help instil/nurture these would be relevant. Identifying high-potential individuals for career development is also an integral part, as is careful recruitment and selection of employees for new roles. And, while HRD may help generate high-performance returns for high performance at all levels, it is necessary to provide pay and benefits that help to attract, motivate and retain the best talent.

Positive experience

The quality of HRD available to and experienced by staff is at the heart of their monitoring of positive experience:

> I have developed my skills over the last six months
> I have recently spoken to my manager about my training/development

The quality of HRD is also an integral part of the other factors measured:

> I feel valued as a member of a team
> My colleagues and I are able to produce high-quality work
> I feel a sense of personal accomplishment in my work
> I am able to act decisively on behalf of the company

The ultimate judgments about experience are clearly based on these constituent parts where HRD is central:

> I am clear about where I add value
> I am proud of what the company is trying to achieve

Training and developing people

The company spends a large amount of money and time on training. Extensive training and development programmes are in place throughout the businesses to implement their policies, procedures and business plan and ensure that they comply with legislation and best practice standards. Improving existing skills and developing new ones provides staff with the opportunity to achieve their potential in their working lives. Providing high-quality training helps to keep people motivated and widens the pool of future high-performance employees. It also fuels confidence, raises ambitions and increases learning power in a cycle that benefits individuals and the company.

PowerCo also links this into the sustainability of communities by sharing its approaches, learning models and resources in a way that provides long-term benefits for the business and the community alike. They deliver both formal and informal learning opportunities in the UK and USA to various groups in their local communities.

Providing equal opportunities to all individuals.

Supporting diversity is said to be a critical component of the employment experience at PowerCo, one that can provide the company with a position of competitive advantage. PowerCo is committed to promoting equal opportunities for all. However, overall, it seems that both women and ethnic minorities are under-represented. They could proactively work with a range of organisations that promote equal opportunities, including the Equal Opportunities Commission, Employers Forum on Age, Employers' Forum on Disability. They could develop

continued overleaf

policies that are broader than the law requires, including sexual orientation protection which applies to all applicants and employees with benefits extended to same-sex domestic partners.

3. Is this strategic HRD?

The descriptions of values and policies seem to suggest that this is an organisation practising strategic HRD. How far is HRD a strategic activity with its own distinct body of knowledge? How far is there is a paradigm shift and practical change occurring about the importance of HRD? Does this change the kind of HRD products and services required? Does strategic focus lead to different performance improvement, core competence issues and different roles for managers? Or is it simply about creating a better climate for learning at work?

Although the traditional reason for dissatisfaction – that HRD was not taken seriously – appears to have subsided, new forms of discontent have arisen to replace the old. Traditionally there have been few strategic issues in people management. Previously important problems such as avoiding strikes, ensuring that wage rises were linked to productivity, and attempting to manage human resource flows through manpower planning, would no longer be thought of as strategic in the modern sense. Such activities reflected what could be called the equilibrium role of people management – that of maintaining a steady state. The flexibility, quality and efficiency of human resources are apparently major concerns of top management. This leads to a greater concern both with the macro-environment that influences human resources (labour markets, education systems) and with the internal environment, where past practices need to be reviewed and changed in order to align and/or integrate HRD practices with strategic aims. There is also the greater concern with 'vision' rather than planning, and with mobilising human resources to achieve that vision. This is the model of strategy in which strategic HRD may be judged.

In this case the senior managers see that business is best served by creating a safe and positive working environment which encourages and supports high personal performance. They seek to achieve that by focusing on issues that matter to their employees. These include safety, training, behaviour-based performance management and the provision of opportunities for growth and development. The safety and well-being of the workforce and the public is PowerCo's number one priority. They believe leadership in their industry will increasingly depend on innovation in the delivery of products and services that provide clear benefits to their customers and their communities. They view their local community initiatives as investments, providing support where their skills, resources and energy will boost local economies, complement customers' ideals and activities, give their staff opportunities for professional development and personal growth, and help them achieve business objectives.

As the business changes, restructuring can place strain on employee relations, and that is an additional concern. Recognising the legitimacy of trade union involvement and having formal agreements that foster open, two-way communication and consultation is then significant in many areas, including the management of HRD. Seeking to achieve necessary workforce changes fairly through processes such as consultation encompasses HRD practices and concerns.

Looking at the issues the HRD Director raised when interviewed reinforces this. Some are about internal HRD matters, of a non-strategic nature – the roles of specialist in-house HRD staff, and changing relations with external training suppliers. Others are linked to strategically central concerns, such as reframing engineer and top talent development. In between these are the more ambiguous areas of HRD strategy, and the desire in this case for learning to be more learner-driven. Is this is a culture change integral with the values, the business and its performance; or is it just a different approach to managing learning processes?

Looking ahead:
the future of HRD

By the end of this chapter you will be able to:

- review key themes and issues of HRD at work using a force field analysis method;
- critically evaluate the place of HRD at work in the context of changes in management and organisation.

Introduction

Having completed your odyssey through this book you will now be aware of and familiar with the challenges facing the learner in this field:

- Contributions from several different academic disciplines are relevant in the study of HRD at work; including psychology, sociology, business policy, social policy and others.
- The boundaries of study of HRD at work can be set differently, according to the definitions employed; ranging from managing training to designing an entire organisation's strategy and purpose.
- Valuable contributions to the literature on HRD at work have been made in all of the last five decades, with the latest not necessarily superseding the earlier. This is particularly true in HRD where new journals have come onto the market.
- The study of HRD at work contains evidence, examples and illustrations generated in a wide variety of organisations and from a diverse range of methodologies with varying degrees of rigour.
- Much material about HRD at work is not readily accessible to non-specialists (for example internal company reviews or background economic policy review papers) and does not readily lend itself to cumulative review.
- The concepts included within the study of HRD at work range in scale from those debated between different academic schools of thought (constructivists and behaviourists), through to methodologies of practice (how to manage HRD) down to discrete single 'tools' (making mentoring work, for example).

My aim in writing this second edition is to help take students through these challenges and present a treatment of HRD that is as integrated, contemporary, evidence-based and open-to-inquiry as possible. This means approaching HRD at work first as a process that is an integral part of the management of an organisation. The general nature of that process is widely recognised, and detailed process analysis of the major phases provides the foundation for understanding HRD. The many and varied practices that arise in the course of managing the HRD process can never be fully and comprehensively covered in a single textbook. Rather, selected representative and prominent practices in HRD at work can be considered, illustrating with case studies what HRD looks like and entails in practice. The third part considers different perspectives on HRD at work – how these embody some very long-standing and some much newer concerns, and to explore the concepts, arguments and evidence. HRD is to be studied as an integrated review of processes, practices and perspectives.

16.1	*Key propositions*

- Effective individual learning is critical if employees are to acquire the knowledge and skill needed to support the organisation's business objectives and delivery targets
- Review of training interventions must ensure that the learning achieved is aligned with business activity
- Many different HR roles are involved in the people development effort, and the boundaries between organisational development, management development and training are becoming increasingly blurred
- The delivery of effective people development practices requires a considerable increase in commitment and enhanced skills from all managers, particularly first-line managers
- A shift is taking place from training, an instructor-led content-based intervention, to learning, which is a self-directed work-based process leading to increased adaptive capacity
- While off-the-job classroom-based training still has a place, it no longer occupies the central role in training provision as other forms of intervention are becoming more important
- Technology is becoming an important enabler in people development, but there are many conceptual and practical issues to be resolved in its implementation
- It is important to demonstrate the value to be derived from people development activities, but traditional hierarchical training evaluation may not be the most appropriate method

Source Sloman 2006.

The propositions of Strategic View Box 16.1 summarise one contemporary review of what matters when looking ahead in HRD. This closing chapter is an opportunity to consider what we have covered and how it connects with these concerns.

HRD at work has been presented in terms of three related dimensions. First, workplace HRD is a process – a series of phases with associated tasks that need to be controlled and completed. There is a core process of observing, planning, acting and reviewing. This is, or should be, integrated with the performance management of the organisation and general HRM policy and practices. These tasks are about managing cognitive capacities, capabilities and behaviours to achieve effective performance. Whatever else changes, this basic process remains constant. Process is constant. The theorising of process does evolve though; the major change being the change from theorising the provision of training to the management of learning.

Second, HRD involves a range of practices for achieving the goals of individuals, groups and organisations. HRD practice has been explored here in terms of HRD strategies, partnerships with providers, the increasing use of e-learning and working with groups. Practices of significance do change from time to time, and from era to era, to fit with changes in the worlds of business, organisations and technology.

Third, there are a range of perspectives for making sense of and understanding HRD at work. These different points of view for looking at and making sense of HRD need to be appreciated, considered and combined to enable a complete picture of strengths, weaknesses, practicalities and potential of HRD at work as an area of problem-solving and decision making of concern to various stakeholders. The perspectives reviewed in this book include the points of view of government and public policy development, the increasing concern with knowledge management, major themes like managing diversity, and new thinking on strategy and the place of HRD in that. Underlying all discussion of process, practice and perspective there is the background of competing conceptions of HRD. These can be described as the realist and constructivist conceptions (see Theory & Research Box 16.1). The future of HRD will continue to be shaped and animated by the presence and rivalry of these different traditions in theory and in practice.

theory & research

| 16.1 | Rival conceptions of HRD |

Realist conception of HRD	Constructivist conception of HRD
HRD is definable as 'one thing' that can be stated explicitly	HRD is many things, a synthesis of changing concerns, evolving socio-economic forces and adaptations to new circumstances
HRD is a means to win–win social ends; its nature is to ameliorate and improve, to drive and achieve progress	HRD is an arena in which shared and distinct interests exist; it is interconnected with the wider balance of power, and its exercise, in societies; some lose.
HRD theory should prescribe what is to be done	HRD theory should offer insights that open options
Good thinking about HRD shows premises and invites critique around empirical evidence	Good thinking about HRD helps to escape the limiting frames of mind inherited from past eras as change occurs
HRD should be based on 'strong' authorities; reputable scholars whose major theoretical and empirical works form a recognised, stable canon	HRD should be about encouraging and participating in 'languaging'; generating meaning anew, in a social context, original for its times, then obsolete

No introduction to HRD should be seen as existing in isolation from the broader world of HRM, and the forces for change in HRM. It is these that lead to HRD mattering as much as it does. By investing in HRD, there are better prospects for success. The fear is that the failure to get HRD right will leave individuals, organisations, nations or regions disadvantaged, and struggling in the wake of others in the future. In other words, getting HRD right can be seen in win–lose terms, with those who gain doing so at the expense of others.

But, as with many other aspects of HRM, getting HRD right can create a win–win situation. Win–win situations through HRD exist for individuals where there are optimum outcomes for each, in the form of fulfilling and rewarding jobs, careers and employment across a wide range of types of capability and interest. They exist for organisations when HRD helps create and sustain employability and a capable workforce, often run in partnership with other stakeholders and meeting their interests rather than conflicting with them. And they exist for nations and regions where, through HRD, each can find a path to integration with world trade and industry by attaining reasonable standards that raise the quality of life above existing levels for the majority.

So HRD at work matters because it is the means to give some individuals good career choices – the capacity to get on in life rather than 'going nowhere' – and it can ensure that the disadvantaged and disenchanted find a place and role rather than being left behind and neglected. HRD matters because the world in which we live in general creates organisations with the capacity to develop their intellectual capital, capabilities and behaviours consistent with core values – organisations that will both compete and collaborate to provide products and services at the quality and cost that customers seek. And HRD matters because the world in which we live is affected by the process of globalisation, which further accelerates the speed at which people need to learn and develop in free-market economies. These circumstances present challenges for nations to compare themselves with the best and compete with each other for inward investment from the major multinationals. Economic imperatives among both developed and developing nations tend to highlight the roles of development and learning in creating and using knowledge, capabilities and behaviours consistent with employment in modern jobs and organisations.

These levels of development and learning interact, and can produce a virtuous or a vicious cycle. In the virtuous cycle the net effect is appropriate levels of investment in HRD that provides high levels of economic and social returns, thus creating a dependence upon development, learning and knowledge. In the vicious cycle a failure at any one level will feed into others. One example of this process is when individuals fail to learn, causing knowledge gaps, capability shortages or behavioural mismatches for organisations. Another is when organisations, already low on knowledge and skill requirements, fail to provide opportunities for educated and capable individuals, which, in turn, leads to frustrated expectations.

There are no value-free, transcendent prescriptions that can be found for HRD – no panacea policies and procedures that can be implemented, to invent or to copy others' success. Practices are embedded in historical, political, social and educational contexts of particular business systems, and cannot be uprooted from these contexts in a predictable manner. And this is also true of perspectives; they too are embedded in history and politics as much as evidence and argument.

The future

It is, in conclusion, helpful to look ahead, and reflect on the future for HRD. Having emphasised the need to take perspectives, cultural and institutional contexts into account, what are the prospects? Views on these questions are divided. One optimistic view, which has clearly been around for some time, is that there is now a greater concern with effective HRD at work. Great economic and social advantages and benefits are to be gained from developing, effectively and efficiently, the kinds and levels of knowledge, capability and behaviour required in the jobs and organisations that are the foundations of a changed, and still changing, world of work. The levers of HRD, from access to greater learning opportunities through reforms within national education and training systems to persuading employers to spend more on training, offer areas for action where the most powerful stakeholders – employers, government, educationalists and employee organisations – can work together on common interests in developing and implementing schemes and initiatives. And in a context where commitments to improved HRM in the workplace are taken for granted, the rationale for investing in people as an integral part of a people-friendly business strategy creates circumstances in which support for HRD will be natural and strong.

What should not be ignored, however, is the alternative and more sceptical and critical view; that there is still a constant, systemic questioning and scepticism around the value of HRD at work. There are uncertainties and difficulties in responding to a changed and changing world of work by seeking, through supporting HRD, to achieve economic and social change of the scale and quality apparently required. And breaking free of an existing economic and social 'status quo', of low skills, low participation in learning and often inefficient systems, is no easy option that can provide overnight returns. Equally, breaking free of the status quo where the HRD 'rich' get richer, with better facilities, support and returns being confined to those in the wealthier classes, nations and regions, is an integral part of the global agenda on change. The debates about pulling the right levers to affect the policies of key institutions, the investments of thousands of organisations and the motivations of millions of people can then become debates that divide stakeholders rather than unite them. Who pays, and where does the money go? Finally, there is the question of the extent to which commitments to HRD can be an integral part of HRM, when it seems that a 'new deal' in employee relations can lead to under-investment in staff because, in the long term, mutually beneficial relations are a thing of the past. If employees may not be within the organisation for any length of time, why develop them? If an organisation cannot provide a career path for an employee, why should they bother to work at learning over time for the benefit of the organisation?

It is tempting to think in terms of one of these perceptions about the future of HRD being right and the other being wrong. But they can be represented, broadly speaking, as describing forces for more, and more effective, HRD and forces against more, or more effective, HRD. Figure 16.1 shows these two views as two sides of a force-field diagram. Force-field diagrams are used to visualise situations in which an equilibrium exists between forces for change and forces against change. Such perceptions are neither right nor wrong. What you see depends on where you looking from. The aim of this book has been to give you several vantage points so that you are better placed to work with a 360 degree view of the area, and not be confined to a limited and partial picture.

The future prospects for HRD can be analysed as fluctuating around an equilibrium 'status quo'. In some situations it may be desirable to change this equilibrium, to seek more – and more effective – HRD at work. And there may be things that individuals, employers, governments, and others can do to achieve that change.

The future of HRD at work ranges from helping the individual struggle to master a subject in a training room to directing the billions spent by employers and government. Developing and improving our understanding of these situations, from the smallest actions carried out in the name of learning to more significant actions, should help shape and influence what is and what is not done. There is then a great span and a great depth to the questions raised by thinking about doing and improving HRD at work, ranging from how best to manage a one-day course in an organisation to the development of policy by government to achieve economic and social goals, and from the evolution of knowledge management in multinational organisations to the improvement of skills in a medium-sized organisation increasing its productivity.

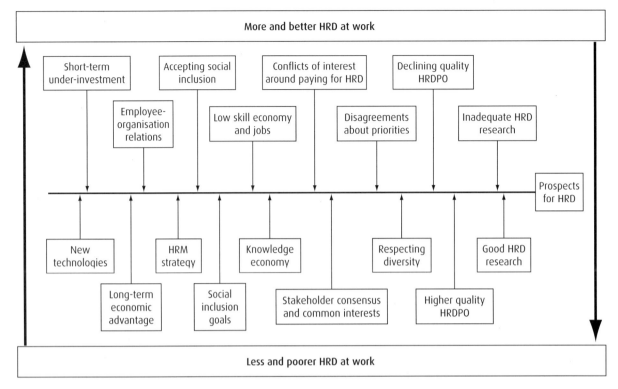

Figure 16.1 A force-field analysis of HRD

Authoritative and universal answers to these questions cannot be found in any text; they need to be researched by thoughtful practitioners each day, and discovered anew wherever the transformational power of learning is to be harnessed.

A way of approaching the daily, monthly, yearly and never-ending tasks of HRD has been offered here: developing a sophisticated understanding of the HRD process, exploring HRD in practice, and using different perspectives.

Q

concluding short case exercise

You are the HRD Director of a large multiple-outlet retail organisation, a supermarket chain. You have been approached by your CEO. The management team is considering acquiring and merging with one of your erstwhile competitors. He wants to know the five key areas from an HRD point of view that will be at the top of the agenda if the merger goes ahead. Identify and explain the five key areas you would suggest.

References

Sloman, M. (2006) 'A New Context for the Trainer', *Impact*, CIPD Policy and Research, Issue 16, pp. 20–1.

Thody, P. (1999) *Researching Human Resource Development: Philosophy, processes and practices*, London, Routledge.

concluding short case answer

This question provides an opportunity to demonstrate a familiarity with themes across the areas of process, practice and perspective. I would expect the better answers to appreciate this, and select a set of areas that show something from each domain, rather than being all about looking at process or practice matters.

In considering process issues, the primary task will be demonstrating that, within the major phase considered (needs, design, delivery, evaluation), what is involved may share common foundations but may also need to be harmonised because the infrastructure of methods, models and practicalities in use in each organisation may be different. Even in the same industry sector differences in history, strategy, values and so on can lead to needs being identified variously (for example, different competence frameworks), design being managed differently (even the language of aims and objectives can vary), in delivery variations (some things in one organisation done on-job and in the other off-job) and evaluation activities being different (in one organisation done in a 'hard'/objective way and in the other more on the 'soft'/subjective side).

I would also expect the better answers to appreciate that in HRD terms such a merger is not just about a takeover with the practices of the purchaser being imported to displace the practices of the purchased. There approach should be to appreciate the possibilities of identifying and protecting best practice, wherever it is seen; and an appreciation that getting understanding and commitment for harmonised HRD systems is something that takes time and resources; it is not a matter of quickly rolling out and imposing new formal practices to replace old ones.

In terms of perspectives the major issue here would probably be that it is an area of change in which there will be various stakeholder concerns to address. Individuals in the workforce will have concerns about HRD ranging from the critical (HRD professionals) to the complacent (many part-time staff). Managers will be interested in issues around their own careers and any changes impacting on them and their role around investment in HRD. Trade unions will be concerned with maintaining and encouraging HRD. Partners, external providers, in both the organisation being acquired and in the acquiring organisation will face major challenges here, that they may see as threats or opportunities. The chance to revisit partnership contracts and improve them is evident. Appreciating that this requires a sensitivity to perspectives is the issue, as much as focusing on, say, the government or partnership concerns.

In the context of process issues, answers might raise the following points:

- Identifying need: focusing on performance improvement, not just merging competence lists/training menus;
- Keeping an eye on all levels of learning from the core capabilities through cognitive concerns to emotional agendas during and after merger;
- Reconsidering learning delivery: learning from the best in each organisation;
- Measuring return on investment (ROI): short-term additional costs and longer-term savings in HRD budgets.

In the context of practices answers might address issues of strategies:

- HRD strategies: same or different?
- Technologies: compatible systems and patterns of use?
- Partnerships: merging or rationalising?
- Coaching/Mentoring: compatible systems and patterns of use?

In the case of perspectives they might include:

- Ethics and opportunities: gender, age, inclusion themes and concerns;
- Collaborating in government/public initiatives: rationalising these;
- Strategy and HRD: organisation development concerns.

Elaborations on these would include the following.

Regarding HRD and needs, on the one hand the business is not going to change, so current competence stays the same. HRD may be contributing to key issues in the merger as a whole, such as reducing costs and restructuring work but maintaining capability. The framework for this will be to determine a new/refreshed

continued overleaf

| concluding short case answer continued |

common HRD vision, with plans that sustain and build on the important role of HRD; talent matters, teams matter, everyone matters. On the other hand, as the organisation is being taken over it is likely that there will be performance shortfalls which can be addressed, and these are likely to include skills gaps in areas like customer handling, team working, communication.

Following this through, the agenda for HRD needs to be to impact on performance: to create entrepreneurial dynamism and, taking advantage of the new enlarged organisation, to drive more company innovation and embed technical advances in production processes; create a skilled and knowledgeable workforce; secure the physical, educational and electronic infrastructure that underpins HRD's contribution to business productivity.

Regarding learning delivery the focus should be on performance and learning, with 'non-training' as well as 'training' solutions an important concern. Aligning performance management systems and processes will be a big task. Adopting a performance analysis perspective rather than a 'training is good' approach is essential here; an opportunity to advance organisational development.

With respect to ROI concerns, the scope for longer-term savings in HRD budgets will arise, alongside costing the additional but short-term HRD costs brought by merging. Savings in HRD spending might arise from rationalising HRD products and services. Should the focus rather be on quality?

Technologies may present a big challenge, with two major systems needing to be merged, or different approaches to learning blended. Issues around the development and use of communication tools, computer-based training (CBT), learning centres and the like will need to be resolved.

As the merger is with a similar organisation there are unlikely to be any new ethical issues, as the profile of employee groups is likely to be pretty much the same. Dealing with concerns around employee groups 'Getting on, getting by, going nowhere' will still be a concern. HRD may either be perpetuating or challenging inequalities around factors like gender and age.At the level of HRD strategy there may be differences, with each organisation favouring a different balance and mix of strategies. There may be two Corporate Universities, for example. HRD responsibilities may lie with different providers, being either concentrated in specialists hands or shared between several stakeholders, not driven by HRD specialists. The existence and use of coaching and mentoring systems may vary.

Regulatory requirements will not be different, but cultures of HRD might. Statutory requirements will be the same, any 'Licence to practise' systems will be familiar, memberships of networks will overlap, as will representative systems and membership of industry skills bodies. This would not then be a major concern.

Appendix 1
Extended CIPD standards

CIPD standards complete

Indicative content

The integration of HRD activity into the organisation

The organisation's business environment and internal context.

The goals of the stakeholders in HRD, and the building and sustaining of partnerships that will produce and communicate effective HRD processes and initiatives.

The formulation of the organisation's HRD goals and strategy, and their implementation at different organisational levels.

The external environment of:

- global, international and more localised trends relevant to the organisation's present position and future progress; the current, planned and emergent position of the organisation in its external environment, and HRD implications;
- national vocational education and training policy, its implementation at regional and local levels, and practical implications and opportunities for the organisation.

The internal environment of:

- corporate and business unit goals, strategies and plans (formal and informal);
- organisational structure and culture
- strategies and plans (formal and informal);
- personnel/HR policy and practice;
- the performance management process.

How to identify and respond to emergent trends and issues relevant to HRD.

How to formulate the HRD plan for the business and align it with wider HR policy and with corporate goals and strategy.

How to identify and respond to new contingencies, and produce relevant divisional, group and individual learning and HRD plans.

CIPD standards complete		Indicative content
The provision of a value-adding HRD function	How the HRD process adds value for the organisation and the individual.	The value chain of the business and: • HRD processes and initiatives with value-adding potential; • the difference between 'value for money' and 'adding value'; • how to create awareness of the value that HRD can add for the organisation.
	The organisation, management and evaluation of the HRD function and roles.	Different structural options to ensure that the HRD process has a business focus and efficient operations.
	The delivery of organisationally-focused projects to time, cost and quality.	Typologies of HRD roles, and their relevance, use and development in different organisational settings.
	Aids and barriers to effective performance as a HRD consultant.	The financial base of HRD in the business: • General measures to ensure cost-efficient and well-regulated HRD operations. • The role of the HRD budget in the provision of a well-managed, organisationally-focused HRD function. • National, regional and local funding opportunities to support and inform HRD operations in the organisation.
		Processes and tools to aid continuous improvement in the HRD field.
		The purpose of marketing the HRD process; marketing methods and approaches.
		How to build, operate and maintain effective business-focused partnerships with internal and external HRD stakeholders: • Interpersonal skills and personal strategies to create and sustain effective business partnerships in different organisational settings; • Identifying and responding to barriers to the partnership process; • Handling issues of power, politics and conflict.
HRD's contribution to the recruitment and performance management processes	Induction, basic skills training and continuous improvement that will motivate learners, achieve competent performance, and build commitment to organisational goals and values.	The value of effective, relevant, well-publicised HRD strategies and practice for the recruitment process.
		The role of marketing in communicating a positive image for HRD to potential applicants.
		The importance for the performance management process of well-planned and effective induction, basic skills training, continuous learning and improvement.
		Problems of balancing control and HRD drivers in the performance management process, and ways of responding to these.

CIPD standards complete		Indicative content
HRD's contribution to the retention of employees	Career and management development processes that help identify, develop and use people's potential and adaptability and aid their continued employability.	The role of career development in aiding employee retention.
		Criteria for effective design and management of career systems and:
		• assessment processes to identify and develop potential;
		• strategies to prepare people for changed career paths, and to increase their employability security.
		The management development process and:
		• how the management development programme (MDP) contributes to current organisational success and builds future organisational competence;
		• different approaches to the design of MDPs, including work-based and more formalised processes and initiatives.
HRD's contribution to building organisational capacity and facilitating change	The skills and attitudes needed to work effectively in changed/changing organisational roles, structures and working environments, and how they can be developed.	Components of organisational capacity: structure, culture, networks, business routines, systems and procedures.
		Helping to expand or contract organisational capacity through HRD strategies for re-skilling, multi-skilling, role and job change.
	HRD strategies for organisational culture change.	HRD initiatives and processes to:
		• ensure effective functioning of personnel in cross-functional, project-based and similar roles;
		• improve workforce adaptability and flexibility;
		• aid and embed change in organisational culture.
		The HRD professional as change agent; the tensions and challenges of that role and ways of responding to these.
The stimulation of strategic awareness and development of knowledge	HRD initiatives and processes to stimulate strategic awareness, creativity and innovation.	Learning initiatives and processes to promote strategic awareness and the identification of strategic issues at all organisational levels.
	Learning strategies and processes to develop, share and disseminate knowledge that is valuable to the organisation.	The importance of unlearning and relearning, and of learning processes that can stimulate challenges to established routines and prescriptions in ways that will help the organisation.
		Barriers and aids to understanding the knowledge process, and to generating, sharing and disseminating knowledge.
		Types of internal and external learning partnership that can produce or expand knowledge valuable to the business.
		Roles and tasks for the HRD professional in 'knowledge management'.

CIPD standards complete		Indicative content
The design and delivery of learning processes and activity	The planning, design and delivery of learning processes and activity that will add value for the organisation and for individuals. The appropriate application of new technology to training and learning.	Principles of effective planning, design and delivery of planned learning events, and their practical application, including: • processes to ensure accurate identification of needs; • how to achieve shared ownership of learning programmes and events by the stakeholders; • how to integrate workplace learning with more formalised training and HRD initiatives, when appropriate; • factors involved in achieving effective transfer of learning. Developments in new technology, and their implications for learning processes and programmes, and for the administration and assessment of learning events. How to monitor ongoing programmes and events to ensure a continued focus on their learning objectives, and the achievement of intended learning outcomes. How to respond to any contingency calling for a change in objectives or strategy in a learning programme or event.
The evaluation and assessment of HRD outcomes and investment	Methods and models for: • evaluating the outcomes of HRD processes and activity; • evaluating the organisation's past HRD investment.	Models and processes to measure and evaluate the specific outcomes of HRD processes and activity. How to assess the relative effectiveness, efficiency and feasibility of different HRD processes and activity in the particular situation. Ways of calculating the 'payback' and 'payforward' of the organisation's overall HRD investment, in order to ensure added value. Essential data and information sources for evaluation and assessment activity.
The role and tasks of the ethical practitioner	The impact on, and implications of, diversity of people, style, and employment contracts for HRD policies and practice and organisational learning strategies. The information and actions needed to identify and achieve legally-compliant and ethical HRD practices and processes.	Sources of information and guidance that help to identify and clarify ethical issues for the HRD practitioner. Ways of creating awareness in the organisation about ethical issues involved in HRD policy and practice, and of gaining commitment to tackle them. Sources of information and advice that clarify legal and ethical responsibilities, and help HRD practitioners to deal fairly and consistently with diversified workforces. How to ensure that all HRD operations and processes conform to relevant statutory, legal and ethical standards.

CIPD standards complete		Indicative content
The importance of continuing professional self-development	Methods and processes of continuing personal and professional development, including coaching, counselling and mentoring. Databases and information sources that provide up-to-date information about current and emergent theory, practice and issues in the field.	National occupational and professional standards in HRD and their implications for the conduct of HRD in the business, and for the enhancement of the HRD practitioner's competence and employability. Methods and processes of continuing personal and professional development, including coaching, counselling and mentoring. Self-assessment and self-development, and tackling barriers to the self-development process. Roles and responsibilities of HRD practitioners in promoting and participating in external sectoral and professional networks, initiatives and programmes. Databases and information sources that enable HRD practitioners to regularly update their knowledge about theory and practice in the field, and about emerging trends and issues.

Appendix 2
Answers to multiple-choice questions

2.1	A or B	7.1.	B and D	12.1	A, B, C, D
2.2	A and B and C	7.2.	D	12.2	E
3.1	D	8.1.	E	13.1	A
3.2	B and C	8.2.	D	13.2	A and C
4.1	C and D	9.1	B	14.1	A, B, C, D
4.2	B and D	9.2.	A	14.2	D
5.1.	D	10.1	D	15.1	B and C
5.2.	A and C	10.2	A, C, D	15.2	A
6.1.	A, B, C, D	11.1	E		
6.2.	A, B, C, D	11.2	C		

Index